D1447361

Discovering Florida

Florida Museum of Natural History:
Ripley P. Bullen Series

FLORIDA MUSEUM
OF NATURAL HISTORY

UNIVERSITY PRESS OF FLORIDA

Florida A&M University, Tallahassee
Florida Atlantic University, Boca Raton
Florida Gulf Coast University, Ft. Myers
Florida International University, Miami
Florida State University, Tallahassee
New College of Florida, Sarasota

University of Central Florida, Orlando
University of Florida, Gainesville
University of North Florida, Jacksonville
University of South Florida, Tampa
University of West Florida, Pensacola

Discovering Florida

First-Contact Narratives from Spanish Expeditions along the Lower Gulf Coast

Edited and Translated by John E. Worth

University Press of Florida

Gainesville • Tallahassee • Tampa • Boca Raton
Pensacola • Orlando • Miami • Jacksonville • Ft. Myers • Sarasota

This book may be available in an electronic edition.

21   20   19   18   17   16   6   5   4   3   2   1

First cloth printing, 2014
First paperback printing, 2016

Library of Congress Control Number: 2014934339
ISBN 978-0-8130-4988-5 (cloth)
ISBN 978-0-8130-6190-0 (pbk.)

University Press of Florida
15 Northwest 15th Street
Gainesville, FL 32611-2079
http://www.upf.com

To Henry

Contents

Illustrations

Preface

If there was a "ground zero" for the earliest European exploration of North America, it was the lower gulf coastline of Florida. Long before Plymouth Rock, Jamestown, Roanoke, and even St. Augustine, the coast and bays of southwestern and western peninsular Florida witnessed a flurry of repeated Spanish visitation, including at least one expedition almost every decade after 1513. Even the founder of Florida's first successful settlement, Pedro Menéndez de Avilés, initially explored and fortified the lower gulf coast within just two years of his 1565 arrival. Indeed, it was only after the failure of Menéndez's forts in 1568 and 1569 that southern Florida was ultimately relegated to virtual isolation for some three centuries, as European exploration and colonization proceeded apace to the north.

The sixteenth century was literally filled with "first-contact" moments along Florida's lower gulf coast. In 1513, Juan Ponce de León finished his exploration of the newly discovered Florida peninsula near the mouth of the Caloosahatchee River and was fought off by Calusa Indians, who would later mortally wound him when he returned to establish a colony there in 1521. In 1528, Pánfilo de Narváez made landfall near modern Tampa Bay, embarking on his disastrous expedition that resulted in the imprisonment of a young Juan Ortiz. In 1539, Ortiz was rescued by Hernando de Soto when he landed at Tampa Bay to launch his nearly four-year trek across the interior southeastern United States, of which only a quarter of his six hundred–man expeditionary force survived. A decade later, in 1549, Dominican friar Luís Cancer de Barbastro made yet another ill-fated attempt to establish contact with the indigenous inhabitants of Tampa Bay but was killed along with several companions before unloading their ship.

That same year, a thirteen-year-old boy named Hernando de Escalante Fontaneda survived a shipwreck in the Florida Keys during a voyage from Cartagena to Spain, and he would spend the next seventeen years as a captive of the Calusa chief at Mound Key in Estero Bay along the gulf coast well below Tampa. It was only upon the 1566 arrival of Pedro Menéndez de Avilés, the founder of Spanish Florida at St. Augustine the previous year, that Escalante Fontaneda was rescued. Although he spent the next three years working as principal interpreter for the Spanish garrison at Fort San Antón de Carlos on Mound Key, when the fort was withdrawn in 1569, he finally traveled to Spain and was able to write about his captivity among the Calusa.

After 1570, Florida's lower gulf coast received only very limited Spanish contact for well over a century, during which time the indigenous chiefdoms of this region gradually declined in population in large part because of European epidemic diseases. They were ultimately chased either to St. Augustine or the remote Florida Keys in response to English-sponsored slave raiding by immigrant Yamasee and Creek Indians armed with flintlock muskets. By the second decade of the eighteenth century, seasonal visits by Cuban fishing vessels represented virtually the only regular human presence in the lower gulf coast region, with the few remaining descendants of its indigenous peoples ultimately destined to settle as refugees around Havana harbor in Cuba. Only toward the end of the eighteenth century did the gradual repopulation of the lower gulf coast by Spanish-allied Creek Indians result in renewed human presence, albeit by immigrants from Georgia and Alabama. The first truly lasting penetration of Florida's lower gulf coast by resident Europeans would take place only at the very end of the colonial era, when Cuban fishermen and immigrant Creek and Yamasee Indians ultimately intermarried during the late eighteenth and early nineteenth centuries, creating an entirely new ethnic group known as "Spanish Indians" on the neutral ground that this region had become (Worth 2012).

The narrative accounts of these initial sixteenth-century contacts between Spaniards and Florida's gulf coast Indians provide a tantalizingly brief glimpse of indigenous cultures that would not survive the colonial era, and as such, they represent a tremendously important record of cultures that are now extinct, ranging from the powerful and geographically extensive Calusa of the Charlotte Harbor region to an assortment of smaller groups bordering Tampa Bay, such as the Tocobaga. Moreover, they provide a detailed documentary record of the initial European exploration of this region and of the situations and circumstances of first contact between Spaniards and Indians. The portrait that emerges from the details of these earliest interactions is one of two sets of disparate but autonomous peoples, indigenous and foreign, sizing up one another along a coastline that would soon be effectively ceded back to Indian control for more than two hundred years. Far from representing yet another instance of American Indians living on the cusp of imminent colonial assimilation and cultural transformation, the first-contact narratives of Florida's lower gulf coast illuminate that shadowy period of tentative and occasionally violent engagement that preceded an even longer period of withdrawal and disengagement. For most of the colonial era, the Calusa and their neighbors remained intentionally isolated from the fast-paced transformations of the colonial era, lending an even greater relevance to the ethnographic information contained in these earliest narratives.

As the modern state of Florida experiences rapid growth, largely spurred by immigration from other parts of the United States, these first-contact narratives provide a vital link between present-day inhabitants of the lower gulf coast and their late prehistoric and early historic predecessors in this same location. The present inaccessibility of most of these narratives to the general public, however, makes this task doubly difficult for historians and anthropologists who are dedicated to increasing the public's appreciation for the human heritage of not just this state but also the United States at large.

Of all the expeditions and accounts just described, narratives from only two—Narváez and Soto—are widely available to both scholars and the general public. The Narváez expedition is chronicled in detail by the published account of Álvar Núñez Cabeza de Vaca, which has received widespread attention in historical and literary circles and which can be found in a number of English editions (e.g., Favata and Fernández 1993; Adorno 1999; Krieger 2003). All known narratives of the Hernando de Soto expedition have recently been published together in a single volume with updated translations (Clayton, Knight, and Moore 1993; Worth 1993a, 1993b). Fortunately, translated narrative accounts of both these expeditions are easily available to modern readers. However, this is not the case with the other first-contact narratives noted previously.

Although details of the Ponce de León expedition have been widely reported using extracts from the 1601 *Historia general de los hechos de los Castellanos en las islas i tierra firme del mar oceano* by Antonio de Herrera y Tordesillas, a full modern translation of the relevant portions of this account is not widely available (but see T. Davis 1935; Kelley 1991). Other accounts by Fernández de Oviedo y Valdés (1851, 1853), López de Gómara (1554), and Las Casas (1875) also form portions of much larger works that are somewhat difficult to find in English translation. Two royal contracts with Ponce de León have appeared in transcribed and translated form (e.g., T. Davis 1935; Lawson 1946) but are not widely available. In addition, two letters authored by Ponce de León just days before his departure for the 1521 expedition have never been published together in translated form (see Lawson 1946: 98–100 for the second letter).

The 1549 Dominican expedition of Luís Cancer de Barbastro is documented by a remarkable firsthand journal written partly in the hand of Fray Cancer himself and finished by Fray Gregorio de Beteta after the murder of the expedition's leader on the shore of Tampa Bay (Cancer and Beteta 1549). Curiously, although a secondary transcription was published in the nineteenth century (Smith 1857: 190–202) and the detailed and lengthy journal has been summarized in print (e.g., Lowery 1911: 411–27; Gannon 1965: 9–14), it has never been published in its entirety (distinguishing both handwritten versions) in a widely accessible English translation. Perhaps more than any of the other accounts, the Cancer-Beteta narrative provides an intensely personal view of first contact, full of drama and suspense.

Two primary texts written by Hernando de Escalante Fontaneda (n.d.b, n.d.c) have been published in translation, most recently by David True (1944b). However, True's edition of five hundred copies is now out of print and difficult to find except at university libraries. Furthermore, based on my own research (Worth 1995), there were at least three additional manuscript sections authored by Escalante Fontaneda (n.d.a, n.d.c) during the 1570s, making True's edition incomplete in any case. These documents have never been published together in their entirety and certainly deserve wider availability because of their pivotal importance in understanding the Calusa Indians of Southwest Florida.

Finally, although historian John Hann (1991) has recently published translations of most of the Jesuit letters associated with the Spanish interaction with the Calusa during the 1560s at Mound Key, one of the most important narratives of first contact between the Calusa and Pedro Menéndez de Avilés was written by Gonzalo Solís de Merás (1893), and this detailed narrative has most recently been published in English translation by Jeannette Thurber Connor (1923). This volume was reprinted in 1964, and the Connor edition remains difficult to obtain outside university libraries. In addition, this translation has long needed updating as well as new analysis and annotations, including additional supplementary documentation.

In sum, while many substantial and important narrative accounts exist regarding first contact between Spaniards and Native Americans along Florida's lower gulf coast, modern English translations of these narratives are generally difficult to find or completely absent altogether, and most of them have never been published together with an introductory historical overview of sixteenth-century Spanish contact with the Native Americans in this region. This book makes all these early narratives easily accessible to both scholars and the general public in a single volume of translations, adding to a small group of recently published volumes of translations for Spanish Florida (e.g., Hann 1986, 1991, 1993; Worth 2007) using the bilingual format that was briefly common in the 1920s (e.g., Connor 1925, 1930; Priestley 2010). Based on the amount of ongoing ethnohistorical and archaeological research into the Calusa and other gulf coast groups (e.g., Hann 2003; Marquardt and Walker 2013), it is my hope that this book of Spanish text with translations will fill an important gap in the available literature regarding first-contact studies along the lower gulf coast of Spanish Florida as well as the broader United States.

An explanation is warranted here regarding the norms that I used for my transcriptions of handwritten manuscript documents and printed publications from the sixteenth to the nineteenth centuries. Spanish handwriting during the early colonial era normally employed little to no punctuation at all (with slashes, equal signs, and dashes sometimes acting in their place), few to no diacritical marks, random capitalization, abundant and inconsistent abbreviations, variable premodern spelling, and extraordinarily lengthy and complex run-on sentences. As a result, while I have attempted to make faithful direct transcriptions of the original letters, words, and sentence structure in sixteenth-century manuscripts, I also adopted certain paleographic conventions for ease in reading by modern Spanish speakers. These include the modernized capitalization of names and the first words of sentences even when not originally present, the proper distinction between *u* as a vowel and *v* as a consonant, the use of the Spanish letters ñ and ç even when not distinguished from *n* and *c* in the original, the elimination of seemingly random capital letters (especially when in the middle of words), the elimination of slashes when used to separate Spanish words from one another (such as their occasional insertion before words beginning with the letter *o*) or their replacement with periods or commas when clearly used by the original author to end sentences or clauses, and the bracketed insertion of appropriate letters when only abbreviations are present in the original manuscript. I have not, however, inserted accents or other diacritical marks in the transcriptions (even though I have inserted them for names in the translations) or punctuation other than periods at original sentence endings. Marginal notes adjacent to the original manuscript text are inserted in my transcriptions at the location they appear and are italicized within brackets. Finally, when folio numbers are present in handwritten manuscripts, they are indicated in brackets at the appropriate location using *r* for "recto" (front) and *v* for "verso" (back).

For transcriptions from printed books, as a general rule I have retained anachronistic orthography present in the original text except in cases where it might make it difficult for modern Spanish readers to sound out the words correctly. For works dating to the sixteenth century, the original spelling, capitalization, punctuation, and diacritical marks generally remain unchanged in my transcriptions, except in the case of the use of the letter *f* in place of *s* and where the letters *u* and *v* have been used interchangeably as both vowel and consonant. In other cases, such as the use of *q* in place of *c*, *y* in place of *i*, and *z* in place of *s* or *ç* or the soft *c*, the original spelling is retained since it does not significantly affect readability. More recent nineteenth-century publications of colonial-era manuscripts possess fewer anachronisms, though I have retained their often-extensive use of accent marks that do not normally appear in modern usage, as well as the use of *ç* in place of the soft *c*.

In all cases, however, my transcriptions are guided by the goal that modern Spanish speakers should be able to sound out the anachronistic version of words as spelled in the historical texts by using modern pronunciation rules and then pick out the modern standardized spelling based on the spoken version. Thus, irregular spellings for personal names and place-names in Spanish are preserved in the Spanish transcriptions but modernized for their corresponding English translations; however, the original spellings of indigenous names are retained for both the transcriptions and translations to allow readers of both to "hear" the phonetic pronunciation of non-Spanish words by their original authors.

In acknowledgment, the translations for this volume were supported in large part by a 2004 Summer Stipend grant from the National Endowment for the Humanities, for which I am extremely grateful. Prior and subsequent research was carried out with the support and encouragement of William H. Marquardt, curator at the Florida Museum of Natural History and director of the Randell Research Center at Pineland, where I worked for six years. Bill's enthusiasm for this project to a large extent made the original manuscript possible. Jennifer Jennings at the Randell Center also deserves special mention for facilitating time at the office for uninterrupted research and writing. In addition, Ed Winn in particular not only was a constant source of moral support and inspiration but also generously provided several important early secondary texts for my library, which were consulted during the course of this project. Over the years during and since my six-year stay in Southwest Florida, I have also been given considerable encouragement to publish this book by many interested avocational historians and archaeologists, to all of whom I offer my thanks. I also thank Patrick Johnson for his help in tracking down microfilm of Buckingham Smith's transcription of the 1539 Hernando de Soto letter and for sharing his own transcriptions of it. Finally, I am grateful to the reviewers from the University Press of Florida, especially J. Michael Francis for his very detailed and thoughtful commentary, which unquestionably strengthened the final product, and for sharing his recent discovery of documentation regarding Hernando de Escalante Fontaneda's activities in Spain with regard to the estate of his father, Juan, in Cartagena (Spanish Crown 1569). While my translations are probably still more literal than he might prefer, it is probably a result of my training as an archaeologist and scientist that I am predisposed to manipulate the original language of the documents as little as possible, even when the result undoubtedly flows a bit less smoothly in modern colloquial English.

I express my considerable gratitude for the support I received at home during the writing of this manuscript from my wife, Concha, and our sons, Christopher and Henry, who all experienced my many long hours of work outside the office on this project. Book projects are never easy to complete, and families inevitably share that burden.

Introduction

Sixteenth–Century Spanish Exploration of Florida's Lower Gulf Coast

When Spanish sailing vessels first began to appear along the beaches and bays of Florida's lower gulf coast during the sixteenth century, what had probably been only rumors and scattered secondhand reports from distant lands was suddenly made very real with the arrival of Spanish explorers, missionaries, soldiers, and would-be colonists. With first contact, peninsular Florida's indigenous societies were suddenly thrust onto the global stage on the periphery of an expanding European-centered world, setting them all firmly on the road to eventual cultural extinction.

Though it was Florida's Atlantic coast that witnessed the first Spanish landfall in 1513, it was the native inhabitants of the lower gulf coast to the west who experienced the vast majority of subsequent landings through 1549. Even after European colonial ventures shifted northward after 1559, Florida's lower gulf coast was still the focus of repeated visitation and fortification between 1566 and 1569, after which almost all European contact in this region was curtailed for well over a century. By the time that increasing numbers of Cuban fishing vessels began to ply these same waters with regularity in the eighteenth century, the indigenous inhabitants of the lower gulf coast had already fled east and south in the face of English-sponsored slave raiding based in Carolina, leaving their homelands open to reoccupation by immigrant Europeans and Indians alike.

The sixteenth century thus represents the primary era of first contact between Spaniards and native Florida Indians along the lower gulf coast. With few notable exceptions, the surviving narrative record of such early interaction is based primarily on the documentary accounts of these sixteenth-century expeditions or on captivity narratives penned years later based on firsthand and secondhand information. For this reason, the sixteenth-century narratives of first contact in this region represent some of our best (and in some cases our only) glimpses of the indigenous cultures that once inhabited the lower gulf coast of Florida. Though most of these narratives have appeared at one time or another in print, either in transcribed Spanish or translated English form, they have never been combined into a single volume with both Spanish and English versions. The following introductory essay is designed to serve as an overview of the historical context of the individual narratives and associated documents that follow. The text intentionally focuses more on the expeditions that framed the events described in the exploration narratives and less on the more anecdotal events reported in captivity narratives, for example. Additionally, more or less detail is provided regarding specific expeditions, in part depending on how well documented each expedition is in the secondary literature. Ultimately, the introductory essay provides a framework for readers to understand the first-contact narratives that form the bulk of this book.

Indigenous Chiefdoms of Florida's Lower Gulf Coast

At the dawn of the sixteenth century, Florida's lower gulf coast was home to tens of thousands of indigenous inhabitants living in dozens of scattered fishing communities along the margins of the rich coastal estuaries between present-day Tampa Bay to the north and Cape Sable to the south. Although they were broadly united by a shared nonagricultural way of life, and probably also by similar patterns of social and political organization, and perhaps even a common language family, these coastal communities were almost certainly not joined as part of a single overarching group or nation. Instead, the lower gulf coast of the Florida peninsula seems to have been generally characterized by considerable diversity and autonomy on a local level, particularly in the environs of modern Tampa Bay, which can perhaps best be characterized as a region of autonomous petty chiefdoms, some allied and some not. To the south, a certain degree of interregional control seems to have been exercised by the Calusa, at least in the mid-1560s. However, even there, other smaller local groupings or "clusters" of communities may have similarly dominated the landscape.

Unfortunately, ethnohistorical data for this coastal region emerged episodically and unevenly through the sixteenth century, as sporadic Spanish exploration and contact gradually added new details to their written knowledge of the various estuarine localities along the lower gulf coast. Compounding this slowly evolving awareness is the fact that direct contact between Spaniards and Indians likely resulted not only in the introduction of at least some European disease pathogens but also in some direct shifts and transformations in local and regional social geography, especially in cases where Spanish military involvement altered the existing balance of power among sometimes-hostile neighbors. For these reasons, our ethnohistorical record is fragmentary throughout the course of the sixteenth century, and these fragments provide only sporadic "snapshots" of a dynamic and changing sociopolitical landscape.

If we recognize these limitations, it is possible to assemble a list of known sixteenth-century communities and chiefdoms for each region or locality within this broader coastal strip (see table 1) and to associate these names with approximate geographic locations on the broader landscape of South Florida (see figure 1). Although it is not the intention of this introductory essay to provide a detailed analysis of the evolving social geography of the lower gulf coast, a few basic conclusions are both warranted and instructive, especially when augmented with late prehistoric archaeological data for these same regions.

Five archaeological regions may be distinguished for the lower gulf coastline during and immediately prior to the sixteenth century, primarily based on preserved aspects of their material culture, particularly pottery (e.g., Milanich 1994: 275–323, 389–412). The northern three are subdivisions of the broader Safety Harbor culture area and include a Northern variant (to the mouth of the Withlacoochee River), a Circum-Tampa Bay variant, and a South-Central variant (to the middle

Table 1 Major named communities and chiefdoms of Florida's sixteenth-century lower gulf coast

Name	Location	Documentation
Pojoy	Tarpon Springs	Cancer era? (and seventeenth–eighteenth centuries)
Tocobaga	Safety Harbor/Old Tampa Bay	Cancer era?, Menéndez era (and seventeenth century)
Mocozo	Alafia River/western Hillsborough Bay	Soto era (and seventeenth century)
Uzita	Little Manatee River/southern Tampa Bay	Soto era
Tampa	Pine Island/southern Charlotte Harbor/northern Pine Island Sound	Menéndez era (and seventeenth century)
Calos	Mound Key/Estero Bay	Menéndez era (and seventeenth–eighteenth centuries)
Muspa	Cape Romano/Marco Island/Goodland	Menéndez era (and seventeenth–eighteenth centuries)

Figure 1 Locations of documented indigenous groups in sixteenth-century Florida. (Map by author.)

of Charlotte Harbor). The southern two regions include the Caloosa-hatchee region (from southern Charlotte Harbor through the southern end of Estero Bay) and the Ten Thousand Islands region (south to Cape Sable). By the sixteenth century, both of these southern regions shared much in common, but their earlier chronologies were clearly distinct.

For the purposes of this book, the lower gulf coast of Florida is defined on the north as the region visited and documented by early Spanish narratives to have had visible coastal habitation by Florida Indians and to have been more or less easily approachable by ship. Based on the diary of the 1549 Luís Cancer expedition (Cancer and Beteta 1549), it seems apparent that the coastal lowlands of present-day Hernando County were north of this boundary, as additionally confirmed by the general paucity of maritime visitation along the upper gulf coastline all the way to the later Apalachee port of St. Mark's (established in the 1630s). To the south, Juan López de Velasco's (1894) geographic descriptions from the 1570s (based on direct information from the late 1560s) additionally suggest that the Ten Thousand Islands region between Cape Romano and Cape Sable was similarly inaccessible, even if somewhat more populated. As a consequence, essentially all of the sixteenth-century expeditions to the western Florida peninsula discussed in this book took place or began between these northern and southern "boundaries": from just north of Tampa Bay to just south of Estero Bay.

Within this broader coastal region, ethnohistorical evidence (in the form of Spanish colonial narratives and other manuscript texts) provides not only names for chiefs and towns but also details regarding the sociopolitical structure and organization of groups living within the five archaeological regions discussed previously. It is not possible to establish a one-to-one correspondence between archaeological regions and named sociopolitical groupings, since the geographic distribution of utilitarian pottery and other items of material culture generally reflects patterns of quotidian social interaction across the landscape and only secondarily (and distantly) mirrors the integration of communities and regions within sometimes short-lived political alliances. Nevertheless, there is at least a rough correspondence between the sixteenth-century social geography of Florida's lower gulf coast and the five archaeological regions, at least in broad terms.

To the north, the Circum-Tampa Bay culture known as Safety Harbor can be unequivocally associated with several groups known from Spanish sources to have inhabited this region, including the Tocobaga, Pojoy, Uzita, and Mocozo, all of which were generally associated with the greater Tampa Bay region, although never all together in the same document at the same time (Milanich and Hudson 1993: 121–27; Hann 2003: 104–38). At the time of Hernando de Soto's 1539 landing, the Uzita and Mocozo occupied the southeastern and eastern margins of the bay, respectively. In fact, they appear to have inhabited these same locations when the Pánfilo de Narváez expedition arrived in 1528. The Uzita disappear from the documentary record not long thereafter; however, the name Mocozo continues to appear in this locality well into the seventeenth century.

Tocobaga clearly occupied the northwestern end of the bay system in the 1560s and were still associated with this location into the early seventeenth century, although they ultimately moved north along the gulf coastline and settled in Northwest Florida near the Apalachee (e.g., Hann 1988, 2003). The name Pojoy appears in the early seventeenth century only in association with Tampa Bay generally, and the first good documentation for the town's exact location is in the last quarter of the

seventeenth century, when two Spanish expeditions provided clues placing it somewhat north to northwest of the bay, perhaps in the vicinity
of Tarpon Springs (Hann 1991: 25–26; 2003: 128). Whether this location corresponds to its placement earlier in the century is not clear from
available documentation.

Importantly, however, all four of these projected villages are in distinct locations in the general vicinity of Tampa Bay and thus could possibly represent four continuously occupied communities or chiefdoms that
extended well back into the sixteenth century. If this were the case, then
all four of these groups—Tocobaga, Pojoy, Uzita, and Mocozo—might
have played a role in the first-contact narratives that follow, whether
or not their name appears in the Spanish text and whether or not the
name was even the same throughout this era. As a consequence, it is at
least possible that the Tampa Bay–area expeditions, for which original
narratives accompany in the chapters that follow, describe one or more
of the four groups. Pánfilo de Narváez's men may have interacted with
the Tocobaga (and possibly the Pojoy and Uzita). Hernando de Soto's
men undoubtedly interacted with the Uzita and Mocozo. A decade later,
Fray Cancer's expedition probably interacted with both the Pojoy and
Tocobaga, and after 1565, Pedro Menéndez and his men had extensive
contact with the Tocobaga. These suppositions cannot be proven without additional data, perhaps archaeological, regarding the continuity of
Safety Harbor occupations in these localities. Nevertheless, it is worth
considering that all four groups may have existed for a considerable time
before their first appearance in the documentary record, even considering the substantial disruptions resulting from Spanish contact throughout the sixteenth century.

To the south, in the vicinity of the Estero Bay and Charlotte Harbor
estuaries of Southwest Florida, there is little ambiguity regarding the
cultural identity of the indigenous groups during at least the latter half
of the sixteenth century. Spanish sources uniformly refer to this region as
the "province of Carlos," a name taken from the chief first met by Spanish authorities in 1566, who had himself adopted it both in reference to
the name of the king of Spain and also apparently based on its similarity
to the indigenous name Calos (also rendered Caalus), meaning "fierce
people" or "fierce town" (Escalante Fontaneda, n.d.c; Rogel 1946e).
Even though Carlos himself was killed in the spring of 1567 and was
replaced by a long line of chiefs named Felipe, the provincial name Carlos remained attached to this region through the eighteenth century and
formed the basis for the modern name used for this group, the Calusa.

Regional subdivisions, or at least important local towns, for the coastal
zone included Tampa on the north (Pine Island Sound/Charlotte Harbor), Calos in the center (Estero Bay), and Muspa to the south (Cape

Romano), as well as the interior district of Mayaimi (Lake Okeechobee) and numerous other named towns scattered across the landscape (e.g., Goggin and Sturtevant 1964; Marquardt 1987, 1988; Widmer 1988; Worth 2006, 2008, 2013). However, while regional hegemony across a vast region of Southwest Florida was clearly exercised by the Calusa from at least the 1540s onward (based in part on Hernando de Escalante Fontaneda's captivity narrative [n.d.c]), there is presently no contemporaneous evidence to indicate whether or not this was the case during the earliest Spanish expeditions to this region during the period between 1513 and 1521. While it has been suggested that Calusa dominance was established only during the decades after early Spanish contact, perhaps even partly in response to this new external threat (e.g., Marquardt 1988: 176–79), archaeological evidence indicates that the region was characterized by broadscale homogeneity in ceramic material culture for several centuries before European contact, so there may have been at least some degree of regional cultural continuity throughout the sixteenth century. Moreover, in light of recent scholarship, there seems no a priori reason to doubt the presence of larger-scale social complexity among coastal fisherfolk and foragers, especially when the Calusa are compared with the comparably well-documented Guale of coastal Georgia, for whom archaeological evidence of hereditary inequality, if on a smaller geographic scale, clearly predates the historic-era reliance on maize agriculture (e.g., Worth 2008; Thompson and Worth 2011).

Much is, of course, known about the Calusa and the Tampa Bay groups, both of which fall into the broader regional designation for "South Florida" cultures (e.g., Hann 2003), as generally distinguished from much of the rest of the southeastern United States, which was characterized by some variant of the widespread "Mississippian" cultural designation. While the Safety Harbor archaeological culture displays some affinities to Mississippian cultures to the north, the general pattern for the entire lower gulf coast of Florida (as defined for this book) is one of nonagricultural (or only minimally agricultural) fisherfolk and hunter-gatherers organized into multicommunity polities with inherited leadership positions who display public architecture in the form of massive community structures, mounds of shell and sand, and canals and waterways (at least in the case of the Calusa). Though clearly not characterized by the level of institutional complexity and surplus food production marking Mississippian chiefdoms in the interior Southeast, these South Florida cultures were clearly comparable in many ways and were perhaps just as powerful, particularly with respect to militarism over great territorial distances (e.g., Goggin and Sturtevant 1964; Marquardt 1987, 1988, 2004; Widmer 1988; Worth 2006, 2008). Although much remains to be learned about these cultures, the narratives in this book provide the great majority of the ethnohistorical detail available for the first-contact era throughout Florida's lower gulf coast.

The Juan Ponce de León Expeditions, 1513–1521

The years 1511–13 were tremendously significant for the indigenous inhabitants of southern peninsular Florida and likewise in aftershock for the rest of the North American continent. In 1511, Spanish forces under Diego Velázquez landed on the eastern end of Cuba in pursuit of the rebel chief Hatuey, who had fled with his followers from the island of Hispaniola. Thus began the military conquest of Cuba, initially culminating with the execution of Hatuey, followed by the subjugation of the remainder of the island and the establishment of several Spanish towns before 1515 (Wright 1970: 23–37; see also Pichardo Viñals 1986; Pichardo Viñals and Portuondo 1947; Sauer 1966; D. Davis 1974). As a result of the Velázquez expedition and others that followed, the island of Cuba was instantly converted from an isolated potential haven for Caribbean Indian refugees into an emergent Spanish colony that ultimately served as an early launching ground for expeditions to Mexico and other mainland locations and later as a way station for treasure-laden ships returning to Spain. Perhaps not long after that initial conquest, at least a small number of indigenous Cuban Indians may have begun to flee northward toward Florida, perhaps even accompanied by some of those who had earlier fled from Hispaniola to Cuba. Whether these refugees from the Spanish conquest arrived in successive waves or in a single migration, at some point they were formally granted permission by the Calusa chief to settle in a single community within the broader Calusa domain in Southwest Florida (Escalante Fontaneda, n.d.c). The location of this refugee village of Cuban Indians has yet to be documented or found, but their presence in Southwest Florida is attested by the fact that at least one of these refugees who spoke a little Spanish was already resident among the Calusa by the summer of 1513, when Spaniards finally made formal landfall along the western coast of Florida.

The earliest documented Spanish expeditions to make direct contact with the indigenous inhabitants of Florida's lower gulf coast were those led by Juan Ponce de León in 1513 and 1521 (e.g., T. Davis 1935; Lawson 1946; Weddle 1985: 38–54; Peck 1992, 1998). Ponce's initial discovery of Florida was actually the unexpected result of a chain of events that led back to political difficulties with allies of Christopher Columbus's son Diego, who upon obtaining the title of admiral and viceroy in the New World in 1511, removed Ponce from his 1509 appointment as the governor of San Juan del Puerto Rico, which he himself had taken the lead in conquering for the Spanish Crown (Spanish Crown 1511; Herrera y Tordesillas 1601; Fernández de Oviedo y Valdés 1851, 1853). Unceremoniously deposed and replaced by his political enemies, Juan Ponce de León subsequently sought and obtained a new royal contract for the exploration and settlement of the rumored island of Binini (Bimini), which had previously been the subject of similar though unfulfilled discussions between Bartholomew Columbus and the Spanish monarch (Spanish Crown 1512b).

One persistent tradition regarding the Ponce de León expedition deserves additional exploration here: the Fountain of Youth. As can be seen in the narratives in this book (Herrera y Tordesillas 1601; Fernández de Oviedo y Valdés 1992; Las Casas 1875; López de Gómara 1554: 37v–39r; Escalante Fontaneda, n.d.c), as well as several other sixteenth-century accounts (Martire d'Anghiera 1530, 1912b; Castellanos 1589: 139–44), the association between Juan Ponce de León and the mythical Fountain of Youth began very early and was fully embedded in the secondary literature and popular consciousness about the discovery of Florida by the end of the sixteenth century. This association seems to have originated in early confusion regarding both the identification of Bimini and Florida and the purported location of the legendary Fountain of Youth. As is detailed later, there is presently no evidence of a connection between the rumored island of Bimini and the legend of a Fountain of Youth prior to Ponce's 1513 discovery of Florida (and some evidence to the contrary), and subsequent documentary references dating to the first decade after Florida's discovery maintain the distinction between all three locations (Bimini, Florida, and the Fountain of Youth). However, beginning no later than 1526, Florida was interpreted by at least one author, Peter Martyr (Pietro Martire d'Anghiera), to have been the location of the Fountain of Youth, and by 1535, Gonzalo Fernández de Oviedo y Valdés asserted that the location was Bimini. Moreover, by no later than 1519, Alonso Alvarez de Pineda, a mapmaker, concluded that Florida was identical to the Bimini of earlier reports, and in 1561, yet another important author, Bartolomé de las Casas, posited that Ponce de León had invented both names (Florida and Bimini) for the same landmass. Finally, about 1575, Florida shipwreck survivor and longtime captive Hernando de Escalante Fontaneda reported the presence in South Florida of Cuban Indians who had come to Florida in the early sixteenth century seeking the Fountain of Youth (which he called the River Jordan). In light of all these sources (including a subsequently lost ship's log or detailed report of the original Ponce de León expedition), Spanish chronicler Antonio de Herrera published his own seminal overview of the expedition, stating unequivocally that in addition to his primary goal of acquiring new lands for the Spanish Empire, Juan Ponce de León set out in search of both the

Fountain of Youth in Bimini and the River Jordan in Florida. In modern times, all this has been consolidated into the single popular legend that Juan Ponce de León came to Florida in search of the Fountain of Youth. A more detailed review of this documentary trail is instructive.

The earliest reference to the "island" called Beinini (more commonly appearing later as Binini, Bimine, and the modern Bimini) prior to the Ponce de León expedition seems to be the woodcut map in Peter Martyr's 1511 book (Martire d'Anghiera 1511: 45v), which gives that name to the large landmass drawn to the north of Cuba, presumably based only on oral accounts obtained directly and indirectly from Caribbean Indians. Peter Martyr also provides the earliest explicit reference to the Fountain of Youth in the first three decades (sets of ten chapters) of his *De Novo Orbe*, published by 1516, which locates the legendary spring some 325 leagues north of Hispaniola on an island called Boiúca or Agnanéo and which mentions neither Bimini nor Florida (Martire d'Anghiera 1530: 35v; 1912a: 274). At this early date, there is no evidence that Bimini was believed to be the location of the Fountain of Youth, especially since the same author was responsible for both named locations.

Over the next few decades, however, the island of Bimini was conflated with that of Florida, and the legend of the Fountain of Youth came to be connected to both the island of Bimini and Florida. As is clear from the Herrera narrative, which is evidently based on a detailed account or log of the first voyage, Juan Ponce de León clearly considered Bimini to be distinct from Florida and, indeed, sent one of his ships separately to identify its location during his return from discovering and exploring Florida (Herrera y Tordesillas 1601). Herrera even says that the ship succeeded in finding the island called Bimini, and though they failed to find the fabled Fountain of Youth on it, the island was described as large, possessing fresh water and trees. Furthermore, Ponce's 1514 contract and title as adelantado specifically noted both islands as distinct by name (Spanish Crown 1514b, 1514c), although his 1521 letters refer only to Florida as the goal of his colonization effort, suggesting he envisioned better colonial prospects there (Ponce de León 1521a, 1521b).

The distinction between Florida and Bimini is further confirmed on the Freducci map of 1514–15, which labels one of the islands off Florida's southeastern coast "Beiminy," consistent with Herrera's later narrative based on Ponce's log (True 1944a; Milanich and Milanich 1996). Peter Martyr also clearly distinguishes Florida from Bimini in the subsequent decades of *De Novo Orbe* written after 1516 but before his death in 1526 (Martire d'Anghiera 1912b: 251). Moreover, Alonso de Chaves's *Espejo de navegantes*, penned between 1520 and 1538, clearly places Bimini exactly in its modern location, along the far western edge of the Bahamas Islands and just twenty leagues across the Bahama Channel from the Florida coast (1977: 21, 89). There seems little doubt that in the immediate aftermath of Ponce de León's 1513 expedition, Florida and Bimini were recognized as distinct from one another, clarifying Martyr's previous 1511 map that portrayed only the then-legendary "Beinini" to the north of Cuba.

The first conflation of the newly discovered Florida with Bimini appears in the 1519 map of the Gulf of Mexico by Alonso Alvarez de Pineda, whose label for the Florida peninsula reads, "Florida, which was called Binini, which Juan Ponce discovered." A later account of Ponce's expeditions was penned by Fray Bartolomé de las Casas before 1561, in which he also equated Bimini with Florida, incorrectly attributing both names to Ponce de León, though failing to mention the Fountain of Youth at all (1875: 459–61).

In addition to the early conflation of Florida and Bimini, several sixteenth-century authors made attempts to identify the location of the legendary Fountain of Youth. Before his death in 1526, Peter Martyr completed five additional decades of *De Novo Orbe*, and in the seventh decade, he explicitly (and for the first time in print) identified the Fountain of Youth that he had previously written about as located in Florida, reporting anecdotal evidence of an elderly Lucayan Indian who had visited the fountain in Florida and returned rejuvenated (Martire d'Anghiera 1530: 97v–98v; 1912b: 293–95). Although Martyr's complete work was not published until 1530, by 1535 Gonzalo Fernández de Oviedo y Valdés (1851, 1853) completed his own account of the voyages, in which he asserted specifically that on his first expeditions Juan Ponce de León had gone in search of what he called the "fountain of Bimini," which was said to restore youth, and although he found these "islands of Bimini" (though not the fountain), while on this expedition he obtained news of the mainland and ultimately named it Florida, where he later returned to settle. Oviedo's work formed a basis for Juan de Castellanos's (1589: 139–44) later poetic expansion on the Ponce de León narrative. In 1554, however, Francisco López de Gómara seems to have blended Martyr's earlier accounts with those of Oviedo, interpreting that Ponce had originally set out in search of the island of Boyuca, where the Fountain of Youth was said to be located, and after failing to find this island, he entered Bimini and also discovered Florida (1554: 37v–39r).

Though the Fountain of Youth was not mentioned in Bartolomé de las Casas's 1561 narrative about Ponce's discovery of Florida, the ca. 1575 account by Hernando de Escalante Fontaneda (n.d.c) recounted the tradition noted previously that during the early sixteenth century, the Indians of South Florida had received many Cuban Indians who traveled north to Florida in search of the miraculous rejuvenating waters of the "River Jordan" and that they and their descendants, as well as the

Florida Indians themselves, were continually in search of such a river. Although Fontaneda also asserted that Juan Ponce de León came to Florida in search of this river, his 1575 account explicitly details only the search by the immigrant Cuban Indians, suggesting that he probably fused existing published narratives or oral traditions regarding Ponce's search for the Fountain of Youth with his own memories of captivity in Florida between 1549 and 1566.

When Antonio de Herrera y Tordesillas (1601) compiled his own comprehensive narrative of the discovery of Florida, in addition to the now-lost ship's log or detailed report that apparently formed the basis for his day-by-day recounting of the 1513 voyage, he also clearly had access to previously published accounts by Martyr, Oviedo, Las Casas, Gómara, possibly Castellanos, and even the handwritten manuscript of Fontaneda, which itself bears Herrera's marginal notes. As a result, Herrera's narrative comprises a blend of many prior renderings of the discovery of Florida, overlaid on a previously unutilized primary source that provided crucial details missing from all prior narratives. Doubtless for this reason, Herrera's addendum about Ponce's search for the Fountain of Youth is placed only after his detailed account of the actual voyage and identifies both the spring in Bimini and the river in Florida, effectively hedging his bets about the identity of the storied Fountain of Youth. Moreover, Herrera is careful to point out that Ponce's primary goal was "to discover new lands, which was what the Castilians understood most in those early times" (1601: 249).

My own analysis of the documentary trail leads me to conclude that Juan Ponce de León's 1513 expedition was precisely what Herrera posited, a voyage of discovery designed to find and settle undiscovered lands reputed to be north of Cuba and west of the inhabited portions of the Lucayos Islands (the Bahamas). The name Bimini was unquestionably attached to such reports, and it is for this reason that Ponce was specifically contracted to find and settle this named location and any others along the way that might be found. While I believe it likely that the so-called Fountain of Youth legend was already in circulation and probably known to Ponce himself prior to his departure, it also seems probable that the exact identity of the island on which this spring was rumored to exist would have been unclear to the Spaniards in 1513. If anything, the legend seems to have been associated with the names Boiúca and Agnanéo, but even if the spring had also become linked with the name Bimini by 1513, there is every reason to suspect that Juan Ponce de León was politically savvy enough to avoid overt mention of the fanciful legend during his contract negotiations in Spain.

Whether or not the mythical Fountain of Youth legend played any role in his personal motivation for the expedition to find the island of Bimini is unlikely ever to be known with certainty, but one thing seems abundantly clear to me after careful review of the documentary evidence: the direct and explicit literary association between Florida and the Fountain of Youth evolved *after* Ponce's 1513 voyage, not before. Independent documentary sources do attest to the early sixteenth-century Lucayan Indian belief in a Fountain of Youth somewhere west of the inhabited Bahamas Islands (Martyr's account) and to the Cuban or Hispaniolan Indian belief in a river with similar properties somewhere north of the island of Cuba during the same period (Fontaneda's account). Furthermore, an archaeological survey of the modern islands of Bimini along the westernmost margin of the Bahamas archipelago indicates that it was never inhabited in prehistory (Granberry 1957; Sears and Sullivan 1978). Although South Florida had been inhabited for millennia, archaeological evidence suggests that there was limited if any direct contact between Florida and Cuba prior to the colonial era (e.g., Knight and Worth 2006). Consequently, both Bimini and Florida seem likely to have been only poorly known, if at all, by most of the Caribbean Indians with whom early sixteenth-century Spaniards interacted, relegating most of their reports to the category of legend and myth. It would therefore seem unsurprising that Juan Ponce de León ventured north from Puerto Rico in 1513 with only the vaguest idea of what he would discover, other than an unconfirmed report of an island called Bimini west of the Bahamas and a shadowy legend of a so-called Fountain of Youth in the same general direction. However, in the aftermath of his discovery of the Florida peninsula and his subsequent death while attempting to settle this same land, these unfocused legends and rumors ultimately crystallized around the persistent myth that surrounds the name of Ponce de León even today and that all researchers must confront.

Returning to the details of Ponce's discovery, the original contract between Juan Ponce de León and the Spanish Crown, dated February 23, 1512, not only granted Ponce administrative privileges and tax breaks for all those who might accompany him on this first voyage of discovery (required to take place within one year of the contract) but also included the same concessions for any and all nearby islands that might be discovered on the journey to Bimini (Spanish Crown 1512a). As a result, when Ponce's expedition of three ships first sighted the coastline of Florida, under the terms of his contract he was legally authorized to claim both the land and its inhabitants under his own lifetime governorship. Naming his discovery after the liturgical season during which it was discovered (*Pasqua Florida*, or Easter, fell on March 27, with the Easter Octave lasting until April 3), Ponce landed and took formal possession of the land during an initial visit to shore along the Atlantic coastline between April 2 and April 8 (Herrera y Tordesillas 1601: 247).

Ponce de León did not immediately presume that the Florida shoreline was part of the rumored island of Bimini. Herrera y Tordesillas's (1601: 248–49) account specifically notes that Ponce was unaware of the identity of the landmass (though he presumed it was a large island) and made efforts to discover its native name while there, which by extrapolation means he must have had some positive criteria for recognizing his contractual goal of Bimini, presumably based on descriptions from Lucayan Indian informants. The original 1512 contract explicitly listed only the island of Bimini as the expedition's direct objective, nonetheless allowing Ponce to claim any subsidiary discoveries in the same manner. In this sense, there seems to have been no obvious advantage to Ponce in feigning ignorance of the identity of the landmass and claiming it as a new and unexpected discovery, although he might possibly have feared renewed interest by Bartholomew Columbus, who had previously expressed interest in exploring Bimini (Spanish Crown 1512b). Consequently, on the surface there would appear to be no reason to dismiss Herrera's description of Ponce de León's first discovery of Florida by positing that the Spaniards were somehow already aware of both Bimini and the Florida peninsula, since only the first was enumerated in the contract, it was never even identified during the main voyage, and it was visited only by a secondary vessel during the return to Puerto Rico (Herrera y Tordesillas 1601: 249). In my own estimation, the most likely explanation is that Florida was truly an unanticipated discovery in 1513.

Establishing the exact point of Ponce's initial landing in Florida is extremely difficult and will likely never be determined with any certainty (see figure 2). Details from what must have been an original log or diary of this first expedition, used by Spanish historian Antonio de Herrera in creating his 1601 narrative of the journey, provide only vague guidance about the precise locations involved, particularly in view of the fact that the latitude measurements are clearly skewed, falling between one and two and a half degrees too far to the north for other locations that can be identified today, averaging just over a degree and a half. With a landing site reported by Herrera at 30 degrees, 8 minutes north latitude, this error factor might place the actual landing site anywhere from as far north as New Smyrna Beach at just over 29 degrees, to as far south as Vero Beach at just over 27½ degrees. My own analysis of the average sailing distances for Ponce's fleet, when they can be tracked, suggests they traveled about forty to fifty miles per day in open water (about twelve to fifteen nautical leagues per day). Although the ships are asserted to have sailed some thirty leagues during the two days after their last sighting of an unnamed island in the Bahamas on March 27, reported bad weather may have slowed their pace until first anchoring near land on April 2.

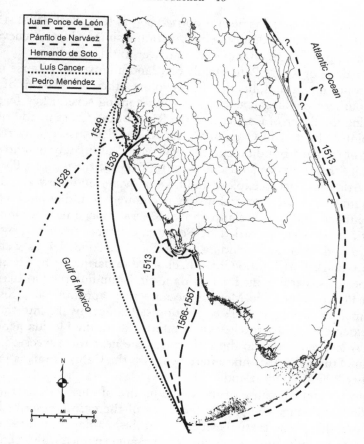

Figure 2 Maritime routes of sixteenth-century Spanish expeditions.
(Map by author.)

One key to Ponce's landing site lies in determining whether or not
the ships passed Cape Canaveral during their southward journey to the
Cape of Florida and the Keys. In my estimation, the one likely candi-
date—Ponce's Punta de Arrecifes (Point of Reefs)—could just as easily
have been located well south of Cape Canaveral. Herrera's text specifically delineates a stretch of coastline between the Point of Reefs on the
north and the Cabo de Corrientes (Cape of Currents, clearly the Cape
of Florida) on the south for a more general description (1601: 247), and
the former feature also appears on the Freducci map of ca. 1514–15
(True 1944a; Milanich and Milanich 1996), but the position and appearance of this point on the map and its only brief mention in Herrera's
narrative make it entirely possible that Ponce never saw Cape Canaveral,

an interpretation that has been proposed before (e.g., Peck 1992, 1998). In the absence of any additional information, I simply do not believe it is possible to provide an unambiguous answer to this question.

Regardless of where Ponce made first landfall, over the course of the next month and a half, his tiny fleet explored the entire sweep of Florida's southern peninsular coast and keys, naming several key features, including the River of Canoes and the River of the Cross in addition to the Point of Reefs and Cape of Currents. The fleet also discovered the strong northward-trending current that would ultimately be known as the Gulf Stream. Ponce landed at least four or five times along Florida's lower Atlantic coast to explore and take on water and firewood, during which time there were several hostile encounters resulting in two Spanish wounded and one Indian captive. Several village names along the Atlantic coast were recorded by Ponce and later transmitted by both Herrera and Freducci, including Abaióa and Chequeschá, as well as a location marked as Cautio/Chautio, claimed in particular by Herrera to have been a general name for Florida itself. Rounding the Florida Keys, which Ponce named the Martyrs because they appeared at a distance to be men drowning, Ponce's expedition sailed northward into the Gulf of Mexico and finally reached the western side of the Florida peninsula on May 23, remaining in the vicinity for the next three weeks. During this time, the Spaniards first interacted with the Calusa Indians in their Southwest Florida homeland.

Unfortunately, because of the vague nature of Herrera's narrative, it is difficult to gauge the precise locations of the events described. Furthermore, there is no textual evidence that the Spaniards under Ponce de León ever actually approached or visited a single named Calusa community, though information from the Freducci map suggests they became aware of the existence of at least two such villages, named Stababa and Juchi (or possibly Suchi or Guchi) during their first voyage (True 1944a; Milanich and Milanich 1996). The combined information from the narrative and map suggests that the first sighting of land along the Florida Gulf Coast occurred somewhere along the barrier islands south of Boca Grande and that the ships sailed southward to eventually land near the mouth of the Caloosahatchee River, probably either on modern Estero Island or Sanibel Island (Herrera y Tordesillas 1601: 303–4). While the actual text is ambiguous enough to allow for landings at any one of a number of island locations along the Southwest Florida coastline, the appearance of Juchi on the Freducci map, independently mentioned by Hernando de Escalante Fontaneda (n.d.b; see also Worth 1995) in the 1570s, strongly suggests that Ponce's expedition landed well north of Cape Romano and Naples (Muspa and Teyo/Tello, respectively, based on other evidence; see Worth 2013), probably just at or not far south of the mouth of the Caloosahatchee River.

Based on this interpretation, it seems likely that after sailing north and northeast from the Florida Keys during the spring of 1513, Ponce's three ships sighted land and turned and sailed south on May 24, skirting Cayo Costa, North Captiva, Captiva, and Sanibel Islands to the mouth of the Caloosahatchee River at San Carlos Bay, where they decided to careen the vessel *San Cristóbal*. Over the course of the next ten days, the Spaniards were approached by several parties of Indians in canoes, sometimes trading skins and guanines (a Spanish term for low-quality gold, though possibly instead referring to native copper) (Herrera y Tordesillas 1601: 303). On June 4, as the Spaniards awaited wind so they could seek out the cacique Carlos (the name provided for this chief may have been a subsequent interpretation by Herrera, writing almost ninety years later, well after the Menéndez era), a canoe arrived carrying an Indian who understood the Spanish language. Ponce de León's party presumed he was originally from Hispaniola or some other Spanish-occupied island, and subsequent evidence suggests he might possibly have been one of the group of Cuban Indian refugees who fled north and were permitted to settle within the Calusa domain (Escalante Fontaneda, n.d.c). This Indian carried a message from the Calusa chief for the Spaniards to wait for his arrival, but it was ultimately discovered to have been a delaying tactic to permit a subsequent attack on the ship by Indians in twenty canoes. The Indians were repulsed, some of whom were killed or captured.

The fact that the Calusa attacked the Spanish visitors almost immediately after their arrival, with only a brief pretense of welcome, almost certainly reflects their foreknowledge of both the Spaniards and their tactics, at the very least conveyed by documented Indian refugees from the brutal conquest carried out by Diego Velázquez during the previous year on the island of Cuba or from previous engagements in Hispaniola or other locations. Furthermore, it is even possible that prior to this time there might have been undocumented indirect or direct contact between South Florida Indians and early Spanish slavers or their victims in the Caribbean or Bahamas (e.g., Marquardt 1988: 176–79), though available documentation strongly suggests that Spaniards had not yet reached Florida itself, if only because there was no attempt to claim or explore this territory until after Ponce's 1513 voyage in search of Bimini. In any case, by 1513 the Calusa had already been conditioned to be wary of Spanish visitors and had almost certainly made a formal decision to mount active military resistance to Spanish exploration and conquest. This policy would ultimately dominate Spanish-Calusa relations for the next 175 years, with only two brief strategic truces until a change of policy in the late 1680s (see Worth 2006, 2013).

Following the initial attack against the Spaniards, two Indian captives were sent by Ponce with a message for Carlos, but the following day, as one of the vessels was sounding the depths of a port (possibly San Carlos Bay), a larger force of eighty shielded canoes attacked the Spaniards. Though the skirmish lasted until dark, both sides retreated without damage. The Spaniards evidently remained in the area until June 14, when they set sail southward on the way back to Puerto Rico, passing by the island where they had first fought the Indians, named Matanzas on account of the Indian deaths (and thus possibly identical to Estero Island, adjacent to Matanzas Pass and just south of San Carlos Bay; see Schober and Torrence 2002: 26–29).

In the aftermath of his accidental discovery of the "island" of Florida, Ponce quickly moved to consolidate and reinforce his claim to the new land, obtaining the title of adelantado of both Florida and Bimini and a revised contract with the Spanish Crown in the fall of 1514 (Spanish Crown 1514a, 1514b). The second contract was broadly similar to the first, but several differences are evident, including a replacement of the clause regarding the "distribution" of Indians to the first settlers with a statement mandating that the Indians be treated well and encouraged to convert voluntarily to the Catholic faith. At the same time as the Florida contract, however, the new adelantado was also named captain of an armada commissioned to search out and destroy the Carib Indians in the lower Caribbean, a task that ultimately occupied the next six years, significantly delaying his return to Florida. During this period, other Spaniards began to encroach on Ponce's newly discovered territories. Exploratory slaving expeditions to the mainland were increasingly common during these years, including at least two that apparently reached the northern coast of what would become greater Spanish Florida by 1516—Diego Miruelo along the northern gulf and Pedro de Salazar along the middle Atlantic coast (Vega 1605: 2–3; Hoffman 1980). At least two formal complaints against such activities were lodged by Juan Ponce de León by 1517, including a lawsuit against Diego Velázquez, lieutenant governor of Cuba, who was accused of having brought back three hundred Indian slaves from the islands of Bimini and Florida, at that time under Ponce's jurisdiction (Spanish Crown 1517a). Similar illegal slaving raids were claimed to have been launched by residents of Hispaniola against the island of Bimini during the same period, and Ponce successfully petitioned to have them restored to their lands (Spanish Crown 1517b). While both these incidents might possibly be identical with the Miruelo and Salazar expeditions, respectively, it is also possible that all were distinct from one another and that illicit slaving in this region became quite common after 1513. Even the happenstance 1517 encounter on an isolated beach along the lower gulf coast of Florida between a group of Indians and the members of a Spanish expedition under Francisco Hernández de Cordoba, taking on water during the return voyage from Yucatán to Cuba, resulted in a pitched battle and several deaths, including three Indian prisoners carried off in the boats (Díaz del Castillo 1939: 65–68).

Only in February 1521 did Juan Ponce de León finally launch his second expedition to Florida, this time with two ships and colonists planning to settle along the coast as originally instructed (Ponce de León 1521a, 1521b; Fernández de Oviedo y Valdés 1853: 621–23). The reason for the eight-year delay of Ponce de León's second expedition is explicitly stated by Ponce himself (1521a) to have been a result of both his service to the king in other places and his desire to await the marriage of his daughters following the death of his wife, though news of discoveries elsewhere on the North American mainland (namely, Mexico) might well be speculated to have played a role in his renewed interest in the colonization of Florida. Still not entirely sure that Florida was a separate landmass from Cuba (despite Alonso de Pineda's 1519 circumnavigation of the Gulf of Mexico; see Weddle 1985), Ponce de León led his ships back to the Southwest Florida coast, evidently landing at or close to their original landing site near the mouth of the Caloosahatchee River and possibly very near the site of the 1517 skirmish (which Ponce's pilot, Antón de Alaminos, had recognized from the 1513 landing). This location was called the Bay of Juan Ponce by the cosmographer Alonso de Chaves (1977: 122) no later than the mid-1530s, and during the early 1570s, cosmographer Juan López de Velasco (1894: 161) made an even more explicit reference to Ponce's mortal wound having been received at the Bay of Carlos (modern Estero Bay). Although primary accounts of this expedition are unavailable, secondary sources agree that the nearby Indians once again attacked the Spaniards not long after their arrival, wounding Ponce de León himself and forcing a retreat to the nearby Spanish town of Havana, where the expedition's leader soon perished from his wound, said by poet Juan de Castellanos (1589: 143) to have been in the thigh. This would be the last official Spanish visit to the Calusa domain for nearly half a century.

The Pánfilo de Narváez and Hernando de Soto Expeditions and the Captivity of Juan Ortiz, 1528–1539

The failure of Juan Ponce de León's 1521 colonial expedition only paved the way for subsequent Spanish expeditions to the southeastern United

States. That very same year a Spanish slaving expedition under Pedro de Quejo and Francisco Gordillo evidently reached the modern coast of South Carolina, which had apparently been visited previously by slaver Pedro de Salazar between 1514 and 1516 (Hoffman 1980, 1990, 1992). These expeditions ultimately paved the way for the second formal Spanish colonial attempt under Lúcas Vázquez de Ayllón five years later along this same stretch of the Atlantic coast, subsequently rendered by contemporary mapmakers as the "Land of Ayllón" to distinguish it from Ponce's Florida until the two were combined under Hernando de Soto in 1537 (Spanish Crown 1537). To the south, however, Spanish colonial efforts continued to focus on the northern rim of the Gulf of Mexico, newly invigorated by Hernando Cortés's rich discoveries in the Valley of Mexico after 1519. Thanks in large part to the circumnavigation of the Gulf of Mexico that same year by Alonso Alvarez de Pineda, seven years later, in 1526, Cuban-conquest veteran Pánfilo de Narváez requested and was granted a new royal contract to settle the region extending between Ponce's Florida and the Río de las Palmas far to the west (Narváez 1526; Spanish Crown 1526; Weddle 1985). Leaving Spain in 1527, Narváez's expedition wintered in Cuba and finally sailed north into the Gulf of Mexico in early 1528, with five ships and some three hundred men. While their original goal was the westernmost margins of the granted territory (nearest to Mexico, as a check on Hernando Cortés's northward expansion), storms and insufficient knowledge of the gulf coast led them to land along the western coast of peninsular Florida, evidently not far north of modern Tampa Bay in the vicinity of John's Pass on Boca Ciega Bay (Hoffman 1994; see figure 2).

Documentary accounts of the Narváez expedition are limited to various versions of a lengthy narrative by the expedition's treasurer, Álvar Núñez Cabeza de Vaca, who stumbled out of the Sinaloan desert in northern Mexico with just three surviving companions some eight years later, having survived an ordeal that ranks among the most remarkable true human odysseys ever recounted in narrative form (Núñez Cabeza de Vaca, n.d., 1989). Cabeza de Vaca's account of interaction between members of Narváez's expedition and the indigenous inhabitants of the Tampa Bay region is unfortunately quite minimal and includes no indigenous names, perhaps largely because neither group could understand the language of the other in this true first-contact situation. On April 18, Thursday of Holy Week, the Spaniards met and bartered with the residents of a village visible on the shores of the coastal bay where they made initial landfall, though the following night the residents evacuated the town and returned on Easter Sunday only to attempt to convince the Spaniards to leave.

Days later, Narváez dispatched a small expedition inland, which by nightfall seems to have reached the western shores of Old Tampa Bay. After returning to the ships for more people and dispatching one vessel to search the coast for the mouth of the bay, the party returned and scoured the coast of the bay, capturing four Indians who led them to a town with cornfields at the very end of the bay, where they found an assortment of Spanish items, including Castilian boxes, cloth, and feathers from New Spain. Based on Cabeza de Vaca's narrative, this town might have been the administrative center of what would later be known as the Tocobaga province at the Safety Harbor archaeological site. The party also discovered what they believed to be signs of gold, which the Indians indicated came from a rich and distant province called Apalachee. Pushing forward ten to twelve leagues, the Spaniards rested at another small town with cornfields before returning to the landing site with the news.

Following considerable debate, the decision was made for the members of the expedition to disembark and travel over land toward the north, with the ships heading north and west along the coastline in search of the bay that Miruelo had described. The route taken by the expedition from this point onward took them northward and into the peninsular interior, outside the region of focus for this book. Reaching Apalachee and eventually skirting the northern gulf coast in crudely constructed barges made along the Apalachee coastline, all but four of the expedition's members ultimately perished in search of New Spain, making the Narváez expedition the most complete disaster of all Spain's earliest colonial attempts in the southeastern United States.

Of no small import, one of the sailing vessels associated with the expedition seems to have entered Tampa Bay not long after the expedition headed north on its overland route, attempting to discover the whereabouts of Narváez's army. The chief of a town on the southern shore of the bay, evidently maimed during an undocumented encounter with Narváez's men, conspired to capture four of the crew in a ruse, among whom was a young man named Juan Ortiz, originally native to Seville, Spain. His subsequent eleven-year captivity among the chiefs of Tampa Bay provided the basis for a unique record of these societies during the era of first contact, including two neighboring but warring chiefdoms: Uzita (erroneously rendered as Hirrihigua in Incan-Spanish writer Garcilaso de la Vega's later narrative of the Soto expedition) on the southeastern side of Tampa Bay and Mocozo on the northeastern side of the bay. Ortiz's captivity also set the stage for the next Spanish expedition to Florida—that of Hernando de Soto in 1539—to have the distinct advantage of an accomplished interpreter, which no previous expedition had available to them.

The discovery of four survivors of the Narváez expedition in Mexico in 1536 and the return of Álvar Núñez Cabeza de Vaca to Spain in 1537 prompted no small measure of renewed interest in the exploration and settlement of Florida. Moreover, shortly before his return, yet another contract had been granted on April 20, 1537, for the colonization of Florida, this time to Hernando de Soto, a successful and wealthy veteran of conquests in Central and South America (Spanish Crown 1537). Soto's expedition, which departed from Spain in the spring of 1538, was larger (ultimately including some six hundred men and nine ships). It regrouped in Cuba (where Soto had also been appointed governor) and sent out a reconnaissance expedition under its accountant Juan de Añasco that winter to search for a suitable port and capture Indians as guides and interpreters. Sailing northward from Havana on May 18, 1539, Soto's fleet sighted land a week later on the feast day of Pentecost (Espíritu Santo), apparently in the vicinity of Longboat Key south of the mouth of Tampa Bay (Hudson 1997: 62–87; see also Clayton, Knight, and Moore 1993: 56–63, 225–26, 252–58). It took them several days to locate and carefully maneuver the ships through the harbor's shallow entrance and to offload horses and men, who approached the village of the local chief Uzita by land. Soto finally took up residence in this shoreline community, probably at the mouth of the Little Manatee River, on June 3 (Milanich and Hudson 1993: 48–70; Hudson 1997: 70–71; see figure 2).

From their base in the recently abandoned town of Uzita (the Indians had fled following early skirmishes with Spaniards set ashore before the ships made landfall), Soto's expedition soon learned of the existence of a sole survivor of the Narváez expedition, which had landed eleven years earlier, later discovered to be Juan Ortiz. Soto dispatched two military detachments in search of villages and people from whom to obtain intelligence regarding the interior. One of these, with only fifty infantrymen, was able to capture four women before being pursued and harassed on the return to camp. The other contingent had forty cavalry and eighty infantry but was led in circles by their guide until finally turning back and encountering Ortiz and his party, who were following the trail left by the Spaniards. The Spaniards charged the group across an open field, but the Indians dispersed into the woods, with the exception of Juan Ortiz and a companion, who ran too slowly. Ortiz's Indian companion was wounded at the edge of the woods, but Ortiz himself was able to block a lance blow with his bow. He shouted a garbled "Sevilla! Sevilla!" and crossed himself before his attacker could return. Despite his appearance, which was by then more Indian than Spanish, he was finally recognized as the Spanish survivor they sought, bringing a peaceful end to the accidental skirmish. After his return to Soto's main camp, Juan Ortiz finally regained effective use of the Spanish language and was gradually able to tell the tale that forms the core of the later captivity narrative penned by Garcilaso de la Vega, which is based on several survivors' accounts (since Ortiz did not survive the Soto expedition).

In the aftermath of Juan Ortiz's rescue, Soto dispatched Indian messengers to express his gratitude to the chief of Mocozo, who arrived three days later leading his own retinue. During the course of his nearly two-week stay with the Spaniards, Soto gathered intelligence and made preparations to push his army into the interior. Not long after Mocozo had returned to his town, the Spaniards sent a detachment of soldiers inland to the province of a chief named Urribarracuxi, to whom both Mocozo and Uzita paid tribute. Though the chief of this interior district successfully avoided contact with the Spaniards, they were nonetheless able to send back intelligence regarding a more distant province called Ocale, rumored to be a rich land, toward which Soto would ultimately march his army. Leaving a hundred men to guard the port at Uzita, where sporadic skirmishes had occasionally erupted throughout this time with the hidden inhabitants, in mid-July the Spaniards pushed inland and eventually northward toward Ocale, turning away from the lower gulf coastline of Florida in search of the phantom riches that Hernando de Soto hoped to find in the southeastern interior. When the Spaniards finally abandoned Uzita in December and transferred the remaining soldiers to their winter encampment in Apalachee, the Tampa Bay Indians would once again enjoy a respite from outside intruders for a full decade. The members of the Soto expedition itself would march inland to a more tragic fate, where they wandered for more than three years, engaging in battles and enduring many hardships, including the death of Hernando de Soto himself along the Mississippi River. The survivors finally escaped on handmade vessels down the Mississippi River and cruised along the western coastline of the Gulf of Mexico to New Spain.

The Luís Cancer Expedition, 1549

In the aftermath of the disastrous Soto expedition of 1539–43, and in concert with the 1542 New Laws outlawing Indian slavery and promoting the "good treatment and conservation" of the Indians, a completely new approach was ultimately authorized with respect to Florida in which the Spanish military would have no role. Spearheaded by Dominican priest Fray Luís Cancer, the next expedition to Florida's lower gulf coast would consist only of missionaries and a single farmer and would focus on conversion instead of conquest.

By the 1540s, Fray Cancer had extensive experience as a missionary in the New World, including several locations in the Caribbean and especially Guatemala, where he came to be renowned in the province of Verapaz and ultimately met fellow Dominican and controversial "Defender of the Indians" Bartolomé de las Casas, bishop of Chiapas. Ultimately developing a plan to mount the peaceful conquest of Florida, Cancer was granted permission to travel to Spain in 1547 and present his petition before the Council of the Indies. Though his journey turned into an adventure itself, since he was captured by a Turkish ship and eventually released in France, he ultimately arrived in Spain and was joined by Las Casas himself in pleading his case (Dávila Padilla 1955). Finally obtaining permission for the Florida expedition, Cancer returned to New Spain to prepare for his voyage.

One of the more curious facets of Fray Cancer's original plan was to gather up surviving Florida Indians brought to Central America as captives of survivors of the Soto expedition and return them to their homeland. As noted in a royal decree dated December 28, 1547, "Fray Luís has related to me that the people who came out of the said provinces of Florida, whom the Adelantado Soto had taken to them, brought out many Indians from those [provinces], and they are scattered in the Province of Guatemala, [and] it is appropriate that they be returned to their land, both in order to serve as interpreters in it, and also for other effects" (Estrada Monroy 1979: 256). While later documentation regarding the expedition confirms that this plan was not brought to fruition, it nonetheless provides some insight into Cancer's mind-set at the time of its planning.

The party chosen to carry out the Florida mission included four Dominican priests (Luís Cancer, Gregorio de Beteta, Diego de Tolosa, and Juan García) and a single lay brother and farmer named Estéban de Fuentes, contracted for a year of service. The ship *Santa María de Encina* was bought in March, and the crew was paid in advance for anticipated service lasting between two and three months (Hernández de Burgos 1549). The ship first sailed from the port of San Juan de Ulua near Veracruz but stopped in Havana to pick up an Indian interpreter named Magdalena, apparently one of those brought back during Juan de Añasco's reconnaissance for the Soto expedition. From Havana the ship made its way north along the gulf coastline of Florida.

The precise location of Cancer's landing can be determined with considerably more accuracy than is the case for any prior expedition to Florida, in large part because Cancer seems to have recorded accurately not only the exact latitude where they first made landfall—28 degrees—but also the northernmost point where they finally turned back—28½ degrees—both of which fit quite well with associated descriptions by Cancer and Beteta (1549) of the physical and social geography of Tampa Bay and the gulf coast to its north. What is perhaps most important in this regard is that through the chain of connections in this general vicinity between captive survivors of previous expeditions—Juan Ortiz between Narváez and Soto, and Juan Muñoz between Soto and Cancer—it is possible to establish a linkage between modern Tampa Bay and all three earlier expeditions, supporting considerable other evidence for these landing sites (e.g., Milanich and Hudson 1993: 39–70). Not least among this supporting evidence are the recollections of the Indians themselves, as reported in Spanish accounts, including the Tocobaga during the 1560s (as reported by Escalante Fontaneda, n.d.c) and the nearby Pojoy as late as 1612 (Fernández de Olivera 1612), both of which placed Soto's landfall in the Tampa Bay vicinity. Cancer's latitudes, however, presumably derived from the pilot of the *Santa María de Encina*, Juan de Arana, thus represent solid and independent evidence for the exact location of his and the two previous expeditions in this vicinity.

The *Santa María de Encina* first sighted land on May 29, 1549, and anchored at 28 degrees latitude, placing the expedition somewhere around Clearwater Harbor or St. Joseph Sound, north of the entrance to Tampa Bay in an area with barrier islands (see figure 2). The following day a small party of five or six sailors was sent toward shore, with orders not to land or go ashore until they had reconnoitered the area for a port. Upon approaching land, they spotted three Indians and beat a hasty retreat in fear of capture, ultimately returning to the ship despite contrary winds.

The expedition decided to sail north, thinking that the port they were searching for was toward the Bay of Miruelo or Apalachee. Arriving as far north as 28½ degrees (near modern Hernando Beach or Weeki Wachee), they sent the shallop to shore, because shallow water prevented the ship from getting any closer than six leagues from shore. Landing at a small bay, Fray Cancer reported that the spot where he wanted to land was an open field where they could have made themselves "lords of the land" and gone into the woods, but instead they landed in a different location where they were met by six Indians who shot arrows at them. They slept that night on a small island some distance from the land, perhaps modern Indian Key, and had to wait until the morning high tide because their shallop was beached at low tide. After proceeding three more leagues northward in search of a port, they returned the nine-league distance to the ship against contrary winds.

Next they retraced their steps and sailed back to the place where they had first sighted land, and the pilot and several sailors, accompanied by Fray Cancer and Fray Tolosa, along with the farmer Estéban de Fuentes, took the shallop to reconnoiter the land and see if there were signs of Indians. They entered an inshore bay, where they saw three or four Indian fishing camps, and dropped anchor. Fray Tolosa went onshore and climbed a tree to look for any signs of people, and soon thereafter as many as fifteen to twenty Indians appeared. Fuentes and Magdalena the Indian interpreter landed, followed by Cancer himself, who handed out gifts. When the entire party kneeled and began reciting litanies, the Indians joined them. In subsequent conversations through the interpreter they quickly learned that the port they searched for was only a day and a half away by land.

Fray Tolosa remained with Fuentes and Magdalena in preparation to make the journey by land, while Cancer returned to the ship to bring food and additional gifts for the chief. An Indian accompanied him to the ship and was clothed and fed before the party returned in the shallop. Upon their arrival, however, none of their party was to be seen, and only a small number of Indians remained, enticing them to come to shore by holding out fish. One of the sailors boldly leaped out of the boat and climbed up to where the Indians were, where he was grasped by the arm and ultimately unable to free himself. Presuming that the others had been captured as well, Cancer returned despondently to the ship, returning the next day with Fray Beteta to find no one left onshore. The party returned to the ship and then weighed anchor, sailing along the coast for the bay where they hoped to find news of their companions.

Similar to the earlier difficulties of the Soto expedition, the *Santa María de Encina* spent more than two weeks navigating through the shallow entrance to Tampa Bay and many leagues into the interior of the bay. Spotting a "little mound" with a house on its summit, the friars attempted to make contact with an Indian at the door but ultimately left a shirt as a gift hanging on a stick over the water and moved a league farther to other huts. After waiting some time, a pair of Indians came forth with a pole topped with white feathers as a sign of peace, and Frays Cancer and Beteta waded near shore and delivered another pair of shirts as gifts. The Indians promised through signs and some Spanish words that they would bring the captive Spaniards and the interpreter the next day.

On the following day, the missionaries found that the Indians had crossed to the other side of the bay, where they made Cancer's party wait before a group of Indians arrived expecting gifts, which were exchanged in a tense encounter in waist-deep water. During this chaotic scene, all three remaining missionaries, as well as many of the sailors, were nearly plundered for clothing and other gifts and were unsure at times whether they would be allowed to leave. The interpreter was among this group but was not recognized at first because she was now naked like the rest of her companions. She claimed that the captive Spaniards were in the chief's house and that the entire land was in a tumult out of fear that a Spanish armada was going to arrive. In the end, the missionaries were sent back and told to return the next day with metal axes, which the Indians desired.

Upon their return to the *Santa María de Encina*, the party's hopes were dashed upon finding that a Spaniard named Juan Muñoz, a survivor of the Soto expedition ten years earlier, had appropriated a canoe to escape and reach the Spanish ship in the harbor. Speaking only fractured Spanish, Muñoz delivered the news that both Fray Diego de Tolosa and Estéban de Fuentes had been killed and that the sailor was alive but a prisoner. He had held the friar's scalp in his hand when the trophy was being passed around by the Indians. The somewhat fanciful 1596 account of the expedition by Agustín Dávila Padilla quotes Muñoz as having stated that the Indians beheaded the murdered Spaniards (including Cancer in his erroneous rendering) and carried their heads "as gifts to a great señor cacique who is in the interior, who drinks from the skulls of his enemies in vengeance, which is the practice they have with the heads, which are esteemed even more when they are from the most renowned people" (Dávila Padilla 1955: 189). Even though it is clear from the Cancer-Beteta diary that Muñoz could only have witnessed such an event for Tolosa and Fuentes, there may still be a grain of truth in the garbled recollections of Dávila Padilla.

In addition to Juan Muñoz's tragic news, the crew of the *Santa María de Encina* was by this time racked with fevers and unable to keep up with the pumps to keep the ship afloat for extended service. Despite the petitions of his remaining companions, who expressed their desire to return to Mexico or Havana and reequip for a mission to a different location, Fray Cancer decided to return and remain alone in Florida. Reasoning that if his mission failed, the resultant Spanish retaliation against the Indians would be far worse than if he had never even arrived, Cancer spent the next day, the Feast of Saint John (June 24), writing letters and making preparations to return to shore.

On the following day, squalls stymied their efforts to reach shore, but despite continuing rain and wind the next day, Wednesday, June 26, the launch finally reached its destination. Despite a tense confrontation in which Juan Muñoz revealed that the murders were no longer a secret, Fray Cancer persisted in his desire to land alone, insisting that the other Spaniards avoid provoking the Indians by shouting or approaching shore. Once onshore, he prayed, embraced the Indian who received him, and was led quickly into the edge of the woods, where he was clubbed to death in sight of the launch.

Thus ended the purely spiritual conquest of Florida. The ship spent another day in search of water before departing on June 28 for Havana. Contrary winds forced the *Santa María* to the Yucatán and finally back to San Juan de Ulua some three weeks later. Fray Beteta (who later became bishop of Cartagena) finished out Cancer's incomplete diary, recopied the entire diary in his own hand, and sent both copies to Spain as a tragic record of the only nonmilitary attempt to colonize Florida.

The Captivity of Hernando de Escalante Fontaneda, 1549–1566

As noted previously, following the failed 1521 colonial attempt by Juan Ponce de León, there is no direct evidence for subsequent visits by Spanish ships to the Calusa domain of Southwest Florida until 1566. Perhaps two full generations had passed during the nearly half century that elapsed between these contacts, and while the Calusa were undoubtedly aware of the sporadic contact between Spaniards (Narváez, Soto, and Cancer) and Indians around present-day Tampa Bay, they nonetheless were not contacted in their homeland, either by choice or chance. This is not to say that they avoided all European contact, however, for during this same period the powerful Calusa chief ultimately became a sort of "magnet" for Spanish shipwreck survivors from the eastern side of the Florida peninsula, drawing as many as several hundred of these captives away from the initial sites of their imprisonment in the Florida Keys or along the lower Atlantic coastline (e.g., True 1944b). While Spanish exploratory ships may have avoided or missed the Calusa homeland throughout the mid-sixteenth century, Spanish treasure fleets routinely passed through the dangerous Florida Straits just off the Atlantic shore, where storms and nearshore reefs took a substantial toll on ships and their crews and passengers, as well as their valuable cargoes.

Historical and archaeological evidence agrees on the fact that during much of the colonial era, there was regular transpeninsular traffic in shipwreck cargo and imprisoned shipwreck survivors. Salvaged Spanish cargo was initially obtained by Atlantic-coast Indians such as the Ais, Jeaga, and Tequesta, who routinely dove on Spanish wrecks to obtain precious metals such as gold and silver, among a range of other objects. The ultimate destination of this material was far to the west, however, as demonstrated by the disproportionately high archaeological frequency of funerary objects crafted from Spanish silver and gold in central and western portions of South Florida, including many from the Calusa heartland along the lower gulf coast (e.g., Allerton, Luer, and Carr 1984; Luer 1994; Wheeler 2000). In part, this westward flow of Spanish goods was certainly a by-product of the political primacy of the Calusa chief in regional affairs across much of South Florida. This was also the likely explanation for the apparent concentration of Spanish captives in the Calusa chief's hands by the 1560s, when it provided the motivation for renewed direct Spanish contact with the Calusa (Solís de Merás 1893).

Among hundreds of other Spanish shipwreck survivors imprisoned in South Florida during the sixteenth century and later, one alone stands out as the author of a detailed narrative of his captivity experiences: Hernando de Escalante Fontaneda. According to his own account, penned about 1575 in Spain, Fontaneda had been shipwrecked in South Florida about 1549, when he was thirteen years old, during a trip from Cartagena to Spain and was imprisoned by the Indians, ultimately spending the next seventeen years living as a Calusa captive (Escalante Fontaneda, n.d.c; True 1944b; Worth 1995). His experiences as a captive between 1549 and 1566, and subsequently as an interpreter at the Spanish fort on Mound Key through 1569 (Escalante Fontaneda 1569), constitute one of the most important records of indigenous Calusa culture available to modern researchers. Even though Fontaneda's primary narrative and other affiliated text fragments represent firsthand recollections long after the fact, they still provide an insider's perspective and window into a period of time during which no Spanish expedition even visited the Calusa.

Since by his own testimony Fontaneda was only thirteen years old when he sailed through Florida waters, documentary evidence regarding his life before captivity is scant to nonexistent. Though his father, Juan de Escalante, who died in Cartagena before 1553, does appear in the documentary record (Spanish Crown 1553, 1569), Hernando remains historically invisible during his youth, with the possible exception of a single name in a list of ship passengers from 1549, the year he would have wrecked in Florida according to his own reckoning. In that year, one "Hernando de Escalante" appeared as a passenger and owner of a total of 2,150 pesos of silver, which arrived in Spain on the ship *Trinidad* owned by Juan Canelas, part of the South American fleet that year ("Relations of the Lots of Gold" 1549). Although the ship and its master made at least one additional round-trip to and from the Indies in 1550–51 (Chaunu and Chaunu 1955: 444, 474), it is possible that this Hernando was a passenger on a different vessel in the fleet, perhaps one that did not survive the crossing.

Whether or not Fontaneda's wreck occurred during the passage of this 1549 fleet through Florida waters, at some point in or about 1549 Fontaneda's life was forever changed by the wreck of the ship on which he was traveling and his subsequent capture by South Florida Indians, most likely in the Keys or in the vicinity of Biscayne Bay (since he specifically noted that he never traveled in Jeaga or Ais to the north, both of which were apparently independent from the Calusa chief). From there, he was eventually brought to the Calusa capital at Mound Key, where he evidently served as an interpreter for newly captured Spaniards. Though his older brother and most of the other Spanish captives during these years were killed or died in captivity, Fontaneda's utility as an interpreter almost certainly contributed to his survival. It also gave him unique access to information at the highest level of the Calusa polity, lending additional depth and reliability to his later narrative.

While the details of his captivity are best recounted in his narrative, the years after his 1566 rescue by Pedro Menéndez de Avilés also provide insight into the eventual content of his writings. Far from being sent immediately back to Cartagena or to Spain, the thirty-year-old Fontaneda was placed by Menéndez on the Florida payroll as an interpreter and sent along with the Spanish garrison dispatched in October 1566 under Captain Francisco de Reynoso to establish Fort San Antón de Carlos at Mound Key (Menéndez de Avilés 1566a, 1566b; Escalante Fontaneda 1569). During the course of the two years and eight months that the fort was maintained there, Fontaneda apparently acted as the principal interpreter for all negotiations and conversations between two successive Calusa chiefs and Spanish officials residing on or visiting the island. This included discussions not only with Pedro Menéndez de Avilés himself but also with Jesuit missionaries such as Juan Rogel, whose subsequent letters to his superiors also contain substantial ethnographic detail regarding Calusa culture (Zubillaga 1946). Given that Rogel (1946f) later admitted that "speaking through interpreters never bore any fruit" in all three of the South Florida missions, all his ethnographic observations based on conversations with the Calusa chief had been filtered through the interpreter Hernando de Escalante Fontaneda. In this sense, both Fontaneda's and Rogel's ethnographic texts are interrelated and cannot be considered independent.

When the Calusa finally withdrew from Mound Key after the death of yet another chief at Spanish hands in 1569, Fontaneda accompanied the members of the Spanish garrison to Havana, Cuba, and followed a number of them to Madrid, Spain, where the fort's former commander Francisco de Reynoso (1569) filed a lawsuit claiming payment for his services at San Antón and where Fontaneda solicited royal aid based on his father's previous service (Spanish Crown 1569). After Fontaneda's testimony in favor of Reynoso's petition, Fontaneda's subsequent activities in Spain are unknown until he put pen to paper about 1575, when internal evidence in his narrative suggests he wrote his manuscript (six years after his departure from Florida). The fact that several of Fontaneda's other text fragments contain marginal notes by the royal cosmographer Juan López de Velasco, who submitted the final version of his manuscript *Geografía y descripción universal de las Indias* in November 1576, strongly indicates that López de Velasco at least consulted Fontaneda's manuscript, or may even have interviewed him, during the preparation of his book (López de Velasco 1894: ix; Worth 1995). Fontaneda himself seems to have died before 1577, when doña María de

Escobar, widow of one Hernando de Escalante, was granted permission to sail from Spain to Cartagena with a daughter named Ana (Romera Iruela and Galbis Díez 1980: 712). His life was brief but eventful, comprising twenty years among the Calusa and twenty years among his fellow Spaniards. Nevertheless, those two decades of captivity provided his posterity a remarkable narrative that fills a significant gap in the Spanish exploration of Florida's lower gulf coast.

The Pedro Menéndez de Avilés Expeditions, 1566–1569

The next phase of Spanish exploration and interaction along the lower gulf coast of Florida, and by far the most intensive throughout the entire early colonial era, began with the 1566 arrival of the founder of St. Augustine and the Florida colony, Pedro Menéndez de Avilés; his rescue of the captive Fontaneda; and the subsequent establishment of three garrisoned forts in South Florida. These forts included Fort San Antón de Carlos (1566–69) at the Calusa capital on Mound Key, as well as additional forts at Tocobaga (1567–68) and Tequesta (1567–68). Though this phase is very commonly referred to as the first Spanish "missions" to the Calusa (e.g., Hann 1991), the Jesuit presence in Fort San Antón was actually only minimal and sporadic, consisting of a single missionary and an open-air chapel and lasting a total of only about fourteen discontinuous months prior to its abandonment. Jesuits stationed only a lay brother at the Tequesta fort during its short life, and Tocobaga was the site of just occasional visits by the resident priest at Mound Key. By far, the forts and their military garrisons represented the most significant and long-lived aspect of Spanish interaction with the South Florida Indians during this period, even though their visibility in the documentary record is considerably less than the Jesuit presence.

During the winter after his 1565 establishment of the first successful Spanish colonial town on the Atlantic coast of Florida at St. Augustine, Pedro Menéndez de Avilés departed from Havana, Cuba, on February 10, 1566, with seven ships in search of the port of Carlos, where he expected to find a number of rumored Christian captives (Solís de Merás 1893: 149–68; Lyon 1976: 147–50). Reaching the Southwest Florida coast four days later, Menéndez left five larger vessels in deeper water offshore and led two smaller brigantines closer to shore (see figure 2). The vessels were first met by the captive Hernando de Escalante Fontaneda in a canoe, claiming to have been sent by the other captive Christians upon learning of the imminent arrival of the Spanish fleet. Fontaneda subsequently led them to the Calusa capital at Mound Key, where they landed adjacent to shore about half a league from the village.

During their initial contact, which was evidently the first official Spanish visit to the Calusa capital town ever (Ponce de León seems never to have reached the town itself), Menéndez lured the principal chief of the Calusa, named Carlos like his father before him after the king of Spain, onto his vessel with twenty nobles and took them out to sea, threatening to have him killed if he refused to turn over the other Spanish captives.

The chief acquiesced and ultimately delivered five men and six women, four of whom (two men and two women) decided to remain with their Calusa families (Menéndez de Avilés 1566c; Solís de Merás 1893: 154–55, 167). Carlos was returned to land with many gifts and requested a reciprocal visit by Menéndez to his village the next day, but Fontaneda later warned him that it was a trap and that Carlos intended to have Menéndez murdered. Sailing around to the village itself, Menéndez found no Indians willing to bring him ashore. He subsequently sailed all the way north to modern Tampa Bay to search for the rest of his fleet and to ransom other captives held there by the Tocobaga. Finding neither, Menéndez returned to Mound Key to find the rest of his fleet already anchored there and some one hundred soldiers under Estéban de las Alas in the village. Having appeared with overwhelming military force at the Calusa capital by surprise, the Spanish fleet met no resistance, and upon Menéndez's return, Chief Carlos displayed a complete change of heart, saying that he wished to consider Menéndez like an elder brother and offered Menéndez his elder sister as a wife in sign of both kinship and political subordination (Solís de Merás 1893: 281). Such elder sibling relationships, both real and fictive, appear to have been common features of the sociopolitical landscape of the southeastern Indians, including both patrilineal groups like the Calusa in South Florida (Goggin and Sturtevant 1964; Marquardt 1987, 1988; Worth 2008) and predominantly matrilineal groups to the north (e.g., Hudson 1990: 61–67; 1997: 11–24; Lankford 2008: 110–11).

Subsequent events detailed by Gonzalo Solís de Merás (1893: 157–68) for Menéndez's first visit to the Calusa capital suggest that Chief Carlos had decided that it was in his best interest to submit himself at least nominally as a vassal of the Spanish Crown (in the governor's name), probably in part out of immediate fear of military domination and perhaps also with designs toward gaining a powerful ally in his ongoing wars with Tocobaga and Tequesta, which he later attempted to exploit to his advantage during a trip to Tocobaga with Menéndez. For his part, Pedro Menéndez clearly needed the allegiance of Chief Carlos and the Calusa domain, in large part because of his plan to establish an inland water route between St. Augustine and South Florida (and ultimately to Havana). Ultimately, this strategic alliance was to be sealed with the political marriage between Carlos's sister (baptized doña

Antonia) and Menéndez himself, which took place before his departure in March in a series of elaborate feasts staged in a large structure belonging to the chief. When the Spanish fleet left Mound Key, Menéndez took all the captives who chose to leave, as well as doña Antonia and seven other Indians, including a cousin and heir of Chief Carlos, who would ultimately be baptized don Pedro. He also left a large cross in the care of Carlos's "captain," or war chief, another cousin and rival who later took the name Felipe (and who would ultimately betray Carlos to the Spaniards and take his place as principal chief).

By mid-October, Menéndez set into motion his plans to consolidate Spanish dominion over the Calusa and all of South Florida. On October 15, 1566, he issued an order to Captain Francisco de Reynoso to lead a detachment of fifty regular soldiers, four old soldiers, two Jesuits, and two boys and sail in a brigantine with a pilot and twelve sailors to the port of San Antón (Estero Bay), where he was to construct a fort at the Calusa capital (Menéndez de Avilés 1566a). Subsequent documents suggest that the initial contingent included only Captain Reynoso, twelve soldiers, and two ex-captives as interpreters, including Fontaneda himself (Menéndez de Avilés 1566c; Rogel 1946a). Upon his arrival, Reynoso also returned Carlos's heir, don Pedro, and delivered a letter from Menéndez for Carlos, along with at least 145 yards of Spanish cloth as a gift, with which he was received in friendship and permitted to begin construction on the fort. He also sent the brigantine to Havana for additional supplies, accompanied by Carlos's sister doña Antonia (who had been returned from Havana in the meantime) and six other nobles who were to act as hostages to ensure the safety of Captain Reynoso and his garrison (Solís de Merás 1893: 277–79, 282).

The following spring, Pedro Menéndez sailed from Havana for Mound Key with six brigantines and 150 soldiers, with the intention of exploring upriver along the Caloosahatchee River to discover if there was a passage to the fabled Lake of Mayaimi (modern Lake Okeechobee) from which he hoped to make his way north through the previously explored St. Johns River valley to St. Augustine (Solís de Merás 1893: 275, 280–83). He brought the promised Jesuit missionaries along with twenty to thirty additional soldiers (see Menéndez de Avilés 1566b), as well as several noble Indians from the Tequesta chiefdom at modern Biscayne Bay to negotiate peace with Carlos under Spanish supervision. These Indians had been sent by their chief as part of his own offer of vassalage to Menéndez de Avilés, sparked by the report of a marriage between the Spanish governor and Carlos's sister, who was said to have been a kinswoman of the Tequesta chief (Solís de Merás 1893: 281–82). By striving to establish peace among all the warring chiefdoms of South Florida, Menéndez ultimately hoped to expand his military dominion over South

Florida by establishing formal Spanish relations with the Calusa chief's two principal enemies at the time—Tocobaga at modern Tampa Bay and Tequesta at the mouth of the modern Miami River.

During his three-day stay at Mound Key, Menéndez built a chapel for Jesuit Father Juan Rogel to say Mass and a separate house for doña Antonia, and he hosted two dinners for Carlos and his wife and nobles. Probably during these meetings, Carlos seems to have intentionally misled Menéndez into believing that the inland waterway to Lake Okeechobee was not the Caloosahatchee River (it was in fact the closest route, though not a continuous waterway) but was instead an estimated fifty leagues north along the gulf coast, in the land of his enemy Tocobaga, for which he readily volunteered Calusa assistance in making war against this province. Clearly designed as a strategic move to gain Spanish military might in asserting Calusa dominion over Tocobaga, Carlos's proposal was turned down by Menéndez, who explained that Spanish policy discouraged such internecine struggles within colonial territories and that he wished to establish peace with Tocobaga. Carlos was said to have "greatly regretted" Menéndez's decision but subsequently acquiesced to Spanish-brokered peace negotiations with the Tequesta delegation, which included the chief's own brother.

Taking Chief Carlos and twenty Calusa with him, Menéndez sailed north to Tocobaga's principal town along the northern margin of present-day Tampa Bay, approaching the village just before dawn, using the help of a Calusa Indian who led them directly to the site on a moonless night. Since the new moon can be calculated to have fallen on March 10, 1567, the date of arrival seems likely to have been March 12, the feast day of Saint Gregory, for which the Bay of San Gregorio was subsequently named (Menéndez de Avilés 1573). Taken by surprise, the Tocobaga chief did not flee but sent a Portuguese captive with a message of his surrender. During his four-day stay, Menéndez negotiated peaceful relations with Tocobaga and between Carlos and Tocobaga (despite the former's continued pleas to let him burn the village and kill its inhabitants). Tocobaga assembled a council of twenty-nine subordinate chiefs and one hundred accompanying nobles, and together with Carlos, they agreed to terms under which either chief would be assisted militarily by the Spaniards against the other, if that chief chose to break the peace established between them (Solís de Merás 1893: 285–91). Menéndez left a garrison of thirty soldiers at Tocobaga before returning to the Calusa capital at Mound Key. Chief Carlos made little pretense of his anger toward Menéndez and the Spaniards and their newfound peace with Tocobaga, and as a result, Menéndez had the fortifications strengthened and left several small artillery pieces (versos, or small culverins), along with fifty additional soldiers. On his way back to Havana, Menéndez returned the Tequesta delegation and left Jesuit lay brother Francisco Villareal as a missionary, also stationing another small Spanish garrison there at Tequesta, later said to have comprised some thirty soldiers (Menéndez de Avilés the Younger 1573; Antonio Pérez 1573).

By the end of March 1567, Spanish forts were garrisoned at San Antón de Carlos, Tocobaga, and Tequesta, and resident Jesuit missionaries had been stationed in Calos and Tequesta. What had been an aboriginal landscape of three warring paramount chiefs was converted, at least superficially, into a fortified Spanish colonial hinterland. But beneath the surface of this imposed peace simmered an undercurrent of anti-Spanish hostility that would ultimately erupt on multiple occasions, usually with tragic results. During the weeks following Menéndez de Avilés's departure, Carlos actively plotted to have all the Spaniards murdered, but in part because of the activities of his cousin the war chief as an informant for the Spanish, the plot was uncovered, and Carlos was lured into the fort and killed along with two other Indians (Rogel 1946b: 306–9). The cousin, who had been deposed as adoptive heir of the chief during his childhood by Carlos's father (309–11), was subsequently emplaced as the new principal chief of the Calusa and became an active proponent of the Spanish alliance, on whose support his chieftaincy was initially predicated. Named Felipe by Juan Rogel (291) in recognition of the reigning king of Spain (Felipe II, who succeeded Carlos I in 1556 after forty years on the throne), the new Calusa chief formally and publicly rendered Calusa vassalage to the Spaniards during ceremonies in July (278, 282). Lengthy personal conversations between Felipe and Father Juan Rogel (entirely through interpreter Hernando de Escalante Fontaneda) took place in the fort between July 1567 and April 1568 and ultimately formed the basis for the Jesuit's theological insights into the indigenous Calusa religion, related in a subsequent letter (Rogel 1946b).

Details about the next two years at Fort San Antón de Carlos under Felipe's rule are not well documented, but important information can be gleaned about the fate of the three South Florida forts and missions from a relative abundance of contemporary and subsequent Jesuit reports (e.g., Rogel 1946b, 1946c, 1946d, 1946e, 1946f, 1946g; Villarreal 1946a, 1946b; Sedeño 1946a, 1946b; Segura 1946a, 1946b, 1946c; Esquivel 1570) and other contemporary accounts (e.g., Menéndez Márquez 1568; Reynoso 1569). The fort was kept in fairly regular contact with Havana by routine supply expeditions, which seem to have occurred roughly every two to five months. Additional Havana supply trips financed by Captain Reynoso himself (and led by his son Jerónimo) may also have been conducted at more frequent intervals (Reynoso 1569). During its existence, Fort San Antón (and its short-lived neighbors at Tocobaga and Tequesta) was supplied with immense quantities of corn, hardtack, wheat flour, cassava, oil, and wine, as well as smaller amounts of vinegar and honey. Large amounts of beef were routinely supplied, and livestock was transported on at least three trips, including three hundred pigs, one hundred hens, and thirty goats. The forts were also provided with arquebuses and small artillery, munitions (such as gunpowder, shot, and match cord), iron tools and nails, and various articles of clothing for the soldiers in garrison. Based on numbers from these supply lists, the relative sizes of each garrison were thirty-five in Calos, twenty-two in Tocobaga, and twelve in Tequesta.

The Jesuits took advantage of the regular ship traffic to travel frequently back and forth to their base in Havana. Father Juan Rogel spent a grand total of only about ten months in Fort San Antón, including stays from March to May and July to December during 1567 and January to April in 1568, as well as an eight-day visit that October. Rogel visited the fort at Tocobaga only once for a few days during late June 1567. Brother Francisco Villarreal remained at the Tequesta fort throughout its eleven-month existence (March 1567 to February 1568, except for a twenty-day trip to Havana) and then replaced Rogel at Calos during April to August 1568. After the arrival of new Jesuits in Havana on June 19, a new priest (Gonzalo del Alamo) was assigned to Fort San Antón in August, but because of sickness he and Villarreal did not return to Mound Key until the following spring of 1569, just before things fell apart completely.

Because of the tenuous nature of Spanish-Indian relations on Mound Key, neither soldiers nor missionaries commonly ventured farther than "a stone's throw" from the walls of the fort, largely in fear of ambush or murder. In part because of his close Spanish alliance, Felipe faced internal resistance and occasional outright rebellion throughout his rule (e.g., Rogel 1946e: 282). Four subordinate towns evidently broke away from Calusa sovereignty during late 1567, rendering obedience to Chief Tocobaga to the north (perhaps including those on the northern fringe of Calusa territory along the northern rim of modern Charlotte Harbor). Perhaps compounding a growing anti-Spanish sentiment among the Tocobaga and the four breakaway Calusa towns, supply shortages at the Spanish fort there reached a critical point during the fall of 1567, apparently prompting the soldiers to have to pressure the Tocobaga more than they would have wished (Rogel 1946e: 292–93, 296–97). Fearing trouble, Father Rogel traveled to Havana to encourage quick aid, but by the time supply ships returned under Pedro Menéndez Márquez in early January 1568, the fort had been overrun and all but three of the roughly twenty to twenty-four soldiers murdered. Upon the arrival of the supply ship, the three remaining prisoners were quickly killed as the Indians of Tocobaga fled their village. Menéndez Márquez subsequently ordered the entire town burned to the ground, along with the temple and its idols

(Rogel 1946e: 295–97; Menéndez Márquez 1568; Villareal 1946a: 415). Felipe vowed to wage war against the Tocobaga, for which the Spaniards this time promised military aid.

After reinforcing Fort San Antón with additional soldiers, Menéndez Márquez returned to Havana and shortly afterward traveled to the Florida Keys to coerce its inhabitants to send their obligatory tribute to the Calusa chief (Menéndez Márquez 1568). While there, he learned that the Calusa chief had had the chief of Tatesta and two other Indians killed, purportedly because of their friendship with the Spaniards (though more likely in an effort to eliminate internal resistance). In addition, and far more urgently, Menéndez Márquez was informed that the Spaniards at the Tequesta fort had killed the old chief on account of some affront to one of the soldiers and that the Indians had risen up against the garrison (Menéndez Márquez 1568; Villarreal 1946a: 415). Upon his arrival, Menéndez Márquez found the Spaniards in the midst of open hostilities with the Indians of Tequesta, who had killed three soldiers (another later died from his wounds), one of whom they disemboweled and impaled on a stake in view of the Spaniards (Menéndez Márquez 1568, 1573; Menéndez de Avilés the Younger 1573; Antonio Pérez 1573). The Indians had taken all the drinking water and fled to the woods, and with little food and munitions left, Menéndez Márquez piled all the surviving soldiers and Brother Villareal into the shallop and delivered it as far as the Keys; he then returned to Havana and sent a larger vessel to bring the refugees to Fort San Antón, where they arrived on April 4 (Menéndez Márquez 1568; Rogel 1946e: 304). Fort San Antón became the final surviving Spanish outpost in South Florida, though under increasingly difficult conditions.

Few details are available for the following months, but by the time Juan Rogel visited Mound Key in October, Felipe seems to have been struggling to survive against open internal rebellion. Rogel noted that "the affairs of that province are arranged and directed in such a manner that the life and reign of that chief depend on the Christians not abandoning him, because he is so disliked by many captains and chiefs, vassals of his, that if it weren't for the favor and rearguard that he has in the Christians, they would have killed him many days ago" (1946c: 337). Felipe had already been forced to kill more than fifteen of "his principal vassals and heads of towns who were trying to kill him," and upon Rogel's arrival, the Indians were feasting and dancing with the severed heads of four rebel chiefs (337). During Rogel's visit, Felipe renewed his promise to become the first Christian Calusa upon the return of Pedro Menéndez de Avilés from Spain.

This long-awaited event finally took place in December 1568, when Menéndez sent word from Havana to the Calusa chief inviting him to come to that city (Rogel 1946d: 380–81; Villarreal 1946a: 416). Felipe and his retinue arrived there sometime by January 1569 and stayed until early February, visiting the Jesuit house several times before returning with the Jesuit priest Gonzalo del Alamo to Mound Key. During his visit, Felipe promised that he would burn his idols and become Christian as soon as he returned to his home, and Menéndez promised to provide military aid to wage war on Tocobaga, which even the Jesuits admitted was justified.

Father Alamo returned to Havana at some point in the spring, and Brother Villarreal apparently returned to Calos, but sometime in the late spring, Pedro Menéndez de Avilés finally returned in person to Mound Key, bringing with him three Jesuits—Father Alamo, Father Antonio Sedeño, and the Vice Provincial Father Juan Bautista de Segura. According to Villarreal (1946a: 416), Menéndez de Avilés spoke alone with Felipe, and the next day the Calusa chief and his Indians finally burned all their idols, admitting later that he had done so out of fear. Leaving Alamo and Villarreal at Mound Key, Menéndez and the other Jesuits returned to Havana, but at some point not long afterward, relations apparently soured between Felipe and the Spaniards, potentially sparked by Menéndez de Avilés's coercion of the Calusa chief into burning the religious objects in the principal Calusa temple. Perhaps attempting to regain lost support from his Calusa subjects, Felipe himself finally turned against the Spaniards and attempted to have them murdered (Rogel 1946g: 610; Villarreal 1946a: 416). Apparently in reference to this incident, Pedro Menéndez Márquez (1573) reported that about four months after the Calusa chief was sent back to his home (in early June), when he sent a ship with supplies for the soldiers there, the chief "gave an order to take the said ship on the coast before it could land, and for this he sent Indians in canoes, and those in the ship defended themselves." When the sailors on the ship returned with news of the attack, the adelantado sent Pedro Menéndez Márquez "to do justice to the said cacique and the rest of the guilty in the case," afterward testifying that he held a trial and executed (literally *degolló*, meaning "cut the throats of") the chief and twenty Indians "of the most guilty" (Menéndez Márquez 1573). Juan Rogel (1946g: 610) provides a nearly identical account, specifying that the Calusa chief Felipe, along with fourteen or fifteen Indians, mostly nobles, were killed by the Spaniards. Brother Villareal (1946a: 416) also notes many others who were badly wounded, presumably referring to those who had participated in the failed surprise attack on the Spanish supply ship.

Other contemporary testimony may also refer to these or other related incidents during this period of rapidly deteriorating relations. Pedro Menéndez de Avilés the Younger (1573) testified that he had heard from knowledgeable people that "the said cacique Carlos had conspired with the aforementioned cacique Tocobaga to kill all the Spaniards that were in the land of the said Carlos instructing the [Christian] doctrine" and that he had implemented this by having "certain Indian vassals of his" carry out a surprise attack on a ship that had entered a port in his territory, entering the ship in friendship and attacking them, casting some of the Spaniards in the water. Portuguese sailor Antonio Pérez (1573) clarified that the attack occurred while he was going to the Calusa fort with supplies and that he and those with whom he was traveling were attacked by "the Indians of Muspataguala, who are subject to the said cacique [of Carlos]" and barely escaped with minor wounds. Shortly after the adelantado had traveled from Havana in three shallops and successfully negotiated peace with the Calusa chief, the cacique suddenly attacked the Spaniards and killed three men, including an ensign and an interpreter, wounded many others, and seized one of the shallops, forcing the rest to return to Havana in the remaining two vessels (Menéndez de Avilés the Younger 1573; Soto 1573; Antonio Pérez 1573). During this attack, Menéndez de Avilés was struck in the chest with a javelin (an *azagaya* or *gorguz*) and survived only because he was wearing armor (Soto 1573; Antonio Pérez 1573).

In response to the executions carried out by Pedro Menéndez Márquez, the inhabitants of the Calusa capital apparently fled the island, leaving the Spaniards without any support or resident labor. On June 15, 1569, Fort San Antón de Carlos was officially abandoned exactly two years and eight months after being commissioned, and the garrison and Jesuits were withdrawn to Havana (Reynoso 1569; Segura 1946b: 385). The Calusa "queens" (including doña Antonia and other noble females) were taken to Havana as well, where they apparently lived out the rest of their lives (doña Antonia, at least, died there several years later, attended by Father Rogel; see Rogel 1946g: 610).

In the aftermath of the fall of Fort San Antón, Captain Reynoso and several other soldiers evidently made their way to Spain, including Hernando de Escalante Fontaneda, whose original childhood trip to Spain had effectively been delayed some twenty years.

The Aftermath

With the 1569 withdrawal of the last Spanish garrison along Florida's lower gulf coast, what had for more than half a century been the scene of many first contacts between Spaniards and Indians was suddenly returned to near complete isolation from the European colonial world, where it would remain for virtually all of the next forty-two years. This seems to have been primarily because of a state of open war that existed between the surviving Calusa and other South Florida Indians after the Spanish withdrawal. Pedro Menéndez de Avilés the Younger later testified that while he was passing the Florida coast as captain of a frigate, "a cacique, his friend, told him that he should not go to Carlos and should go away immediately from there, because the aforementioned cacique and all the Indians of that coast had made many weapons and sworn by their gods to kill all the Spaniards and take the ships and boats that they traveled in" (1573). He later found out that this same cacique "rose up with the rest of the Indians in the Martyrs, and they are at war." He and other witnesses reported a number of subsequent attacks by South Florida Indians against Spaniards during the early 1570s, including not just the capture and murder of shipwreck survivors but also several ambushes of ships both large and small while at anchor, using overwhelming forces armed with bows and arrows, spears, and war clubs (Menéndez Márquez 1573; Menéndez de Avilés the Younger 1573; Soto 1573; Antonio Pérez 1573; Ruíz 1574).

Importantly, these declarations were assembled as part of a new proposal by Florida governor Pedro Menéndez de Avilés, who in 1573 petitioned the king for permission to implement the military conquest of all of South Florida. The testimony gathered in both Havana and Madrid during 1573 and 1574 included not just a recounting of recent attacks but also a review of the reported treatment of Spanish shipwreck survivors from previous decades. Anticipating Fontaneda's later written account, Pedro Menéndez Márquez testified regarding the sacrifice of some 250 Christian prisoners at the hands of the Calusa, noting that "on certain days of the year when they gather for their festivities, they sacrifice them little by little," reducing their number to just eighteen by the time that they were liberated (Menéndez Márquez 1573). A number of the witnesses revealed gruesome details of what they had seen and heard from the Spanish captives when they first arrived in 1566, including several who reported seeing the heads of many Christians displayed on poles (Soto 1573; Alvaro Pérez 1573) and one who reported that he had "counted and seen at the foot of a tree more than fifty heads of Christians that the said cacique [Carlos] had sacrificed" (Antonio Pérez 1573).

Together, all of this formed part of a proposal that represented a truly radical change in Menéndez's strategy for South Florida, one that reflected his complete loss of hope for the colonial assimilation of its native peoples. In it, he lamented:

Although all the Indians from the Mosquito River [Mosquito Inlet] at the beginning of the Bahama Channel down to the Martyrs [Florida Keys], and returning up to Tocobaga Bay [Tampa Bay], have been approached in great friendship, and have been given many gifts and brought many times to Havana and returned to their lands, and have rendered obedience to His Majesty, they have many times ruptured the peace, killing many Christians, and they have been pardoned, and despite everything they have not taken advantage of this. . . . I have established peace with them three times, and they have broken it. (Menéndez de Avilés 1573)

Describing details of these depredations drawn from the testimony he had assembled, Menéndez offered a bold proposal:

From now on, in order to protect the service of God our lord, and of His Majesty, it is suitable . . . that war be waged on them with all rigor, in blood and fire, and that those who are taken alive can be sold as slaves, removing them from the land and carrying them to the neighboring islands of Cuba, Santo Domingo, and Puerto Rico, because in this manner . . . it will remain clean and depopulated . . . and it will be a great example and fear for the friendly Indians who maintain and fulfill our friendship. (Menéndez de Avilés 1573)

Although the Spanish Crown ultimately denied Menéndez's request to enslave the South Florida Indians, it nevertheless proposed that Spanish soldiers "should go into the interior and apprehend all those guilty for the murders and sacrifices that have been committed against Christians under pretense of peace and friendship" but that the rest "should be brought to the islands of Cuba, Hispaniola, and Puerto Rico and turned over to the justices of those islands so that they are distributed among the people that seem most suitable to instruct them in government, and to become Christians, or to give them places to make their villages with the government of people who will occupy them in labor, and to have regulation and catechesis" (Menéndez de Avilés 1573). In all cases, however, the Spanish Crown commanded "that neither one nor the other should be slaves." Though this plan was never implemented, it demonstrates staunch legal support for the prohibition of any Indian slavery in Spanish colonies after the early sixteenth century. It also reveals the depth of Menéndez de Avilés's frustration with the indigenous groups of South Florida.

When Spaniards finally returned to Florida's lower gulf coast during the period between 1611 and 1614, it would be in response to several aggressive moves by the coastal Indians in this region against Spanish expansion from the north, including newly established Franciscan missions along the lower Suwannee River near the coast and along the Oklawaha River in the peninsular interior (Worth 1998a: 65–69; 1998b: 17–18;

2013). The chiefs of Pojoy and Tocobaga were executed in 1611 in response to an attack on Christian Timucua Indians, and war was waged against the Calusa in 1614 in response to their near annihilation of the Spanish-allied Mocozo west of Tampa Bay. While hostilities diminished during subsequent decades, Spanish relations with these groups would not improve until the 1680s, though Spanish visits to the lower gulf coast continued to be rare into the eighteenth century. The Tocobaga are documented to have moved north along the gulf coast during the seventeenth century, while the Pojoy, Calusa, and other gulf coast groups survived through the arrival of English-sponsored Indian slave raiders between 1704 and 1711, which ultimately led to the evacuation and abandonment of the entire lower gulf coast of Florida (Worth 2003, 2013; Hann 2003). In the end, Cuban fishermen and immigrant Creek Indians resettled Florida's lower gulf coast during the eighteenth and early nineteenth centuries (Boyd and Navarro Latorre 1953; Covington 1954; Almy 2001; Worth 2004). Without exception, the indigenous groups occupying this region during the sixteenth century did not survive to the present day or even past the eighteenth century. As a result, the narratives of first contact during the sixteenth century provide an unparalleled glimpse of cultures extinguished during the European colonial era, allowing the witnesses of this traumatic era to speak directly to posterity through their written words.

1

The Juan Ponce de León Expeditions, 1513–1521

Despite their pivotal importance in terms of first contact between the indigenous peoples of North America and early sixteenth-century European explorers, the Juan Ponce de León expeditions remain among the most poorly documented exploratory ventures in Florida history. No contemporary narrative accounts of the expeditions have yet been discovered, though we are fortunate to have a secondhand account of the 1513 expedition by late sixteenth-century historian Antonio Herrera, which seems to have been based on now-lost primary source materials. Gonzalo Fernández de Oviedo y Valdés also briefly recounted the events of the 1513 expedition and the 1521 colony in his mid-sixteenth-century work. In addition, as supplements to these more comprehensive narrative accounts, the Archivo General de Indias in Seville preserves not only the original royal contracts authorizing both expeditions (among other related documents) but also two original letters written by Ponce de León himself just days before his departure for the second expedition, all of which are presented here.

Narratives

The 1601 Antonio Herrera Account

The Herrera narrative of the Ponce de León expedition, appearing in Decade I, Libro IX of his *Historia general de los hechos de los Castellanos en las islas i tierra firme del mar oceano* (Herrera y Tordesillas 1601: 246–50), was written some eight decades after the events described in the text, though presumably based on one or more extremely detailed original sources, probably including an original log or detailed report of the expedition, none of which is known to have survived to the present day. It nevertheless remains the best available source for the exact route of the expedition as well as the sequence of events during its course. Some details, such as the name "Carlos" used in reference to the chief near the landing site, were undoubtedly additions by Herrera based on subsequent information available to him (no such name appears on the 1514–15 Freducci map, which nonetheless includes several names not within Herrera's narrative). Regardless of such insertions, until earlier sources emerge, Herrera's narrative is pivotal for understanding the moment of true first contact in Florida (see also Kelley 1991).

The transcription here follows the norms detailed in the preface, generally preserving anachronistic orthography present in the original text except in cases where it might make it difficult for modern Spanish readers to sound out the words correctly or follow the intended sentence structure.

Spanish

Cap[itulo] X. De la navegacion de Juan Ponce de Leon, al Norte de la isla de San Juan, y descubrimiento de la Florida, y porque la llamo assi.

Hallandose Juan Ponce de Leon sin oficio, por aver sido restituydos en los de la isla de San Juan, Juan Ceró[n], y Miguel Diaz: y viendose rico, determino de hazer alguna cosa con que ganar honra, y acrecentar hazienda: y como avia nueva que se hallava tierras a la vanda del Norte, acordó de yr a descubrir hazia aquella parte: para lo qual armó tres navios, bien proveydos de vituallas, gente, y marineros, que para efeto de descubrir son los mas necessarios. Salio de la isla Jueves en la tarde, a tres de Março, partiendo del puerto de San German. Fue al Aguada, para tomar de alli su derrota. La noche siguie[n]te salio a la mar, al Norueste, quarta del Norte, y anduvieron los navios ocho leguas de singladura, hasta que salio el sol. Fueron navega[n]do hasta que el Martes a ocho del dicho, llegaron a surgir a los baxos de Babueca, a una isla que dizen el Viejo, que esta en veynte y dos grados y medio. Otro dia surgiero[n] en una isleta de los Lucayos, dicha Caycos. Luego surgieron en otra dicha la Yagúna, en veinte y quatro grados. A los onze del mismo, llegaron a otra isla dicha Amaguáyo, y alli estuvieron al reparo: passaron a la isla dicha Maneguá, que está en veinte y quatro grados y medio. A los catorze llegaron a Guanahani, que está en veinte y cinco grados, y quarenta minutos, adonde aderezaron un navio para atravesar el golvo Barlovento de las islas de los Lucayos. Esta isla Guanahani fue la primera que descubrio el Almirante don Christoval Colon, y a donde en su primer viaje salio a tierra, y la llamó San Salvador. Partieron de aqui corrie[n]do por el Norueste, y Domingo a veinte y siete, que era dia de Pasqua de Resurecion, que comunmente dizen de Flores, vieron una isla, y no la reconocieron, y el Lunes a veinte y ocho corrieron quinze leguas por la misma via, y el Miercoles anduvieron de la misma manera, y despues con mal tie[m]po hasta dos de Abril, cortiendo [sic] a Luesnorueste, yendo disminuyendo el agua hasta nueve braças, a una legua de tierra, que estava en treynta grados y ocho minutos, corrieron por lue[n]go de costa, buscando puerto, y la noche surgieron cerca de tierra, a ocho braças de agua. Y pensando que esta tierra era isla, la llamaron la Florida, porque tenia muy linda vista de muchas y frescas arboledas, y era llana, y pareja: y porque tambien la descubrieron en tiempo de Pasqua Florida, se quiso Juan Ponce co[n]formar en el nombre, con estas dos razones. Salio a tierra a tomar lengua, y possession. Viernes a ocho hizieron vela, corrieron por la misma via: y Sabado navegaron al Sur, quarta al Sueste: y navegando por el mismo Rumbo, hasta los veynte de Abril, descubrieron unos Bohios de Indios, adonde surgieron: y el dia siguiente, yendo del borde de la mar todos tres navios, vieron una corirente [sic], que aunque tenian viento largo no podian andar adelante, sino atras, y parecia que andavan bien: y al fin se conocio que era tanta la corriente, que podia mas que el viento. Los dos navios que se hallavan mas cerca de tierra surgieron, pero era tan grande la corriente, que hazian rehilar los cables: y el tercer navio, que era bergantin, que se halló mas a la mar, no devio de hallar fondo, o no conocio la corriente, y le desabrazo de la tierra, y le perdiero[n] de vista siendo el dia claro, y co[n] bona[n]ça.

Salio aqui Juan Ponce a tierra, llamado de los Indios: los quales luego procuraron de tomar la barca, los remos, y las armas, y por no romper con ellos se les sufrio, y por no escandalizar la tierra: pero porque dieron a un marinero con un palo en la cabeça, de q[ue] quedó amortezido, se huvo de pelear co[n] ellos: los quales co[n] sus flechas y baras armadas, las puntas de agudos huessos, y espinas de pescados, hiriero[n] a dos Castellanos, y los Indios recibiero[n] poco daño, y despartendolos la noche, Juan Ponce recogio con harto trabajo a los Castellanos. Partiose de alli a un rio, adonde tomó agua y leña, y estuvo esperando el berga[n]tin, acudieron a estorvarlo sesenta Indios, tomose uno dellos para piloto, y para que aprendiesse la lengua: puso a este rio el nombre de la Cruz, y dexo en el labrada una de canteria con un letrero, y no acabaro[n] de tomar el agua por ser salobre. Domingo ocho de Mayo doblaron en el cabo de la Florida, que llamaron cabo de corrientes, porque alli corre tanto el agua, que tiene mas fuerça que el viento, y no dexa yr los navios adelante, aunque den todas las velas, surgieron detras de un cabo, ju[n]to a un pueblo dicho Abaióa. Toda esta costa, desde punta de Arrazifes, hasta este cabo de corrie[n]tes, se corre Norte Sur quarta del Sueste, y es toda limpia, y de hondura de seys braças, y el cabo está en veinte y ocho grados, y quinze minutos: navegaro[n] hasta que hallaron dos

islas al Sur en veynte y siete grados: a la una, que tiene una legua de cumplido pusieron Santa Marta, hizieron agua en ella. El Viernes a treze de Mayo
hizieron vela, corriendo por la costa de un banco e Arrazife de islas, hasta el
paraje de una isla q[ue] llamaron Pola, q[ue] esta en veinte y seys grados y
medio, y entre el baxo y Arrazife de islas, y la tierra firme, va la mar grande
a manera de vahia. El Domingo dia de Pasqua de Espiritu Santo quinze de
Mayo, corriero[n] por la costa de los Isleos diez leguas hasta dos Isleos
blancos, y a todo este restringe de islas y isleos, pusieron por nombre los
Martires, porque vistas de lexos las peñas que se levantan, parecen hombres
que estan padeciendo, y el nombre ha quadrado tambien, por los muchos
que en ellas se han perdido despues: estan en veinte y seys grados, y quinze
minutos, fueron navegando unas vezes al Norte, y otras al Nordeste, hasta
los veinte y tres de Mayo, y a los veinte y quatro corriero[n] por la costa al
Sur (no echando de ver que era tierra firme) hasta unas isletas, que se hazian
fuera a la mar: y porque parecio q[ue] avia entrada entre ellas, y la costa para
los navios, para tomar agua y leña, estuviero[n] alli hasta los tres de Junio,
y dieron carena a un navio, que se llamava San Christoval, y en este tie[m]po
acudieron Indios en canoas a reconocer a los Castellanos, la primera vez
viendo, que aunque los llamavan los Indios, los Castellanos no salian a tierra,
queriendo leva[n]tar un ancora para enmendarla, pensaron que se yvan, se
metieron en la mar en sus canoas, y echaron mano del cable para llevarse el
navio: por lo qual fue tras ellos la barca, y saliendo en tierra los tomaron quatro mugeres, y los quebraron dos canoas viejas, las otras vezes que acudieron
no llegaron a rompimiento, porq[ue] no vieron aparejo, antes rescataro[n]
cueros y guanines.

Cap[itulo] XI. Que Juan Ponce de Leon acabada su navegacio[n] por la costa de la Florida, bolvio a la isla de S[an] Juan.

El Viernes a los quatro, esperando viento para yr en busca del Cazique Carlos, que dezian los Indios de los navios que tenia oro, llegó una canoa a los
bageles, y un Indio que entendia los Castellanos, q[ue] se creyó que devia
de ser de la Española, o de otra isla de las habitadas de Castellanos, dixo
que aguardassen, que el Cazique queria embiar oro para rescatar, y aguardando parecieron hasta veinte canoas, y algunas atadas de dos en dos, unas
fuero[n] a las ancoras, otras a los navios, y començaron a pelear desde sus
canoas, y no pudiendo levantar las ancoras, quisieron cortar los cables,
salio a ellos una barca armada, y los hizo huyr y desamparar algunas canoas,
tomaron cinco, y mataro[n] algunos Indios, y se pre[n]dieron quatro, dos
dellos embio Juan Ponce al Cazique, para que le dixessen, que aunque le
avian muerto un Castellano de dos flechazos, haria paz con el. El dia siguiente fue la barca a sondar un puerto que alli avia, y salio la gente a tierra,
acudieron Indios, que dixeron, que otro dia yria el Cazique a rescatar (pero

era engaño) mientras juntava la gente, y canoas: y assi fue, que a los onze salieron ochenta empavesadas, sobre el navio que estava mas cerca, pelearo[n]
desde la mañana hasta la noche, sin daño de los Castellanos, porque no
alcançavan las flechas, que por las ballestas y tiros del artilleria no se osavan
acercar, y al cabo los Indios se retiraron: y los Castellanos despues de averse
detenido nueve dias, Martes a catorze acordaron de bolver a la Española, y a
San Juan, con fin de descubrir en el camino algunas islas, de que davan noticia los Indios que llevavan. Bolvieron a la isla, a donde tomaron el agua, que
se llamó de Matança, por los Indios q[ue] mataron. Miercoles fueron en demanda de los onze Isleos, que dexaron al Hueste, Jueves y Viernes corriero[n]
por la misma via, hasta el Martes a veinte y uno, que llegaron a los Isleos,
que no[m]braron las tortugas, porque en un rato de la noche tomaron en una
destas islas ciento y sesenta tortugas, y tomaran muchas mas si quisieran, y
tambie[n] tomaron catorze lobos marinos, y se mataron muchos Alcatrazes, y
otras aves, que llegaron a cinco mil. El Viernes a los veinte y quatro corrieron
al Sudueste, quarta del Hueste, el Domingo vieron tierra, el lunes anduvieron
por luengo della para reconocerla, y el Miercoles tomaron puerto en ella, y
adobaron las entenas y las velas, aunque no pudieron saber que tierra era,
los mas la tuvieron por Cuba, porque hallaron canoas, perros, cortaduras de
cuchillos, y de herramientas de yerro, y no porque ninguno conociesse que
era Cuba, sino por dezir q[ue] a Cuba tenian aquella derrota, y que se corria
Leste Hueste como ella, salvo que se hallava diez y ocho leguas largos de
derrota para ser Cuba. El Viernes salieron de aqui en busca de los Martires;
Domingo llegaron á la Isla de Achecambéi: i pasando por Santa Pola, i Santa
Marta, llegaron á Chequeschá, navegaron hasta unas Islatas, que son en los
Baxos de los Lucayos, mas al Hueste, i surgieron en ellas á diez i ocho de
Julio, adonde hicieron aguada, i las pusieron Nombre la Vieja, por una India
Vieja, sin otra Persona alguna, que hallaron, i estén en veinte i ocho Grados.
    No se pudo saber en el principio el Nombre que tenia la Florida, al pare-
cer, de los Descubridores: porque viendo que aquella punta de Tierra salia
tanto, la tenian por Isla, i los Indios, como era Tierra-firme, decian el nombre
de cada Provincia, i los Castellanos pensaban que los engañaban: pero al
cabo, por sus importunaciones, dixeron los Indios, que se llamaba Cautió,
nombre que los Indios Lucayos pusieron á aquella Tierra, porque la Gente de
ella trae sus partes secretas cubiertas con hojas de Palma, texidas á manera
de pleita. A veinte i cinco de Julio salieron de las Isletas, en demanda de
Bimini, navegando por entre Islas, que parecian anegadas: i estando parados,
no sabiendo por donde pasar con los Navios, embió Juan Ponce la Barca,
á reconocer una Isla, que tenia por anegada, i halló ser la de Baháma, i asi
lo dixo la Vieja que llevaban, i Diego Miruelo, Piloto, que encontraron con
un Barco de la Española, que iba á sus Aventuras, aunque otros dicen, que
con su fortuna havian aportado alli. Salieron Sabado á seis de Agosto, por
donde havian ido, i hasta hallar la hondura corrieron al Norueste, quarta

del Hueste, hasta un Isleo de peñas solo al canto de la hondura: mudaron derrota, corrieron por canto debaxo al Sur. Mudaron esta derrota otro Dia, aunque no estaba Bimini en aquella via: i por temor de las corrientes, que otra vez hechaban los Navios á la Costa de la Florida, ó Cautió (como entonces decian) se bolvieron la buelta de la Isla de San Juan de Puerto Rico; i haviendo navegado hasta los diez i ocho de Agosto, se hallaron al amanecer dos Leguas de una Isla de los Lucayos, i corrieron tres Leguas, hasta la punta de esta Isla, adonde á los diez i nueve surgieron, i se estuvieron hasta los veinte i dos. De aquí tardaron quatro Dias en llegar á Guanimá, porque les faltó el viento, i la travesía, i bolvieron huiendo de la Costa á la Isla de Guatáo: i por las Tormentas, se entretuvieron en ella, sin poder salir de ella, veinte i siete Dias, hasta los veinte i tres de Septiembre, i alli se perdió el Barco de la Isla Española, que se havia juntado con ellos, aunque la Gente se salvó. Adobados los Navios, pareciendo á Juan Ponce, que se havia trabajado mucho, determinó, aunque contra su voluntad, de embiar al uno á reconocer la Isla de Bimini, porque lo quisiera hacer él mismo, por la Relacion que tenia de la riqueça de esta Isla, i en especial de aquella señalada Fuente, que decian los Indios, que bolvia á los Hombres, de viejos, moços, la qual no havia podido hallar, por baxos, i corrientes, i tiempos contrarios. Embió, pues, por Capitan del Navio, á Juan Perez de Ortubia, i por Piloto á Anton de Alaminos. Llevaron dos Indios para Pilotos de los baxos, porque son tantos, que con mucho peligro se puede andar por ellos: i partió este Navio á diez i siete de Septiembre, i Juan Ponce otro Dia para su viage, i en veinte i un Dias llegó á reconocer á San Juan, i fue á tomar Puerto á la Baía de Puerto Rico, adonde despues de haver hallado á Bimini, aunque no la Fuente, llegó el otro Navio con Relacion, que era Isla grande, fresca, i de muchas Aguas, i Arboledas: i este fin tuvo el Descubrimiento de Juan Ponce en la Florida, sin saber que era Tierra-firme, ni algunos Años despues se tuvo de ello certificacion.

Cap[itulo] XII. Del engaño que tuvieron los Indios de Cuba, acerca de la fuente de Bimini, y rio Jordan, y de la causa de los movimientos de la mar.

Es cosa cierta, que demas del principal proposito de Juan Ponce de Leon, para la navegacion q[ue] hizo (q[ue] se ha referido en el capitulo precedente) q[ue] fue descubrir nuevas tierras, q[ue] era en lo que mas entendian los Castellanos, en aquellos primeros tiempos. Fue a buscar la fuente de Bimini, y en la Florida un rio, dando en esto credito a los Indios de Cuba, y a otros de la Española, q[ue] dezian q[ue] bañandose en el, o en la fue[n]te, los ho[m]bres viejos se bolvia moços, y fue verdad que muchos Indios de Cuba, tenie[n]do por cierto que avia este rio passaro[n], no muchos años antes q[ue] los Castellanos, descubriessen aquella isla a las tierras de la Florida en busca del, y alli se quedaron, y poblaron un pueblo, y hasta oy dura aquella generacion de los de Cuba. Esta fama de la causa que movio a estos para entrar en la Florida, movio tambien a todos los Reyes, y Caziques de aquellas comarcas, para tomar muy a pechos, el saber que rio podria ser aquel, que tan buena obra hazia, de tornarlos viejos en moços, y no quedó rio ni arroyo en toda la florida, hasta las lagunas y pantanos, a donde no se bañassen, y hasta oy porfian algunos en buscar este misterio: el qual vanamente algunos pie[n]san, que es el rio que aora llaman Jordan en la pu[n]ta de Santa Elena, sin co[n]siderar q[ue] fueron Castellanos los q[ue] dieron el nombre el año de veinte, quando se descubrio la tierra de Chicora.

English

Chapter X. Of the navigation of Juan Ponce de León, to the north of the island of San Juan, and the discovery of Florida, and why it was called thus.

Juan Ponce de León finding himself without an official position, on account of Juan Cerón and Miguel Díaz having been restored in their positions on the island of San Juan, and seeing himself rich, he determined to do something with which to gain honor, and enrich his estate. And as there was news that lands were to be found to the north, he decided to go discover in that direction, for which he equipped three ships, well provided with victuals, people, and sailors, which are the most necessary for the purpose of discovery. He left the island Thursday afternoon, the third of March, leaving from the port of San Germán. He went to El Aguada, in order to begin his journey from there. The following night he ventured seaward, northwest and by north,[1] and the ships traveled eight leagues in a day's run,[2] until sunrise. They continued navigating until Tuesday the eighth of [March], and arrived to anchor at the shoals of Babueca, at an island called El Viejo, which is at twenty-two and a half degrees [latitude]. The next day they anchored at a little island of the Lucayos, called Caycos.[3] Next they anchored at another called La Yagúna, at twenty-four degrees. On the eleventh of [March], they arrived at another island called Amaguáyo, and they were there making repairs. They passed to the island called Maneguá, which is at twenty-four and a half degrees. On the fourteenth they arrived at Guanahani, which is at twenty-five degrees, forty minutes, where they careened a ship in order to traverse the gulf to the windward of the Lucayos Islands. This island of Guanahani was the first discovered by Admiral don Christopher Columbus, and where he set foot on land during his first voyage, and he named it San Salvador. They left here running to the northwest, and Sunday the twenty-seventh, which was the day of the Feast of the Resurrection, which is commonly called [the Feast] of Flowers, they saw an island that they did not recognize. On Monday the twenty-eighth they ran fifteen leagues in the same direction, and on Wednesday they traveled in the same manner, and afterward with bad weather until the second of April, running to the west-northwest, the water diminishing until nine fathoms at one league from land, which was at thirty degrees, eight minutes. They ran the length of the coast looking for a port, and at night they anchored near land in eight fathoms of water. And thinking that this land was an island, they called it Florida, because it had a very pretty view of many cool groves of trees, and it was flat and level, and also because they discovered it in the time of the Feast of Florida, Juan Ponce wished the name to correspond with both these reasons. He disembarked to examine the land and take possession of it. On Friday the eighth they set sail, and ran in the same direction. And on Saturday they navigated to the south, a quarter to the southeast, and navigating in the same direction until the twentieth of April, they discovered some Indian huts, where they anchored. And the next day, all three ships withdrawing from the edge of the sea, they saw a current, in which although they had a strong wind, they could not move forward, but rather backward, and it seemed that they were traveling well, and in the end they found out that the current was such that it was stronger than the wind. The two ships that found themselves closer to land anchored, but the current was so strong that it made the cables quiver, and the third ship, which was a brigantine that found itself farther out to sea,[4] must not have found the bottom, or did not recognize the current, and it was drawn away from land, and it was lost to sight on a clear day, and with fair weather.

Juan Ponce came forth on land here, called by the Indians, who then endeavored to take their rowboat,[5] the oars, and their weapons, and in order to avoid conflict and disturb the land they put up with it. But because they struck a sailor on the head with a club,[6] which knocked him unconscious, they had no choice but to fight. [The Indians], with their arrows and spears tipped with pointed bones and fish spines,[7] wounded two Castilians, and the Indians received little damage. When they separated at night, Juan Ponce gathered the Castilians with great effort and left from there to a river, where he took on water and firewood. While waiting for the brigantine, sixty Indians turned up to impede them, and they took one of them as a navigator, and in order to learn the language.[8] He gave this river the name of the Cross, and they left at it a stone with a sign,[9] and they did not finish taking on water on account of it being brackish. Sunday the eighth of May they rounded the Cape of Florida, which they called the Cape of Currents, because here the water runs so fast that it is stronger than the wind, and does not permit ships to go forward, even if they unfurl all their sails. They anchored behind a cape, next to a town called Abaióa. All this coast, from the Point of Reefs down to the Cape of Currents, runs north-south, a quarter to the southeast, and it is all clean, and of six fathoms in depth. The cape is at twenty-eight degrees, fifteen minutes. They navigated until they found two islands to the south at twenty-seven degrees. One, which is one league in length, they named Santa Marta, where they took on water. On Thursday, the thirteenth of May, they set sail running along the coast of a bank and reef of islands down to the place of an island that they called Pola, which is at twenty-six and a half degrees. Between the shoal and reef of islands and the mainland, the sea grows wide in the manner of a bay. On Sunday, the day of the Feast of the Holy Spirit, the fifteenth of May, they ran along the coast of the keys ten leagues down to two white keys. They gave the name Los Martires to all this reef of islands and keys, because seen from a distance the rocks that they project up seem to be men who are drowning, and the name has also conformed with the many [men] who have been lost in them afterward. They are at twenty-six degrees, fifteen minutes. They went navigating sometimes to the north, others to the northeast, until the twenty-third of May. On the twenty-fourth they ran along the coast toward the south (not realizing that it was the mainland) down to some little islands that were located off the seashore.[10] Because it seemed that there was an entrance between them and the coast for the ships to take on water and firewood, they remained there until the third of June, and careened a ship called *San Christobal*. During this time Indians showed up in canoes to see the Castilians, the first time seeing that although the Indians called them, the Castilians did not come forth on land. When [the Castilians] wished to raise an anchor to repair it, [the Indians] thought they were going away and set out to sea in their canoes and grabbed hold of the cable to carry off the ship, because of which the rowboat went after them. Coming forth on land, they took four women, and broke up two old canoes. The other times that they showed up there were no hostilities, because they saw no ship's tackle, but instead they bartered skins and base gold.[11]

Chapter XI. Having finished his navigation on the coast of Florida, Juan Ponce de León returned to the island of San Juan.

Friday the fourth [of June], while awaiting wind in order to go in search of the Chief Carlos, whom the Indians on the ships said had gold, a canoe arrived at the vessels. An Indian who understood the Castilians, who it was believed must have been from Hispaniola, or another of the islands inhabited by Castilians, said that they should wait, and that the Chief wished to send gold to barter. And while waiting, there appeared up to twenty canoes, some tied two by two, and some went to the anchors, and others to the ships, and they began to fight from their canoes, and unable to raise the anchors, they wished to cut the cables. An armed rowboat came forth to them and made them flee and abandon some canoes. They took five [canoes], and killed some Indians and captured four. Juan Ponce sent two of them to the Chief to tell him that although they had killed a Castilian with two arrow wounds, he would make peace with him. The next day, the rowboat went to sound the depths of a port that was there, and the people disembarked on land, and Indians showed up who said that the Chief would come the next day to barter (but it was a trick) while the people and canoes were gathered. And thus it was, that at eleven o'clock eighty shielded [canoes] came upon the ship that was closest. They fought from morning until night, without injury to the Castilians, because the arrows did not reach them, since [the Indians] did not dare approach nearer because of the crossbows and artillery shots. In the end the Indians retreated, and after having detained themselves nine days, on Tuesday the fourteenth the Castilians decided to return to Hispaniola and to San Juan, with the goal of discovering along the way some islands about which the Indians they were carrying told them. They returned to take on water from the island they called Massacre Island, because of the Indians that they killed. Wednesday they went in search of the eleven keys that were off to the west. On Thursday and Friday they ran in the same direction, until on Tuesday the twenty-first they arrived at the keys, which they named the Tortugas, because in the space of one night at one of these islands they took one hundred and sixty turtles, and they would have taken many more if they had wished. They also took fourteen sea-wolves, and killed many pelicans, and others that reached five thousand. On Friday the twenty-fourth they ran southwest and by west, and on Sunday they saw land. On Monday they traveled alongside its length in order to reconnoiter it, and on Wednesday they entered a port in it, and repaired the yards and sails. Although they could not discover what land it was, most of them took it for Cuba, because they found canoes, dogs, cut marks from knives and from iron tools. This was not because anyone knew that it was Cuba, but rather because they were aiming for Cuba, and it ran east-west like this [land], save that it was found to be eighteen leagues farther in distance than Cuba should have been.[12] On Friday they departed from here in search of the Martyrs. Sunday they arrived at the Island of Achecambéi, and passing by Santa Pola and Santa Marta, they arrived at Chequeschá. They navigated up to some little islands that are on the shoals of the Lucayos, more to the west, and anchored in them on the eighteenth of July, where they took on water. And they gave it the name La Vieja, for an old Indian woman, without any other person, whom they found, and [these islands] are at twenty-eight degrees.

At first it could not be discovered what name Florida had, in the opinion of the discoverers, because seeing that that peninsula extended so far, they held it to be an island, and the Indians, since it was mainland, called it the name of each province, and the Castilians thought they were deceiving them. In the end, as a result of their incessant questions, the Indians said that it was called Cautió, a name that the Lucayos Indians gave to that land, because its people cover their private parts with palm leaves woven from strips. On the twenty-fifth of July, they left the little islands in search of Bimini, navigating between islands that appeared flooded. While they were stopped, not knowing where to pass with the ships, Juan Ponce sent the rowboat to reconnoiter an island that he thought was flooded, and it was found to be that of Baháma, and thus it was called by the old woman that they carried, and Diego Miruelo, the pilot, whom they encountered with a bark from Hispaniola, and who was going exploring, although others say that he had arrived there by accident. They left on Saturday, the sixth of August, by the way they had come, and until finding deep water they ran northwest and by west up to a solitary island of rocks at the edge of the deep water. They changed bearing, running along the edge beneath them toward the south. The next day they changed this bearing, although Bimini was not in that direction, and on account of fear that the currents would push the ships again to the coast of Florida, or Cautió (as they then called it), they turned in the direction of the island of San Juan de Puerto Rico. Having navigated until the eighteenth of August, they found themselves at dawn two leagues from one of the Lucayos Islands, and they ran three leagues up to the point of this island, where they anchored on the nineteenth and remained until the twenty-second. From here they spent four days arriving at Guanimá, because they lacked wind, and [because of] the distance. And they turned, fleeing from the coast to the island of Guatáo, and due to the storms, they were held up for twenty-seven days without being able to leave, until the twenty-third of September. There they lost the bark from the island of Hispaniola that had joined with them, although the people were saved. When the ships were repaired, it seeming to Juan Ponce that he had labored greatly, he determined to send one [ship] to reconnoiter the island of Bimini, although against his will, because he wished to do so himself because of the account he had of the richness of this island, and especially of the renowned Fountain that the Indians said turned old men young, which he had not been able to find through shoals and currents and contrary weather. Therefore he sent Juan Pérez de Ortubia as captain of the ship, and Antón de Alaminos as pilot. They took two Indians as navigators of the shoals, because there are so many that it is very dangerous to travel through them. And this ship departed on the seventeenth of September, and Juan Ponce on the next day for his voyage, and in twenty-one days he arrived in sight of San Juan, and went to take port at the Bay of Puerto Rico. There, after having found Bimini, but not the Fountain, the other ship arrived with an account that it was a large island, cool, and with much [fresh] water and groves of woods. This was the end of the discovery of Juan Ponce in Florida, without knowing that it was the mainland, nor was it certified to be such for some years.

Chapter XII. Of the deception that the Indians of Cuba had regarding the spring of Bimini and the River Jordan, and of the causes of the motions of the sea.

It is a certain thing, that in addition to the principal goal of Juan Ponce de León for the navigation that he made (which has been covered in the preceding chapter), which was to discover new lands, which was what the Castilians understood most in those early times, he also went to look for the spring of Bimini, and in Florida a river, giving credit in this to the Indians of Cuba and others of Hispaniola.[13] They said that bathing in the [river], or in the spring, old men would become young, and it was true that many Indians from Cuba, holding it for certain that this river existed, crossed to the lands of Florida in search of it not many years before the Castilians discovered that island, and there they remained and settled a town, and up to this day there remain descendants of those from Cuba.[14] This rumor about the reason that provoked these [Cuban Indians] to enter in Florida, also provoked all the Kings and Chiefs of those districts to take to heart knowing which river it could be that had such a wonderful effect, of making old men young, and there was not a river or stream in all of Florida, up to the lakes and swamps, where they did not bathe themselves, and some persist even today in seeking out this mystery. Some vainly believe that it is the river now called the Jordan, at the point of Santa Elena, without considering that it was Castilians who gave it that name in the year of [fifteen] twenty,[15] when the land of Chicora was discovered.

The Oviedo Account of the 1513 and 1521 Expeditions

The following text is from several disparate chapters in Oviedo's monumental work *General and Natural History of the Indies*. The manuscript was begun as early as 1515 and was completed by its author in 1548, but because of his death it was not published in its entirety until 1851–55 by the Spanish Royal Academy of History, as edited by José Amador de los Rios (and in a more recent edition edited by Juan Pérez de Tudela Bueso; Fernández de Oviedo y Valdés 1992). Though it must be considered a secondary source, its early date of composition gives it even greater chronological priority than the later work by Antonio Herrera. Oviedo presumably had access both to documents and probably even survivors of the original 1521 expedition, but his text also inserts significant personal commentary that must be taken into account. The narrative provides the best details available regarding the events of the 1521 colony and Ponce's death in Havana, in addition to providing further information regarding the rationale for and historical context of the expedition. Both the 1513 and 1521 expeditions are mentioned in chronological order in the two separate sections of Oviedo's work quoted here, but each gives slightly different emphasis and details.

The transcription of the Oviedo account follows the exact spelling used in the first publication of Oviedo's work (Fernández de Oviedo y Valdés 1851: 482, 486; 1853: 621–23), including extensive use of accents that do not normally appear in modern usage, as well as the use of ç in place of the soft c. In addition, a portion of the text at the end of the chapter has been omitted here, since it simply refers the reader to the other books and chapters that recount the Hernando de Soto expedition.

Spanish

Libro XVI, Capitulo XI

Cómo el gobernador Johan Ponçe acordó deyr a descubrir por la vanda o parte del Norte, é fue á la Tierra-Firme, en la costa de las islas de Bimini, é halló la isla dicha Bahamá; é cómo fue removido de la gobernaçión é volvieron á gobernar los que él avia enviado presos á Castilla; y de otros gobernadores que ovo despues en la isla de Sanct Johan.

Ya tenía el gobernador Johan Ponçe de Leon quassi conquistada é pacífica la isla de Sanct Johan, aunque no faltaban algunos sobresaltos é acometimientos de los indios caribes, los cuales eran resistidos, é Johan Ponçe estaba muy rico. É cómo las cosas llegaron á este estado, siguióse que aquel alcalde mayor del almirante, llamado Johan Çerón, y el aguaçil mayor Miguel Diaz, que Johan Ponçe avia enviado presos á España, negoçiaron sus cosas é libertad; y su prinçipal motivo, demas de desculparse á sí, fue culpar á Johan Ponçe, diciendo que demas de los aver injustamente preso, él avia cometido otras culpas y hecho otros errores mayores. É aquestos eran favoresçidos por el almirante, porque como Johan Ponçe era afiçionado al comendador mayor, é por su respecto avia avido el cargo contra la voluntad del almirante, y echado sus ofiçiales de la isla, y enviádolos en prisiones, sintiéndose desto, procuró que Johan Ponçe fuesse removido, pues que el almirante era gobernador é visorrey, é decía que aquella administraçion de la justicia en la isla de Sanct Johan le pertenesçia por sus previlegios. É mandó el Rey Cathólico que volviessen á la isla de Sanct Johan é se les entregasen las varas é officios; é assi tornados, quitaron el cargo al dicho Johan Ponçe, porque finalmente el Rey mandó que el almirante pusiesse allí los ofiçiales de justiçia que él quisiesse. É sabido esto por Johan Ponçe, acordó de armar é fue con dos caravelas por la vanda del Norte, é descubrió las islas de Bimini, que están en la parte septentrional de la isla Fernandina; y estonçes se divulgó aquella fábula de la fuente que haçia rejovenesçer ó tornar mançebos los hombres viejos; esto fue el año de mill é quinientos y doçe. É fue esto tan divulgado é certificado por indios de aquellas partes, que anduvieron el capitan Johan Ponçe y su gente y caravelas perdidos y con mucho trabajo más de seys meses, por entre aquellas islas, á buscar esta fuente: lo cual fue muy gran burla deçirlo los indios, y mayor desvario creerlo los cripstianos é gastar tiempo en buscar tal fuente. Pero tuvo notiçia de la Tierra Firme, é vídola é puso nombre á una parte della que entra en la mar, como una manga, por espaçio de çient leguas de longitud, é bien çincüenta de latitud, y llamóla la *Florida*. La punta ó promontorio de la qual está en veinte é cinco grados de la equinoçial de la vanda de nuestro polo ártico, y se extiende y ensancha háçia el viento Norueste: la qual tiene á par de la dicha punta muchas isletas y baxos, que llaman los *Mártyres*. . . .

Libro XVI, Capitulo XIII

De la muerte del adelantado Johan Ponçe de Leon, primero conquistador de la isla de Boriquen, que agora llaman Sanct Johan, y otras cosas tocantes á la mesma isla.

Dicho se há cómo Johan Ponçe de Leon fué removido del cargo é gobernaçion de la isla de Sanct Johan, y de cómo fue á descubrir á la vanda del Norte, é cómo anduvo en busca de aquella fabulosa fuente de Bimini, que publicaron los indios que tornaba á los viejos moços. Y esto yo lo he visto (sin la fuente), no en el subgeto é mejoramiento de las fuerças, pero en el enflaqueçimiento del sexo, é tornarse en sus hechos moços y de poco entender: y destos fué uno el mismo Johan Ponçe, en tanto que le turó aquella vanidad de dar crédito á los indios en tal disparate, é á tanta costa suya de armadas de navíos y gentes, puesto que en la verdad él fué honrado caballero é noble persona é trabaxó muy bien en la conquista é paçificaçión de aquesta Isla Española y en la guerra de Higuey; y tambien fué el primero que començó a poblar é pacificar la isla de Sanct Johan, como tengo dicho, donde él é los que con él se hallaron padesçieron muchos trabajos, assi de la guerra como de enfermedades é muchas nesçesidades de bastimentos é de todas las otras cosas nesçesarias á la vida.

Halló, pues, como ya he dicho, este capitan, aquella tierra que llaman la Florida, é tornó á la isla de Sanct Johan, é fué á España, é dió relaçion de todo al Rey Cathólico: el qual, aviendo respecto á sus serviçios, le dió titulo de adelantado de Bimini y le hizo otras merçedes, para lo qual le aprovechó mucho el favor de su amo, Pero Nuñez de Guzman comendador mayor de Calatrava, ayo del sereníssimo infante don Hernando, que es agora la Majestad del rey de los romanos. É después se tornó á la isla de Sanct Johan é armó de mas propóssito para yr á poblar en aquella tierra de su adelantamiento y gobernaçion que alli se le dió, é gastó mucho en el armada é volvió de allá desbaratado y herido de una flecha, de la qual herida vino á morir á la isla de Cuba. É no fué selo él quien perdió la vida y el tiempo y la haçienda en esta demanda: que muchos otros por le seguir, murieron en el viaje, é despues de ser allá llegados, parte á manos de los indios, é parte de enfermedades; é assi acabaron el adelantado y el adelantamiento.

Libro XXXVI, Capitulo I

En el qual se tracta del armada quel adelantado Johan Ponçe de Leon hiço, con que fué á poblar é conquistar en la Tierra-Firme, á la parte del Norte, la provinçia que llaman la Florida, quél avia antes descubierto, é cómo le desparataron los indios é le hirieron de una flecha, de que vino á morir á la isla de Cuba, alias Fernandina; é assimesmo se tractan otras particularidades dessa tierra.

Como se dixo en el libro XVI de la primera parte destas historias, Johan Ponçe de Leon avia conquistado é pacificado la isla de Boriquen, que agora se llama de Sanct Johan, y en aquella isla por su industria é grangerias vino á ser muy rico hombre, é á tener mucho ganado de vacas é ovejas é puercos é yeguas, é cogio mucho oro de minas, é allego tantos bienes, que pudiera muy bien passar esta vida (é aun ayudar á otros en sus miserias). É cómo era hidalgo é hombre de gentiles é altos pensamientos, paresçióle que quitándole el cargo de la gobernacion de la isla de Sanct Johan (como se lo quitaron por la diligençia é sagaçidad de sus émulos) quél no podia estar ni vivir contento donde otros le mandassen; é assi por esto como por emplear bien el tiempo, é pensando que con él é sus dineros (que tenia hartos) podria, sirviendo á Dios é al Rey con ellos, doblar é haçerlos muchos mas, é acresçentar su persona en titulos de honor y estado: é para este efetto, ó mejor diçiendo para aquel que su ventura le tenia guardado, despues que descubrio á Bimini é le dió el Rey titulo de adelantado por lo que avia gastado é servido en sus armadas é buscando aquella fuente de Bimini, que los indios avian dado á entender que haçia renovar é retoñesçer é refrescar la edad é fuerças del que bebia ó se lavaba en aquella fuente, cómo todo aquello paró en la vanidad que debia de parar una cosa tan fabulosa é mendaçe, é vido que avia seydo burlado é mal informado, no cansado por gastos ni trabaxos, volvió á armar con más acuerdo y expensas, é proveyó é puso en órden ciertos navios para entrar por la Tierra-Firme en la banda del Norte, en aquella costa é punta que entra en la mar çient leguas de longitud é çinqüenta de latitud, poco más ó menos. É paresçióle que demás de lo que se podia alcançar é saber de las islas que por alli hay, que tambien en la Tierra-Firme se podrian saber otros secretos é cosas importantes, é convertir aquellas gentes á Dios con utilidad grande de su persona en particular é generalmente para todos los que con él yban, que eran dosçientos hombres é çinqüenta caballos en los navios, ques dicho. É hasta poner en efetto essa armada, dispendió mucho: é passó á aquella tierra por el mes de _____[16] del año de mill é quinientos é veynte años: é como buen poblador, llevó yeguas é terneras é puercos é ovejas é cabras é todas las maneras de animales domésticos é útiles al serviçio de los hombres; é tambien para la agricoltura é labor del campo fué proveydo de todas simientes, como si el negoçio de su poblaçion no estoviera en más de llegar é cultivar la tierra é apaçentar sus ganados. Pero el temple de la region era muy diferente é desconviniente á lo quel llevaba imaginado, é los naturales de la tierra gente muy áspera é muy salvage é belicosa é feroz é indómita é no acostumbrada á quietud ni á dexar su libertad tan façilmente en discreçion ó voluntad extrangera de otros hombres, ni en eleçion de aquellos frayles é clérigos de que yba acompañado para el exerçiçio del culto divino é serviçio de la iglesia, aunque predicassen quanto quisiessen, ni pudieran ser entendidos con la brevedad que se les figuraba á ellos é al que allá los llevó, si Dios de poder absoluto no los hiçiera ser entendidos de aquellas gentes barbarissimas é salvages ydólatras é colmadas de delictos é viçios. Quiero deçir, que aunque, como en la verdad todo lo que paresçe dificultoso es façil de obrar á Dios, quando le plaçe, es bien que pensemos que no somos meresçedores de essa façilidad, ni tan á pié enjuto se tomen essas truchas: é quiere que primero se reformen las personas de los pescadores, para que caygan en conosçimiento de la verdad los que los han de escuchar é seguir. Non obstante que con este capitan yban personas religiosas é de buena dotrina; pero pues todo se erró, é se perdió el armada y el capitan y el tiempo é haçienda juntamente y en breves dias, de pensar es que no era Dios servido ni el tiempo llegado de la conversion de aquella tierra é provinçia á nuestra sancta fée cathólica, pues permite quel diablo aun los tenga engañados é por suyos á aquellos indios, é que se aumente la poblaçion infernal con sus ánimas.

Esta armada llegó á aquella tierra el año que está dicho; é luego el adelantado Johan Ponçe, cómo se desembarcó, dió, como hombre proveydo, órden en que la gente de su armada descansasse; é quando le paresçió, movió con su gente y entró por la tierra y en una guaçábara ó batalla que ovo con los indios, cómo él era animoso capitan, é se halló de los primeros, é no tan diestro en aquella tierra como en las islas, cargaron tantos é tales de los enemigos, que no bastó su gente é su esfuerço á los resistir. Y en fin le desbarataron é mataron parte de los chripstianos, é murieron más que doblados de los indios, y él salió herido de un flechaço malamente; é acordó de se yr á la isla de Cuba para se curar, si pudiesse, é con más gente é pujança volver á essa conquista. É assi se embarcó é llegó á la isla al puerto de la Habana, donde despues de allegado, vivió poco; pero murió como cathólico é resçebidos los sacramentos, é tambien murieron otros que yban heridos, é otros de enfermedades. Pero porque este gobernador vido poco de aquella tierra, é despues andando el tiempo, passó á ella otro adelantado, que fué Hernando de Soto, é con más gente é poder, é no con mejor ni tal ventura, pues allá quedó muerto, é se supo mucho más de aquella tierra de la Florida . . . en la conquista de la Nueva España, que una caravela de las deste adelantado Johan Ponçe de Leon, aportó á la Nueva España, é aquella llevó poca gente de los que escaparon del otro peligro de la Florida.

English

Book XVI, Chapter XI

How the governor Juan Ponce decided to go to discover toward the direction or region to the north, and went to the mainland, on the coast of the islands of Bimini, and found the island called Bahama; and how he was removed from the government and those whom he had sent as prisoners to Castille returned to govern; and of other governors that there were afterward on the island of San Juan.

Governor Juan Ponce de León already had the island of San Juan almost conquered and pacified, although surprises and assaults from the Carib Indians were not lacking, though they were resisted, and Juan Ponce was very rich. And as affairs had reached this state, it followed that the senior magistrate of the Admiral [Diego Columbus], named Juan Cerón, and the senior bailiff Miguel Díaz, whom Juan Ponce had sent as prisoners to Spain, negotiated their affairs and liberty; and their principal motive, apart from removing their guilt, was to assign guilt to Juan Ponce, saying that apart from having unjustly imprisoned them, he had committed other crimes and made other greater errors. Juan Ponce was a friend of the senior knight commander, and on his behalf he had obtained his office against the will of the Admiral, and had thrown his officials off the island, and sent them away in chains. And since those [two] were favored by the Admiral, smarting from this, he endeavored to have Juan Ponce removed, given that the Admiral was governor and viceroy, and he said that the administration of justice on the island of San Juan pertained to him on account of his privileges.

And the Catholic King [Ferdinand] commanded that they should return to the island of San Juan, and that their staves and offices should be given back to them.[17] Having thus returned, they removed the aforementioned Juan Ponce from his office, because in the end the King ordered the Admiral to emplace whatever judicial officials that he might wish. And when he found this out, Juan Ponce decided to arm up and depart with two caravels toward the north, and he discovered the islands of Bimini, which are to the north of the island of Fernandina [Cuba]; and then was divulged that fable of the fountain that rejuvenates, or turns old men into lads; this was the year of fifteen twelve.[18] And this was so extensively divulged and certified by the Indians of those regions, that captain Juan Ponce and his people and caravels traveled lost and with great hardship more than six months among those islands in search of that fountain. All this was told as a great mockery among the Indians, and an even greater delirium for the Christians to believe it and spend time in looking for such a fountain. But he obtained news of the mainland, and saw it and gave a name to a part of it that enters in the sea, like a sleeve, for the space of one hundred leagues in longitude, and a good fifty in latitude, and he called it La Florida. The point or promontory of this is at twenty-five degrees from the Equator, on the side of our arctic pole, and it extends and broadens toward the northwest wind; even with the stated point it has many islets and shoals that are called the Martyrs. . . .

Book XVI, Chapter XIII

Of the death of the adelantado Juan Ponce de León, first conqueror of the island of Boriquén, which is now called San Juan, and other affairs regarding the same island.

It has been related how Juan Ponce de León was removed from the office and government of the island of San Juan, and how he went to discover toward the north, and how he traveled in search of that fabled fountain of Bimini, which the Indians publicized as turning the old young. And this I have seen (without the fountain), not with regard to the improvement of strength, but in the weakening of the brain, and by one's deeds turning into children of little understanding. One of these was the very same Juan Ponce, inasmuch as he persisted in that vanity of giving credit to the Indians regarding such rubbish, and at such a cost to him in armadas of ships and people. Despite this, in truth, he was an honorable gentleman and a noble person, and labored very well in the conquest and pacification of the island of Hispaniola, and in the war of Higüey; and he was also the first who began to settle and pacify the island of San Juan, as I have said, where he and those who found themselves with him experienced many hardships, both in war and sickness, and many shortages of food and all the other things necessary for life.

Well, as I have already stated, this captain found that land that is called Florida, and returned to the island of San Juan, and went to Spain and gave a relation of everything to the Catholic King, who in respect for his services, gave him the title of adelantado of Bimini, and gave him other mercies. For this, [Ponce] took great advantage of the favor of his sponsor, Pedro Núñez de Guzmán, knight commander of Calatrava, manservant of the most serene Infante don Hernando, who now is the Majesty of the King of the Romans. And afterward, he returned to the island of San Juan and armed himself more suitably in order to go and settle in that land of the adelantadoship[19] and government that was given to him there, and he spent much in the armada, and returned from there ruined and wounded from an arrow, from which he came to the island of Cuba to die. And it was not just he who lost his life and time and estate in this enterprise: many others, in following him, died on the voyage, and after having arrived there, some at the hands of the Indians, and some from illnesses; and thus ended the adelantado and his adelantadoship.

Book XXXVI, Chapter I

In which is discussed the armada that the Adelantado Juan Ponce de León formed, with which he went to the northern mainland to settle and conquer the province called Florida, which he had discovered before, and how the Indians thwarted him and wounded him with an arrow, from which he came to die on the island of Cuba, alias Fernandina; and likewise other details of that land are discussed.

As was stated in book XVI of the first part of these histories, Juan Ponce de León had conquered and pacified the island of Boriquen, which is now called San Juan, and on that island, through his industry and husbandry he became a very rich man, and had many livestock of cows and sheep and pigs and horses, and he gained much gold from mines, and he gathered so many possessions that he could live his life comfortably (and even help others in their miseries). And since he was a gentleman, and a man of genteel and high thoughts, it seemed to him

that when they took the government of the island of San Juan away
from him (as was done through the diligence and shrewdness of his
rivals), he could not remain or live content where others commanded
him. It was on account of this, and in order to make good use of his
time, and thinking that with himself and his money (which he had
plenty of) he could, by serving God and the King with them, double it
and make much more, and promote his person in titles of honor and
estate. And with this goal, or better said with what his fate had in store
for him, after having discovered Bimini, and the King gave him the title
of adelantado on account of what he had spent and how he had served
in his armadas, and searching for that spring of Bimini, which the
Indians had given to understand renewed and regrew and refreshed the
age and strength of he who drank or bathed in that spring. Since all of
that ended up being vanity, as should anything so fabulous and untrue,
and having seen that he had been deceived and poorly informed, not
weary of expenses or labors, he arranged again with greater accord and
expense, and equipped and arranged certain ships in order to enter the
mainland to the north, on that coast and point that enters in the sea
one hundred leagues in longitude, and fifty in latitude, a little more or
less. And it seemed to him that in addition to what could be achieved
or discovered about the islands there were there, other secrets and
important things could be also be discovered on the mainland, and
he could convert those peoples to God with great utility to his person in
particular, and generally to all those who went with him, who were two
hundred men and fifty horses on the aforementioned ships. And until
putting this armada into use, he squandered much. And he crossed to that
land in the month of [February][20] in the year of fifteen twenty[-one].[21]
And like a good settler, he carried mares and calves and pigs and sheep
and goats and all manner of domestic animals useful to human service,
and all types of seeds were also provided for agriculture and labor in
the fields, as if the matter of his settlement consisted in no more than
arriving and cultivating the land and grazing his livestock. But the
temper of the region was very different and incongruous with what he
had imagined, and the natives of the land a people very harsh and very
savage and warlike and ferocious and indomitable, and not accustomed
to quietude, or to abandoning their liberty so easily upon the discretion or foreign will of other men, or upon the election of those friars
and clerics who accompanied him for the exercise of the divine cult
and service of the church. Although they might preach as much as they
wished, they could not be understood with the brevity that they or he
who led them there had anticipated, if God in his absolute power did
not make them understood by those supremely barbarous and savage idolators,[22] brimming over with crimes and vices. What I mean to

say is that while it is true that everything that appears difficult is easy for God to perform when it pleases him, it is good for us to think that we are not deserving of that facility, nor are those fish taken without getting the feet wet. And he first desires the personal reform of the fishermen, so that those who are to hear and follow them fall into an understanding of the truth. Regardless of the fact that religious persons of good doctrine went with this captain, everything still went astray, with the loss of the armada and the captain and the time and money together, and in a few short days. One must think that God was not served, nor had the time arrived for the conversion of that land and province to our holy Catholic faith, since he permits that the devil still deceives them, holding those Indians as his, and that the population of hell increases with their souls.

This armada arrived at that land in the aforementioned year, and then the adelantado Juan Ponce, as a dignified man, gave an order upon disembarking that the people of his armada should rest, and when it seemed suitable to him, he moved with his people and entered into the land, and in a skirmish or battle that there was with the Indians, as he was a brave captain and found himself among the first, and not so dexterous in that land as on the islands, the enemies that charged were so many and such that neither his people nor his strength was enough to resist them. And in the end they routed them and killed part of the Christians, and more than twice as many Indians died, and he [Juan Ponce] was wounded badly with an arrow. And he decided to go to the island of Cuba to cure himself if he could, and return to the conquest with more people and strength. And thus he embarked and arrived at the island at the port of Havana, where after having arrived, he lived only a short time. But he died as a Catholic and received the sacraments, and others who were wounded also died, and others from sicknesses. But because this governor saw little of that land, and later with the passage of time, there crossed to [that land] another adelantado, who was Hernando de Soto, and with more people and power, and not with better or even equal fortune, since he remained dead there, and much more was learned about that land of Florida . . . and during the conquest of New Spain, one of the caravels of this adelantado Juan Ponce de León showed up in New Spain, carrying few people of those that escaped from the other danger of Florida.

The López de Gómara Account of the 1513 and 1521 Expeditions

The following brief narrative of the Ponce de León expeditions was written by sixteenth-century Spanish historian Francisco López de Gómara as part of chapter 45 in his 1554 *Historia general de las Indias* (68v–69r). Although it is only a secondary source, there are details within his narrative that do not appear in other sources.

The transcription here follows the norms detailed in the preface, generally preserving anachronistic orthography present in the original text except in cases where it might make it difficult for modern Spanish readers to sound out the words correctly or follow the intended sentence structure.

Spanish

Cap[itulo] XLV
El Descubrimiento de la Florida

Quito el Almirante del govierno del Boriquen a Juan Ponce de Leon, y el viendose sin cargo y rico, armo dos caravelas, y fue a buscar la ysla Boyuca, donde dezia[n] los Indios estar la fuente q[ue] tornava moços a los viejos. Anduvo perdido, y ha[m]briento seys meses, por entre muchas yslas sin hallar rastro de tal fuente, entro en Bimini, y descubrio la Florida en Pascua florida del año de doze, y por esso le puso aq[ue]l no[m]bre y espera[n]do hallar en ella grandes riquezas, vino a España. Do[n]de negocio con el rey do[n] Fernando todo lo que pidia, con intercession de Nicolas de Ovando, y de Pero Nuñez de Guzman, ayo del infante don Fernando, cuyo paje avia sido. Assi que le dio el rey titulo de adelantado de Bimini, y de governador de la Florida y con tanto armo en Sevilla tres navios muy de proposito, el año de quinze. Toco en Guacana, q[ue] llaman Guadalupe, echo en tierra gente a tomar agua y leña, y algunas mugeres q[ue] lavassaen los trapos y ropa suzia. Salieron los Caribes, q[ue] se avian puesto encelada, y flecharo[n] co[n] sus saetas enerboladas los Españoles, mataron los mas q[ue] a tierra saliero[n], y cativaron las lava[n]deras. Con este mal principio, y aguero, se partio Juan Po[n]ce al Boriquen, y de alli a la Florida, salto en tierra con sus soldados para buscar assiento, donde fundar un pueblo. Vinieron los Indios a defenderle la entrada y estada, pelearon con el, desbarataronlo y aun le mataro[n] hartos Españoles, y le hiriero[n] a el con una flecha. De cuya herida uvo de morir en Cuba, y assi acabo la vida, y consumio gran parte de la mucha hazienda, que allegara en San Juan del Borique[n].

English

Chapter XLV
The Discovery of Florida

The admiral removed Juan Ponce de León from the government of Boriquen, and seeing himself without employment and rich, he outfitted two caravels and went to look for the island of Boyuca, where the Indians said the fountain was that turned old men young. He traveled lost and hungry for six months among many islands without finding a trace of such a fountain, entered Bimini, and discovered Florida on Easter of the year [15]12, and for that he gave it that name. Hoping to find great riches in it, he came to Spain, where he negotiated everything he asked for with the king don Fernando, with the intercession of Nicolás de Ovando, and of Pedro Núñez de Guzmán, tutor of the prince don Fernando, who had been his page. Thus the king gave him the title of adelantado of Bimini, and of governor of Florida, and with this he outfitted three very suitable ships in Seville in the year of [15]15. He landed in Guacana, which is called Guadalupe, [and] disembarked people on land to take on water and wood, and some women to wash their rags and dirty clothes. The Caribe [Indians], who became jealous, came forth and shot the Spaniards with their poisoned arrows, killing most of those who had gone on shore, and captured the washerwomen. With this bad beginning and omen, Juan Ponce departed for Boriquen, and from there to Florida. He leapt forth on land with his soldiers in order to look for a site to found a town. The Indians came to defend against his entrance and stay, fought with him, broke up [the town], and even killed plenty of Spaniards, and wounded him with an arrow. From this wound he would die in Cuba, and thus was finished off his life, and a large part of the great wealth that he had gathered in San Juan del Boriquen.

The Las Casas Account of the 1513 and 1521 Voyages

The following narrative was penned by Fray Bartolomé de las Casas, bishop of Chiapas and famed sixteenth-century "Protector of the Indians," as part of his lengthy work *Historia de las Indias*. A contemporary of Juan Ponce de León, Las Casas participated in the conquest of Cuba immediately prior to Ponce's first journey to Florida and was so affected by the atrocities he witnessed there that he became a lifelong advocate for American Indian rights throughout the Spanish Empire. Though his writings are strongly flavored by his advocacy, some aspects of his recounting of Ponce's Florida expeditions (Las Casas 1875: 459–61) are unique to his narrative, which is thus important to consider as a predecessor to the more famous Herrera narrative published two generations later.

The transcription here follows the norms detailed in the preface, generally preserving anachronistic orthography present in the original text except in cases where it might make it difficult for modern Spanish readers to sound out the words correctly or follow the intended sentence structure.

Spanish

Capitulo XX

Deste salto hace mencion Pedro Mártir, en la Década 7.ª [septima] capitulo 2.º [segundo], donde da cuenta de muchas cosas que oyó referir por dichos de los indios que de alli trujeron, asi de las costumbres y ritos de las gentes de allí, como de la calidad de la tierra y cosas que en ella habia, en especial perlas. Al olor, por ventura, desta nueva, en este tiempo, al principio del año de [1]511, debió moverse Juan Ponce de Leon, algunas veces nombrado, y el que arriba en el libro II dijimos que habia sido el primero que habia ido á inquietar y tiranizar los vecinos naturales de la isla de Sant juan, porque como el almirante D[on] Diego Colon le hobiese quitado la gobernacion de aquella isla y puesto otro Gobernador, y se hallase rico de los sudores, sangre y angustias de tantos hombres y gentes que habia tenido en servidumbre, así en esta isla, en la provincia de Higuey, como en la dicha isla de Sant Juan, fué necesario que para mostrase Dios la justicia y razon con que lo habia todo hecho y ayudado á hacer, emprendiese negocio y empresa donde malgastase lo robado y en muchos dias amontonado, y al cabo, con mala suerte, feneciese. Este armó dos navíos bien proveidos y aparejados de gente, que por la mayor parte, para descubrir, son marineros, y bastimentos de las otras cosas necesarias, y viniendo hácia el Norte desta isla Española, pasando las islas de los Lucayos, quiso tomar más arriba á mano izquierda del viaje que los dichos dos navíos havian llevado, y á pocos dias vido tierra, y ésta fué un cabo muy grande que sale á la mar del Norte, hácia el Sur, más de noventa leguas de toda la otra tierra, el cual hace el estrecho que llamamos agora la canal de Bahama, entre él y la isla de Cuba; luégo, como la vido, llegóse á reconoscella y púsole por nombre la tierra Florida, porque debiera parecerle fresca y florida como esté en 25° de la equinocial, como lo están las islas dichas de los Lucayos, que son fresquísimas y felícimas. Esta misma tierra llamó el mismo Juan Ponce Bimine, no supe de dónde ó por qué causa tal nombre le puso, ó de dónde le vino, ó si la llamaron así los indios, porque no creo que saltó en tierra ni tuvo deste viaje habla con indios. Descubierta esta tierra, tornosé á la isla de Sant Juan, donde tenia sus haciendas, y de allí fué á Castilla y pidió al Rey merced, por el descubrimiento de nueva tierra que habia hecho, le hiciese Adelantado de Bimine y le diese la gobernacion della, porque él á su costa la queria poblar, con otras más preeminencias y provechos que debiera de pedir, como hombre acá experimentado, que yo no supe; lo cual, todo le concedió el Rey. Tornó de Castilla muy favorecido con título de Adelantado y Gobernador de Bimine, que él llamó por otro nombre la Florida, y que agora llamamos tambien Florida, aunque deste nombre decimos toda la tierra y costa de la mar que comienza desde aquel cabo grande que él descubrió, hasta la tierra de los Bacallaos, y por otro nombre la tierra de Labrador, que no está muy lejos de la isla de Inglaterra. Llegado á la isla de Sant Juan, tomó de allí de sus haciendas todo lo que habia menester y vínose á esta isla y puerto de Sancto Domingo, donde se rehizo de gente y navíos. Partióse deste puerto en el año de [1]512, y váse á su Bimine, y queriendo entrar en la tierra como habia entrado en estas islas, y las nuevas del salto que hicieron más abajo, en la misma tierra, los que habemos dicho, que debieran todas aque- llas regiones de haber cundido y alborotado, los de Bimine defendieron su patria cuanto pudieron, y, peleando con sus pocas armas y flacas fuerzas, en- tre los primeros hirieron con una flecha al Juan Ponce, Adelantado y Gober- nador. Parece que aunque no tienen hierba ponzoñosa por aquella tierra, fué la herida en tal lugar, que juzgó de sí mismo tener peligro, por lo cual mandó que todos se recogiesen á los navíos, y dejasen la tierra y lo llevasen á la Isla de Cuba, que era la tierra más propincua de donde estaban. En llegando á ella, y creo, si no me he olvidado, al puerto que hoy se llama del Príncipe, que es en la dicha isla, pasó desta vida puesto en tanto trabajo; y por esta manera perdió el cuerpo, gastó gran suma de pesos de oro, que, como dije, habia allegado con muchas muertes y vidas dolorosas y amargas de indios, y padeció trabajos muy grandes yendo y viniendo á Castilla, y á descubrir, y á querer poblar, y el ánima no sabemos cómo le ha ido. Y así feneció el adelan- tamiento de Bimine con todo lo demas.

English

Chapter XX

Peter Martyr makes mention of this assault in Decade 7, Chapter 2, where he relates many things that he heard said by the statements of the Indians that were brought from there, both about the customs and rituals of the people there, and about the quality of the land and the things that there were in it, especially pearls. Upon the hint, by chance, of this news in this time, at the beginning of the year of 1511 Juan Ponce de León must have been inspired. He has been mentioned some- times above, and we noted in Book II that he had been the first who had gone to disturb and tyrannize the native residents of the island of San Juan [de Puerto Rico]. Admiral don Diego Columbus had removed the government of that island from him and emplaced another gover- nor, and he found himself rich from the sweat, blood, and tears of so many men and people that he had held in servitude both on this island [of Hispaniola] in the province of Higuey, and also on the stated island of San Juan. Because of all this, and so that God might demonstrate the justice and reason with which he had done and helped do everything, it was necessary for him to undertake an affair and enterprise where he would misspend that which he had robbed and accumulated in many days, and in the end, with bad fortune, pass away. This [Ponce] armed two well-provided ships furnished with people, who are in large part sailors, and provisions of other necessary things. Coming toward the north from this island Hispaniola, passing the Lucayos Islands, he wished to go farther up on the left-hand side of the voyage that the aforementioned two ships had taken, and in a few days he sighted land, and this was a very large cape that extends into the northern sea toward the south, more than ninety leagues from all the other land, which makes the strait that we now call the Bahama Channel, between it and the island of Cuba. As soon as he saw it, he approached to reconnoiter it and gave it the name of the land of Florida, because it must have seemed cool and florid, since it is at 25° of latitude, as are the aforementioned Lucayos Islands, which are very cool and pleasant. This same land was called Bimine by the very same Juan Ponce, [and] I did not discover from where or for what cause he gave it such a name, or from where it came, or if the Indians called it thus, because I do not believe that he disembarked or spoke with Indians during this voyage. Having discovered this land, he returned to the island of San Juan, where he had his haciendas, and from there he went to Castille and requested of the King, on account of the discovery of new land that he had made, the favor of making him adelantado of Bimine, and that he be given its government, because he wished to settle it at his cost, with other preeminences and benefits that he must have requested as a man of experience here, which I did not discover. All of this the King granted him. He returned from Castille very fortunate with the title of adelantado and governor of Bimine, which he called by the other name Florida, and which we also call Florida now, although with this name we speak of all the land and seacoast that begins from that large cape that he discovered up to the land of the Bacallaos, and by another name the land of Labrador, which is not very far from the island of England. Having arrived at the island of San Juan, he took everything he needed from his haciendas there and came to this island and port of Santo Domingo, where he again assembled people and ships. He left from this port in the year of [1]512 and went to his Bimine,[23] wishing to enter the land as he had entered these islands. The news of the landing that they made farther south in the same land, which we have stated, must have spread and stirred up all those regions. Those of Bimine defended their homeland as much as they could, and fighting with their few weapons and meager forces, among the first wounded with an arrow was Juan Ponce, adelantado and governor. It seems that although they do not have poison herbs in that land, the wound was in such a place that he judged himself on his own to be in danger, because of which he ordered everyone to return to the ships and leave the land and take him to the island of Cuba, which was the land nearest to where they were. Upon arriving there, and I believe, if I have not forgotten, it was at the port that today is called [Puerto] del Principe, which is on the stated island, he passed from this life placed in so much hardship. In this manner he lost his body, spent a great sum of pesos of gold that, as I said, he had gathered with many deaths and painful and bitter lives of Indians, and endured very great labors in going and coming from Castille, and in discovering, and in attempting to settle, and we do not know the disposition of his soul. And thus passed away the adelantadoship of Bimine with everything else.

Supplementary Documents

1512 Royal Contract with Juan Ponce de León

On February 23, 1512, Juan Ponce de León was officially granted permission to undertake an exploratory expedition in search of the island of Bimini, about which there seems to have been considerable interest, if little clear information, at the time. The following contract, transcribed in a bound volume of such contracts (Spanish Crown 1512a), outlines the details of the official agreement between Ponce and the king of Spain. The contract provides instruction about the responsibilities and rights of each party, including dispensations granted to those who accompanied the explorer on his first voyage of discovery, which was to be undertaken within the first year of a three-year period in which the discovery was Ponce's exclusive right. Of considerable importance, the contract granted him identical rights to any "nearby" islands or territories, which of course established the foundation for his claim to Florida itself. Amendments to this contract were recorded two and a half years later, after the initial voyage had been successfully undertaken.

Contracts such as these were standard practice for early Spanish voyages of discovery and conquest, and their texts provide important insights into the exact nature of these privately financed but royally incentivized endeavors, later examples of which can be characterized as public-private partnerships with direct monetary contributions from private and royal funds. Contracts such as these represent legal delineations of rights and responsibilities of each party, and salient features include the privileges granted to initial participants in these expeditions, such as time-limited tax breaks, titles, and grants of Indian labor (*repartimiento*), as well as requirements and limitations imposed under Crown authority.

The transcription here follows the norms detailed in the preface, generally preserving anachronistic orthography present in the original text except in cases where it might make it difficult for modern Spanish readers to sound out the words correctly or follow the intended sentence structure.

Spanish

Por quanto vos Juan Ponce de Leon me enbiastes a suplicar e pedir por m[e]r[ce]d vos diese licencia y facultad para yr a descubrir y poblar la ysla de Binini con ciertas condiciones que adelante seran declaradas. Por ende por vos hazer m[e]r[ce]d vos doy licencia y facultad para que podais yr a descubrir y poblar la d[ic]ha ysla contanto que no sea de las q[ue] hasta agora estan descubiertas y con las condiciones y segun que adelante sera contenido en esta guissa.

Primeramente que podais con los Nabios que quisierdes llevar a vuestra costa y minsion yr a descubrir y descubrais la d[ic]ha ysla y para ello tengais tres años de termino q[ue] se quenten desde el dia que vos fuere presentada esta mi capitulacion o se tomare el asiento con vos sobre la dicha poblacion contanto q[ue] seais obligado para la yr a descubrir dentro del primer año de los d[ic]hos tres años e que a la yda podais tocar en qualles quier yslas e tierra firme del mar oceano asi descubiertas como por descubrir contanto que no sean de las yslas e tierra firme del mar oceano que pertenescan al serenissimo Rey de Portugal Nuestro muy caro y muy amado hijo y entiendese aquellas que [e]stuvieren dentro de las limites que entre nos y el estan señaladas ni dellas ni de alguna dellas podais tomar ni [h]aber ynteresse ni otra cosa alguna salvo solamente las cossas que para vuestro mantenimiento y provision de navios y gente que ovierdes menester pagando por ellos lo que valieren.

Yten que podais tomar y se tomen por vuestra parte en estos Reynos de Castilla o en la d[ic]ha ysla [E]spañola para lo suso dicho los navios mantenimientos y officiales y marineros y gente que ovierdes menester pagandolo todo segun se acostumbra y siendo a vista en la ysla Española de nuestros officiales que al presente residen y residieren en nuestra Casa de la Contratacion della y en [f. 9v] Castilla a vista de los nuestros officiales que residen y residieren en la nuestra Casa de la Contratacion de Sevilla.

Yten por vos hazer m[e]r[ce]d mando que durante el d[ic]ho tiempo de los d[ic]hos tres años no podais yr ni vaya ninguna persona a descubrir la d[ic]ha ysla de Binini y si alguno fuere a la descubrir o por acertamiento la descubriere se cunpla con vos lo en esta mi capitulacion contenido y no con la persona que ansi la descubriere e que por la descubrir otro no perdais vos nada del derecho que a ella teneis contanto que como d[ic]ho es os hagais a la vela para la yr a descubrir dentro del d[ic]ho primero año e que de otra manera no balga y contando que no sea de las q[ue] se tiene ya noticia y sabiduria cierta.

Yten que hallando y descubriendo la d[ic]ha ysla en la manera que dicha es vos hago m[e]r[ce]d de la gobernacion y justicia della por todos los dias de vuestra vida y para ello vos doy poder cunplido y jurisdicion civil y criminal con todas sus ynsidencias y dependencias anexidades y conexidades.

Yten que hallando la d[ic]ha ysla segun dicho es seais obligado a la poblar a vuestra costa en los lugares y asiento que mejor lo podais hazer e que gozeis de las casas y estancias y poblaciones y heredades que halli hizierdes y del prove- cho que en la d[ic]ha ysla oviere conforme a lo contenido en este asiento.

Yten que si fortalezas se ovieren de hazer en la dicha ysla ayan de ser y sean a nuestra costa e pongamos en ellas nuestros alcaydes como mas vieremos que a nuestro servicio cunpla y [f. 10r] si entre tanto que se hazen las d[ic]has fortalezas vos facides alguna cassa e casas de morada e para defension de los yndios que [e]stas sean vuestras propias y si de [e]llas huviere necesidad para nuestro servicio las ayais de dar pagando lo que valieren.

Yten que vos haze m[e]r[ce]d y por la presente vos la hago por tienpo de doze años contados desde el dia que descubrierdes la d[ic]ha ysla de Binini del diesmo de todas las rrentas e provechos que a nos pertenescan en la dicha ysla no siendo de los diezmos de n[uest]ra granjeria porque de [e]sto no aveis de llevar cosa alguna sino de lo que vos y los que poblaren y estovieren en la d[ic]ha ysla por el dicho tiempo obierdes por granjeria o en otra qualquier manera.

Yten que [e]l repartimiento de los Yndios que oviere en la d[ic]ha ysla se haga por la persona o personas que por mi fueren nombrados y no de otra manera.

Yten que yo mandare y por la presente mando que los Yndios que huviere en la dicha ysla se rrepartan segun las personas que oviere y que primero se cunpla y sean probeydos los primeros descubridores que otras personas algunas e que a estos se haga en ello toda la ventaja que buenamente huviere lugar.

Yten que yo hago m[e]r[ce]d por tienpo de los d[ic]hos diez años que gozen las personas que fueren a descubrir la d[ic]ha ysla y poblaren de aquel viaje del oro e otros metales e cosas de provecho que en la d[ic]ha ysla oviere sin nos pagar de [e]llos mas derecho del diezmo el [f. 10v] primer año e el segundo el nobeno y el tercero el ochavo y el quinto [sic] el setimo y el quinto año la sesta parte y los otros cinco años benideros pagando el quinto segun e por la forma y manera que hagora se paga en la ysla Española e que los otros pobladores que despues fueren que no sean de los descubridores paguen desde el primer año el quinto, porque a estos yo les mandare dar otra franqueça de otras cosas que no sea del oro.

Yten por hazer mas bien y m[e]r[ce]d a vos el dicho Juan Ponce de Leon es mi m[e]r[ce]d y voluntad que todas las yslas que estuvieren comarcanas a la dicha ysla de Binini que vos descubrierdes por vuestra persona y a vuestra costa y minsion en la forma suso dicha y no siendo de las que se tiene noticia como dicho es tengais la gobernacion y poblacion de [e]llas con las condiciones e segund que en esta mi capitulacion se contiene e como por virtud de [e]lla la abeys de tener de la d[ic]ha ysla.

Yten que vos hago m[e]r[ce]d del titulo de nuestro adelantado de la dicha ysla e de las otras que en la forma suso dicha descubrierdes.

Yten que se coxa el oro si lo huviere por la forma q[ue] en la Española se coxe agora e por la forma y manera que yo mandare.

Yten que no podais llevar en vuestra conpañia para lo suso dicho persona ni personas algunas q[ue] sean estrangeros de fuera de nuestros reynos e señorios.

Yten que para seguridad que vos el dicho Juan Ponce e las personas que con vos fueren hareis [f. 11r] y cunplireis e pagareis y sera cunplido y pagado e guardado lo en esta capitulacion contenido que a vos pertenesce guardar y cunplir antes que fagais el dicho viaje deis fianças llanas y abonadas a contentamiento de los n[uest]ros offi[ciale]s que rresiden en la ysla [E]spañola.

Yten que vos el dicho Juan Ponce e las otras personas que con vos fueren e alli estuvieredes hareis y guardareis e pagareis todo lo contenido en esta dicha mi capitulacion y cada cossa y parte de [e]llo y no hareis fraude ni engaño alguno ni dareis fabor ni ayuda ni consentimiento para ello e si lo supierdes lo notificareis a nos e a n[uest]ros officiales en n[uest]ro nonbre sopena que vos o otros qualesquier personas que lo contrario hizieredes por el mismo fecho el que asi no lo cunpliere aya perdido qualquier m[e]r[ce]d o officio que de nos toviere e pague por su persona y bienes todas las penas que nos por bien tovieremos de mandar executar en sus personas y bienes de aquellos y lo hicieren consintieren o encubrieren.

Yten que despues de allegados a la ysla y sabido lo que en ella ay me embiere relacion de [e]llo e otra a los n[uest]ros officiales que residen en la ysla [E]spañola para que nos sepamos lo que se oviere fecho e se probea lo que mas a n[uest]ro servi[ci]o cunpla.

Por ende cunpliendo vos el dicho Joan Ponce todo lo que d[ic]ho es y cada cosa y parte de [e]llo e dadas las dichas fianças e guardando y pagando las cosas suco d[ic]has vos prometo y seguro por la presente de mandar guardar e cunplir todo lo en esta cappitulacion contenido e cada cossa y parte de [e]llo e mando a los n[uest]ros officiales que rresiden en la ysla Española que en n[uest]ro nonbre conforme a lo suso dicho tomen con vos el dicho asiento y capitulacion e rrescivan las dichas fiançças e para v[uest]ro despacho mando a Don Diego Colon n[uest]ro almirante y governador [f. 11v] de la dicha ysla Española e a los n[uest]ros juezes de apelacion e a los officiales de n[uest]ra hazienda que rresiden en ella y a todas las justicias de la dicha ysla Española que vos den todo el fabor e ayuda que ovierdes menester sin que en ello ni en cosa alguna ni parte de [e]llo se vos ponga ningun ympedimiento. Fecha en Burgos a XXIII de hebrero de DXII a[ñ]os. Yo el Rey. Por mandado de su al[tez]a Lope Conchillos señalada del obispo de Palencia.

English

Inasmuch as you, Juan Ponce de León, sent to me to request and ask for the mercy that I should give you license and faculty to go to discover and settle the Island of Binini with certain conditions that will be declared hereafter, therefore in order to grant you this mercy, I give you license and faculty so that you may go to discover and settle the stated island, noting that it should not be one of those that has been discovered up to now, and with the conditions and according to what will be contained hereafter, in this manner:

First, that with the ships that you might wish to take at your cost and expense, you may go and discover the stated island. For this you have a limit of three years that are counted from the day that this my agreement is presented to you, or the contract is made with you about the stated settlement, noting that you are obligated to go to discover within the first year of the aforementioned three years. On the journey you may touch on whichever islands and mainland of the ocean sea, both discovered and yet to be discovered, noting that they should not be among the islands and mainland of the ocean sea that belong to the most serene King of Portugal, our very cherished and very beloved son. And it is understood regarding those that might be within the limits that are assigned between him and us, that neither from them nor from any of them should you take or have any interest or any other thing, excepting only the things that might be necessary for your sustenance and provision of ships, paying for them what they are worth.

In addition, you may take on your behalf in these Kingdoms of Castille or in the stated island of Hispaniola for the aforementioned [journey] the ships, supplies, and officials and sailors and people that might be necessary, paying for all of them as is customary. On the island of Hispaniola this must be under the oversight of our officials who at the present reside or might reside in our House of Trade there, and in Castille under the oversight of our officials who reside and might reside in our House of Trade of Seville.[24]

In addition, in order to grant you mercy, I command that during the aforementioned time of the stated three years, no person may go to discover the stated island of Binini, and if anyone goes to discover it or discovers it by accident, they will fulfill with you the contents of this my agreement, and not with the person who might discover it thus, and that if another discovers it, you will not lose any of the right that you have to it. As is stated, it should be noted that you should make sail to go and discover within the first year, and in any other manner it is invalid. I also note that it should not be one of those [islands] for which news and certain understanding already exists.

In addition, upon finding and discovering the stated island in the manner that is stated, I grant you the mercy of the government and judiciary for all the days of your life, and for this I give you full power, and civil and criminal jurisdiction, with all its incidences and dependencies, annexes and connections.

In addition, upon finding the aforementioned island, as is stated, you are obligated to settle at your cost in the best places and site that you can, and that you will reap the benefits of the houses and establishments and settlements and estates that you might make there, and that might be of value on the stated island, in conformity with the contents of this contract.

Also, if fortresses need to be made on the stated island, they must be and are at our cost, and we will place in them our magistrates as we see fit to our service, and if while the stated fortresses are being made, you make some house or residence for defense against the Indians, these will be your own, and if there is need of them for our service, you must provide them, being paid what they are worth.

In addition, I grant you the mercy, and for the present I do so for the time of twelve years, counted from the day that you discover the stated island of Binini, of the tithe of all the rents and benefits that pertain to us on the stated island,[25] not being from the tithes of our earnings; because of this you will not take anything, but rather from that which you and those who settle and remain on the aforementioned island for the stated time might have as earnings, or in whatever other manner.

In addition, the *repartimiento* of the Indians that might be on the stated island will be made by the person or persons that are named by me, and not in any other manner.[26]

In addition, I will command, and for the present I command, that the Indians that might be on the stated island shall be distributed among the people that there might be, and that the first to be fulfilled and provided will be the first discoverers, before any other persons, and that these [persons] will be given all the advantage that is suitably appropriate.

In addition, I grant the mercy for the time of the aforementioned ten years that the persons who go to discover the stated island and settle from that voyage should benefit from the gold and other metals and things of value that might be on the stated island, without paying us more tax from them than the tenth part in the first year, and the ninth part in the second [year], and the eighth part in the third [year], and the seventh part in the [fourth], and the sixth part in the fifth, and the following five years paying the *quinto* according to and in the form and manner that is paid on the island of Hispaniola,[27] and that the other settlers who might go later, who are not part of the discoverers, will pay the *quinto* from the first year, because I will command them to be given other allowances from other things that are not from gold.

In addition, in order to grant more benefit and mercy to you, the aforementioned Juan Ponce de León, it is my mercy and will that all the islands that might be nearby the stated island of Binini, which you might discover in person, and at your cost and expense, in the afore-mentioned form, and not being those that are already known, as is stated, you shall have the government and settlement of them with the conditions, and according to what is contained in this my agreement, and as by virtue of it, you should have from the stated island.

In addition, I grant you the mercy of the title of our adelantado of the stated island, and of the other ones that in the aforementioned manner you might discover.

In addition, if there is gold, it will be obtained in the manner it is obtained now on Hispaniola, and by the form and manner that I command.

In addition, you may not take in your company for the aforementioned [voyage] any person or persons who are foreigners from outside our kingdoms and lordships.

In addition, for the security of you, the aforementioned Juan Ponce, and the persons that might go with you, you will do and fulfill and pay, and have fulfilled and paid and guarded that which is contained in this agreement, since it pertains to you to guard and fulfill, before you make the stated voyage, giving plain sureties and guaranties to the satisfaction of our officials who reside on the island of Hispaniola.

In addition, you, the aforementioned Juan Ponce, and the other persons who go with you and remain there, will do and guard and pay all that contained in this my stated agreement, and each thing and part of it, and you will not commit any fraud or deceit, nor will you give favor or help or consent for the same, and if you are aware of such, you will notify us and our officials in our name, on penalty that if you or any other persons do the contrary, by the very act he who does not fulfill it has lost whatever mercy or office that he has from us, and will pay by his person and goods all the penalties that we might hold for good effect to order executed on the persons and goods of those who do so, consent, or cover up the same.

In addition, after having arrived at the island and found out what there is on it, you will send me a relation of this, and another to our officials who reside on the island of Hispaniola, so that we find out what has been done, and provide what is most suitable to our service.

Therefore, upon you, the aforementioned Juan Ponce, fulfilling what is stated, and each thing and part of it, and having given the stated sureties, and guarding and paying the aforementioned things, I promise and assure for the present to command guarded and fulfilled all that which is contained in this agreement, and each thing and part of it, and I command our officials who reside on the island of Hispaniola that in our name, in conformity to the aforementioned, they establish with you the stated contract and agreement, and receive the stated sureties, and for your dispatch I command Don Diego Colon, our Admiral and Governor of the stated island of Hispaniola, and our appellate judges, and the officials of our treasury who reside in it, and all the justices of the stated island of Hispaniola, to give you all the favor and help that is needed, without placing any impediment in this, or in any thing or part of it. Dated in Burgos on February 23, 1512. I the King. By order of his highness, Lope Conchillos. Sealed by the Bishop of Palencia.

1514 Royal Contract with Juan Ponce de León

On September 27, 1514, the following contract was issued as a supplement to the 1512 contract regarding Juan Ponce de León's expedition to discover the island of Bimini, effectively renewing and updating the original agreement. Updated to include both Bimini and Florida, the new contract extended Ponce's window of opportunity to implement colonization and specified in explicit terms the treatment of "caciques and Indians" in the new land, prohibiting their enslavement by anyone operating outside the consent of Ponce himself. This new component of the contract was doubtless a response to the newly issued Laws of Burgos, which were promulgated during December 1512, more than ten months after the original Ponce de León contract, and which provided specifics regarding the proper treatment of the Indians (Hussey 1932; Altamira 1938). Copies of the contract are found in two bound volumes in the Archivo General de Indias (Spanish Crown 1514a, 1514b).

The transcription here follows the norms detailed in the preface, generally preserving anachronistic orthography present in the original text except in cases where it might make it difficult for modern Spanish readers to sound out the words correctly or follow the intended sentence structure.

Spanish

El asiento q[ue] se tomo por n[uest]ro mandado con vos Joan Ponce de Leon para yr a poblar a la ysla de Bimini e la ysla Florida que vos descubristes por n[uest]ro mandado demas de la capitulaçion y asiento que con vos se tomo quando las fuistes a descubrir es el siguiente.

1. Primeramente por quanto en la dicha capitulaçion e asiento que con vos por mi mandado se tomo sobre el descubrir y poblar de las d[ic]has yslas vos di licencia y facultad para que por tienpo y termino de tres años que començasen desde el dia que vos fuese entregada la dicha capitulaçion pudiesedes llevar a v[uest]ra costa y mansion los navios que quisiesedes

contanto que fuesedes obligado a descubrir dentro del primero año y porque hasta agora os abeis ocupado en cosas de nuestro servicio y no abeis tenido tienpo para entender en ello es mi m[e]r[ce]d y voluntad que los dichos tres años comiençen a correr y se cuenten desde el dia q[ue] enbarcardes para yr a las dichas yslas.

2. Yten que luego que fuerdes o enviardes a las dichas yslas hagais requerir a los caçiques e yndios dellas por la mejor maña o mañas que se les pueda dar a entender lo que se les dixere conforme a un rrequerimiento questa hordenado por muchos letrados el qual se vos dara firmado del muy r[everen]do yn xpo[28] padre obispo de Burgos Arçobispo Derrosano nuestro capellan maior y de nuestro consejo y de Lope Conchillos n[uest]ro secretario y del m[ism]o consejo y procuradores por todas las vias y mañas que pudierdes e que bengan en conosçimiento de n[uest]ra sancta fee catholica y en obedeçer y serbir como son obligados y tomareis por escripto por ante dos o tres escrivanos si los oviere y ante los mas testigos y mas abonados que halla se hallaren para que aquello sirva para n[uest]ra justificaçion y enbiarmeis las dichas scripturas y requirimientos que asi se hizieren y estos dichos requirimientos se an de hazer una y dos y tres vezes.

3. E si despues de lo suso dicho [no][29] quisieren obedesçer lo contenido en el dicho rrequirimiento en tal caso les podeis fazer guerra y prenderlos y traerlos por esclavos pero si obedesçieren hazedles el buen tratamiento que fuere posible y travajad como d[ic]ho es por todas las maneras que pudierdes como ellos se conviertan a nuestra sancta fee catholica y si por bentura despues de aver obedesçido una bez el dicho requirimiento ellos se tornasen a rrebelar en tal caso mando que les torneis a fazer el dicho rrequirimiento antes de les fazer guerra ni mal ni daño.

4. Otro si que ningun mercader ni otra persona alguna no pueda armar para yr ni enbiar a las d[ic]has yslas por esclavos ni por gente ninguna y que si oviere de yr sea de consentimiento del d[ic]ho Juan Ponçe y no de otra manera contando que nos paguen el quinto e otros derechos que ovieremos de aver y nos pertenesçiere de las armadas y cosas suso d[ic]has.

5. Otros por quanto en la dicha capitulaçion e asiento que con vos mande tomar al tienpo que yvades a descubrir la d[ic]ha ysla yo fize m[e]r[ce]d a las personas que fuesen a descubrir la d[ic]ha ysla y poblasen de aquel viaje que por tienpo y termino de doze años contados desde el dia que la d[ic]ha ysla se descubriese y del oro y otros metales y cosas de provecho que oviesen nos pagasen de d[e]r[ech]o el primer año el diezmo y el segundo el nobeno el terçero el o[c]tavo y el quarto el seteno y el quinto la sesta parte y los otros años siguientes el quinto segun y como se paga en la ysla Española por ende

por la presente confirmo y apruevo lo suso dicho y es mi m[e]r[ce]d que aya hefeto por tienpo de los dichos doze años los quales comiençan desde que se començaren a poblar las dichas yslas.

6. Otro si que yo dare liçencia y por la presente la doy al d[ic]ho Juan Ponçe de Leon para que pueda hazer y hedificar cassas en las dichas yslas y pueblos de las casas de morada de la manera que se hazen y labran en estos reinos contanto que los çimientos dellas sean de una tapia en alto de piedra y lo otro de tierra y asimismo pueda hazer qualesquier labranças de pan y bino y poner qualesquier arboles frutuosos e ynfrutuosos y otras cosas que en la dicha tierra se dieren.

7. Yten que despues que ayais fecho guerra a los d[ich]os Caribes o asegurado los caçiques e yndios y fecho los de paz podais yr o enbiar con los navios y gente de la dicha armada a bisitar las d[ic]has yslas de Binini e ysla Florida quando no aya nesçesidad de v[uest]ra persona e hazer sobre ello lo que mejor paresçiere que conbiene a nuestro serviçio.

8. Yten que para seguridad que vos el dicho Juan Ponce y las personas que con vos fueren hareis y cunplireis y sera cunplido guardado y pagado lo en esta capitulaçion contenido que a vos pertenesce guardar y cunplir antes que hagais el dicho viaje deis fianças y abonadas a contentamiento de los nuestros offiçiales que rresiden en la dicha ysla de San Jua[n].

Por ende cunpliendo vos el dicho Juan Ponçe todo lo que dicho es e cada cossa y parte dello e dadas las dichas fianças y guardando y pagando las cosas suso dichas vos prometo y seguro por la presente de mandar guardar y cunplir todo lo en esta capitulaçion contenido e cada cossa y parte dello y mando a los mas offiçiales que rresiden en la ysla de Sant Juan que en n[uest]ro nonbre conforme a lo suso dicho tomen con vos el dicho asiento y capitulaçion y resçiban las d[ic]has fianças y para v[uest]ro despacho mando a don Diego Colon n[uest]ro almirante visorrey y gover[na]dor de la ysla Española e a los n[uest]ros juezes de apelaçion que en ella rresiden e a los n[uest]ros offiçiales que rresiden en la dicha ysla de Sant Juan e a todas las justiçias de las dichas yslas que vos den todo el fabor e ayuda que obierdes menescer sin que en ello ni en cossa alguna ny parte dello se vos ponga ningun ynpedimiento. Fecha en Vall[adol]id a XXVII de Setienbre de DXIIII años. Yo el Rey. Refrendada de Conchillos. Esta señalada del obispo y quitose la señal porquesto es cosa de crimen.

English

The contract that was made by our command with you, Juan Ponce de León, in order to go and settle the Island of Bimini and the Island of

Florida, which you discovered by our order, in addition to the agreement and contract that was made with you when you went to discover, is the following:

1. First, inasmuch as in the aforementioned agreement and contract that was made by my command with you about the discovery and settlement of the stated islands, I gave you permission and faculty so that for the time and limit of three years that would begin from the day on which you were given the aforementioned agreement, you could take at your cost and estate whatever ships that you might wish, noting that you were obligated to discover within the first year, and because until now you have occupied yourself in affairs of our service, and have not had time to delve into this, it is my favor and will that the stated three years begin to run and are counted from the day that you embark to go to the aforementioned islands.

2. In addition, as soon as you go or send to the aforementioned islands, you will require their caciques and Indians, by the best skill or skills that can make them understand what is told to them, in conformity with a *Requerimiento*[30] that is ordered by many degreed individuals, which will be given to you, signed by the Very Reverend in Christ Father Bishop of Burgos, Archbishop De Rosano, our principal chaplain, and that of our Council, and by Lope Conchillos, our secretary, and that of the same Council, and you will endeavor by all ways and skills that you are capable of that they should come to the understanding of our holy Catholic faith, and obey and serve as they are obligated, and you will take down in writing before two or three notaries, if they are available, and before as many witnesses and trustworthy [people] that find themselves there, so that this serves for our justification, and you will send me the stated writings and *Requerimientos* that are done thus, and these *Requerimientos* must be performed one and two and three times.

3. And if after the aforementioned they do not wish to obey that which is contained in the aforementioned requirement, in such a case you may make war against them and imprison them and bring them as slaves, but if they obey, you will give them the best treatment possible, and work as is stated in all ways you can that they should convert to our holy Catholic faith, and if by chance after having obeyed the stated requirement one time, they should rebel, in that case I command that you make the aforementioned requirement once again, before making war against them, or harm or damage.

4. In addition, no merchant or any other person may arm to go or send to the aforementioned islands for slaves, or for any people, and if they do go it will be with the consent of the aforementioned Juan Ponce, and in no other manner, noting that they must pay us the *quinto* and other taxes that must be paid to us, and that pertain to us from the armadas and aforementioned affairs.

5. In addition, inasmuch as in the aforementioned agreement and contract that I ordered made with you at the time that you went to discover the stated island, I granted the provision that for the persons that should go to discover the stated island and settle on that voyage, during the time and limit of twelve years, counted from the day that the aforementioned island might be discovered, of the gold and other metals and items of value that there might be, they should pay us as tax in the first year the tenth part, and in the second [year] the ninth, in the third [year] the eighth, in the fourth [year] the seventh, and in the fifth year the sixth part, and in the following years the *quinto* according to and how it is paid on the island of Hispaniola, which for the present I confirm and approve the aforementioned, and it is my provision that this be in effect for the time of the stated twelve years, which will begin from the commencement of the settlement of the stated islands.

6. In addition, I will give permission, and for the present I give it, to the aforementioned Juan Ponce de León so that he may make and build houses on the stated islands, and towns of the houses of residence, of the manner that are made and crafted in these kingdoms, noting that their masonry should be of the measurement of one *tapia* in height of stone,[31] and the rest of earth, and likewise that he may make whatever factories of bread and wine, and plant whatever trees, with or without fruit, and other things that might be needed in the aforementioned land.

7. In addition, after you may have made war against the aforementioned Caribes, or securing the caciques and Indians, and having made peace, you may go or send with the ships and people of the stated armada to visit the aforementioned islands of Bimini and island of Florida, when there is no necessity for your person, and do in this what seems most suitable to our service.

8. In addition, for the security of you, the aforementioned Juan Ponce, and the persons who might go with you, you will do and fulfill, and have fulfilled, guarded, and paid, that which is contained in this agreement, which pertains to you to guard and fulfill, before you should

make the aforementioned voyage, sureties and guarantors to the satisfaction of our officials who reside on the stated island of San Juan.

Therefore, if you, the aforementioned Juan Ponce, fulfill all that is stated, and each matter and part of it, and given the stated sureties and guarding and paying the aforementioned things, I promise and assure you for the present that I will command that everything contained in this agreement, and each thing and part of it, shall be guarded and fulfilled. And I command the rest of the officials who reside on the island of San Juan that, in conformity with the aforementioned, in our name they will establish with you the stated contract and agreement, and receive the stated sureties. And for your dispatch, I command Don Diego Columbus, our Admiral, Viceroy and Governor of the Island of Hispaniola, and our appellate judges who reside on it, and our officials who reside on the stated island of San Juan, and all the justices of the stated islands, to give you all the favor and help that is needed, without placing any impediment against you in this, or in any matter, or part of it. Dated in Valladolid on September 27, 1514. I, the King. Countersigned by Conchillos. It is sealed by the Bishop, and the seal should not be removed because this is a criminal matter.

1521 Letter from Juan Ponce de León to the Spanish Crown

The following letter is an original handwritten piece of correspondence written by Juan Ponce de León just days before his anticipated departure with two ships to colonize the southwestern coast of Florida. While it provides few details regarding the expedition itself, it nonetheless reveals the background, context, and even the thoughts and hopes of the expedition's leader. This letter and an accompanying one were filed together in the Archivo General de Indias (Ponce de León 1521b). Given Ponce's tendency for lengthy run-on sentences, periods have been added at apparent sentence breaks where no conjunction appeared.

Spanish

Al muy poderoso señor enperador y rrey de españa don carlos n[uest]ro señor.

Muy poderoso señor

Como quiera q[ue] my husança y costumbre aya sido servir en estas partes a la Corona real por m[anda]do del Rey Catolico y en acrescentami[ent]o de sus rentas y señorios agora aunq[ue] con pobreza e querido continuar el servir a V[uest]ra Mag[es]tad y esperar m[e]r[ce]d[e]s como las espero entre

los quales servicios q[ue] d[ic]ho tengo descobri a my costa y mynsion la ysla
Florida y otras en su comarca de q[ue] no se haze myncion por ser pequ[eñ]as
e ynhutiles y agora yo buelbo aq[ue]lla ysla plaz[i]do a la voluntad de dios a
poblar podiendo lebar copia de gente con q[ue] lo poder hazer porq[ue] alli
sea alabado el nonbre de Xpto[32] y b[uest]ra mag[esta]d sea servido del fruto
q produziere aq[ue]lla t[ie]rra y tanbien entiendo de descobrir mas la costa
de la d[ic]ha ysla y saber sy lo es o sy confina con la t[ie]rra donde esta Di[eg]o
Velazquez o con otra alguna y procurare de saber todo lo q[ue] mas podiere.
Partirme de aqui p[ar]a seguir mi biaje de aqui a cinco o seys dias. De lo q[ue]
se heziere o se viere en aq[ue]llas partes po[r] donde andoviere hare relacion
a la buelta a v[uest]ra mag[esta]d y pidire m[e]r[ce]d[e]s y desde agora suplico me las haga por q[ue] yo no osaria enprender tan gran cosa ny de tanta
costa ni podria salyr con ello syno mediante el favor y m[e]r[ce]d[e]s
de v[uest]ra cesaria magestad y hasta aqui e dexado de las pedir a sydo por
ver q[ue] v[uest]ra magestad tenya poco rreposo y mucho trabajo q[ue] de
v[er]dad lo syento como sy por ello pasase. Guarde n[uest]ro señor su muy
rreal persona a acrescentami[ent]o de larga vida y otros muchos reynos y señorios como por v[uest]ra mag[es]t[a]d es deseado. Desta ysla de San Jua[n]
en ciubdad de Pue[r]to Rrico q[ue] es en las yndias del mar oceano a X dias
del mes de hebrero de iUdxxi años.

A v[uest]ra mag[es]t[a]d.
Esclavo y servidor q[ue] sus muy rreales pies y manos besa,
Jua[n] Po[n]ce de Leo[n]

English

To the very powerful Lord emperor and king of Spain
Don Carlos, our Lord.

Very powerful lord,

As you wish, my usage and custom has been to serve the Royal Crown
in these parts by order of the Catholic King, and in the increase of his
income and domains, although now in poverty, I have wished to continue to serve Your Majesty and await your favors, as I hope, among
which I served you, as I have stated, in discovering at my cost and
expense the island of Florida, and others in its district. No expense is
made because they are small and useless, and now I am returning to
that island to settle, with great pleasure at the will of God, being able
to carry many people with which to do so, so that the name of Christ
is worshipped, and so that Your Majesty is served by the fruit that that
land will produce, and I also intend to discover more of the coast of the
aforementioned island, and find out if it is [an island], or if it borders

on the land where Diego Velázquez is, or some other [land], and I will
endeavor to find out everything I can. I will depart from here in pursuit of my journey in five or six days from now. I will make a relation
to Your Majesty of whatever is done or seen in those parts upon my
return. I will ask for favors, and from now on I implore that they be
granted, because I would not dare to undertake such a great affair, or
at such great cost, nor could I go forth with it, were it not by means of
the kindness and favors of Your Caesarian Majesty, and I have left off
asking for them until now, which has been on account of seeing that
Your Majesty had little rest and much work, for which I am truly sorry
if for this reason it should happen. Our Lord guard your very royal
person in the augmentation of long life, and many other kingdoms and
dominions, as is desired for Your Majesty. From this island of San Juan,
in the city of Puerto Rico, which is in the Indies in the Ocean Sea, on
the 10th day of February, 1521.

To Your Majesty.
Slave and servant, who kisses your very royal feet and hands,
Juan Ponce de León

1521 Letter from Juan Ponce de León to the Cardinal of Tortosa

Like the previous letter, the following one was written by Juan Ponce
de León a few days before his departure to colonize the southwestern
coast of Florida, this time to the Cardinal of Tortosa, who was governing
Spain at the time as regent for the king though was soon to be elected
Pope Adrian VI (1522–23). The letter was filed together with the previous one in the Archivo General de Indias (Ponce de León 1521a).

Spanish

Al ylustre y muy revere[n]disimo S el señor cardenal de tortosa
gob[er]nador en estos reynos y señorios po[r] su cesaria
mag[esta]d n[uest]ro señor en la corte de españa.

Yllustre y muy reverendisimo Señor

Yo e servydo mucho en estas partes de las yndias a la corona rreal po[r]
m[anda]do del rrey catolico y hasta aqui an estado suspensos mys servicios
ansy aca en la continuacion q[ue] yo avre de hazer como alla de tener memoria dellos y hazerme m[e]r[ce]d[e]s. P[er]o esto tambien creo lo a causado
el t[ie]npo y trabajos q[ue] an ocorrido ansy a my por ab[er] enbihudado y
ab[er]me q[ue]dado hijas y yo no las osar dexar ni descompañar hasta casar-
las y agora ya las e casado y a dios pliego pues alla bien. Se q[ue] no an fal-

tado trabajos y pena ansy a su mag[es]t[a]d como a v[uest]ro s[eñor] p[er]o
como espero en dios pues alla a bien y el estado y señorio de su mag[es]t[a]d
en mucha aumentacion y q[ue] me hara m[e]r[ce]d[e]s. Yo e acordado con la
pobreza q[ue] me q[ue]dava de servir a su mag[es]t[a]d en yr a la ysla florida
y sus comarcas y poblar q[ue] podiere y descobrir todo lo q[ue] mas podiere.
Partirme de aqui a cinco o seys dias p[ar]a alla con dos navios y con la gente
q[ue] podiere lebar. De lo q[ue] por alla se hiziere hare relacion a su mag[es]-
t[a]d y a v[uest]ro s[eñor] y le suplico tenga memoria como e servido y como
syrbo y como e gastado quanto e tenido por servir y agora no me q[ue]do en
la posada. A v[uest]ra s[eñor] suplico q[ue] por su mano reciba yo m[e]r-
[ce]d[e]s de su mag[es]ta[d] pa[ra] con q[ue] yo pueda servir q[ue] de v[er]-
dad no deseo q[ue] me las haga pa[ra] atesorar ni pa[ra] pasar esta vida miserable syno pa[ra] servir con ello y con my pe[r]sona en lo q[ue] yo tuviere a
su mag[es]t[a]d y poblar a aq[uel]la t[ie]rra q[ue] descobri y desfruto q[ue]
de alli produziere sea dios servido y su magestad y este entencion de servir y
pa[ra] me ayudar pedir m[e]r[ce]d[e]s a su mag[es]t[a]d q[ue] si me oviese
de rretraer con lo q[ue] tengo mas bien tengo q[ue] a dios meresca. A
v[uest]ra s[eñor] suplico juzgue mi yntencion y se ynforme de quien soy y lo
q[ue] e servido y myre como syrvo y conforme a ello me ayude y haga haze[r]
m[e]r[ce]d[e]s pa[ra] q[ue] pueda servir.

Señor a todos es notorio mis servicios p[er]o doy por autores al señor obispo
de burgos y al secretario conchillos y al señor comendador mayor de la hor-
den y caballeria de calatrava y a la mano de quien se podra ynformar pues le
tiene ay a la mano v[uest]ra s[eñor] de todo lo q[ue] digo. Guarde n[uest]ro
señor la yllustre y muy revere[n]disima persona de v[uest]ra s[eñor] con
acrescentami[ent]o de mucha prosperidad y mayor estado como por v[uest]ra
s[eñor] es deseado. Desta ysla de San Jua[n] y ciudad de pue[r]to rico q[ue]
es en las yndias del mar oceano a X dias de hebrero de iUdxxi años.

Criado y servidor de v[uest]ra ylustrysima y revere[n]disima s[eño]r
Jua[n] Po[n]ce de Leo[n]

English

To the illustrious and most reverend Señor Cardinal
of Tortosa, governor in these kingdoms and dominions
for His Caesarian Majesty our lord in the court of Spain.

Illustrious and very revered Lord,

I have served much in these parts of the Indies of the Royal Crown by
order of the Catholic King, and until now my services have been sus-
pended, both here in the continuation that I will have to do, and also

there [in Spain] with having a memorial of [my services] and granting me favors. But I also believe that [the delay] has been caused by the time and hardships that have likewise occurred to me by having been widowed and been left with daughters, and I did not dare leave or stop supporting them until marrying them, and now I have married them off, and I pray to God that it goes well. I know that hardships and distress have not been lacking for both His Majesty and Your Lordship, but as I hope in God that all goes well, and the estate and dominion of His Majesty augment greatly, and that he will grant me favors. I have decided in the poverty that I remain to serve His Majesty by going to the island of Florida and its district to settle what I can, and discover all that I can. I will depart from here to go there in five or six days with two ships and the people that I can carry. I will give a relation of whatever is done there to Your Grace, and I request that it be recalled how I have served, and how I serve, and how I have spent as much as I had in order to serve, and even now I am not remaining at home. I ask Your Lordship that by your hand I might receive favors from His Majesty with which I can serve, since in truth I do not desire that he grants me [favors] in order to hoard wealth, or in order to spend this miserable life [better], but rather in order to serve His Majesty with what I have and with my person, and to settle that land that I discovered, and enjoy whatever is produced from there, if God and His Majesty are pleased to do so. And this intention to serve helps me request favors from His Majesty, and if I were to have to withdraw with what I have, I have to deserve it from God. I ask Your Lordship to judge my intention and inform yourself about who I am, and how I have served, and to look at how I serve, and in conformity with this help me and have favors granted to me so that I might be able to serve.

Lord, my services are well known to everyone, but I present as references the Señor Bishop of Burgos, and Secretary Conchillos, and the Señor Encomendador Mayor of the Order and Cavalry of Calatrava, and you can inform yourself best about everything I have said since you have them all there at hand. Our Lord guard the illustrious and most reverend person of Your Lordship with the increase of much prosperity and greater estate, as is desired for Your Lordship. From this island of San Juan and city of Puerto Rico, which is in the Indies of the Ocean Sea, on the 10th of February, 1521.

Servant of Your illustrious and most reverend Lordship,
Juan Ponce de León

2

The Pánfilo de Narváez and Hernando de Soto Expeditions and the Captivity of Juan Ortiz, 1528–1539

The captivity narrative of Juan Ortiz effectively bridges two of the earliest Spanish expeditions to the lower Florida gulf coast: those of Pánfilo de Narváez in 1528 and Hernando de Soto in 1539. Having been captured during the first expedition, he was subsequently liberated during the second. Apart from demonstrating relatively clearly the proximity between the landing sites of these two expeditions, the narrative provides intricate details of what essentially constituted one of the earliest first-contact situations in Spanish Florida. While the text of Garcilaso's narrative must be viewed as a secondary source based on interviews with several survivors of the Soto expedition, as well as several contemporary narrative accounts (most of which have not survived to the present day), there is still much to be learned from Garcilaso's moving account of Juan Ortiz's lengthy captivity along the margins of Tampa Bay, particularly as a virtually unique ethnographic record of the daily life of its indigenous inhabitants during the early sixteenth century. In particular, although many names attached to specific individuals and locations in Garcilaso's text have long been recognized to have been confused with the correct ones, and his lengthy "speeches" and other literary devices are generally viewed with suspicion (e.g., Swanton 1985: 4–11; Hudson 1997: 448–53; Galloway 1997: 27–39; see also Chang-Rodríguez 2006), his descriptions of events and indigenous customs observed are nonetheless likely to have been based in large part on the real memories of expedition survivors.

The documents in this chapter include selections from Álvar Núñez Cabeza de Vaca's published narrative of the Pánfilo de Narváez expedition and from Garcilaso de la Vega's account of Hernando de Soto's landing and the Juan Ortiz captivity. Although both of these narratives have been translated and published multiple times by other authors, they are presented here in new translations as companions and complements to the other narratives of first contact for this period along Florida's lower gulf coast.

Narratives

Cabeza de Vaca's Account of the Narváez Expedition

The following text is extracted from a much more lengthy narrative of the travails of Álvar Núñez Cabeza de Vaca (1989: 82–91) as a result of his participation in the expedition of Pánfilo de Narváez to Florida (and points beyond) between 1528 and 1536. The volume was originally published in Spain in 1542 and in revised format in 1555, from which the text for the present extract was selected. An earlier handwritten manuscript, penned by Cabeza de Vaca (n.d.) himself, exists today in the Archivo General de Indias and contains basically the same information as that contained in the later *Naufragios* narrative, though in considerably shorter format. Given that he was only one of four survivors who reached Mexico some eight years later, the Cabeza de Vaca narrative is the only detailed account that survives regarding the initial events of the Narváez expedition along the lower gulf coast of Florida, setting the stage for the captivity narrative of Juan Ortiz.

The transcription here follows the norms detailed in the preface, generally preserving anachronistic orthography present in the original text except in cases where it might make it difficult for modern Spanish readers to sound out the words correctly or follow the intended sentence structure.

Spanish

Capitulo II. Como el Governador vino al Puerto de Xagua, i truxo consigo à vn piloto.

. . . anduvimos con tiempo contrario, hafta llegar á doce leguas de la Habana; i estando otro dia para entrar en ella, nos tomó vn tiempo de Sur, que nos apartó de la tierra, i atravesamos por la costa de la Florida, i llegamos á la tierra, Martes, doce dias del mes de Abril, i fuimos cofteando la via de la Florida: i Jueves Santo surgimos en la misma costa, en la boca de una baía, al cabo de la qual vimos ciertas casas, i habitaciones de Indios.

Capitulo III. Como llegamos á la Florida.

En este mismo dia salió el Contador Alonso Enriquez, i se puso en vna isla, que está en la misma baía, i llamó á los Indios, los quales vinieron, i estuvieron con él buen pedaço de tiempo, i por via de rescate le dieron pescado, i algunos pedaços de carne de venado. Otro dia siguiente, que era Viernes Santo, el Governador se desembarcó con la mas gente, que en los bateles que traía, pudo sacar; i como llegamos á los buhíos, ó casas, que haviamos visto de los Indios, hallamóslas desamparadas, i solas, porque la Gente se havia ido aquella noche en suscanoas. El uno de aquellos buhíos era mui grande, que cabrian en él mas de trecientas personas: los otros eran mas pequeños, i hallamos alli una sonaja de oro, entre las redes. Otro dia el Governador levantó pendones por V[uestra] Mag[estad] i tomó la posesion de la tierra en su Real Nombre, presentó sus provisiones, i fue obedescido por Governador, cómo V[uestra] Mag[estad] lo mandaba. Asimismo presentamos nosotros las nuestras ante él, i él las obedesció, como en ellas se contenia. Luego mandó, que toda la otra gente desembarcase, i los caballos que havian quedado, que no eran mas de quarenta i dos, porque los demás, con las grandes tormentas, i mucho tiempo que havian andado por la Mar, eran muertos: i estos pocos que quedaron estaban tan flacos, i fatigados, que por el presente poco provecho podiamos tener de ellos. Otro dia los Indios de aquel pueblo vinieron á nosotros, i aunque nos hablaron, como nosotros no teniamos lengua, no los entendiamos: mas hacian nos muchas señas, i amenaças, i nos paresció, que nos decian, que nos fuesemos de la tierra; i con esto nos dexaron, sin que nos hiciesen ningun impedimento, i ellos se fueron.

Capitulo IV. Como entramos por la tierra.

Otro dia adelante, el Governador acordó de entrar por la Tierra, por descubrirla, i vér lo que en ella havia. Fuimonos con él, el Comisario, i el Veedor, i yo, con quarenta hombres, i entre ellos seis de caballo, de los quales poco nos podiamos aprovechar. Llevamos la via del norte; hasta que á hora de visperas llegamos á vna baía mui grande, que nos paresció que entraba mucho por la tierra, quedamos alli aquella noche, i otro dia nos bolvimos donde los navios, i gente estaban. El Governador mandó, que el vergantin fuese costeando la via de la Florida, i bufcafe el puerto, que Miruelo el piloto havia dicho que sabia: mas iá él lo havia errado, i no fabia en qué parte estabamos, ni adonde era el puerto; i fuele mandado al vergantin, que si no lo hallase, travesase á la Habana, i buscase el navio, que Alvaro de la Cerda tenia, i tomados algunos bastimentos, nos viniesen á buscar. Partido el vergantin, tornamos á entrar en la tierra los mismos que primero, con alguna gente mas, i

costeamos la baía, que haviamos hallado: i andadas quatro leguas, tomamos
quatro Indios, i mostramosles maíz, para vér si lo conoscian, porque hasta
entonces no haviamos visto señal de él. Ellos nos dixeron, que nos llevarian
donde lo havia, i asi nos llevaron á su pueblo, que es al cabo de la baía,
cerca de alli, i en él nos mostraron vn poco de maíz, que aun no estaba para
cogerse. Alli hallamos muchas caxas de mercaderes de Castilla, i en cada
una de ellas estaba un cuerpo de Hombre muerto, i los cuerpos cubiertos
con unos cueros de venados, pintados. Al Comisario le paresció, que esto era
especie de idolatría, i quemó las caxas con los cuerpos. Hallamos tambien
pedaços de lienço, i de paño, i penachos, que parescian de la Nueva España:
hallamos tambien muestras de Oro. Por señas preguntamos á los Indios, de
adonde havian havido aquellas cosas? Señalaron nos, que mui lexos de alli
havia una provincia, que se decia Apalache, en la qual havia mucho Oro, i
hacian seña de haver mui gran cantidad de todo lo que nosotros estimamos
en algo. Decian, que en Apalache havia mucho, i tomando aquellos Indios por
guia, partimos de alli: i andadas diez, ó doce leguas, hallamos otro pueblo
de quince casas, donde havia buen pedaço de maíz sembrado, que iá estaba
para cogerse, i tambien hallamos alguno, que estaba iá seco; i despues de
dos dias, que alli estuvimos, nos bolvimos donde el Contador, i la gente, i
navios estaban, i contamos al Contador, i pilotos lo que haviamos visto, i las
nuevas, que los Indios nos havian dado. Y otro dia, que fue primero de Maio,
el Governador llamó á parte al Comisario, i al Contador, i al Veedor, i á mi, i
á vn marinero, que fe llamaba Bartolomé Fernandez, i á vn escrivano, que se
decia Geronimo de Alaniz, i asi juntos, nos dixo, que tenia en voluntad de entrar por la tierra adentro, i los navios se fuesen costeando, hasta que llegasen
al puerto, i que los pilotos decian, i creían, que iendo la via de las Palmas,
estaban mui cerca de alli, i sobre esto nos rogo, le diesemos nuestro parescer. Yo respondia, que me parescia, que por ninguna manera debia dexar los
navios, sin que primero quedasen en puerto seguro, i poblado, i que mirase,
que los pilotos no andaban ciertos, ni se afirmaban en una misma cosa, ni
sabian á qué parte estaban: i que allende de esto, los caballos no estaban
para que en ninguna necesidad que se ofreciese, nos pudiesemos aprovechar
de ellos: i que sobre todo esto, ibamos mudos, I sin lengua, por donde mal
nos podiamos entender con los Indios, ni saber lo que de la tierra queriamos,
i que entrabamos por tierra, de que ninguna relacion teniamos, ni sabiamos
de qué suerte era, ni lo que en ella havia, ni de qué gente estaba poblada, ni
á qué parte de ella estabamos: i que sobre todo esto, no teniamos bastimentos para entrar adonde no sabiamos; porque visto lo que en los navios havia,
no se podia dár á cada hombre de racion, para entrar por la tierra, mas de
una libra de vizcocho, i otra de tocino; i que mi parescer era, que se debia
embarcar, i ir á buscar puerto, i tierra; que fuese mejor para poblar, pues lo
que haviamos visto, en sí era tan despoblada, i tan pobre, quanto nunca en
aquellas partes se havia hallado. Al Comisario lo paresció todo lo contrario;

diciendo, que no se havia de embarcar, sino que iendo siempre ácia la costa, fuesen en busca del puerto, pues los pilotos decian, que no estaria sino diez, ó quince leguas de alli, la via de Panuco; i que no era posible, iendo siempre á la costa, que no topasemos con él, porque decian, que entraba doce leguas adentro por la tierra, i que los primeros que lo hallasen, esperasen alli á los otros, i que embarcarse era tentar á Dios, pues desque partimos de Castilla tantos trabajos haviamos pasado, tantas tormentas, tantas pérdidas de navios, i de gente haviamos tenido, hasta llegar alli: i que por estas raçones él se debia de ir por luengo de costa, hasta llegar al puerto: i que los otros navios, con la otra gente, se irian la misma via, hasta llegar al mismo puerto. A todos los que alli estaban, paresció bien que esto se hiciese asi, salvo al escrivano, que dixo, que primero que desamparase los navios, los debia de dexar en puerto conoscido, i seguro, i en parte que fuese poblada: que esto hecho, podria entrar por la tierra adentro, i hacer lo que le pareciese. El Governador siguió su parescer, i lo que los otros le aconsejaban. Yo, vista su determinacion, requerile de parte de V[uestra] Mag[estad] que no dexase los navios, sin que quedasen en puerto, i seguros, i asi lo pedí por testimonio al escrivano, que alli teniamos. El respondió, que pues él se conformaba con el parescer de los mas de los otros oficiales, i Comisario, que yo no era parte para hacerle estos requerimientos; i pidió al escrivano le diese por testimonio, como por no haver en aquella tierra mantenimientos para poder poblar, ni puerto para los navios, levantaba el pueblo que alli havia asentado, i iba con él en busca del puerto, i de tierra, que fuese mejor; i luego mandó apercibir la gente, que havia de ir con él, que se proveiesen de lo que era menester para la jornada; i despues de esto proveído, en presencia de los que alli estaban, me dixo: Que pues yo tanto estorvaba, i temia la entrada por la tierra; que me quedase, i tomase cargo de los navios, i la gente, que en ellos quedaba, i poblase, si yo llegase primero que él: yo me escusé de esto; i despues de salidos de alli aquella misma tarde, diciendo, que no le parescia, que de nadie se podia fiar aquello, me embió á decir, que me rogaba, que tomase cargo de ello; i viendo que importunandome tanto, yo todavia me escusaba, me preguntó, qué era la causa porque huía de aceptallo? A lo qual respondí, que yo huía de encargarme de aquello, porque tenia por cierto, i sabia; que él no havia de vér mas los navios, ni los navios á él; i que esto entendia, viendo que tan sin aparejo se entraban por la tierra adentro, i que yo queria mas aventurarme al peligro, que él; i los otros se aventuraban, i pasar por lo que él, i ellos pasasen, que no encargarme de los navios, i dár ocasion que se dixese, que como havia contradicho la entrada, me quedaba por temor, i mi honra anduviese en disputa, i que yo queria mas aventurar la vida, que poner mi honra en esta condicion. El, viendo que conmigo no aprovechaba, rogó á otros muchos, que me hablasen en ello, i me lo rogasen: á los quales respondí lo mismo que á él; i asi proveió por su teniente, para que quedase en los navios, á un alcalde, que traía, que se llamaba Caravallo.

Capitulo V. Como dexó los navios el Governador.

Sabado, primero de Maio, el mismo dia que esto havia pasado, mandó dár á cada uno de los que havian de ir con él, dos libras de vizcocho, i media libra de tocino; i ansi nos partimos para entrar en la tierra. La suma de toda la gente que llevabamos, era trecientos hombres, en ellos iba el comisario Frai Juan Suarez, i otro Fraile, que se decia Frai Juan de Palos, i tres clerigos, i los oficiales. La gente de caballo, que con estos ibamos, eramos quarenta de caballo; i ansi anduvimos con aquel bastimento que llevabamos, quince dias; sin hallar otra cosa que comer, salvo palmitos, de la manera de los de Andalucia. En todo este tiempo no hallamos Indio ninguno, ni vimos casa, ni poblado. . . .

English

Chapter II. How the Governor came to the Port of Xagua, and brought with him a pilot.

. . . we traveled with contrary weather until arriving twelve leagues from Havana. On the next day, waiting to enter inside [the bay], a southerly storm struck us that separated us from land. We crossed to the coast of Florida and arrived at land on Tuesday, the twelfth of the month of April, and we cruised along the coast of Florida. On Holy Thursday we anchored on the coast itself, in the mouth of a bay, at the end of which we saw certain houses and Indian habitations.

Chapter III. How we arrived at Florida.

This same day the Accountant Alonso Enríquez came forth and landed on an island that is in the same bay, and called to the Indians, who came out and were with him a good space of time. And as barter, they gave him fish, and some pieces of deer meat. The next day, which was Good Friday, the governor disembarked with as many people as he could get in the rowboats he brought. And when we arrived at the Indian huts, or houses, that we had seen, we found them abandoned and alone, because the people had gone away that night in their canoes. One of those huts was very large, in which more than three hundred people could fit. The others were smaller, and we found there a gold bell among the nets. The next day the governor raised banners for His Majesty and took possession of the land in his royal name, presented his commissions, and was obeyed as governor, as His Majesty commanded. Likewise, we presented our [commissions] before him, and he obeyed them as was contained in them. Then he ordered that all the rest of the people should disembark, and the surviving horses. There were no more than forty-two [horses], because the rest were dead, on account of the great storms and lengthy time that they had been traveling on the sea, and these few that remained were so thin and weak that for the present, we could expect little benefit from them. The next day the Indians of that town came to us, and although they spoke to us, we could not understand them, since we had no interpreter. They also made many signs to us, and threats, and it seemed to us that they were telling us to go away from the land. With this they left us, without making any hindrance to us, and they went away.

Chapter IV. How we entered in the land.

On a later day, the governor decided to enter in the land in order to discover it, and see what there was in it. With him went the commissioner, the overseer, and I,[1] with forty men, and among them six on horseback, of the few horses that were of any value. We went in a northerly direction, until at the hour of vespers we arrived at a very large bay, which seemed to us that it entered far into the land. We remained there that night, and the next day we returned to where the ships and people were. The governor commanded that the brigantine should cruise along the coast of Florida and look for the port that the pilot Miruelo had said he knew about, though he had erred, and did not know where we were, or where the port was. The brigantine was ordered that if it did not find it, it should cross to Havana and look for the ship that Alvaro de la Cerda had, and after having taken on some supplies, it should come and look for us. The brigantine having departed, the same ones as at first entered in the land again, with some additional people. We traveled along the coast of the bay that we had found, and having walked four leagues, we took four Indians, and we showed them corn in order to see if they recognized it, because up to that point we had not seen any sign of it. They told us that they would take us where there was [corn], and thus they took us to their town, which is at the end of the bay, near there, and in it they showed us a little corn, which was not ready to be harvested yet. There we found many boxes from merchants of Castille, and in each one of them was the body of a dead man, and the bodies covered with some painted deerskins. It seemed to the commissioner that this was a type of idolatry, and he burned the boxes with the bodies. We also found pieces of linen, and cloth, and feathers that seemed to be from New Spain. We also found signs of gold. By signs, we asked the Indians where they had gotten those things. They signaled that there was a province called Apalache, very far from there, in which there was much gold, and they made signs of there being a great quantity of everything that we esteem. They said that in Apalache there was much, and taking those Indians as guides, we departed from there. And having traveled ten or twelve leagues, we found another town of fifteen houses, where there was a good field of corn sown, which was then ready for harvest, and we also found some that was already dry. And after we were there two days, we returned to where the accountant and the people and ships were. We told the accountant and pilots what we had seen, and the news that the Indians had given us. And the next day, which was the first of May, the governor called aside the commissioner, the accountant, the overseer, and I, and a sailor named Bartolomé Fernández, and a notary called Gerónimo de Alaniz. While there together, he told us that he wished to enter in the interior, and the ships should go along the coast until they arrived at the port, and that the pilots said and believed that going in the direction of Las Palmas, they were very close to it.[2] He implored us to give our opinion about this. I responded that it seemed to me that in no way should he leave the ships without first leaving the port secure and settled, and that he should attend to the fact that the pilots were not certain, nor did they affirm one single thing, nor did they know in what place they were. Beyond this, the horses were not ready for us to make use of in case of any need that might arise. And beyond all this, we were traveling mute, and without an interpreter, for which there could be poor understanding between us and the Indians, and they could not know what we wanted from the land. And we were entering in land that we had no account of, nor did we know what kind it was, or what there was in it, or what people populated it, or in what part of it we were. And above all this, we did not have supplies in order to enter an unknown land, because seeing what there was in the ships, no more than one pound of biscuit and another of bacon could be given to each man as rations. And that my opinion was that he should embark and go to look for a port and land that was better to settle, because what we had seen was more unpopulated and more poor than had ever been found in those parts. To the commissioner it seemed exactly the opposite, saying that he should not disembark, but rather that going always facing the coast, they should go in search of the port, since the pilots said that it would not be more than ten or fifteen leagues from there in the direction of Pánuco,[3] and that by going always along the coast, it was impossible not to run across it, because they said that it entered twelve leagues within the land, and that the first ones who found it should wait there for the others. And to embark was to tempt God, because ever since we left Castille we had experienced so many hardships, so many storms, and so many losses of ships and people until arriving here. For these reasons he should go alongside the coast until arriving at the port, and the other ships should go in the same direction with the other people until arriving at the same port. It seemed good to do this in this way to everyone else who was there, except for the notary, who said that before abandoning the ships, they should leave them in a known and secure port, and in a place that was settled, and that having done this, he could enter in the interior and do what seemed best to him. The governor followed his opinion, and that which the others counseled. Seeing his determination, I required him on behalf of His Majesty not to leave the ships unless they remained in a port, and secure, and thus I requested this of him in writing with the notary we had there. He responded that since he was in conformity with the opinion of the majority of the other officials, and the commissioner, that I did not have the power to make these requirements. And he asked the notary to give him in writing that since in that land there were neither supplies to be able to settle, nor a port for the ships, that he was removing the town that he had established there, and was going with it in search of the port, and of land that was better. And then he ordered the people who were to go with him to get ready, and provide themselves with whatever was necessary for the journey. After having provided this, in the presence of those who were there, he told me that since I was such an obstruction, and feared to enter in the land, that I should remain and take charge of the ships and the people who remained in them, and settle if I should arrive before him. I excused myself from this. After having departed from there that very same afternoon, saying that it seemed to him that he could not trust that task to anyone else, he sent word to tell me that he implored that I should take charge of it. And seeing that it bothered me so much, that I still excused myself, he asked me what was the reason that I avoided accepting it. To this I responded that I was avoiding taking charge of that because I held it for certain and knew that he would not see the ships again, nor the ships him. And understanding this, seeing that they were entering into the interior so unprepared, I wished to risk the danger more than he and the others were risking, and pass through what he and they might experience, instead of taking charge of the ships, giving occasion for him to say that since I had contradicted the entrance, I remained behind out of fear. Since my honor was in dispute, I wished to risk my life and place my honor in this condition. Seeing that he could not take advantage of me, he implored many others to speak with me about it, and that they should implore me. I responded to them the same thing that I had to him, and thus he provided a magistrate that he brought, called Caravallo, as his lieutenant to remain in the ships.

Chapter V. How the governor left the ships.

Saturday, the first of May, the same day that this had happened, [the governor] ordered each one of those who were to go with him to be given two pounds of biscuit, and half a pound of bacon, and thus we departed to enter in the land. The sum of all the people that we carried was three hundred men. Among them went the commissioner Fray Juan Suárez and another friar called Fray Juan de Palos, and three clerics, and the officials. The people on horseback with whom we went numbered forty. And thus we traveled fifteen days with those supplies that we were carrying, without finding anything else to eat except for hearts of palm, like those from Andalucia. In all this time we did not find one Indian, nor did we see a house or settlement. . . .

Garcilaso's Account of the Ortiz Captivity and Soto Landing

The following text is a secondary historical narrative constructed by Garcilaso de la Vega (1605: 28r–51v), the Inca, and represents one of the earliest examples of indigenous New World literature during the European colonial era (e.g., Chang-Rodríguez 2006). Originally published in Lisbon in 1605, the Garcilaso account is the most lengthy narrative that survives of the Hernando de Soto expedition. Unfortunately, it is also generally regarded as the least trustworthy in terms of names and details, even though Garcilaso clearly indicated his heavy reliance on several original narratives by survivors of the expedition (including Alonso de Carmona and Juan de Coles), as well as direct and intensive interviews with several others (including Gonzalo Silvestre). Nevertheless, the narrative still has significant value from an ethnographic perspective, despite its flaws, extrapolations, and potential exaggerations. For this book, Chapter XI and part of Chapter XII are omitted, since they focus on internal affairs of Soto's army.

For the extract that follows, it is important to note that the name of one of the principal figures in Garcilaso's narrative, the cacique Hirrihigua, is named in other more reliable chronicles, such as those by Rodrigo Rangel and the Gentleman of Elvas (see Clayton, Knight, and Moore 1993: 33–219, 247–306) as Oçita (or Ucita). On several occasions throughout his narrative, Garcilaso transposes certain aboriginal names for one another, presumably based on the flawed memories of his sources. Hirrihigua was indeed mentioned (as Orriygua) in the Rangel account as one of four nearby rivals of Mocoço, probably accounting at least in part for the error.

The transcription here follows the norms detailed in the preface, generally preserving anachronistic orthography present in the original text except in cases where it might make it difficult for modern Spanish readers to sound out the words correctly or follow the intended sentence structure.

Spanish

[f. 28r] Primera Parte del Libro Segundo de la Historia de la Florida del Ynca.

Donde se trata de como el Governador llegó á la Florida, y halló rastro de Pamphilo de Narbaez, y un Christiano cautivo: los tormentos y la cruel vida que los Indios le dava[n]: las generosidades de un Indio, Señor de vasallos: Las preve[n]ciones que para el descubrimie[n]to se hizieron: los sucezos que acaescieron en las primeras ocho provincias que descubrieron: y las desatinadas bravezas en palabras y obras de un Cacique temerario. Contiene treynta capitulos.

Cap[itulo] I. El Governador llega a la Florida, y halla rastro de Pamphilo de Narvaez.

El Governador Hernando de Soto, que como diximos, yva navegando en demanda de la Florida, descubrió tierra della el postrer dia de Mayo, aviendo tardado diez y nueve dias por la mar, por averle sido el tiempo [f. 28v] contrario. Surgieron las Naos en una baia honda, y buena, que llamaron del Spiritu Sancto, y por ser tarde no desembarcaron gente alguna aquel dia. El primero de Junio echaron los bateles a tierra, los quales bolvieron cargados de yerva para los cavallos, y truxeron mucho agraz de parrizas incultas, que hallaron por el monte, que los Indios de todo este gran reyno de la Florida no cultivan esta planta, ni la tienen en la veneracion que otras naciones, aunque comen la fruta de ella, quando esta muy madura, o hecha passas. Los nuestros quedaron muy contentos de las buenas muestras, que trujeron de tierra, por asemejarse en las uvas á España, las quales no hallaron en tierra de Mexico, ni en todo el Peru. El segundo dia de Junio mando el Governador, que saliessen a tierra trezientos infantes al auto, y solemnidad de tomar la posession della por el Emperador Carlos Quinto, Rey de España. Los quales despues de el auto, anduvieron todo el dia por la costa sin ver Indio alguno, y a la noche se quedaron a dormir en tierra. Al quarto del alva dieron los Indios en ellos con tanto impetu, y denuedo, que los retiraro[n] hasta el agua; y como tocasen arma, salieron de los navios infantes, y cavallos a los socorrer con tanta presteza, como si estuvieran en tierra.

El tiniente general Vasco Porcallo de Figueroa fue el caudillo del socorro halló los infantes de tierra apretados, y turbados, como visoños, q[ue] unos á otros se estorvava[n] al pelear, y algunos de ellos ya heridos de las flechas. Dado el socorro, y seguido un buen trecho el alcançe de los enemigos, se

bol[f. 29r]vieron a su alojamiento, y apenas avian llegado a el, qua[n]do se
les cayó muerto el cavallo del tiniente general de un flechazo, q[ue] en la refriega le dieron sobre la silla, que passando la ropa, tejuelas, y bastos e[n]tró
mas de una tercia por las costillas a lo hueco. Vasco Porcallo holgo mucho de
que el primer cavallo, que en la conquista se empleo, y la primera lança que
en los enemigos se estreno, fuesse el suyo.

Este dia y otro siguiente desembarcaron los cavallos, y toda la gente salio
a tierra, y aviendose refrescado, ocho o nueve días, y dexado orden en lo
q[ue] a los navios convenia, caminaron la tierra a de[n]tro poco mas de dos
leguas hasta un pueblo de un Caçique llamado Hirrihigua, co[n] quien
Pa[m]philo de Narvaez, quando fue a conquistar aquella provincia avia tenido
guerra: aunque despues el Indio se avia reducido, a su amistad, y durante
ella no se sabe porque causa, enojado Pamphilo de Narvaez le avia hecho
ciertos agravios que por ser odiosos no se cuentan.

Por la sin razon, y ofensas quedó el Caçique Hirrihigua tan amedrentado, y
odioso de los Españoles, que, quando supo la yda de Hernando de Soto a su
tierra, se fue a los montes, desamparando su casa, y pueblo, y por caricias,
regalos, y promesas, que el Governador le hizo, embiandoselas por los Indios
sus vasallos, que prendia, nunca jamas quiso salir de paz, ni oyr recaudo
alguno de los que le embiavan; antes se enfadava con quien se los llevava,
diziendo que; pues sabian quan ofendido, y lastimado estava de aquella nacion, no tenian para que ll[e]varle sus mensages: que si fueran sus cabeças,
essas recibiera el de muy buena gana; mas [f. 29v] que sus palabras, y nombres, no les querria oyr. Todo esto y mas puede la infamia, principalmente, si
fue hecha sin culpa del ofendido: y para que se vea mejor la ravia, que este
Indio contra los Castellanos tenia, será bien dezir aqui algunas crueldades, y
martyrios, que hizo en quatro Españoles, q[ue] pudo aver de los de Pamphilo
de Narvaez, que aunque nos alarguemos algun tanto, no saldremos del proposito, antes aprovechará mucho para nuestra historia.

Es de saber, que passados algunos dias despues que Pamphilo de Narvaez
se fue de la tierra deste Caçique, avie[n]do hecho lo que dexamos dicho,
acerto a yr a aquella baía un Navio de los suyos en su busca, el qual se avia
quedado atras, y como el Caçique supiese q[ue] era de los de Narvaez, y que
los buscaba, quisiera coger todos los que yvan dentro, para quemarlos vivos,
y por asegurarlos, se fingio amigo de Pa[m]philo de Narvaez, y les embió a
dezir, como su capitan avia estado alli, y dexado orden de lo que aquel navio
devia de hazer, si aportasse a aquel puerto: y para persuadirles a que le
creyesse[n], mostró desde tierra dos o tres pliegos de papel blanco, y otras
cartas viejas, que de la amistad pasada de los Españoles, o como quiera que
huviesse sido, avia podido aver, y las tenia muy guardadas.

Los del navio, con todo esto se recataron, y no quisieron salir a tierra.
Entonces el Caçique embio en una canoa quatro Indios principales al navio,
dicie[n]do, que pues no fiavan del, les embiavan aquellos quatro hombres

nobles, y cavalleros (este nombre cavallero en los Indios, parece improprio porque no tuviero[n] cavallos de los quales se deduxo el no[m]bre, mas por que en España se entiende [f. 30r] por los nobles, y entre Indios los uvo no-bilissimos, se podra ta[m]bien decir por ellos) en rehenes, y seguridad: para que del navio saliesen los Españoles q[ue] quisiesen yr a saber de su capi-tan Pamphilo de Narvaez, y que sino se aseguravan, que les embiaria mas prendas: viendo esto salieron quatro Españoles, y entraron en la canoa con los Indios, que avian llevado las rehenes. El Caçique, q[ue] los quisiera todos, viendo que no yvan mas de quatro, no quiso hazer mas instancia en pedir mas Castellanos, porque essos pocos que yvan a el, no se escandalizassen, y se bolviese[n] al navio.

Luego que los Españoles saltaron en tierra, los quatro Indios q[ue] avia[n] quedado en el navio por rehenes, viendo que los Christianos estaban ya en poder de los suyos se arrojaron al agua, y dando una larga çabullida, y nadando como peçes, se fueron a tierra, cu[m]pliendo en esto el orde[n] que su señor les avia dado. Los del navio viendose burlados, antes que les acaeciesse otra peor, se fueron de la baía con mucho pesar de aver perdido los compañeros tan indiscretamente.

Cap[itulo] II. De los tormentos que un Caçique dava a un Español esclavo suyo.

El Cacique Hirrihigua mandó guardar a buen recaudo los quatro Españoles, para que con la muerte de ellos, sole[m]nizar una gran fiesta, que segun su ge[n]tilidad esperava celebrar de[n]tro de pocos dias. Venida la fiesta los mandó sacar desnudos a la plaça, y que uno a uno, corriendolos de una parte a otra, los flechassen como a fieras, y que no les tirasen muchas flechas juntas porque tardassen mas en morir, y el torme[n]to les fuese mayor, y a los Indios su fiesta, y regozijo mas larga [f. 30v] y solenne. Assi lo hizieron con los tres Españoles recibiendo el Caçique gra[n] contento, y plazer de verlos huyr a todas partes, buscando remedio, y que en ninguna hallassen socorro sino muerte. Quando quisieron sacar el quarto que era moço, que apenas llegava a los diez y ocho años, natural de Sevilla, llamado Juan Ortiz, salio la muger del Caçique, y en su compañia s[a]có tres hijas suyas moças, y puestas dela[n]te del marido le dixo, que le suplicava se contentasse con los tres Cas-tellanos muertos, y que perdonasse aquel moço, pues ni el, ni sus compa-ñeros avian tenido culpa de la maldad, que los passados avian hecho, pues no avian venido con Pamphilo de Narvaez: y q[ue] particularme[n]te aquel muchacho era digno de perdo[n]: porque su poca edad le librava de culpa, y pedia misericordia, que bastava quedasse por esclavo, y no que lo matassen tan crudamente sin aver hecho delicto.

El Caçique por dár contento á su muger, y hijas, otorgo por entonçes la vida a Juan Ortiz: aunque despues se la dio tan triste, y amarga, que muchas

veces uvo embidia á sus tres co[m]pañeros muertos: porque el trabajo
continuo sin cessar de acarrear leña y agua era tanto y el comer y dormir
ta[n] poco, los palos, bofetadas, y açotes de todos los dias tan crueles, sin
los demás torme[n]tos, que a sus tie[m]pos en particulares fiestas le davan,
q[ue] muchas veçes, sino fuera Christiano, tomara por remedio la muerte
co[n] sus manos. Porque es assi que sin el tormento cotidiano, el Caçique
por su passatiempo muchos dias de fiesta mandaba, que Juan Ortiz co-
rriesse todo el dia sin parar (de Sol a sombra) en una plaça larga, que en el
pueblo avia, donde flecharon a sus compañeros; y el mis[f. 31r]mo Caçique
salia a verle correr, y con el yvan sus Gge[n]tiles ho[m]bres, apercibidos de
sus arcos y flechas, para tirarle en dexando de correr. Juan Ortiz empeçava
su carrera en salie[n]do el Sol, y no parava de una parte a otra de la plaça
hasta que se ponia el Sol, que este era el tiempo que le señalavan. Y quando
el Caçique se yva a comer dexaba sus gentiles hombres, q[ue] le mirassen:
para que en dexando de correr lo matassen. Acabado el dia quedava el triste
qual se puede imaginar, tendido en el suelo mas muerto, que vivo: la piedad
de la muger y hijas del Caçique le socorria[n] estos tales dias, porque ellas
lo tomavan luego, y lo arropavan, y hazia[n] otros beneficios, co[n] que le
sustentavan la vida, q[ue] fuera mejor quitarsela, por librarle de aquellos
muchos trabajos. El Caçique viendo que tantos y tan continuous torme[n]tos
no bastava[n] a quitar la vida a Juan Ortiz, y cresciendole por horas el odio
que le tenia, por acabar con él, mandó un dia de sus fiestas hazer un gran
fuego en medio de la plaça, y quando vio mucha brasa hecha, mandó ten-
derla, y poner encima una barbacoa, que es un lecho de madera de forma de
parrillas, una vara de medir alta del suelo, y que sobre ella pusiessen a Juan
Ortiz, para assarlo vivo.

Assi se hizo donde estuvo el pobre Español mucho rato tendido de
un lado, atado a la barbacoa. A los gritos que el triste dava en el fuego,
acudiero[n] la muger y hijas del Caçique, y roga[n]do al marido, y aun ri-
ñiendo su crueldad, lo sacaron del fuego ya medio assado, que las bexigas
tenia por aquel lado como medias naranjas: y algunas de ellas rebentadas
por donde le corria mucha sangre que era lastima verlo. El Caçique passo
por ello, por[f. 31v]que eran mugeres, que el tanto queria: y quiçá lo hizo
tambien, por tener adelante en quien exercitar su ira, y mostrar el desseo de
su vengança, porque huviesse en quien la exercitar, que aunque tan pequeña
para como la deseava, todavia se recreava con aquella poca: y assi lo dixo
muchas veces, que le avia pesado de aver muerto los tres Españoles tan brevemente. Las mugeres llevaron a Juan Ortiz a su casa, y con çumos de yervas
(que las Indias é Indios como careçen de Medicos son grandes hervolarios) le
curaron con gran lastima de verle, qual estava. Que vezes y vezes se avia[n]
arrepentido ya, de averlo la primera vez librado de muerte; por ver que tan a
la larga, y con tan crueles tormentos se la davan cada dia. Juan Ortiz al cabo

de muchos dias quedó sano, aunque las señales de las quemaduras del fuego le quedaron bien grandes.

El Caçique, por no verlo assi, y por librarse de la molestia, que su muger, y hijas con sus ruegos le davan, mandó, porque no estuviesse ocioso, exercitarlo en otro tormento, no tan grave como los passados: y fue que guardasse de dia y de noche los cuerpos muertos de los vezinos de aquel pueblo, que se ponian en el campo dentro en un monte, lexos de poblado, lugar señalado para ellos. Los quales ponian sobre la tierra en unas arcas de madera, que servian de sepulturas, sin gonzes, ni otro mas recaudo de cerradura, que unas tablas con que las cubrian, y encima unas piedras, o maderos; de las quales arcas por el mal recaudo, que ellas tenian de guardar los cuerpos muertos, se los llevavan los leones, que por aquella tierra ay muchos, [f. 32r] de que los Indios recibian mucha pesadumbre y enojo. Este sitio mandó el Caçique a Juan Ortiz, q[ue] guardasse con cuydado, que los leones no le llevasen algun difuncto, o parte del, con protestacion y jurame[n]to que le hiço, si lo llevava[n] moriria assado sin remedio alguno: y para con que los guardasse, le dió quatro dardos, que tirasse a los leones, o a otros salvaginas, que llegassen a las arcas. Juan Ortiz, dando gracias a Dios, que le huviesse quitado de la continua presencia del Cacique Hirrihigua su amo, se fue a guardar los muertos, esperando tener mejor vida con ellos q[ue] con los vivos. Guardavalos con todo cuydado principalmente de noche, porque entonçes avia mayor riesgo. Sucedio que una noche de las que assi velaba, se durmio al quarto del alva, sin poder resistir al sueño: porque a esta ora suele mostrar sus mayores fuerças contra los q[ue] velan. A este tiempo acertó a venir un leon, y derribando las compuertas de una de las arcas, sacó un niño, que dos dias antes avian echado en ella, y se lo llevo. Juan Ortiz recordó al ruydo, que las compuertas hiciero[n] al caer, y como acudio al arca, y no hallo el cuerpo del niño, se tuvo por muerto: mas con toda su ansia, y congoja no dexo de hacer sus diligencias, buscando al leon: para si lo topase, quitarle el muerto, o morir a sus manos. Por otra parte se encomendava a nuestro Señor le diesse esfuerço para morir otro dia, confessando, y llamando su nombre: porque sabia, que luego que amaneciesse, avian de visitar los Indios las arcas, y no hallando el cuerpo del niño, lo avian de quemar vivo. Andando por el mo[n]te de una parte á otra con las ansias de la muerte, salio a un camino ancho, q[ue] por [f. 32v] medio del passava, y ye[n]do por el un rato co[n] determinacion de huyrse, aunque era impossible escaparse, oyó en el monte, no lexos de donde yva, un ruydo como de perro, que roia huessos: y escuchando bien, se certifico en ello, y sospecha[n]do que podia ser el leo[n], que estuviesse comiendo el niño, fue con mucho tiento por entre las matas, acercandose a donde sentia el ruydo, y a la luz de la Luna, que hazia aunque no muy clara, vio cerca de si al leon, que a su plaçer comia el niño. Juan Ortiz llamando a Dios, y cobrando animo le tiró un dardo; y aunque por entonces no vio, por causa de las matas el tiro, que avia hecho, todavia sintio que no avia sido malo, por quedarle la mano sabrosa, qual dizen los caçadores, que la sie[n]ten quando an hecho algu[n] bue[n] tiro a las fieras de noche: con esta esperança aunque tan flaca, y tambien por no aver sentido que el leon se huviesse alexado de donde le avia tirado, aguardó a q[ue] amaneciese, encome[n]dandose a nuestro Señor, le socorriesse en aquella necessidad.

Cap[itulo] III. Prosigue la mala vida del Cautivo Christiano, y como se huyó de su Amo.

Con la luz del dia se certifico Jua[n] Ortiz del buen tiro, que a tiento avia hecho de noche, porque vio muerto el leon, atravessadas las entrañas, y el coraçon por medio (como despues se hallo quando lo abrieron) cosa que el mismo, aunque la veya, no podia creer. Con el contento y alegria, que se puede imaginar, mejor que dezir, lo llevo arrastra[n]do por un pie, sin quitarle el dardo, para q[ue] su Amo lo viesse assi, como lo avia hallado: avie[n]do primero recogido, y buelto al [f. 33r] arca los pedaços que del niño halló por comer. El Caçique, y todos los de su pueblo se admiraron grandemente de esta hazaña, porq[ue] en aquella tierra en general se tiene por cosa de milagro matar un hombre a un leon: y assi tratan co[n] gra[n] veneracion, y acatamiento al que acierta a matarlo. Y en toda parte por ser animal tan fiero se deve estimar en mucho, principalme[n]te si lo mata sin tiro de ballesta, o arcabuz como lo hizo Juan Ortiz, y aunq[ue] es verdad que los leones de la Florida, Mexico, y Peru no son tan grandes ni tan fieros como los de Africa, al fin son Leones, y el nombre les basta, y aunque el refrán comun diga, q[ue] no son tan fieros como los pinta[n]: los que se an hallado cerca de ellos dizen, que son tanto mas fieros que los dibuxados, quanto va de lo vivo a lo pintado.

Con esta buena suerte de Juan Ortiz tomaro[n] mas animo, y osadia la muger, y hijas del Caçique, para interceder por el, que lo perdonasse del todo, y se sirviesse del en oficios honrados, dignos de su esfuerço, y valentia. Hirrihigua de alli adelante por algunos dias trató mejor a su esclavo, assi por la estima y favor que en su pueblo, y casa le hazia[n], como por acudir al hecho hazañoso, que ellos en su vana religion tanto estima[n], y honran: que lo tienen por sagrado, y mas que humano. Empero (como la injuria no sepa perdonar) todas las vezes que se acordava, que á su madre avian echado a los perros y dexadola comer dellos: y quando se iva a sonar y no hallava sus narizes, le tomava el diablo por vengarse de Juan Ortiz, como si el se las huviera cortado: y como siempre truxesse la ofensa delante de los ojos, y con la memoria della de dia en dia le creciesse la ira, rancor, y desseo de tomar ve[n]gança: [f. 33v] aunque por algun tiempo refrenó estas passiones, no pudiendo ya resistirlas, dixo un dia a su muger, y hijas, que le era impossible sufrir, que aquel Christiano viviesse, porque su vida le era muy odiosa, y abominable, que cada vez que le veia, se le refrescaban las injurias pasadas y de nuevo se dava por ofendido. Por tanto les mandava que en ninguna manera intercediessen mas por el, sino querian participar de la misma saña, y enojo: y que para acabar del todo con aquel Español avia determinado, que tal dia de fiesta (que presto avian de solennizar) lo flechassen y mata-sen, como avian hecho á sus compañeros: no obstante su valentia, q[ue] por ser de enemigo se devia antes aborrescer que estimar. La muger y hijas del Caçique, porque le vieron enojado, y entendieron q[ue] no avia de aprovechar intercessio[n] alguna: y tambie[n] porque les parescio, que era demasia im-portunar, y dar tanta pesadumbre al señor por el esclavo, no osaron replicar palabra en contra. Antes con astucia mugeril acudieron a dezirle, que seria muy bien que assi se hiziesse, pues el gustava dello. Mas la mayor de las hijas, por llevar su intencion adelante y salir co[n] ella, pocos dias antes de la fiesta en secreto, dio noticia a Juan Ortiz de la determinacion de su Padre co[n]tra él: y que ella, ni sus hermanas, ni su madre ya no valian, ni podian cosa alguna con el padre: por averles puesto silencio en su favor, y amenaça-dolas, si lo quebrantassen.

A estas nuevas tan tristes, queriendo esforçar al Español: añadio otras en contrario, y le dixo: porque no desconfies de mi, ni desesperes de tu vida, ni temas que yo dexe de ha[f. 34r]zer todo lo que pudiere, por dartela: si eres hombre, y tienes animo para huyrte, yo te daré favor y socorro para que te escapes, y te pongas en salvo. Esta noche que viene a tal hora, y en tal parte, hallarás un Indio, de quien fio tu salud, y la mia; el qual te guiará hasta una puente, que está dos leguas de aqui, llegando a ella, le mandaras, que no pase adelante, sino que se buelva al pueblo antes que amanezca, porque no le echen menos, y se sepa mi atrevimiento, y el suyo, y por averte hecho bien, a el y a mi nos venga mal. Seys leguas mas allá de la puente está un pueblo, cuyo señor me quiere bien, y dessea casar conmigo, llamase Mucoço, dirasle de mi parte que yo te embio a el, para que en esta necesidad te socorra, y favorezca, como quien es. Yo se que hará por ti todo lo que pudiere, como veras. Encomiendate a tu Dios, que yo no puedo hazer mas en tu favor. Juan Ortiz se echo a sus pies, en reconocimiento de la merced, y beneficio que le hazia, y siempre le avia hecho, y luego se apercibio para caminar la noche siguiente. Y a la hora señalada, quando ya los de la casa del Caçique, estavan repossados, salio a buscar la guia prometida, y con ella salio del pueblo sin que nadie los sintiesse, y en llegando a la puente dixo al Indio, que con todo recato se bolviesse luego a su casa aviendo primero sabido de el, que no avia donde perder el camino hasta el pueblo de Mucoço. [f. 34v]

Capitulo IIII. De la magnanímidad del Curaca o Caçique Mucoço, a quien se encome[n]dó el cautivo.

Juan Ortiz, como ho[m]bre que yva huyendo, llegó al lugar antes q[ue] amaneciese; mas por no causar algu[n] alboroto, no osó entrar en el, y

quando fue de dia, vio salir dos Indios del pueblo por el mismo camino, que
el llevava. Los quales quisieron flecharle, que sie[m]pre andan apercibidos
destas armas. Juan Ortiz que tambien las llevava, puso una flecha en su arco,
para defenderse dellos, y tambien para, ofenderles. O quanto puede un poco
de favor, y mas si es de dama; pues vemos, que el que poco antes no sabia
donde esconderse temiendo la muerte; aora se atreve a darla a otros de su
propria mano, solo por verse favorecido de una moça hermosa discreta y
generosa, cuyo favor eccede á todo otro favor humano, con el qual aviendo
cobrado animo y esfuerço, y aun sobervia, les dixo, que no era enemigo, sino
q[ue] yva con embaxada de una señora para el señor de aquel lugar.

Los Indios oyendo esto no le tiraron, antes se bolvieron con el al Pueblo, y
abisaron a su Caçique como el esclavo de Hirrihigua estaba alli con mensage
para el. Lo qual sabido por Mucoço, o Mococo, q[ue] todo es uno, salio hasta
la plaça, a reçebir el recaudo, que Juan Ortiz le llevava. El qual despues de
le aver saludado como mejor supo, a la usança de los mesmos Indios, en
breve le co[n]to los martyrios, que su amo le avia hecho, en testimonio de
los quales, le mostro en su cuerpo las señales de las quemaduras, golpes y
heridas que le avian dado; y como aora ultimamente su señor estava determinado de matarle: para con [f. 35r] su muerte regocijar, y solennizar tal dia
de fiesta que esperava tener presto. Y que la muger y hijas del Caçique su
amo, au[n]que muchas veces le avia[n] dado la vida, no osavan agora hablar
en su fabor: por averla impedido el señor sopena de su enojo, y que la hija
mayor de su señor con desseo que no muriesse, por ultimo y mejor remedio,
le avia mandado y puestole animo, que se huyesse; y dadole guia, que le encaminasse a su pueblo y casa, y dichole, que en nombre della se presentasse
ante el: la qual le suplicaba por el amor, que le tenia, lo recibiese debaxo de
su amparo, y como a cosa encomendada por ella, le favoreciesse como quien
era. Mucoço lo recibió afablemente, y le oyó con lastima de saber los males,
y tormentos que avia passado, que bien se mostraban en las señales de su
cuerpo, que segun su trage de los Indios de aquella tierra, no llevava mas de
unos pañetes.

En este passo, demas de lo que hemos dicho añade Alonso de Carmona,
que lo abraço, y beso en el rostro en señal de paz.

Respondióle que fuesse bien venido, y se esforçase a perder el temor de la
vida passada: que en su compañia, y casa la tendria bien diferente, y contraria, y que por servir a quien lo avia embiado, y por el, que avia ydo a soco-
rrerse de su persona, y casa, haria todo lo que pudiesse, como por la obra
lo veria: y que tuviesse por cierto, que mientras el viviesse, nadie seria parte
para enojarle.

Todo lo que este bue[n] Caçique dixo en favor de Juan Ortiz cumplio, y
mucho mas de lo que prometio, porque luego lo hizo su Camarero y siempre
de dia, y de noche lo traia consigo haziendole mucha honra, [f. 35v] y muy
mucha mas, despues que supo, que avia muerto al leon con el dardo. En

suma le trató como a propio hermano muy querido (q[ue] hermanos ay que se aman como el agua y el fuego) y aunque Hirrihigua sospechando que se fue a valer de Mocoço, se lo pidió muchas veces; siempre Mucoço se escuso de darlo, diziendo entre otras razones por ultima respuesta, que lo dexasse, pues se le avia ydo á su casa, que muy poco perdia en perder un esclavo que tan odioso le era, lo mesmo respondio a otro Caçique cuñado suyo, llamado Urribarracuxi, de quien el Hirrihigua se valio, para lo pedir, el qual viendo que sus mensages no aprovechavan, fue personalmente a pedirselo, y Mocoço le respondio en presencia lo mismo que en ausencia, y añadio, otras palabras con enojo, y le dixo, que pues era su cuñado, no era justo, le mandasse hacer cosa contra su reputacion, y honra; que no haria el dever si a un afligido, que se le avia ydo a encomendar, entregasse a su proprio enemigo, para que por su entretenimiento y passatiempo lo martyrizasse, y matasse, como a fiera.

Destos dos Caçiques, que con mucha instancia, y porfia, pedian a Juan Ortiz, lo defendio Mocoço con tanta generosidad, que tuvo por mejor perder (como lo perdio) el casamiento, que aficionadamente desseava hazer con la hija de Hirrihigua, y el parentesco, y amistad del cuñado, que bolver el esclavo a quien lo pedia, para matarlo, al qual tuvo siempre consigo muy estimado, y regalado hasta que el Governador Hernando de Soto entró en la Florida.

Diez años fueron los que Juan Ortiz estuvo en[f. 36r]tre aquellos Indios, el uno y medio en poder de Hirrihigua, y los demas con el buen Mocoço, el qual, aunque barbaro lo hizo con este Christiano mui de otra manera, que los famosissimos varónes del triumuirato, que en Layno lugar cerca de Bolonia, hizieron aquella nunca jamas bastantemente abominada, proscripcion y concierto de dar, y trocar los parientes, amigos, y valedores, por los enemigos y adversarios; y lo hizo mucho mejor, que otros Principes Christianos, que despues acá han hecho otras tan abominables, y mas que aquella, considerada la inocencia de los entregados, y la cálidad de alguno de ellos, y la fé, que devian tener, y guardar los entregadores: que aquellos eran Gentiles, y estos se preciaban del nombre y religion christiana. Los quales quebrantando las leyes y fueros de sus Reyno[s], y sin respetar su proprio ser, y grado, que eran Reyes, y grandes Principes, y con menos precio de la Fé jurada, y prometida (cosa indigna de tales nombres) solo por vengarse de sus enojos, entregaron los que no les avian ofendido, por aver los ofensores, dando inocentes por culpados: como lo testifican las historias antiguas, y modernas, las quales dexaremos por no, ofender, oydos poderosos, y lastimar los piadosos.

Basta representar la magnanimidad de un infiel, para que los Principes fieles se esfuerçen a le imitar y sobrepujar, si pudieren: no en la infidelidad, como lo hazen algunos indignos de tal nombre, sino en la virtud y gra[n]dezas semejantes, a que por la mayor alteza de estado, q[ue] tienen, y están mas obligados. Que cierto consideradas [f. 36v] bien las circunstancias del hecho valeroso deste Indio, y mirado por quien, y contra quien se hizo, y lo mucho, que quiso posponer, y perder, yendo aun co[n]tra su proprio amor y desseo, por negar el socorro, y favor, demandado, y por el prometido, se vera que nascio de animo generosissimo, y heroíco: indigno de aver nascido, y de vivir en la barbara gentilidad de aquella tierra: mas Dios, y la naturaleza humana, muchas vezes en desiertos tan incultos, y esteriles produzen semeja[n]tes animos, para mayor confusion y verguença de los que nascen, y se crian en tierras fertiles y abundantes de toda buena doctrina, sciencias, y religion Christiana.

Cap[itulo] V. Embia el Governador por Juan Ortiz.

La relacion, que hemos dado de la vida de Juan Ortiz tuvo el Governador, aunque confusa, en el Pueblo del Caçique Hirrihigua, donde al presente lo tenemos: y antes la avia tenido, aunque no tan larga en la Havana, de uno de los quatro Indios, que diximos, avia preso el Contador Juan de Añasco, quando le embiaron a que descubriesse la costa de la Florida, que acertó a ser vasallo deste Caçique: el qual Indio, quando en su relacio[n] nombrava en la Havana a Juan Ortiz, dejando el no[m]bre Juan, porque no lo sabia, dezia Ortiz, y como a este mal hablar del Indio, se añadiesse el peor entender de los buenos interpretes, que declaraban, lo que el queria dezir, y como todos los oyentes tuviessen por principal intento el yr a buscar oro, oyendo decir al Indio Orotiz, sin buscar otras declaraciones entendian, que llanamente dezia, que en su tierra avia mucho oro, y se holgavan, [f. 37r] y regocijava[n] solo co[n] oyr lo nombrar: aunque en tan diferente significacion, y sentido.

Pues como el Governador se certificasse, que Juan Ortiz estaba en poder del Caçique Mucoço, le parescio seria bien embiar por el: assi por sacarlo de poder de Indios, como por que lo avia menester, para lengua e interprete, de quien se pudiesse fiar. Para lo qual eligio un cavallero natural de Sevilla nombrado Baltasar de Gallegos, que yva por Alguazil mayor de la armada, y del exercito; el qual por su mucha virtud, esfuerço, y valentia merescia ser General de otro mayor exercito, que aquel: y le dixo que con sesenta la[n]ças, que llevase en su compañia, fuesse a Mucoço, y de su parte le dixesse, quan agradescidos estavan, el y todos los Españoles, q[ue] consigo tenia, de la honra, y beneficios, que a Juan Ortiz avia hecho; y quanto deseaba que se ofreciesse en q[ue] gratificarselos. Y que al presente le rogava se lo diesse, que para cosas que importavan mucho, lo avia menester; y quando le pareciesse, viniesse a visitarle, que holgaria mucho de lo conoscer, y tener por amigo. Baltasar de Gallegos con las sesenta lanças, y un Indio que lo guiasse, salio del real en cumplimiento de lo que se le mando.

Por otra parte, el Caçique Mucoço, aviendo sabido la yda del Governador Hernando de Soto co[n] tanta pujança de gente, y cavallos, y que avia to-mado tierra tan cerca de la suya, temiendo no le hiziessen daño en ella, quiso con prude[n]cia, y buen consejo prevenir el mal, q[ue] podria venirle y para

lo remediar, llamó á Juan Ortiz, y le dixo. Aveys de saber hermano, q[ue] en
el pueblo de vuestro bue[n] amigo Hirrihigua está un capitan Español co[n]
mil ho[m]bres de guerra, y muchos [f. 37v] cavallos, que vienen a conquistar esta tierra: bien sabeys lo que por vos [h]e hecho, y como por salvaros
la vida, y no entregaros al que os tenia por esclavo, y os queria para matar,
elegí caer antes en desgracia de mis deudos, y vezinos, que hacer lo que
ellos contra vos me pedian. Aora se ofrece tiempo, y occasion en que podreys
gratificarme la buena acogida, regalo, y amistad, que os [h]e hecho: aunque
nunca yo lo hize con esperança de galardon alguno, mas pues la ventura lo ha
encaminado assi, será cordura no perder lo que ella nos ofrece.

Yreys al General Español, y de vuestra parte, y mia le suplicareys, que en
remuneracion de lo que a el, y a toda su nacion en vos he servido (pues por
qualquiera de todos ellos hiziera lo mismo) tenga por bien de no hazerme
daño en esta poca tierra que tengo, y se digne de recebirme en su amistad
y servicio, que desde luego le ofrezo mi persona, casa, y estado, para que la
ponga debaxo de su proteccion, y amparo, y porque vays acompañado, como
a vos, y a mi conviene, llevareys cinquenta gentiles hombres de mi casa, y
mirareys por ellos, y por mi, como nuestra amistad os tiene obligado.

Juan Ortiz con regozijo de la buena nueva, dando interiormente gracias a
Dios por ella, respondio a Muçoço, que holgava mucho se huviesse ofrecido
tiempo, y occasion en que servir la merced y beneficios, que le avia hecho,
no solo de la vida, sino tambien de mucho favor, estima, y honra, que de su
mucha virtud, y cortesia avia recebido; de modo lo qual daria muy larga relacion, y cuenta al Capitan [f. 38r] Español, y a todos los suyos: para que se lo
agradeciessen, y pagassen en lo que al presente en su nombre les pidiesse,
y en lo porvenir se ofreciesse, que el yva muy confiado: que el General haria
lo que de su parte le suplicasse, porq[ue] la nacion Española se preciava
de gente agradescida, de lo q[ue] por los suyos se huviesse hecho: y assi
seguramente quedasse con espera[n]ça de alcançar lo que embiava a pedir
al Governador. Luego viniero[n] los cinquenta Indios, que el Caçiq[ue] avia
mandado apercebir los quales y Juan Ortiz tomaron el camino real, que va de
un pueblo al otro, y salieron el mismo dia que Baltasar de Gallegos salio del
real a buscarle.

Sucedio que despues de aver andado los Españoles mas de tres leguas por
el camino real ancho, y seguido que yva al pueblo de Muçoço, el Indio, que
los guiava paresciendole que no era bien hecho usar de tanta fidelidad con
gente, que venia a les sujetar, y quitar sus tierras, y libertad, y que de mucho
atras se avia[n] mostrado enemigos declarados, aunque de aquel exercito,
hasta entonçes no avian recibido agravios, de que se poder quexar, mudó
el animo de guiarles, y a la primera se[n]da, que vio atravessar, dexando el
camino real, la tomo, y a poco trecho que por ella anduvo la perdio, que no
era seguida, y assi los truxo gran parte del dia descaminados, y perdidos,
llevandolos siempre en arco hazia la costa de la mar, con desseo de topar al-

guna çienaga, cala, o baia en que, si pudiesse, los ahogasse. Los Castellanos, como no sabian la tierra, no sentian el engaño del Indio hasta que uno dellos por entre los arboles de un monte claro, por donde yvan, acertó a ver las gavias de los navios, que avian dexado: y [f. 38v] vio que estavan muy cerca de la costa, de que dio aviso al Capitan Baltasar de Gallegos. El qual vista la maldad de la guia le amenazo con muerte, haziendo ademan que lo queria alançear. El Indio temie[n]do no le matassen, por señas, y palabras como pudo, dixo, que los bolveria al camino real; mas que era menester desandar todo lo que fuera de camino avian andado, y assi bolvieron por los mismos passos a buscarlo.

Cap[itulo] VI. Lo que sucedio a Juan Ortiz, con los Españoles, que por el yvan.

Juan Ortiz caminando por el camino real llego a la senda por donde el Indio avia descaminado a Baltasar de Gallegos, y a sus cavalleros; y sospechando lo que fue, y temiendo no fuessen los Castellanos por otra parte, é hiziessen daño en el pueblo de Mucoço, consultó con los Indios lo que harian; acordaron todos que seria bien siguiessen a toda priessa el rastro de los cavallos hasta los alcançar, y que no tomassen otro camino, porq[ue] no los errassen.

Pues como los Indios siguiessen el rastro de los Españoles, y bolviessen por el mismo camino, que avian llevado, se dieron vista los unos a los otros en un gra[n] llano, que a una parte del avia un monte çerrado de matas espessas. Los Indios vie[n]do los Castellanos dixeron a Jua[n] Ortiz q[ue] seria cordura asegurar sus personas y vidas co[n] meterse en aq[ue]l mo[n]te hasta q[ue] los christianos los reconociessen por amigos: porq[ue] teniendolos por enemigos no los ala[n]çeasse[n] e[n] lo raso del ca[m]po. Jua[n] Ortiz no quiso tomar el bue[n] co[n]sejo de los Indios, co[n]fiado en q[ue] era Español, y q[ue] los suyos le avia[n] de conocer luego q[ue] le viese[n] como si viniera vestido a la Española, o estuviera en [f. 39r] alguna cosa difere[n]ciado de los Indios: para ser conoscido por Español. El qual como los demas no llevava sino unos pañetes por vestidura, y un arco y flechas en las manos, y un plumage de media braça en alto sobre la cabeça por gala y ornamento.

Los Castellanos como noveles y ganosos de pelear viendo los Indios arremetieron a ellos a rienda suelta; y por muchas v[oc]es, que el Capitan les dio, no basto a los detener. Quien podrá con visoños quando se desmandan?

Los Indios como viese[n] quan denodada e inconsideradamente yvan los Castellanos a ellos, se arrojaron todos en el monte, que no quedó en el campo mas de Juan Ortiz, y un Indio que no se dio tanta priessa, como los otros, a meterse en la guarida, al qual hirio un Español que avia sido soldado en Italia, llamado Francisco de Morales, natural de Sevilla, de una lançada en los lomos, alcançandole a las primeras matas del monte. Con Juan Ortiz arremetio otro Español llamado Alvaro Nieto, natural de la villa de Albuquerque, uno de los mas rezios, y fuertes Españoles, q[ue] yvan en todo el exercito, el qual cerrando con el, le tiró una brava la[n]çada, Jua[n] Ortiz tuvo buena ventura, y destreza, que rebatiendo la lança con el arco, dio un salto al traves, huyendo a un mismo tie[m]po del golpe de la lança, y del encue[n]tro del cavallo; y viendo q[ue] Alvaro Nieto rebolvia sobre el dio grandes vozes, diziendo Xibilla, Xibilla por dezir Sevilla Sevilla.

En este passo añade Jua[n] Coles que no acertando Juan Ortiz a hablar Castellano hizo con la mano y el arco la señal de la Cruz para que el Español viesse q[ue] era Christiano. Porque con el poco o ningu[n] uso, que entre los Indios avia tenido de la le[n][f. 39v]gua Castellana, se le avia olvidado hasta el pronunciar el no[m]bre de la propria tierra, como yo podre dezir tambien de mi mesmo, que por no aver tenido en España con quien hablar mi lengua natural, y materna, que es la general, que se habla en todo el Peru (aunque los Yncas, tenian otro particular, que hablavan ellos entre si unos con otros) se me ha olvidado de tal manera, que con saberla hablar ta[n] bien y mejor, y con mas elegancia, que los mismos Indios que no son Yncas, porque soy hijo de Palla y sobrino de Yncas, que son los que mejor y mas apuradame[n]te la hablan, por aver sido lenguage de la Corte de sus Principes, y aver sido ellos los principales cortesanos, no acierto aora a concertar seys o siete palabras en oracion, para dar a entender lo que quiero dezir; y mas, que muchos vocablos se me han ydo de la memoria, que no se quales son, para nombrar en Indio, tal, o tal cosa. Aunque es verdad que si oyesse hablar a un Ynca, le ente[n]deria todo lo que dixesse, y si oyesse los vocablos olvidados, diria lo q[ue] significan. Empero de mi mesmo por mucho que lo procuro no acierto a dezir quales son, esto he sacado por esperiencia del uso, o descuydo de las lenguas, que las agenas se aprenden con usarlas, y las proprias se olvidan no usandolas.

Bolviendo a Juan Ortiz que lo dexamos en gra[n] peligro de ser muerto, por los que mas desseava[n] verlo vivo. Como Alvaro Nieto le oyesse dezir Xibilla, le preguntó si era Juan Ortiz, y como le respondiesse que si, lo afio por un braço, y echó sobre las ancas de su cavallo, como a un niño, porque era rezio y fuerte este buen soldado, y con mucha alegria de aver hallado lo que yva a buscar, dan[f. 40r]do gracias á Dios de no averle muerto, aunque le parecia que todavia lo veia en aquel peligro, lo llevó al Capitan Baltasar de Gallegos. El qual recibio a Juan Ortiz con gran regozijo; y luego mandó llamassen a los demas cavalleros, que por el monte andavan, ansiosos por matar Indios, como si fueran venados; para que todos se juntassen a gozar de la buena suerte, que les avia sucedido: antes que hiziessen algun mal en los amigos por no conoscerlos. Juan Ortiz entro en el monte a llamar los Indios, diziendoles a gra[n]des vozes que saliessen, y no huviessen miedo. Muchos de ellos no pararon hasta su pueblo, a dar aviso a su Caçique de lo que avia passado. Otros, que no se avian alexado tanto, bolvieron de tres en tres, y de quatro en quatro, como acertavan a hallarse, y todos, cada uno de por sí

con mucha saña, y enojo reñian a Juan Ortiz su poca advertencia, y mucha
visoñeria. Y quando vieron al compañero Indio, herido por su causa, se en-
cendieron de manera, que apenas se contenian de poner las manos en el, y
se las pusieran si los Españoles no estuvieran presentes: mas vengavan su
enojo con mil afrentas, que le dezian, llamandole tonto, necio, impertinente,
que no era Español, ni hombre de guerra, y que muy poco, o nada le avian
aprovechado los duelos; y toda la malaventura pasada, que no embalde se
la avian dado, y que la merescia mucho peor: en suma ningun Indio salio del
monte q[ue] no riñesse co[n] el, y todos le dezia[n] casi unas mismas palabras, y el proprio las declaraba a los demas Españoles, para su mayor [f. 40v]
afrenta. Juan Ortiz quedó bien reprehe[n]dido, de aver sido bien confiado,
mas todo bie[n] empleado, atrueque de verse entre Christianos. Los quales
curaron al Indio herido, y ponie[n]dole sobre un Cavallo, se fuero[n] co[n] el,
y con Juan Ortiz, y con los demás Indios al real, deseosos de ver al Governador, por llevar en ta[n] breve tiempo, tan buen recaudo de lo que les avia
mandado, y antes que saliessen del puesto despacho Juan Ortiz un Indio con
relacio[n] a Muçoço de todo lo sucedido, porque no se escandalizasse de lo
que los Indios huydos le huviessen dicho.

Todo lo que hemos referido de Juan Ortiz lo dize[n] tambien Juan Coles y
Alonso de Carmona en sus relaciones, el uno de ellos dize, que le cayeron gusa-
nos en las llagas, que el fuego le hizo, quando lo assaron. Y el otro que es Juan
Coles dize, que el Governador le dio luego un vestido de terciopelo negro, y que
por estar hecho a andar desnudo, no lo pudo sufrir: que solame[n]te traia una
camisa, y unos calçones de lienço, gorra y çapatos, y que anduvo assi mas
de veynte dias, hasta que poco a poco se hizo a andar vestido, dize[n] mas
estos dos testigos de vista, que entre otras mercedes y favores, que el Caçique Muçoço hizo a Juan Ortiz, fue una, hazerle su Capita[n] general de mar
y tierra.

Cap[itulo] VII. La fiesta que todo el exercito hizo a Juan Ortiz, y como vino Muçoço a visitar al Governador.

Buena parte de la noche era ya passada qua[n]do Baltasar de Gallegos y
sus compañeros entraro[n] en el real. El Governador que los sintio, y recibio
sobresalto, temiendo, que pues bolvian tan presto, les avia acaecido alguna
desgra[f. 41r]cia; porque no los esperava hasta el dia tercero; mas certificado
del buen recaudo, que traian, toda la congoxa se convirtio en fiesta y regozijo,
rindio las gracias al Capitan, y a sus soldados de que lo huviessen hecho ta[n]
bien, recibio a Juan Ortiz como a proprio hijo con lastima, y dolor de acordarse de tantos trabajos, y martyrios como avia dicho, y su mismo cuerpo
mostrava aver passado: porq[ue] las señales de las quemaduras de quando
lo assaron eran tan grandes, que todo un lado no era mas q[ue] una quema-
dura, o señal della. De los quales trabajos, dava gracias a Dios, le huviesse

librado, y del peligro de aquel dia, que no avia sido el menor de los q[ue] avia pasado. Acaricio los Indios que con el viniaro[n] mandó que co[n] gran cuydado y regalo curassen al herido. Despachó aq[ue]lla mesma hora dos Indios al Caçique Mucoço co[n] mucho agradescimie[n]to, por los beneficios, que avia hecho a Juan Ortiz, y por averselo embiado libremente; y por el ofrecimiento de su persona y amistad: la qual dixo q[ue] en no[m]bre del Emperador y Rey de España su señor, que era el principal y el mayor de toda la Christiandad; y en nombre de todos aquellos capitanes, y cavalleros, que con el estavan, y en el suyo aceptaba para le agradescer, y pagar lo que por todos ellos avia hecho, en aver escapado de la muerte a Juan Ortiz, que todos ellos le rogavan los visitasse, que quedava[n] con desseo de le ver y conoscer.

Los Capitanes y ministros assi del exercito, como de la hazie[n]da real y cavalleros, y todos los demas soldados en comun, y particular festejaron grandemente a Juan Ortiz, que no se tenia por co[m]pañero, el que no llegava a le abraçar, y dar la enorabuena [f. 41v] de su venida. Assi passaron aquella noche q[ue] no la durmieron con este general regozijo.

Luego el dia siguiente llamo el General a Jua[n] Ortiz para informarse de lo q[ue] sabia de aquella tierra, y para que le contasse particularmente lo que por el avia passado en poder de aq[ue]llos dos Caçiques. Respondio que de la tierra, aunq[ue] avia ta[n]to tiempo que estava en ella sabia poco, o nada: porque en poder de Hirrihigua su amo, mientras, no le atormentavan con nuevos martyrios, no le dexava desmandarse un passo del servicio ordinario que hazia, acarrea[n]do agua, y leña para toda la casa: y que en poder de Mucoço, aunque tenia libertad para yr donde quisiesse, no usava della porque los vasallos de su amo viendolo apartado de Mucoço, no le matassen, que para lo hazer tenian su orden, y mandato: y que por estas causas no podia dar buena noticia de las calidades de la tierra: mas que avia oydo dezir q[ue] era buena: y quanto mas adentro era mejor y mas fertil, y que la vida que co[n] los Caçiques avia passado, avia sido en los dos estremos de bien y de mal, que en este siglo se puede tener: porque Mucoço se avia mostrado con el tan piadoso y humano, quanto el otro cruel, y vengativo, sin poderse encarecer bastantemente la virtud del uno, ni la passion del otro: como su Señoria avria sido ya informado, para prueva de lo qual mostro las señales de su cuerpo; descubrie[n]do las que se podian ver, y amplio la relacion, q[ue] de su vida hemos dado, y de nuevo relató, otros muchos tormentos, que avia passado, que causaron compassion a los oyentes: y lo dexaremos por escusar prolixidad.

El Caçique Mucoço, al dia tercero de como se le [f. 42r] avia hecho el recaudo con los Indios, vino bie[n] acompañado de los suyos: beso las manos del Governador con toda veneracion y acatamiento. Luego habló al tiniente general, y al maesse de campo, y a los demas capitanes, y cavalleros, que alli estavan, a cada uno, co[n]forme a la calidad de su persona: preguntando primero a Juan Ortiz quien era este, aquel, y el otro: y aunque le dixesse por alguno de los que le hablavan, que no era cavallero, ni capitan sino soldado particular, le tratava con mucho respecto, pero con mucho mas a los que eran nobles, y a los ministros del exercito: de manera que fue notado por los Españoles. Mocoço, despues de uvo hablado, y dado lugar a que le hablassen los que presentes estavan, bolvio a saludar al Governador con nuevos modos de acatamiento. El qual aviendole recibido con mucha afabilidad, y cortesia le rindio las gracias de lo que por Juan Ortiz avia hecho, y por averselo embiado tan amigablemente, dixole que le avia obligado a el, y a su exercito, y a toda la nacion Española, para que en todo tiempo se lo agradesciessen. Mucoço respondio, que lo que por Juan Ortiz avia hecho, lo avia hecho por su proprio respeto, porque aviendosele ydo a encomendar, y socorrer de su persona y casa con necessidad de ella, en ley de quien era estava obligado, a hazer lo que por el avia hecho, y que le parescia todo poco; por que la virtud, esfuerço, y valentia de Juan Ortiz por sí solo sin otro respecto alguno merescia mucho mas, y que el averlo embiado a su señoria, mas avia sido por su proprio interes y beneficio que por servir a su señoria; pues avia sido, para que [f. 42v] como defensor y abogado con su intercession, y meritos, alcançasse merced y gracia: para que en su tierra no se le hiziesse daño. Y assi ni lo uno ni lo otro, no tenia su señoria q[ue] agradescer ni recebir en servicio: mas q[ue] el se holgava, como quiera que huviesse sido, de aver acertado a hacer coza de que su Señoria, y aquellos cavalleros, y toda la nacio[n] Española, cuyo aficionado servidor el era, se huviesse[n] agradado, y mostrado aver recebido contento. Suplicava a su Señoria, que co[n] el mismo beneplacito lo recibiesse en su servicio, debaxo de cuya proteccion y amparo ponia su persona y casa, y estado, reconosciendo por principal señor el Emperador, y Rey de España, y segundariamente a su Señoria como a su capitan general, y Governador de aquel Reyno, que con esta merced, que se le hiziesse se tendria por mas aventajadamente gratificado, q[ue] avia sido el merito de su servicio, hecho en beneficio de Juan Ortiz, ni el averlo embiado libremente cosa que su Señoria tanto avia estimado: á lo qual dezia que el estimava y tenia en mas verse como aquel dia se veia, favorescido, y honrado de su Señoria, y de todos aquellos cavalleros, que quanto bueno avia hecho en toda su vida: y que protestava esforçarse a hazer de alli adelante cosas semejantes en servicio de los Españoles: pues aquellas le avian salido a tanto bien.

Estas, y otras muchas ge[n]tilezas dixo este Caçique con toda la buena gracia, y discrecion, que en un discreto cortesano se puede pintar, de que el Governador, y los que con él estava[n] se admiraron, no menos, q[ue] de las generosidades, que por Juan Ortiz avia hecho a las quales imitavan las palabras.

Por todo lo qual el Ade[f. 43r]lantado Hernando de Soto, y el teniente general Vasco Porcallo de Figueroa, y otros cavalleros particulares, aficionados de la discrecion y virtud del Caçique Mucoço, se movieron a corresponderle en lo que de su parte, en agradescimiento de tanta bondad, pudiessen premiar. Y assi le dieron muchas dadivas, no solo a el, sino tambien a los gentiles-hombres, que con el vinieron: de que todos ellos quedaron muy contentos.

Cap[itulo] VIII. Viene la madre de Mucoço muy ansiosa por su hijo.

Dos dias despues de lo q[ue] hemos dicho, vino la madre de Mucoço muy ansiosa y fatigada, de q[ue] su hijo estuviese en poder de los Castellanos; la qual por aver estado ause[n]te no supo la venida del hijo a ver al Governador, q[ue] no se lo co[n]sintiera; y assi las primeras palabras q[ue] al General dixo fuero[n], q[ue] le diesse el hijo, antes q[ue] hiziesse del, lo q[ue] Pamphilo de Narvaez avia hecho de Hirrihigua, y q[ue] si pe[n]sava hazer lo mismo, q[ue] diesse libertad a su hijo q[ue] era moço, y en ella q[ue] era vieja hiziesse lo q[ue] quisiesse, que ella sola llevaria la pena de ambos.

El Governador la recibio co[n] muchas caricias, y respo[n]dio, q[ue] su hijo por mucha bo[n]dad y discrecio[n] no mereçia q[ue] le hiziesse mal, sino q[ue] todos le sirviesse[n], y ella lo mismo, por ser madre de tal hijo: q[ue] perdiesse el temor que traia, porq[ue] ni a ella ni a su hijo, ni a persona de toda su tierra, se le haria mal ninguno, sino todo el plaxer, y regalo q[ue] fuesse possible. Co[n] estas palabras se quieto algu[n] tanto la buena vieja, y estuvo co[n] los Españoles tres dias, mas sie[m]pre ta[n] maliciosa, y reca- tada, que comie[n]do a la mesa del Governador, pregu[n]taba a Jua[n] Ortiz si osaria comer de lo q[ue] la dava[n], q[ue] dezia se rezelava, y temia [f. 43v] le diessen ponçoña para matarla.

El Governador y los q[ue] co[n] el estava[n] lo riero[n] mucho, y le dixero[n], q[ue] segurame[n]te podia comer, q[ue] no la querian matar, sino regalar: mas ella todavia, no fiandose de palabras de estra[n]geros, au[n]q[ue] le daban del mesmo plato del Governador, no queria comerlo ni gustarlo, si primero no le hazia la salva Jua[n] Ortiz. Por lo qual le dixo un soldado Español, que como avia ofrescido poco antes la vida por su hijo: pues se recatava tanto de morir? Respo[n]dio q[ue] no aborrescia ella el vivir, sino q[ue] lo amava como los demas ho[m]bres, mas q[ue] por su hijo daria la vida todas las vezes que fuesse menester, porq[ue] lo q[ue]ria mas que al vivir, por ta[n]to suplicava al Governador se lo diesse, q[ue] queria yrse y llevarlo co[n]sigo, q[ue] no osaria fiarlo de los christianos.

El General respo[n]dio, que se fuesse qua[n]do ella quiesiesse, q[ue] su hijo gustava de quedarse por algunos dias entre aquellos cavalleros, q[ue] eran moços y soldados ho[m]bres de guerra como el, y se hallava bie[n] con ellos; q[ue] qua[n]do le pareciesse, se yria libreme[n]te, sin q[ue] nadie lo enojasse. Con esta promessa se fue la vieja, au[n]que mal co[n]te[n]ta de que su hijo quedasse en poder de Castellanos: y a la partida dixo a Juan Ortiz, que librasse a su hijo de aquel Capitan, y de sus soldados, como su hijo lo avia librado a el de Hirrihigua, y de sus vasallos: lo qual rio muy mucho, el

Governador, y los demas Españoles, y el mismo Mucoço ayudava a reyr las ansias de su madre.

Despues de aver passado estas cosas de risa y co[n]tento estuvo el buen Caçique en el exercito ocho dias, en los quales visito en sus posadas al tinie[n]te general, y al maesse de ca[m]po, y a los capitanes y oficiales de hazie[n]da imperial, y a muchos cavalleros particulares por su noble[f. 44r]za, co[n] los quales todos hablava ta[n] familiarme[n]te, con ta[n] buena de-se[m]boltura, y cortesia, q[ue] parescia averse criado entre ellos. Pregu[n]-tava cosas particulares de la Corte de Castilla, y por el Emperador, por los señores, damas, y cavalleros della, dezia holgara verla, si pudiera venir a ella. Passados los ocho dias se fue a su casa; despues bolvio otras vezes a visitar al Governador, traiale sie[m]pre de los regalos q[ue] en su tierra avia. Era Mucoço de edad de veynte y seis o veinte y siete años, lindo ho[m]bre de cuerpo y rostro.

Cap[itulo] IX. De las preve[n]ciones q[ue] para el descubrimie[n]to se hiziero[n], y como pre[n]diero[n] los Indios un Español.

No estava ocioso el Governador, y Adela[n]tado Herna[n]do de Soto e[n]treta[n]to q[ue] estas cosas passava[n] entre los suyos, antes co[n] todo cuidado, y dilige[n]cia hazia oficio de capita[n], y caudillo, porq[ue] luego q[ue] los bastime[n]tos, y municiones se dese[m]barcaro[n] y pusieron en el pueblo del Caçique Hirrihigua, por ser el mas çercano a la baia del Es-piritu Sa[n]cto, porq[ue] estuviesse[n] cerca del mar, ma[n]do q[ue] de los onze navios, q[ue] avia llevado bolviesse[n] los siete mayores a la Havana, a orde[n] de lo q[ue] doña Isabel de Bovadilla su muger, dispusiesse dellos, y quedasse[n] los quatro menores para lo q[ue] por la mar se les ofresciesse, y huviesse menester. Los vasos q[ue] quedaro[n] fuero[n] el navio Sa[n] Anton, y la caravela, y los dos vergantines, de los quales dio cargo al capita[n] Pedro Caldero[n], el qual e[n]tre otras eccele[n]cias, q[ue] tenia era aver militado muy moço debaxo del bastó[n] y govierno del gran Capita[n] Gonzalo Fer-nandez de Cordova. Procuró co[n] toda dilige[n]cia y cuydado atraer de paz, y co[n]cordia al Caçique Hirrihigua, porq[ue] le parescia q[ue] co[n]forme al exe[m]plo q[ue] este Caçique diesse de si, poderia esperar o temer q[ue] haria[n] los de[f. 44v]mas Caçiques de la comarca: desseava su amistad, porque con ella ente[n]dia tener ganada la de todos los de aquel Reyno, porq[ue] dezia q[ue] si aquel, q[ue] tan ofendido estava de los Castellanos, se reco[n]çiliasse y hiciesse amigo dellos, qua[n]to mas ayna lo seria[n] los no ofendidos? demas de la amistad de los Caçiques esperava q[ue] su reputacio[n] y ho[n]ra se aume[n]taria generalmente entre Indios, y Españo-les, por aver aplacado este ta[n] ravioso enemigo de su nascio[n]; por todo lo qual sie[m]pre q[ue] los Christianos, corrie[n]do el ca[m]po, açertava[n] a pre[n]der de los vasallos de Hirrihigua, se los embiava co[n] dadivas, y

recaudos de buenas palabras roga[n]dole con la amistad, y co[m]bidan-
dole co[n] la satisfacio[n], que del agravio hecho por Pamphilo de Narvaez,
desse[a]va darle. El Caçique, no solame[n]te no salio de paz ni quiso aceptar
la amistad de los Españoles, ni au[n] respo[n]der palabra alguna a ningu[n]
recaudo de los q[ue] le embiaro[n]. Solo dezia a los me[n]sageros, q[ue] su
injuria, no sufria dar buena repuesta, ni la cortesia de aquel capitan merescia
que se la diessen mala; y nunca a este proposito habló otras palabras: mas
ya que las buenas diligencias, que el Governador hazia por aver el amistad de
Hirrihigua, no aprovecharo[n] para los fines, é inte[n]to, q[ue] el desseava, a
lo menos sirviero[n] de mitigar en parte la ira y ra[n]cor q[ue] este Cacique
tenia co[n]tra Españoles: lo qual se vio en lo que diremos luego.

La ge[n]te de servicio del real yva cada dia por yerva para los cavallos, en
cuya guarda y defensa solian yr de co[n]tino quinze o veynte infantes, y ocho
o diez cavallos. Acaecio un dia q[ue] los Indios q[ue] andava[n] en asse-
cha[n]ça destos Españoles, diero[n] en ellos ta[n] de sobresalto co[n] ta[n]ta
grita, y alarido, q[ue] sin usar de las armas solo co[n] la vozeria los asombra-
ron: y [f. 45r] ellos, q[ue] estava[n] descuydados y desordenados se turbaro[n], y antes q[ue] se recogiese[n], pudiero[n] aver los Indios a las manos un
Soldado llamado Grajales, co[n] el qual, sin q[ue]rer hazer otro mal en los
demas Christianos se fueron mui co[n]te[n]tos de averlo preso.

Los Castellanos se recogiero[n] tarde, y uno de los de acav[a]llo fue
corrie[n]do al real, da[n]do arma, y aviso de lo q[ue] avia passado; por cuya
relacio[n] a toda dilige[n]cia, saliero[n] del Exercito veynte cavallos bie[n]
apercebidos, y halla[n]do el rastro de los Indios q[ue] yva[n] co[n] el Español
preso, lo siguiero[n], y al cabo de dos leguas, q[ue] corriero[n], llegaron a un
gra[n] cañaveral, q[ue] los Indios por lugar secreto, y apartado, avia[n] ele-
gido, do[n]de tenia[n] esco[n]didas sus mugeres, y hijos. Todos ellos chicos
y grandes co[n] mucha fiesta y regozijo de la buena presa hecha, estava[n]
comie[n]do a todo su plazer descuydados de pe[n]sar, q[ue] los Castellanos
hiciesse[n] ta[n]ta diligencia por cobrar un Español perdido. Decia[n] a Grajales que comiesse, y no tuviesse pena q[ue] no le daria la mala vida q[ue] a
Juan Ortiz avian dado.

Lo mesmo le dezia[n] las mugeres y niños, ofrecie[n]dole cada uno dellos
la comida que para si tenia, roga[n]dole q[ue] la comiesse por el, y se
co[n]solase q[ue] ellos le haria[n] buena amistad y compañia.

Los Españoles sintiendo los Indios entraro[n] por el cañaveral, hazie[n]do
ruydo de mas ge[n]te, q[ue] la que yva; por asombrar con el estrue[n]do á los
q[ue] estava[n] dentro: porque no se pusiessen en defensa.

Los Indios oye[n]do el tropel de los cavallos huyero[n] por los callejones,
q[ue] a todas partes tenia[n] hechos por el cañaveral para entrar y salir del,
i e[n] medio del cañaveral tenia[n] roçado un gran pedaço para esta[n]cia de
las mugeres, y hijos, los quales quedaro[n] e[n] poder de los Españoles por
esclavos del q[ue] poco antes lo era dellos: la variedad de los sucessos de la

gue[f. 45v]rra, y la inco[n]stancia de la fortuna della es ta[n]ta, q[ue] en un punto se cobra lo q[ue] por mas perdido se tenia, y en otro pierde lo q[ue] en nuestra opinio[n] mas asegurado está.

Grajales reconocie[n]do las vozes de los suyos, salio corrie[n]do a recebirlos, dando gracias á Dios q[ue] ta[n] presto le huviese[n] librado de sus enemigos. Apenas le conosciero[n] los Castellanos, porq[ue] au[n]q[ue] el tie[m]po de su prisio[n] avia sido breve, ya los Indios le avia[n] desnudado, y puestole no mas que co[n] unos pañetes como ellos trae[n], regozijaro[n]se co[n] él, y recogie[n]do toda la gente q[ue] en el cañaveral avia de mugeres y niños, se fuero[n] con ellos al exercito, do[n]de el Governador los recibio co[n] alegria de q[ue] se huviesse cobrado el Español: y con su libertad preso ta[n]ta gente de los enemigos.

Grajales co[n]tó luego todo lo q[ue] avia sucedido, y dixo, como los Indios, qua[n]do saliero[n] de su emboscada no avia[n] querido hazer mal a los Christianos: porque las flechas, q[ue] les avia[n] tirado mas avia[n] sido por amedre[n]tarlos, q[ue] no por matarlos ni herirlos, q[ue] segu[n] los avia[n] hallado descuydados, y desmandados pudiera[n], si quisiera[n] matar los mas de ellos. Y q[ue] luego q[ue] lo pre[n]dieron se conte[n]taro[n] con el, y sin hazer otro mal, se fuero[n], y dexaron los demas Castellanos, y q[ue] por el camino, y en el alojamie[n]to del cañaveral le avia[n] tratado bien, y lo mismo sus mugeres, y hijos, dizie[n]dole palabras de co[n]suelo, y ofrecie[n]- dole cada qual lo q[ue] para su comer tenia: lo qual sabido por el Governador mandó traer ante sí las mugeres muchachos, y niños, q[ue] truxero[n] presos, y les dixo q[ue] les agradescia mucho el buen tratamie[n]to, q[ue] a aquel Español avia[n] hecho, y las buenas palabras, q[ue] le avian dicho: en reco[m]- pensa de lo qual les dava libertad, para q[ue] se fuesse[n] a sus casas, y les encargava que de alli adela[n]te no huyese[n] de los Castellanos, ni [f. 46r] les oviese[n] temor, sino que tratassen, y co[n]tratassen co[n] ellos como si todos fuera[n] de una misma nacio[n], q[ue] el no avia ydo alli a maltratar naturales de la tierra, sino a tenerlos por amigos y hermanos, y que assi lo dixesse[n] a su Caçique, a sus maridos, parie[n]tes, y vezinos: sin estos halagos les diero[n] dadivas, y las embiaro[n] muy co[n]tentas del favor q[ue] el general i todos los suyos les avian hecho.

Entre otros dos la[n]ces pre[n]dieron despues estos mesmos Indios otros dos Españoles, el uno, llamado Herna[n]do Vintimilla gra[n]de ho[m]bre de la mar; y el otro Diego Muñoz, que era muchacho, page del capita[n] Pedro Caldero[n], y no los mataron, ni les diero[n] la mala vida q[ue] avia[n] dado a Jua[n] Ortiz, antes los dexaro[n] andar libreme[n]te, como a qualquiera Indio dellos: de tal manera que pudieron despues estos dos Christianos con buena maña que para ello tuvieron, escaparse de poder de los Indios en un navio que co[n] torme[n]ta acerto a yr a aquella baia del Espiritu Sancto, como adelante diremos. De manera que co[n] las buenas palabras que el Governador embio a dezir al Caçique Hirrihigua y co[n] las buenas obras que a sus vasallos hizo le forç ó que mitigasse y apagasse el fuego de la saña y ravia que contra Castellanos en su coraçon tenia. Los beneficios tienen ta[n]ta fuerça, que aun a las fieras mas bravas hazen trocar su propria y natural fiereza.

Capitulo X. Como se empieça el descubrimimento, y la entrada de los Españoles la tierra adentro.

Aviendo passado estas cosas, que fueron en poco mas de tres semanas, el Governador mandó al Capitan Baltasar de Gallegos, que con sesenta lanças [f. 46v] y otros tantos infantes entre arcabuzeros, ballesteros, y rodeleros fuessen a descubrir la tierra adentro, y llegasse hasta el pueblo principal del Caçique Urribarracuxi, que era la provincia mas cercana a las dos de Mu- coço y Hirrihigua. Los nombres de estas provincias no se ponen aqui porque no se supo si se llamavan de el nombre de los Caçiques, o los Caçiques del nombre de sus tierras, como adelante veremos, que en muchas partes deste gran Reyno se llama de un mismo nombre el señor y su provincia, y el pueblo principal della.

El capitan Baltasar de Gallegos eligio las mismas sesenta lanças, que avian ydo con el quando fue en busca de Juan Ortiz, y otros sesenta infantes, y entre ellos al mismo Juan Ortiz, para que por el camino les fuesse guia, y con los Indios interprete. Assi fueron hasta el pueblo de Mucoço, el qual salio al camino a recibirlos, y con mucha fiesta, y regozijo de verlos en su tierra los [h]ospedó y regaló aquella noche, el dia siguie[n]te le pidio el capitan un Indio, que los guiasse hasta el pueblo de Urribarracuxi. Mucoço se escusó dicie[n]do, que le suplicava no le mandasse hazer cosa contra su mesma reputacion y ho[n]ra, que pareceria mal, que a ge[n]te estrangera diesse guia contra su proprio cuñado, y hermano. Los quales se quexaria[n] del, co[n] mucha razon, de que á su tierra y casa les huviesse embiado sus enemigos. Que ya q[ue] el era amigo, y servidor de los Españoles, queria serlo sin per- juyzio ageno, ni de su honor. Y dixo mas, que aunque Urribaracuxi no fuera su cuñado como lo era, sino muy estraño, hiziera por el lo mismo: qua[n]to mas sie[n]do deudo ta[n] cercano de afinidad, y vezindad: y q[ue] asimismo le suplicava muy en[f. 47r]carescidamente, no atribuyessen aquella resisten- cia a poco amor y menos voluntad de servir a los Españoles, q[ue] cierto no lo hazia sino por no hazer cosa fea, por la qual fuesse notado de traydor a su patria, parientes, vezinos, y comarcanos, y que a los mismos Castellanos paresceria mal, si en aquel caso, o en otro semejante el hiziesse lo q[ue] le ma[n]dassen, aunque fuesse en servicio dellos, porque en fin era mal hecho, por lo qual dezia que antes eligiría la muerte, que hazer cosa q[ue] no de- viesse a quien era.

Juan Ortiz por orde[n] del capitan Baltasar de Gallegos respondio, y dixo, que no tenian necesidad de la guia para que les mostrasse el camino, pues era notorio que el que avian traido hasta alli era camino r[ea]l, que passava

adelante hasta el pueblo de su cuñado: mas que pedian el Indio para mensagero, que fuesse dela[n]te a dar aviso al Caçique Urribarracuxi, para que no
se escandalizasse de la yda de los Españoles, temie[n]do no llevasen animo
de hazerle mal y daño: y para que su cuñado creyesse al mensagero, que
siendo amigo no le engañaria, querian q[ue] fuese vasallo suyo, y no ageno,
para q[ue] lo fuesse mas fidedigno, el qual de parte del Governador dixesse
a Urribarracuxi, que el y toda su gente desseava[n] no hazer agravio a nadie,
y de parte del Capitan Baltasar de Gallegos, que era el que yva a su tierra,
le avisasse como llevava orden y espreso mandato del General, que aunque
Urribarracuxi no quisiesse paz, y amistad con el, y sus soldados, ellos la man-
tuviessen con el Caçique, no por su respeto, que no le conocia[n], ni les avian
merecido cosa alguna, sino por amor de Mucoço, a quien los Españoles y su
capitan General deseavan dar contento, y por el a todos sus deudos, amigos
[f. 47v] y comarcanos, como lo avian hecho co[n] Hirrihigua el qual, aunque
avia estado y estava muy rebelde no avia recebido, ni recebiria daño alguno.

Mocoço, con mucho agradescimiento respo[n]dió, que al Governador,
como a hijo del Sol, y de la Luna y a todos su capitanes, y soldados por el
semejante besava las manos muchas vezes por la merced, y favor que con
aquellas palabras le hazian, que de nuevo le obligavan a morir por ellos; que
ahora que sabia para que querian la guia, holgava mucho darla; y para q[ue]
fuesse fidedigno a ambas partes, mandava, que fuese un Indio noble, que
e[n] la vida passada de Juan Ortiz avia sido gra[n]de amigo suyo, con el qual
saliero[n] los Españoles del pueblo de Mucoço muy alegres y contentos, y
aun admirados de ver que e[n] un barbaro huviesse en todas ocasiones tan
buenos respectos.

En quatro dias fueron del pueblo de Mucoço al de su cuñado Urribarracuxi. Avria del un pueblo al otro diez y seys o diez y siete leguas. Hallaronla
desamparada, que el Caçique, y todos sus vasallos se avian ydo al monte,
no embargante que el Indio amigo de Juan Ortiz les llevó e[l] recaudo mas
acariciado q[ue] se les pudo embiar, y aunque despues de llegados los Españoles al pueblo bolvio otras dos vezes con el mismo recaudo, nunca el Curaca
quiso salir de paz, ni hizo guerra a los Castellanos ni les dio mala respuesta.
Escusose co[n] palabras comedidas y razones q[ue] aunq[ue] frivolas y vanas
le valiero[n].

Este no[m]bre Curaca en le[n]gua general de los Indios del Peru, significa
lo mismo q[ue] Caçique en le[n]guage de la Isla Española y sus circu[n]vezi-
nas, q[ue] es señor de vasallos y pues yo soy Indio del Peru y no de S[anto]
Domingo, ni sus comarcanas, se me permi[f. 48r]ta, que yo introduzga
algunos vocablos de mi le[n]guage en esta mi obra, porq[ue] se vea q[ue] soy
natural de aquella tierra y no de otra.

Por todas las veynte y cinco leguas, que Baltasar de Gallegos, y sus compañeros desde el pueblo de Hirrihigua hasta el de Urribarracuxi anduvieron,
hallaron muchos arboles de los de España que fueron parrizas, como atras

diximos, nogales, enzinas, morales, çiruelos, pinos, y robles, y los campos apazibles, y deleytosos, que participavan tanto de tierra de monte como de campiña. Avia algunas çienagas, mas tanto menores quanto mas la tierra adentro, y apartado de la costa de la mar.

Con esta relacio[n] embio el capitan Baltasar de Gallegos quatro de a cavallo, entre ellos a Gonçalo Sylvestre para que la diessen al Governador de lo que avian visto, y como en aq[ue]l pueblo y su comarca avia comida para suste[n]tar algunos dias el exercito. Los quatro cavalleros anduviero[n] en dos dias las veynte y cinco leguas, q[ue] hemos dicho sin q[ue] en el camino se les ofreciesse cosa digna de memoria; do[n]de los dexaremos, por co[n]tar lo q[ue] entre tanto sucedio en el real.

Cap[itulo] XII. La relacion que Baltasar de Gallegos embió de lo que avia descubierto.

. . . El dia siguie[n]te a la partida de Vasco Porcallo llegaron al exercito los quatro cavalleros, q[ue] Baltasar de Gallegos embió co[n] la relacio[n] de lo q[ue] avia[n] visto, y oydo de las tierras q[ue] avia[n] andado. Los quales la dieron muy cu[m]plida, y de mucho co[n]te[n]to para los Españoles; porq[ue] todas las cosas, q[ue] dixero[n] en favor de su prete[n]sion, y conquista; salvo una que dixeron, que adelante del pueblo de Urribarracuxi avia una grandissima çienaga y muy mala de passar. Todos se alegraro[n] co[n] las buenas nuevas, y a lo de la çienega respo[n]dieron, que Dios avia dado al ho[m]bre ingenio y maña para allanar, y passar por las dificultades que se le ofreciessen.

Con esta relacion ma[n]dó el Governador echar va[n]do, q[ue] se apercibiesse[n] para caminar passados los tres dias siguie[n]tes. Ordenó q[ue] Go[n]çalo Sylvestre co[n] otros veynte de a cavallo bolviesse a dar aviso a Baltasar de Gallegos como al quarto dia saldria el exercito en su seguimiento.

Avie[n]do de salir el Governador del pueblo de Hirrihigua, era necessario dexar presidio, y ge[n]te de guarnicio[n], q[ue] defendiesse, y guardasse las armas, bastimentos y municiones, q[ue] el exercito tenia, porq[ue] de todo esto avia llevado mucha ca[n]tidad, y ta[m]bie[n] q[ue] la caravela y los dos ve[r]gantines, q[ue] estava[n] e[n] [f. 51r] la baia no quedassen desa[m]parados. Para lo qual nombró al capitan Pedro Calderon que quedase por caudillo de Mmar y tierra, y tuviesse a su cargo lo que en ambas partes quedava, para cuya defensa y guarda dexó quarenta lanças; y ochenta infantes (sin los marineros de los tres navios) co[n] orde[n] que estuviessen quedos sin mudarse a otra parte, hasta que les embiassen a mandar otra cosa: y que con los Indios de la comarca procurassen tener siempre paz, y en ninguna manera guerra, aunque fuessen sufrie[n]doles mucho desden; y particularmente regalassen, y hiciessen toda buena amistad a Mucoço.

Dexada esta orden, la qual el capitan Pedro Calderon guardó como buen capitan y soldado, salio el Governador de la baia del Espiritu Sancto y pueblo de Hirrihigua, y caminó hazia el de Mucoço al qual llegó a dár vista la mañana del dia tercero de su camino. Mucoço que sabia su venida salio a recebirle co[n] muchas lagrimas y sentimiento de su partida, y le suplicó se quedasse aquel dia en su pueblo; el Governador que desseava no molestarle con tanta gente, le dixo, que le convenia passar adelante, porque llevava las jornadas contadas, que se quedasse con Dios, y huviesse por encomendados al capitan y soldados, que en el pueblo de Hirrihigua quedavan, rindiole de nuevo las gracias de lo que por el y su exercito, y Juan Ortiz avia hecho: abraçole con mucha ternura, y señales de grande amor que lo merescia la bo[n]dad de este famoso Indio, el qual con muchas l[a]grimas, aunque procuraba retenerlas, besó las manos al Governador, y entre otras palabras que para significar la pena de su ausencia, le habló, dixo: que no sabria dezir qual avia sido mayor, [f. 51v] o el contento de averle conoscido, y recebido por señor, o el dolor de verle partir sin poder seguir a su señoría, que le suplicava por ultima merced, se acordase del. Despedido del General, habló a los demas capitanes y cavalleros principales, y por buen termino les dixo, la tristeza y soledad en que le dexavan, y que el Sol les encaminasse, y prosperasse en todos sus hechos. Con esto se quedó el buen Mucoço. Y el Governador passó adelante en su viage hasta el pueblo de Urribarracuxi sin que por el camino se le ofreciesse cosa digna de memoria.

De la baia de Espiritu Sancto al pueblo de Urribarracuxi, caminaron siempre al Nordeste, que es al Norte torcie[n]do un poco hazia donde sale el Sol. En este rumbo y en todos los demas que en esta historia se dixeren, es de advertir que no se tomen precisamente para culparme si otra cosa pareçiere despues quando aquella tierra se ganare siendo Dios servido: que aunque hize todas las diligencias necessarias, para poderlos escrevir con certidumbre, no me fue possible alcançarla: porque, como el primer intento que estos Castellanos llevavan era conquistar aquella tierra, y buscar oro, y plata, no atendian a otra cosa que no fuesse plata, y oro: por lo qual dexaron de hazer otras cosas, que les importavan mas, que el demarcar la tierra. Y esto basta para mi descargo de no aver escrito con la certenidad, que he desseado, y era necessario.

English

[f. 28r] First Part of the Second Book of the History of Florida, by the Inca.

Where it is discussed how the Governor arrived in Florida, and found evidence of Pánfilo de Narváez, and a captive Christian; the tortures and cruel life that the Indians gave him; the generosities of an Indian lord of vassals; the preparations that were made for the discovery; the events that happened in the first eight provinces that they discovered; and the foolish ferocity, in words and deeds, of a reckless chief. It contains thirty chapters.

Chapter I. The Governor arrives in Florida, and finds evidence of Pánfilo de Narváez.

The Governor Hernando de Soto, who as we stated, was sailing in search of Florida, discovered its land on the last day of May, having spent nineteen days on the sea, on account of the weather being [f. 28v] contrary. The ships anchored in a deep and good bay, which they called [the Bay] of the Holy Spirit, but since it was late, they did not land any people that day. On the first of June they sent the rowboats to land, which returned loaded with grass for the horses, and they brought many sour grapes from wild vines that they found in the woods. The Indians of all this great kingdom of Florida do not cultivate this plant, nor do they hold it in veneration like other nations, although they eat its fruit when it is very ripe, or having become raisins. Our [men] were very happy from the good samples that they brought from the land, since they resembled the grapes of Spain, which are not found in the land of Mexico, or in all of Peru. The second day of June the Governor ordered three hundred infantrymen to come forth on land for the *auto* and solemnity of taking possession of it for the Emperor Charles the Fifth, King of Spain.[4] After the *auto*, they traveled all day long along the coast, without seeing any Indian, and at nightfall they slept on land. At the dawn watch the Indians came upon them with such force, and with such intrepidity, that they withdrew back to the water, and when they sounded the call to arms, infantry and horses came forth to help them from the ships with as much quickness as if they were on land.

The Lieutenant General Vasco Porcallo de Figueroa was the leader of this assistance, and found the infantrymen on land distressed and disconcerted like recruits, such that they disturbed each other while fighting, and some of them were already wounded from the arrows. Having provided aid, and followed their enemies for a good distance, they returned [f. 29r] to their camp, and had barely just arrived at it when the horse of the Lieutenant General fell dead from an arrow wound that had been received during the skirmish in the saddle. Passing through the cloth, tree, and saddle pad, [the arrow] entered more than a third of its length through the ribs into the body cavity. Vasco Porcallo greatly lamented that the first horse that was employed in the Conquest, and the first lance that was tested against the enemies, was his own.

During this day and the next one, the horses disembarked and all the people came forth on land. Having refreshed themselves for eight or nine days, and having left orders regarding what was suitable for the ships, they traveled inland a little more than two leagues, up to the town of a cacique named Hirrihigua, with whom Pánfilo de Narváez had warred when he went to conquer that province, although afterward the Indian had been reduced to his friendship. During [the Conquest], for some unknown reason, Pánfilo de Narváez became angered and had done certain grievances against him, which are not recounted here on account of being hateful.

Because of the unjustness and offenses, the cacique Hirrihigua remained so intimidated and hateful of the Spaniards, that when he found out about the journey of Hernando de Soto to his land, he went away to the woods, abandoning his house and town. And regardless of the favors, gifts, and promises that the governor made him, sending them with the Indian vassals of his that he captured, he never ever wanted to come forth in peace, or hear any message of those that they sent him. Instead, he became angry with those who carried the messages, who since they knew how offended and wounded he was from that nation, should not have carried him their messages. If they were [the Spaniards'] heads, those he would receive with great pleasure, but [f. 29v] their words and names he refused to hear. The infamy was all this and more, principally if it was done without guilt of the offended, and so that the rage of this Indian against the Castilians is better seen, it will be good to recount some cruelties and martyrdoms that he performed against four Spaniards that he obtained from those of Pánfilo de Narváez. Although we may prolong [the narrative] somewhat, we will not depart from its intention, but instead take great advantage for our History.

It is to understand that, a few days after Pánfilo de Narváez left the land of this cacique, having done what we left off saying, one of his ships that had remained behind managed to get to that bay in his pursuit. When the cacique found out that it was one of Narváez's, and that it was searching for them, he desired to capture all those who were on it in order to burn them alive. In order to assure this, he pretended to be a friend of Pánfilo de Narváez, and sent to tell them how their captain had been there, and had left orders about what that ship should do if it reached port there. In order to persuade them so that they would believe him, he displayed from land two or three folds of blank paper, and other old letters that he had been able to obtain from the past friendship of the Spaniards, or in some manner, which he had guarded well.

With all this, those of the ship grew wary, and refused to come forth on land. Then the cacique sent four principal Indians to the ship in a canoe, saying that since they did not trust him, they were sending those four noble men, and knights (this name knight appears inappropriate, because they had no horses, from which the name derives, and even more because in Spain it is understood [f. 30r] as nobles, and among Indians there were high nobles, which one could also say for them)[5] as hostages, and as security so that the Spaniards would come out of the ship if they wished to go and find out about their captain Pánfilo de Narváez, and if they were not certain, he would send them more captives. Seeing this, four Spaniards came forth and entered in the canoe with the Indians who had brought the hostages. The cacique, who wanted all of them, seeing that no more than four were going, did not wish to insist further in asking for more Castilians, so that these few that were going to him would not be startled and return to the ship.

As soon as the Spaniards set foot on land, the four Indians who had remained on the ship as hostages, seeing that the Christians were now in the power of their own, threw themselves in the water, making a long dive. Swimming like fish, they went to land, fulfilling with this the order that their lord had given them. Those of the ship, seeing themselves deceived, went away from the bay before something worse should happen, with great remorse for having lost their companions so indiscreetly.

Chapter II. Of the torments that a cacique gave to a Spanish slave of his.

The cacique Hirrihigua ordered the four Spaniards guarded closely, so that he could solemnify a great feast that, according to his heathenism, he expected to celebrate within a few days. The feast having arrived, he ordered them taken out naked to the plaza, and that one by one, running them from one place to another, they should be shot with arrows like animals. And they should not be shot with many arrows all at once, so that they would delay more in dying, and so that the torment would be all the greater, and so that the delight of the Indians would be lengthier [f. 30v] and more complete. They did so with the three Spaniards, the cacique receiving great pleasure, and in whom none of them found aid, but rather death. When they wished to bring out the fourth, who was a young man, who had barely reached eighteen years, a native of Seville named Juan Ortiz, the wife of the cacique came forth in the company of three of his young daughters, and having placed themselves in front of the husband, she told him that she begged him to be content with the three dead Castilians, and that he should pardon that young man, since neither he nor his companions had held the guilt of the evil that the previous [Spaniards] had done, since they had not come with Pánfilo de Narváez. And that young man in particular was worthy of pardon, because his youthful age liberated him from guilt, and she asked for mercy, and that it was enough for him to remain as a slave, and that they should not kill him so crudely, without having committed any crime.[6]

The cacique, in order to make his wife and daughters happy, granted for the time being the life of Juan Ortiz. However, afterward he [Ortiz] became so sad and bitter that many times he was envious of his three dead companions, because the continuous and incessant labor of carrying firewood and water was so much, and the eating and sleeping so little, and the blows, slaps, and lashings every day so cruel, not to speak of the rest of the tortures that they gave him at times on particular feast days, for which many times he would have taken death at his own hands as a remedy, if he had not been Christian. And it was thus, that beyond the daily torture, on many feast days the cacique commanded, as his hobby, that Juan Ortiz should run the entire day without stopping (from sunrise to sunset) in a long plaza that was in the town, where they shot arrows in his companions. [f. 31r] The cacique himself came out to watch him run, and with him came his nobles prepared with their bows and arrows in order to shoot him if he stopped running. Juan Ortiz began his race upon the sunrise, and he did not stop going from one side to the other of the plaza until the sun set, which was the time that they indicated. And when the cacique went away to eat, he left his nobles to watch him, so that if he stopped running they would kill him. At the end of the day, as one can imagine, the poor man was left sprawled on the ground, more dead than alive. The piety of the wife and daughters aided him on such days, because they took him immediately, and clothed him, and provided other help for him, with which they sustained his life, though it might have been better to take it away from him, in order to liberate him from those many hardships. Seeing that so many and so continuous tortures did not suffice to take away the life of Juan Ortiz, and his hatred toward him increasing hour by hour, in order to finish him off, the cacique commanded on one of his feast days that a great fire be made in the middle of the plaza. And when he saw many coals, he ordered it to be spread out, and that over it should be placed a *barbacoa*, which is a bed of wood in the form of a grill, one yard in height over the ground,[7] and that Juan Ortiz should be placed upon it in order to roast him alive.

This was done, where the poor Spaniard remained a long time spread out on one side, tied to the *barbacoa*. The wife and daughters of the cacique attended to the cries that the poor man made in the fire, and imploring her husband, and even scolding his cruelty. They took him out of the fire already half roasted, so that the blisters he had on that side were like half oranges, and some of them ruptured, from which ran much blood, which was pitiful to see. The cacique consented to this because [f. 31v] they were women that he loved so much. And perhaps he also did so in order to have someone in the future on whom to exercise his wrath, and show the desire of his vengeance, so that there would be someone on whom to exercise it. Even though it was so small compared to what he desired, he still enjoyed even that little. And he said so many times, that he regretted having killed the three Spaniards so quickly. The women took Juan Ortiz to their house, and with juices of herbs (since they lack doctors, the Indian women, and men, are great herbalists) they cured him, with great pity in seeing him in that state. How many times they had now repented having freed him from death that first time, on seeing how lengthy and cruel were the tortures that they gave him each day. At the end of many days, Juan Ortiz became well, although the signs of his burns remained very large.

The cacique, in order not to see him thus, and in order to liberate himself from the bother that his wife and daughters caused him with their petitions, ordered that he be employed in another torment, not so grave as the past ones, so that he would not be useless. And it was that he should guard, day and night, the dead bodies of the residents of that town, which were placed in the outdoors, within a forest, far from any settlement, in a place designated for them. They placed [the bodies] upon the ground in some chests of wood that served as sepulchres, without hinges or any other form of closure than some boards with which they covered them, and on top some stones or logs. Because of the poor security these chests had for guarding the dead bodies, they were carried off by lions, of which there are many in that land,[8] [f. 32r] from which the Indians received great sorrow and anger. The cacique ordered Juan Ortiz to guard this place with care, so that the lions would not carry off some dead person, or a part of them, with the warning and oath he made to him that if they carried them off, he would die roasted, without any possible remedy. And in order to guard them, he gave him four darts for him to throw at the lions,[9] or at other wild animals that might reach the chests. Giving thanks to God that he had removed him from the continual presence of the cacique Hirrihigua, his master, Juan Ortiz went to guard the dead, expecting to have a better life with them than with the living. He guarded them with all care, principally at night, because then there was greater risk. It happened that one night of those that he stood watch, he fell asleep at the dawn watch, without being able to resist sleep, because at this hour it shows its greatest force against those who keep watch. At this time a lion was fortunate enough to arrive, and scattering the inner doors of one of the chests, it pulled out a boy who had been placed there two days earlier, and carried him off. Juan Ortiz awoke with the noise that the doors made upon falling, and when he reached the chest and did not find the body of the boy, he knew it had been taken. Even with all his anxiety and worry, he did not fail to spring into action by looking for the lion, so that if he found it he could take back the dead body or die at [the lion's] hands. On the other hand, he commended himself to Our Lord to give him the strength to die another day, confessing and calling his Name, because he knew that as soon as the sun rose, the Indians would visit the chests, and not finding the body of the boy, they would burn him alive. Traveling through the forest, from one place to another, with the anxiety of death, he came forth to a wide road that [f. 32v] passed through the middle of it, and going on it for a short while with the determination of fleeing, although it was impossible to escape, he heard in the forest, not far from where he was going, a noise like a dog gnawing on bones. Listening well, he confirmed it, and suspecting that it could be the lion that was eating the boy, he went with much care through the bushes, approaching where he heard the noise. In the light that the moon cast, though not very clearly, he saw near himself the lion, which was eating the boy at its pleasure. Juan Ortiz, calling to God, and gathering courage, threw a dart at it, and although at that time he could not see the throw that he had made because of the bushes, he still sensed that it had not been bad, because of the "taste of his hand," as the hunters say they feel when they have made a good shot at wild animals at night.[10] With this hope, though so weak, and also by not having heard the lion withdraw from where he had thrown, he waited for the sunrise, commending himself to Our Lord to help him in that time of need.

Chapter III. The bad life of the captive Christian continues, and how he fled from his master.

With the light of the day, Juan Ortiz confirmed the good throw that he had made blindly at night, because he saw the lion dead, with its entrails traversed, and the heart in the middle (as was afterward found when they opened it), a fact which he himself could not believe, even though he saw it. With the satisfaction and happiness that one can imagine better than saying, he dragged it off by its foot, without removing the dart, so that his master would see it just as he had found it, having first gathered and returned to the [f. 33r] chest the pieces of the boy that had not been eaten. The cacique, and all those of his town, greatly admired this deed, because in that land, in general it is held as a miraculous thing for a man to kill a lion, and thus they treat with great veneration and respect he who manages to kill one. And because it is such a fierce animal, it ought to be esteemed greatly everywhere, principally if it is killed without the shot of a crossbow or arquebus, as Juan Ortiz did. And although it is true that the lions of Florida, Mexico, and Peru are not as large or fierce as those of Africa, in the end they are lions, and the name suffices. And although the common proverb says that they are not as fierce as they are painted, those who have found themselves near them say that they are just as much fiercer than those that are sketched as the difference between the live and the painted.

With the good fortune of Juan Ortiz, the wife and daughters of the cacique took more courage and audacity to intercede for him, and that he should be pardoned for everything, and that his services should be employed in honorable offices, worthy of his effort and valor. From then onward, for some days, Hirrihigua treated his slave better, both for the esteem and favor that was afforded him in his town and house, and in order to recognize the valiant deed that they, in their vain religion, esteem and honor so much that they hold it as sacred, and more than human. However (since injury does not know how to forgive), every time he remembered that they had thrown his mother to the dogs, and let them eat her, and when he tried to blow his nose and did not find his nose, the devil prompted him to avenge himself against Juan Ortiz, as if he had cut it off. Since he held the offense always before his eyes, with the memory of it, from day to day grew his ire, rancor, and desire to take vengeance, [f. 33v] although for some time he restrained these passions. Not being able to resist any longer, one day he told his wife and daughters that it was impossible for him to tolerate that that Christian should live, because his life was hateful and abominable to him, and each time he saw him, his past injuries were refreshed, and his offense renewed. Therefore he commanded that in no way should they intercede again for him, if they did not wish to participate in the same fury and anger. And in order to finish off with that Spaniard, he had determined that on a certain feast day (which they would celebrate soon) they would shoot him with arrows and kill him, as they had done to his companions, irrespective of his valor, because since he was an enemy, he should be abhorred instead of esteemed. Because the wife and daughters of the cacique saw him angered, and understood that their intercession would be of no benefit, and also because it seemed to them that it was too inopportune, and would give such grief to their lord on behalf of the slave, they did not dare reply with a single word of opposition. To the contrary, the women astutely told him that it would be very good for him to do thus, and that this pleased them. In addition, the oldest of the daughters, in order to carry her intention forward and achieve it, a few days before the feast, notified Juan Ortiz in secret about the determination of her father against him. Neither she nor her sisters nor her mother was worth anything [to him], nor could they do anything with the father, on account of them having remained silent in his favor, and threatening them if they should break it.

To this sad news, wishing to encourage the Spaniard, she added other different [news], and told him: So that you will not lose faith in me, or despair of your life, or fear that I might fail [f. 34r] to do everything I can to give it to you, if you are a man, and have the will to flee, I will give you favor and aid so that you may escape, and save yourself. Tonight, at a certain time and place, you will find an Indian whom I trust with your health and mine, who will guide you to a bridge that is two leagues from here. When you reach it, you will command him not to pass onward, but rather that he should return to the town before dawn, so that they do not miss him and discover my audacity and his, and as a result of having done good to you, evil would befall him and me. Six leagues farther beyond the bridge is a town, the lord of which loves me greatly, and wishes to marry me, named Mucoço. Tell him on my behalf that I am sending you to him, so that in this need he will aid and favor you, as [the lord] he is. I know that he will do everything he can for you, as you will see. Commend yourself to your God, since I cannot do more in your favor. Juan Ortiz threw himself at her feet in recognition of her mercy, and the benefit that she gave him, and had always done, and immediately he prepared himself to travel the following night. And at the assigned hour, when those of the cacique's house were already asleep, he left in search of the promised guide, and with him he left the town without anyone noticing them. Upon reaching the bridge, he told the Indian with all humility that he should return immediately to his house, having first found out from him that there was no way to stray from the road up to the town of Mucoço. [f. 34v]

Chapter [IV]. Of the magnanimity of the curaca, or cacique, Mucoço, to whom the captive commended himself.

Juan Ortiz, as a man who was fleeing, reached the village before dawn, and in order not to cause any disturbance, he did not dare to enter it. When it was daytime, he saw two Indians come forth from the town by the same road he had taken, and they wished to shoot him with arrows, since they always travel with these weapons prepared. Juan Ortiz was also carrying them, and placed an arrow in his bow in order to defend himself, and also in offense. Oh how valuable is a little favor, and even more if it is from a Lady, since we see that he who a little earlier did not know where to hide himself, fearing death, now dares to strike others with his own hand, only by seeing himself favored by a beautiful, discreet, and generous young woman, whose favor exceeds all other human favor. With this, having gathered will, strength, and even pride, he told them that he was no enemy, but rather that he was on a diplomatic mission from a lady, for the lord of that village.

Upon hearing this, the Indians did not shoot at him, but instead returned with him to the town and advised their cacique that a slave of Hirrihigua was there with a message for him. [The cacique], known as Mucoço, or Mocoço, which are both the same, came forth to the plaza to receive the message that Juan Ortiz carried. After having greeted him in the best manner he knew in the usage of the Indians themselves, he briefly recounted the tortures that his master had inflicted on him, in testimony of which he showed him on his body the signs of the burns, blows, and wounds that he had given him. And [he told him] how now, at the end, his lord was determined to kill him, so that with [f. 35r] his death he might rejoice and solemnify the feast day that they were awaiting soon. And [he related] that although the wife and daughters of the cacique, his master, had given him his life many times, they did not dare speak in his favor now, on account of the lord having prohibited it, on pain of his anger. And as a final and best remedy, the eldest daughter of this lord, with the desire that he should not die, had commanded and encouraged him to flee, and had given him a guide to set him on the road to his town and house. And she told him that in her name he should present himself before [the cacique], and that she begged him, on the love that he held for her, to receive [Ortiz] under his protection, and that as a matter commended by her, he should favor him, as [the lord] he was. Mucoço received him affably, and listened to him with pity upon learning of the evils and tortures that he had experienced, which were well displayed in the marks on his body, since according to the dress of the Indians of that land, he was not wearing more than some light cloths.

At this point, apart from what we have said, Alonso de Carmona adds that [the cacique] embraced him and kissed him on the face, in sign of peace.[11]

[Mucoço] responded that he was welcome, and that he should endeavor to lose the fear of his past life, and that in his company and house he would have a significantly different and better life, and that in order to serve her who had sent him, and for him, who had gone to seek aid from his person and house, he would do all that he could, as he would see by his deeds, and that he should hold it as certain that as long as he lived, no one would have cause to disturb him.

All that this good cacique said in favor of Juan Ortiz he fulfilled, and much more than what he promised, because later he made him his steward, and he always took him with him, by day and by night, giving him much honor, [f. 35v] and very much more after he found out that he had killed the lion with the dart. In sum, he treated him as his own brother, very beloved (and there are brothers who love each other like water and fire), and although Hirrihigua, suspecting that [Ortiz] had availed himself of Mocoço, asked for him many times, always Mucoço excused himself from returning him, saying among other reasons, for his last reply, that he should leave him alone, since he had gone from his house, and that he lost very little in losing a slave that was so hateful for him. He responded the same to another cacique, a brother-in-law of his called Urribarracuxi, of whom Hirrihigua availed himself in order to ask for [Ortiz]. Seeing that his messages were of no use, [Urribarracuxi] went personally to ask for him, and Mocoço responded the same in his presence as in his absence, and added other words in anger. He told him that since he was his brother-in-law, it was not just that he should command him to do something against his reputation and honor, and that he would not be doing his duty if he turned over an afflicted [person], who had come to commend himself to him, to his very enemy, so that for his entertainment and recreation he might torture and kill him, like a beast.

Mocoço defended him with such generosity from these two caciques, who asked for Juan Ortiz with much insistence and obstinacy, that he held it as best to lose (as he lost) the marriage that he enthusiastically desired to have with the daughter of Hirrihigua, and to lose the kinship and friendship of the brother-in-law, rather than return the slave he asked for in order to kill him. [Mocoço] always had [Ortiz] with him, esteeming and regaling him greatly, until Governor Hernando de Soto entered into Florida.

Juan Ortiz was among [f. 36r] those Indians for ten years, one and a half in the power of Hirrihigua, and the rest with the good Mocoço. Although he was a barbarian, he treated this Christian in a very different manner than the very famous Barons of the Triumvirate, who in Layno, a village near Bolonia, made that never ever sufficiently abhorred proscription and agreement to give away and barter their relatives, friends, and protectors in exchange for their enemies and adversaries. And he acted much better than other Christian princes, who since then have done other abominations even worse than that one, considering the innocence of those they turned over, and the quality of some of them. Those who delivered them should have held and guarded their faith, since those [Barons] were gentiles, and these [princes] boasted of the Christian name and religion. They broke the laws and charters of their kingdoms, without respecting their own condition and rank, since they were kings and great princes, and with even less appreciation of their sworn and promised faith (a thing unworthy of such names). Just in order to avenge themselves of their anger, they turned over those who had not offended them, because the offenders had declared the innocent guilty, as the ancient and modern histories testify. We will leave off from this in order not to offend powerful ears, and injure pious ones.

It is sufficient to represent the magnanimity of a pagan, so that the believing princes make an effort to imitate him, and surpass him if they can, not in his unbelief, as some unworthy of that name do, but rather in his virtue, and similar grandeur, to which the greater height of their estate that they have makes them more obligated. How certain it is, considering [f. 36v] well the circumstances of the valorous deed of this Indian, and having seen for whom, and against whom, he did it, and how much that he wished to postpone and lose, going even against his own love and desire. In denying the aid and favor demanded, and promised by him, it will be seen that it was born of a very generous and heroic will, unworthy of having been born and lived in the barbarous gentility of that land. But many times God and human nature produce such souls in deserts so uncultured and sterile, for the greater confusion and shame of those who are born and raised in fertile lands, and abundant in all good doctrine, science, and Christian religion.

Chapter V. The Governor sends for Juan Ortiz.

The relation that we have given of the life of Juan Ortiz was obtained by the Governor, although confused, in the town of the cacique Hirri-higua, where at the present we have him. And he had already had it in Havana, although not as lengthy, from one of the four Indians that we recounted had been imprisoned by the Accountant Juan de Añasco when they sent him to discover the coast of Florida, and who ended up being a vassal of this cacique. When he named Juan Ortiz in his account in Havana, this Indian left off the name Juan, because he did not know it, and said Ortiz. In addition to the poor speech of the Indian was added the worse understanding of the good interpreters who testified as to what he wished to say. Since all the listeners had as their principal intent to go in search of gold, upon hearing the Indian say *Orotiz*, without seeking other declarations they understood that he plainly said that in his land there was much gold,[12] and they were pleased [f. 37r] and rejoiced only with hearing the name, although with such a different significance and meaning.

Well, since the governor certified that Juan Ortiz was in the power of the cacique Mucoço, it seemed to him that it would be good to send for him, both in order to remove him from the power of the Indians, and also for what he had need of in the way of a translator and interpreter in whom he could trust. For this he selected a knight native to Sevilla, named Baltasar de Gallegos, who went as senior bailiff of the armada and of the army, who on account of his great virtue, strength, and valor deserved to be the general of another army, larger than that one. And he told him that with sixty lancers that he would take in his company, he should go to Mucoço, and on his behalf he should say how thankful he and all the Spaniards he had with him would be of the honor and benefits that he had made to Juan Ortiz, and how much he desired that he could reward him for them. For the present he prayed that he would give [Ortiz] to him, since there was need for him for affairs that were very important. And whenever it seemed suitable to him, he [Mocoço] should come to visit him [Soto], and that he would be very pleased to meet him, and to consider him as a friend. In fulfillment of what he was ordered, Baltasar de Gallegos left the army with sixty lancers and an Indian who would guide him.

On the other side, the cacique Mucoço was fearful, having found out about the arrival of Governor Hernando de Soto with such a force of people and horses, and that he had made landfall so close to his [land]. And so that they might not do him any damage, he wished to avoid this evil that might befall him with prudence and good council. And in order to remedy it, he called to Juan Ortiz and told him: You should know, brother, that in the town of our good friend Hirrihigua there is a Spanish captain with a thousand men of war and many [f. 37v] horses, and they come to conquer this land. You know well what I have done for you, and how in order to save your life, and not to deliver you to he who held you as a slave, and who wished to have you in order to kill you, I chose instead to fall in the disgrace of my kin and neighbors, rather than do what they asked me against you. Now the time and occasion are here in which you can reward me for the good reception, gifts, and friendship that I have given you, although I never did so with the expectation of any award. But since fortune has led things in this way, it would be sensible not to miss out on what she [fortune] offers us.

You will go to the Spanish general, and on your behalf and mine, you will request that in remuneration of what I have done for him and for all your nation in you (since for any one of them I would do the same), he should consider it good not to do me any damage in this small land that I have, and should deign to receive me in his friendship and service, since from now on I offer him my person, house, and estate, so that he might place it beneath his protection and shelter. And so that you may be accompanied, as is suitable to you and to me, you will take fifty nobles from my house, and you will look out for them and for me, as our friendship obligates you.

Juan Ortiz, rejoicing with the good news, giving thanks to God for it on the inside, responded to Mucoço that he was very pleased that the time and occasion had been offered to serve the mercy and benefits that he had made him, not only of his life, but also for the great favor, esteem, and honor that he had received from his great virtue and courtesy. He would give a very long relation and account of this to the Spanish [f. 38r] captain, and to all his [people], so that they would be grateful and would repay him in what at the present he would request in his name, and in what might be offered in the future. He was very confident that for his part the general would do what was asked of him, because the Spanish nation valued people who had done something for their [people], and thus he could certainly remain with the expectation of receiving what he had asked for from the Governor. Presently there came the fifty Indians whom the cacique had commanded to prepare themselves, with whom Juan Ortiz took the Royal Road, which goes from one town to the other. And they left on the same day that Baltasar de Gallegos came forth from the army to look for him.

It happened that after the Spaniards had traveled more than three leagues along the Royal Road, wide and straight, which went to the town of Mucoço, the Indian that was guiding them changed his mind about guiding them, and at the first sign of a footpath that he saw intersect, he took it, leaving the Royal Road, it seeming to him that it was not appropriate to be so loyal to people who came to subjugate them and take away their lands and liberty, and who long ago had shown themselves to be declared enemies, although up to that point they had not received any wrongs of which to complain from that army. After traveling a short distance along [the footpath], he lost it, since it was not straight, and thus he brought them most of the day off-road and lost, leading them always in a curve toward the coast of the sea, with the desire of running across some swamp, cove, or bay, in which he would drown them if he could. Since they did not know the land, the Castilians did not notice the deceit of the Indian until one of them managed to see the topsails of the ships they had left through the trees of an open forest, [f. 38v] and saw that they were very near the coast, of which he informed Captain Baltasar de Gallegos. Seeing the malice with which the guide threatened their death, he made a gesture that he wished to catch up with him. The Indian, fearing that they would kill him, told them by signs and words as best he could that he would return them to the Royal Road, for which it was necessary to retrace their steps along all the route they had traveled, and thus they returned along the same steps in search of it.

Chapter VI. What happened to Juan Ortiz with the Spaniards who were going for him.

Juan Ortiz, traveling along the Royal Road, arrived at the footpath through which the Indian had misguided Baltasar de Gallegos and his knights, and suspecting what it was, and fearing that the Castilians would go by another route and do damage in the town of Mucoço, he consulted with the Indians what they would do. They all agreed that it would be good to follow the signs of the horses with all speed until reaching them, and that they should not take another road, so that they would not miss the mark.

Well, since the Indians were following the sign of the Spaniards, and they were returning by the same road that they had followed, they sighted each other in a great plain, in which on one side of it there was a closed forest of dense shrubs. The Indians, seeing the Castilians, told Juan Ortiz that it would be sensible to secure their persons and lives by entering that forest until the Christians might recognize them as friends, because in having them as enemies, they should not meet them in the open part of the field. Juan Ortiz refused to take the good counsel of the Indians, confident that he was a Spaniard, and his [people] would have to recognize him as soon as they saw him, as if he had come dressed in Spanish style, or were [f. 39r] distinguishable in some way from the Indians, in order to be recognized as a Spaniard. But he, like the rest, did not wear anything other than some light cloths as clothing, and a bow and arrows in his hands, and a plumage half a fathom high upon his head,[13] as adornment and ornament.

The Castilians, as novices, and anxious to fight, upon seeing the Indians, launched at them with open reins, and despite many commands the captain gave them, it was insufficient to detain them. Who can control greenhorns when they go on a rampage?

The Indians, seeing how boldly and rashly the Castilians came at them, all plunged into the woods, so that there in the field there only remained Juan Ortiz and an Indian who did not hurry as much as the rest in getting into the haven. Upon reaching the first shrubs of the forest, [this Indian] was wounded in the loins by a lance blow from a Spaniard named Francisco de Morales, who had been a soldier in Italy. Against Juan Ortiz lunged another Spaniard, named Alvaro Nieto, a native of the villa of Albuquerque, one of the stoutest and strongest Spaniards who were in the entire army, and who, upon closing in, gave him a fierce lance blow. Juan Ortiz had good luck and dexterity, and blocking the lance with his bow, he leaped to the side, simultaneously fleeing from the blow of the lance and from the collision with the horse. And seeing that Alvaro Nieto was coming back against him, he shouted loudly, saying "Xibilla, Xibilla," which is to say "Sevilla, Sevilla."

At this point, adds Juan Coles,[14] since Juan Ortiz could not manage to speak Castilian, made the sign of the cross with his hand and the bow, so that the Spaniard would see that he was Christian. With the little, or nonexistent, use of the [f. 39v] Castilian language that he had practiced among the Indians, he had forgotten even the name of the land itself. I could say the same of myself, on account of not having anyone in Spain with whom I could speak my native and maternal language, which is the general [language] spoken in all of Peru (although the Incas had another particular one that they spoke among themselves, one with another). I knew how to speak it well, and better and with greater elegance than the Indians themselves who are not Incas, because I am a son of Palla, and nephew of Incas, who are those who speak it better and more exactly, on account of it having been the language of the court of its princes, and they were the principal courtiers. I had forgotten in such a manner that now I cannot manage to string together six or seven words in oration in order to communicate what I want to say. Beyond this, many words have disappeared from my memory, and I do not know which ones they are, in order to name one thing or another in Indian, although it is true that if I were to hear an Inca speak, I would understand everything he said, and if I heard the forgotten words, I could say what they mean. But on my own, no matter how much I try, I cannot manage to say which [words] they are, [and] this I have learned in the experience of using, or not using, languages that are learned by using them, and are forgotten by not using them.

We return to Juan Ortiz, whom we left in great danger of being killed by those who most desired to see him alive. When Alvaro Nieto heard him say Xivilla, he asked him if he were Juan Ortiz, and when he responded yes, he took him by the arm and lifted him upon the haunches of his horse like a child, because this good soldier was stout and strong, and very happy to have found what he was looking for, giving [f. 40r] thanks to God that he had not killed him. Although it seemed to him that he still saw himself in danger, he took him to Captain Baltasar de Gallegos, who received Juan Ortiz with great joy, and immediately ordered to be called together all the rest of the knights, who were wandering through the forest anxious to kill Indians, as if they were deer, in order for everyone to enjoy the good luck that had befallen them, before they should do harm to friends by not recognizing them. Juan Ortiz entered in the forest to call the Indians, telling them in a loud voice that they should come out, and that they should not be afraid. Many of them did not stop until reaching their town, in order to give news to their cacique about what had happened. Others, who had not gone as far, returned by threes and fours, as they managed to find themselves. All of them, each one on his own, with great fury and anger scolded Juan Ortiz for his little caution, and great naïveté. And when they saw his Indian companion, wounded on account of him, they became fired up in a manner that they were almost unable to contain themselves from laying hands on him, and they would have done so had the Spaniards not been there. In addition, they avenged their anger with a thousand affronts that they said to him, calling him stupid, foolish, flippant, and that he was neither a Spaniard nor a man of war, and that all his past challenges and misfortunes had served for little, or nothing, and that they had not been given to him in vain, and that he deserved much worse. In sum, not a single Indian came out of the woods who did not scold him, and everyone told him almost the same words, and he himself repeated them to the rest of the Spaniards, for his greater [f. 40v] shame. Juan Ortiz was left well reprimanded on account of having been so gullible, and above all well used, in exchange for seeing himself among Christians. [The Christians] healed the wounded Indian, and placing him on a horse, they went with him and Juan Ortiz and the rest of the Indians to the army, desirous of seeing the governor, since in such a brief time they brought such good news regarding what he had ordered them. And before they left from that place, Juan Ortiz dispatched an Indian to Mucoço with an account of everything that had happened, so that he would not be disturbed by what the Indians who fled [earlier] told him.

All that we have referred to regarding Juan Ortiz is also stated by Juan Coles and Alonso de Carmona in their accounts. One of them says that worms got in the wounds that he got from the fire when they were roasting him. And the other, which is by Juan Coles, says that later the governor gave him a suit of black velvet, and that on account of having been forced to go naked, he could not tolerate it, and that he only wore a shirt and some linen underwear, a hat, and shoes, and that he remained that way for more than twenty days, until little by little he returned to using clothes. Both these eyewitnesses also say that among other mercies and favors that the cacique Mucoço made to Juan Ortiz, one of them was to make him his captain-general of land and sea.

Chapter VII. The celebration that all the army made for Juan Ortiz, and how Mucoço came to visit the Governor.

A good part of the night had already passed when Baltasar de Gallegos and his companions entered the army's camp. The governor seated them, and received a shock, fearing that since they had returned so quickly, some mishap had befallen them, [f. 41r] because he did not expect them until the third day. But having certified the good news that they brought, all the anguish converted into celebration and joy. He offered thanks to the captain and his soldiers for having done so well, [and] received Juan Ortiz like his own son, with pity and pain from remembering so many hardships and martyrdoms, as he related, and as his own body showed he had experienced, because the signs of the burns from when they roasted him were so large that one entire side was nothing more than a burn, or scar from it. He gave thanks to God for having freed him from these hardships, and from the danger of that day, which had not been the least of those that he had experienced. [The governor] fawned on the Indians who came with him, and commanded that the wounded Indian should be healed with great care and comfort. At that very hour, he dispatched two Indians to the cacique Mucoço with great appreciation for the benefits that he had made to Juan Ortiz, and for having sent him freely, and for the offer of his person and friendship. He said that in the name of the Emperor and King of Spain, his lord, who was the principal and greatest of all Christianity, and in the name of all those captains and knights who were with him, and in his own name, he accepted this in order to thank him and repay him for what he had done for all of them in having liberated Juan Ortiz from death. And all of them requested that he should visit them, since they had the desire to see him and get to know him.

The captains and ministers, both from the army and the royal treasury, and the knights and all the rest of the soldiers, in common and individually, greatly celebrated Juan Ortiz, and there was no one in the company who did not manage to embrace him and congratulate him [f. 41v] on his arrival. Thus they spent that night, in which they did not sleep with this general exhilaration.

Then on the following day, the general called Juan Ortiz in order to inform himself about what he knew about that land, and so that he would recount in particular what had happened to him in the power of those two caciques. He responded that although he had been in the land so much time, he knew little, or nothing, because while he was in the power of Hirrihigua his master, when they were not tormenting him with new martyrdoms, they did not let him slack off even one step from the ordinary service that he performed, carrying water and wood for all the house. And while he was in the power of Mucoço, although he had liberty to go wherever he might wish, he did not make use of it, so that the vassals of his [former] master, seeing him separated from Mucoço, would not kill him, because they had his order and command to do so. For these reasons, he could not give a good description of the qualities of the land beyond the fact that he had heard it said that it was good, and that farther inland it was better and more fertile. The life that he had spent with the caciques had been on the two extremes of good and bad that could be had in this century, because Mucoço had shown himself just as merciful and humane with him as the other was cruel and vindictive, without being able to stress sufficiently the virtue of the one, or the passion of the other, as his lordship had already been informed. In proof of this, he showed the signs on his body, showing those that could be seen, and amplified the account of his life that we have given, and newly related many other torments that he had suffered, which provoked compassion among the hearers, and which we will leave off in order to avoid tediousness.

On the third day after word [f. 42r] was sent to him with the Indians, the cacique Mucoço came well accompanied by his own [Indians], kissing the hands of the governor with all veneration and respectfulness. Then he spoke to the lieutenant general, and the field master, and the rest of the captains and knights who were there, to each one in conformity with the quality of his person, first asking Juan Ortiz who was this, that, and the other one. And even if he told him that one of those with whom he was speaking was not a knight or a captain, but rather an individual soldier, he treated him with great respect, but with even more to those who were nobles, and the ministers of the army, in a manner that was noticed by the Spaniards. Mucoço, after having spoken, and given the opportunity for those who were present to speak with him, once again greeted the governor with new manners of reverence. Having received [Mucoço] with great affability and courtesy, [the governor] gave him thanks for what he had done for Juan Ortiz, and for having sent him so amicably, [and] told him that he had obligated him and his army, and all the Spanish nation, to be grateful for all time. Mucoço responded that what he had done for Juan Ortiz, he had done for his own respect, because in his having gone in need to entrust himself and receive aid from his person and house, because of who he was, by custom he was obligated to do what he did for him. And it seemed little to him, because the virtue, effort, and valor of Juan Ortiz, on its own, without any other respect, deserved much more. And his having sent him to his lordship had also been more in his own interest and benefit than to serve his lordship, since it had been so that, [f. 42v] as defender and advocate, with his intercession and merits, he might obtain mercy and amnesty, so that no damage would be done to him in his land. And thus, neither for the one thing nor the other did his lordship have to be grateful, nor receive him in service, beyond the fact that he rejoiced in having managed to do something that his lordship and those knights, and all the Spanish nation, were grateful for, and received with satisfaction. He requested of his lordship that with the same approval, he should receive him in his service, under whose protection and favor he placed his person, and house, and estate, recognizing as principal lord the emperor and king of Spain, and secondarily his lordship as his captain-general, and governor of that kingdom. And with this mercy that he might offer him, he would hold himself as more extraordinarily gratified than had been the merit of his service made in benefit to Juan Ortiz, or having sent him freely, a thing that his lordship had esteemed so much. To this he said that he esteemed and regarded as greater to see himself, as he did that day, favored and honored by his lordship, and by all those knights, and that whatever good he had done in all his life, he declared that he would strive to do from now onward similar things in service of the Spaniards, since those things had come out so well.

This cacique said these and many other genteel things, with all the good grace and discretion that a discreet courtesan could depict, which the governor and those who were with him admired no less than the generosities that he had done for Juan Ortiz, which his words imitated.

For all of this, the [f. 43r] Adelantado Hernando de Soto, and the Lieutenant General Vasco Porcallo de Figueroa and other individual knights, fond of the discretion and virtue of the cacique Mucoço, were moved for their part to reciprocate in whatever they could reward him in gratitude for so much goodness. And thus they gave him many gifts, not just to him, but also to the nobles who came with him, from which all of them remained very satisfied.

Chapter VIII. The mother of Mucoço comes, very anxious for her son.

Two days after what we have said, the mother of Mucoço came, very anxious and grief-stricken that her son was in the power of the Castilians. On account of having been absent, she did not know about her son having come to see the governor, which she would not have consented to. And thus the first words that she said to the general were that he should give her son back before he did to him what Pánfilo de Narváez did to Hirrihigua, and that if he intended to do the same, that he should free her son, who was young, and do whatever he wanted with her, who would take the suffering of them both.

The governor received her with much kindness, and responded that her son, on account of his goodness and discretion, did not deserve to have anything evil done to him, but rather that all were in service to him, and to her as well, by being the mother of such a son. And she should abandon her fear, because neither to her nor her son nor to any other person in all their land would any evil be done, but instead all the pleasure and courtesy that was possible. With these words the good old lady was somewhat calmed, and remained with the Spaniards three days, though always so mistrustful and cautious that while eating at the table of the governor, she asked Juan Ortiz if she should dare to eat what they gave her, and said that she had misgivings, and feared [f. 43v] that they would give her poison to kill her.

The governor and those who were with him laughed greatly at this, and told her that she could eat safely, that they did not wish to kill her, but instead regale her. Still not trusting the words of foreigners, even when they gave it to her from the governor's own plate, she refused to eat or even taste it until Juan Ortiz had tried it. To this a Spanish soldier asked her how it was that a little before she had offered her life for her son, when she was so afraid of dying? She responded that she did not detest life, but instead loved it like all other people, but more than this she would give her life for her son whenever it was necessary, because she loved him more than life. For all this, she implored the governor to give him to her, and that she wished to go away and take him with her, because she did not dare trust him with the Christians.

The general responded that she could go away whenever she wished, but that her son wished to remain for some days among those knights, who were young men and soldiers, men of war, like him, and he enjoyed being among them, and that whenever it seemed suitable to him he could leave freely, without anyone becoming angry. With this promise the old lady went away, although discontented that her son remained in the power of the Castilians. Upon her departure Juan Ortiz told her that he would free her son from that captain and his soldiers, just as her son had liberated him from Hirrihigua and his vassals, at which the governor and the rest of the Spaniards laughed very much, and Mucoço himself helped to laugh away the anxieties of his mother.

After having passed these matters of laughter and happiness, the good cacique remained with the army eight days, during which he visited the lieutenant general, and the field master, and the captains, and the officials of the imperial treasury, and many individual knights for their nobility, all in their lodgings, [f. 44r] and he spoke with such familiarity, and such ease and courtesy, that it seemed that he had been raised among them. He asked specific things about the court of Castille, and about the emperor, and about its lords and ladies and knights, and said that he would like to see it, if it could come to that. After the eight days had passed, he went away to his home. Afterward he came other times to visit the governor, and always brought some of the gifts that there were in his land. Mucoço was twenty-six or twenty-seven years old, handsome in body and countenance.

Chapter IX. Of the preparations that were made for the discovery, and how the Indians captured a Spaniard.

The governor and adelantado Hernando de Soto was not idle while these affairs happened among his own, but rather with all care and diligence he performed the office of captain and leader, because as soon as the supplies and munitions were unloaded and placed in the town of the cacique Hirrihigua, on account of being the closest to the Bay of Espiritu Santo so that they would be near the sea, he ordered that of the eleven ships that he had taken, the largest seven should return to Havana to be at the order of whatever Doña Isabel de Bobadilla, his wife, should arrange, and that the smallest four should remain for whatever might occur or be necessary by sea. The vessels that remained were the navio *San Antón*, and the caravel, and the two brigantines, of which he gave command to Captain Pedro Calderón, who, among other excellent qualities that he had, had served under the staff and command of the great Captain Gonçalo Fernandez de Cordova. He endeavored with all diligence and care to attract the cacique Hirrihigua to peace and amity, because it seemed to him that in conformity to the example of this cacique, whatever he did could be expected, or feared, would be done by the rest [f. 44v] of the caciques of the district. He desired his friendship, because with it he understood that he would have earned that of all those in that kingdom, because he said that if that [cacique], who was so offended by the Castilians, should reconcile himself and make himself their friend, how much more quickly would those who had not been offended? Apart from the friendship of the caciques, he hoped that his reputation and honor would grow generally among the Indians and Spaniards on account of having placated such a rabid enemy of his nation. For all of this, whenever the Christians who traveled in the field managed to apprehend vassals of Hirrihigua, they were sent with gifts and messages of kind words, entreating him with friendship, and inviting him with the reparation that [the governor] desired to make him for the offense of Pánfilo de Narváez. Not only did the cacique not come forth in peace, nor did he wish to accept the friendship of the Spaniards, nor even respond a single word to any of the messages that were sent to him, he only told the messengers that his injury would not suffer providing a good answer, nor did the courtesy of that captain deserve a bad one. Never did he speak other words in this regard, though despite the fact that the good tasks that the governor performed to obtain the friendship of Hirrihigua were not taken advantage of for the goals and intentions that he desired, at least they served to mitigate in part the anger and rancor that this cacique had against Spaniards, which was seen in what we will state later on.

The service people of the army went out each day for grass for the horses, in whose guard and defense normally went fifteen or twenty infantrymen and eight or ten cavalry. It happened one day that the Indians who were trying to ambush these Spaniards struck upon them so alarmingly, with such shouting and yelling, that without even making use of weapons, they were startled by the clamor alone, and [f. 45r] heedless and disordered, they were broken up, and before they gathered themselves together, the Indians laid hands on a soldier named Grajales, with whom, without desiring to do any other evil to the remaining Christians, they went away very satisfied at having captured him.

The Castilians gathered themselves late, and one of those on horseback went racing to the army's camp, firing his weapon and giving news of what had happened. Upon his account, with all diligence there came forth from the army twenty horsemen, well prepared, and upon finding the trail of the Indians who were going away with the captive Spaniard, they followed it, and at the end of two leagues that they raced, they reached a large canebrake that the Indians had selected as a secret and remote place, where they had their women and children hidden. All of them, small and large, with great festivity and rejoicing for the good capture that had been made, were eating with all pleasure, heedless of thinking that the Castilians would perform such diligence in recovering a lost Spaniard. They told Grajales that he should eat, and he should not be distressed, because they would not give him the bad life that Juan Ortiz had been given.

The women and children said the same, each one offering him the food they had for themselves, imploring him to eat it for his own good, and that he should console himself, that they would give him good friendship and company.

The Spaniards, noticing the Indians, entered the canebrake, making noises of more people than they had, in order to startle those who were within with the clamor, so that they would not put themselves in a defensive posture.

Hearing the throng of the cavalrymen, the Indians fled through the passageways that they had made throughout all parts of the canebrake in order to enter and leave from it, and in the middle of the canebrake they had cleared a large piece of it for the residence of the women and children, who remained in the power of the Spaniards as slaves, as he who had been [a slave] of them a little before. The variety of the fortunes of war, [f. 45v] and the inconstancy of its fortune, is such that at one point there is obtained that which was held as completely lost, and in another there is lost that which is most secure in our opinion.

Recognizing the voices of his own, Grajales came forth running to receive them, giving thanks to God that they had liberated him so quickly from his enemies. The Castilians almost did not recognize him, because although the time of his imprisonment had been brief, the Indians had already stripped him of his clothes, and placed on him nothing more than a loincloth like they wear. They rejoiced with him, and gathering all the people that were in the canebrake, women and children, they went away with them to the army, where the governor received them with joy that they had recovered the Spaniard, and with his liberty, captured so many people of the enemies.

Grajales then recounted everything that had happened to him, and told how the Indians, when they came forth in their ambush, had not wished to do damage to the Christians, because the arrows that they had fired were more to intimidate them than to kill them or wound them. Since they had found them so heedless and disordered, if they had wanted to they could have killed the majority of them, and as soon as they captured him, they were satisfied with him, and without doing any other evil, they went away and left the rest of the Castilians. And in their quarters in the canebrake they had treated him well, and their women and children the same, speaking words of consolation to him, and offering him everything that they had for their own sustenance. Finding this out, the governor ordered to be brought before him the women, young people, and children that they had brought as prisoners, and he told them that he was very grateful for the good treatment they had made to that Spaniard, and for the good words that they had spoken to him, in recompense for which he gave them their freedom, so that they could go to their homes. And he charged them that from then onward, they should not flee from the Castilians, nor [f. 46r] should they have fear of them, but rather that they should interact and trade with them, as if they were all from one single nation, and that he had not gone there to mistreat the natives of the land, but instead to have them as friends and brothers, and thus they should tell this to their cacique, and to their husbands, relatives, and neighbors. Beyond these compliments, they gave them gifts, and sent them away very satisfied with the favor that the general and all his people had shown them.

Among others, two lancers were captured afterward by these same Indians, one named Hernando Vintimilla, a great seaman, and the other Diego Muñoz, who was a boy, a page of Captain Pedro Calderón. They did not kill them, nor did they give them the bad life that they had given to Juan Ortiz, but instead they let them walk around freely, like any of their own Indians, in such a manner that afterward these Christians, with the good knack that they had for it, were able to escape from the power of the Indians in a ship that managed to go to the Bay of Espiritu Santo during a storm, as we will tell farther on. In this manner, with the good words that the governor sent to the cacique Hirrihigua, and with the good deeds that his vassals did, he forced him to mitigate and quench the fire of the fury and rage that he held in his heart against Castilians. Such benefits have as much force as to make even the bravest beasts change their own natural ferocity.

Chapter X. How the discovery was begun, and the entrance of the Spaniards into the interior.

These things having happened, which occurred during a little more than three weeks, the governor sent Captain Baltasar de Gallegos, who went with sixty lancers [f. 46v] and just as many infantrymen, between arquebusiers, crossbowmen, and shield men, to discover the interior and arrive as far as the principal town of the cacique Urribarracuxi, which was the province closest to the two [provinces] of Mucoço and Hirrihigua. The names of these provinces are not put here, because it was not found out if they were called by the name of the caciques, or the caciques by the name of their lands, as we will see farther on, since in many parts of this great kingdom the lord and his province, and its principal town, are all named the same.[15]

Captain Baltasar de Gallegos selected the same sixty lancers who had gone with him when he went in search of Juan Ortiz, and another sixty infantrymen, among them the very same Juan Ortiz, so that he would be their guide on the road and their interpreter with the Indians. Thus they went up to the town of Mucoço, who came forth to the road to receive them, and with great festivity and joy upon seeing them in his land. He housed them and regaled them that night. The following day the captain asked for an Indian to guide them to the town of Urribarracuxi. Mucoço excused himself, saying that he implored that they should not order him to do something against his own reputation and honor, since it would appear bad that he gave to foreign people a guide against his own brother-in-law, and brother, and that those [of Urribarracuxi] would complain against him, with good cause, for having sent his enemies to his land and home. And now that he was a friend and servant of the Spaniards, he wished to be so without disservice to another, or to his honor. And in addition he said that even if Urribarracuxi was not his brother-in-law, as he was, but instead a total stranger, he would do the same for him, and thus even more with his being such a close relative by kin and proximity. And he likewise implored him very [f. 47r] insistently not to attribute that resistance to little love and less will to serve the Spaniards, which he was certainly not doing, but rather in order not to do something unsightly, for which he would be marked as a traitor to his native land, his relatives, his citizens, and his neighbors. And it would seem bad to the Castilians themselves if in that case, or another similar one, that he should do what they were ordering, even if it were in their service, because in the end it was badly done. For all this he said that he would sooner choose death than do something that he ought not to whomever it might be.

By order of Captain Baltasar de Gallegos, Juan Ortiz responded and said that they did not have need of the guide in order to show them the road, since it was well known that [the road] that had brought them up to there was the Royal Road, which passed onward up to the town of his brother-in-law, but instead that they asked for the Indian as a messenger who would go forward to notify the cacique Urribarracuxi, so that he would not be scandalized by the arrival of the Spaniards, fearing that they were intending to do him evil and damage, and so that his brother-in-law would believe the messenger, who as a friend would not deceive him. They wanted [the messenger] to be a vassal of [Urribarracuxi], and not an outsider, so that he would be more trustworthy. [This messenger] should tell Urribarracuxi, on behalf of the governor, that he and all his people did not desire to do wrong to anyone, and on behalf of Captain Baltasar de Gallegos that it was he who was going to his land. And he should advise [the cacique] how he carried order and express command from the general that even if Urribarracuxi did not wish peace and friendship with him and his soldiers, they would maintain it with the cacique, not for his respect, since they did not know him, nor had he deserved anything, but instead out of love for Mucoço, whom the Spaniards and their captain-general desired to make happy, and through him to all his relatives, friends, [f. 47v] and neighbors. And they had [already] done so with Hirrihigua, who, although he had been and still was very rebellious, had not received, nor would he receive, any damage.

With great thankfulness, Mucoço responded that he kissed the hands many times of the governor, as a son of the sun and the moon, and of all his captains and soldiers for the same reason, on account of the mercy and favor that they did him with those words, and that they newly obligated him to die for them. And now that he knew why they wanted the guide, he was very happy to provide him, and so that he would be trustworthy to both sides, he commanded that he should be an Indian noble who had been a great friend of Juan Ortiz in his previous life, with whom the Spaniards left from the town of Mucoço very happy and content, and even impressed upon seeing that a savage should have such great respect in all occasions.

In four days they went from the town of Mucoço to that of his brother-in-law Urribarracuxi, which were about sixteen or seventeen leagues apart from one another. The found it abandoned, since the cacique and all his vassals had gone away to the woods, despite the fact that the Indian friend of Juan Ortiz had taken them the most diplomatic message that could have been sent. Although after the Spaniards arrived at the town he returned another two times with the same message, the *curaca* never wished to come forth in peace, nor did he make war with the Castilians or give them a bad response. He excused himself with moderate words and reasons that, although frivolous and worthless, availed him.

This name *curaca*, in the general language of the Indians of Peru, means the same as cacique in the language of the island of Hispaniola and its neighbors, which is a lord of vassals, and since I am an Indian from Peru, and not from Santo Domingo or its district, permit me [f. 48r] to introduce some words from my language in this my work, so that it may be seen that I am a native of that land, and not from another.

For all the twenty-five leagues that Baltasar de Gallegos, and his companions traveled, they found many trees like those in Spain, which were grapes, as we stated before, walnuts, willows, live oaks, mulberries, plums, pines, and oaks, and the fields mild and delightful, which were as much like backcountry as farmland. There were some swamps, which were smaller farther into the interior, and separated from the seacoast.

With this account Captain Baltasar de Gallegos sent four on horseback, among them Gonçalo Silvestre, so that they should relate to the governor what they had seen, and how in that town and its district there was enough food to feed the army for several days. The four knights traversed the twenty-five leagues that we have spoken of in two days, without the road offering them anything worthy of memory, where we will leave them in order to recount what happened in the army's camp in the meantime.

[Sections of the Garcilaso narrative that deal with internal affairs of Soto's army are omitted here.]

Chapter XII. The account that Baltasar de Gallegos sent of what he had discovered.

. . . The following day, upon the departure of Vasco Porcallo, there arrived at the army the four knights that Baltasar de Gallegos sent with an account of what he had seen and heard of the lands that they had crossed. They gave a very complete account, and very pleasing to the Spaniards, because everything they said was in favor of their goal and conquest except one, which was that they said that beyond the town of Urribarracuxi there was a very large swamp, and very difficult to cross. Everyone rejoiced with the good news, and regarding the swamp, they responded that God had given Man the ingenuity and skill to smooth out and pass through all the difficulties that might arise.

With this account, the governor ordered a proclamation issued that they should prepare to travel after the next three days. He ordered that Gonçalo Silvestre, with another twenty on horseback, should return to Baltasar de Gallegos with the news that the army would leave in his pursuit on the fourth day.

Since the governor had to leave the town of Hirrihigua, it was necessary to leave a presidio, and people in garrison to defend and guard the weapons, supplies, and munitions that the army had, because a great quantity of all this had been brought, and also so that the caravel and the two brigantines that were in [f. 51r] the bay should not remain abandoned. For this he named Captain Pedro Calderón to remain as commander of land and sea, and that he should have under his charge whatever remained on both sides [of the shore]. For its defense and guard he left forty lancers and eighty infantrymen (not counting the sailors of the three ships) with an order that they should remain still, without moving to another place until some other order might be sent to them, and that they should endeavor always to have peace with the Indians of the district, and in no manner war, even if they should suffer much disdain, and in particular that they should regale and make all friendship with Mucoço.

Having left this order, which Captain Pedro Calderón observed as a good captain and soldier, the governor left from the Bay of Espiritu Santo and the town of Hirrihigua, and traveled toward that of Mucoço, which he sighted on the morning of the third day of his journey. Mucoço, who knew about his arrival, came forth to receive him with many tears and regret at his departure, and implored him to remain that day in his town. The governor, who wished not to disturb him with so many people, told him that it was more suitable to pass onward, because he was counting the days of his journey, and that he should remain with God, and that he entrusted to him the captain and soldiers who remained in the town of Hirrihigua. Again he offered thanks for what he had done for him and his army, and for Juan Ortiz, and embraced him with great tenderness, and signs of great love, which the goodness of this famous Indian deserved. With many tears, although he endeavored to retain them, [Mucoço] kissed the hands of the governor, and among other words that he spoke in order to signify the distress of his absence, he said that he did not know how to say which had been greater, [f. 51v] the pleasure of having met him and received him as lord, or the pain of seeing him leave, without being able to follow his lordship, and he pleaded that as a final mercy he should remember him. Having said good-bye to the general, he spoke with the rest of the captains and principal knights, and as a final gesture he told them of the sadness and solitude in which they left him, and that [he prayed that] the sun would guide them, and that they would prosper in all their deeds. With this the good Mucoço stayed behind, and the governor passed forward in his journey up to the town of Urribarracuxi, without anything happening on the road worthy of memory.

From the Bay of Espiritu Santo to the town of Urribarracuxi they traveled always to the northeast, which is to the north, turning a little in the direction of the sunrise. In this direction, and in all the rest that are stated in this history, it must be noted that they should not be taken as precise in order to blame me if something else should appear afterward, when that land is conquered, if God is so served. Although I performed all the tasks necessary in order to write about them with certainty, it was not possible for me to achieve it, because since the primary goal that these Castilians had was to conquer that land, and to look for gold and silver, they did not attend to anything that was not silver and gold, on account of which they left off doing other things that were more important for them, such as demarcating the land. And this is sufficient for my acquittal in not having written with certainty, which I have desired, and which was necessary.

Supplementary Document: Letter of Hernando de Soto to the Royal Officials of Santiago de Cuba, July 9, 1539

The text of the following letter was written by Hernando de Soto himself while still at the Bay of the Holy Spirit (modern Tampa Bay), where he made landfall just a few days before the army began their march inland and northward. Soto's original letter was first transcribed in 1539 for inclusion in a letter sent by the Royal Officials of Santiago de Cuba to the Spanish Crown and was then retranscribed by eighteenth-century Spanish historian Juan Bautista Muñoz, whose papers were ultimately left in the Spanish Royal Academy of History. In 1855, American historian Buckingham Smith had yet another transcript of the Muñoz transcription made by his wife, and this transcript presently resides in the New York Public Library, from which microfilm copies have been made. A set of the microfilm copies is archived in the Coker Collection of the University of West Florida Special Collections Department. I have not found the original 1539 transcript in the Archivo General de Indias; thus, the present transcript was made from Buckingham Smith's transcript of the Muñoz version. Nevertheless, it seems to be the first publication of the Spanish text as transcribed by Smith's wife and the first direct translation of the original since Smith's, published in 1854 and 1866 (Smith 1854, 1866: 284–87). The importance of the letter is obvious, in part since it represents the last known text written by Soto himself and sent to Cuba before his eventual death along the Mississippi River three years later. Beyond this, the letter contains details regarding the first weeks of the expedition along Florida's lower gulf coast, confirming and augmenting what is known from other more comprehensive narratives of the expedition.

The transcription here follows the norms detailed in the preface, generally preserving anachronistic orthography present in the original text except in cases where it might make it difficult for modern Spanish readers to sound out the words correctly or follow the intended sentence structure.

Spanish

[f. 1r][16] Traslado de una carta que el Adel[antad]o Soto escrivio a la just[ici]a i reg[imien]to de la c[iuda]d de Santiago de la isla de Cuba.

Mui Noble Señor

En estar en nueva tierra aunque no mui lejos desa enpero con algun mar en medio me parece que ha mill años que no he sabido de v[uest]ras m[e]r[ce]-d[e]s porque a la verdad tambien a mucho que no he visto carta i aunque por tres vias les dexe escrito en la Havana enpero por agora se ha ofrecido de me dar cuenta ques una cosa que yo siempre tengo de hacer; dexe aqui lo que me parece i creo que les sera agradable como a personas que conosco yo i e siempre conoscido que tienen buena voluntad; yo parti de la Havana con toda mi armada Domingo 18 de Mayo aunque escrevi que a 25 del anticipé me por no perder un buen tiempo que teniamos que se nos convirtio en calmas estando engolfados en pero no tan continuas que en ocho dias no llegasemos a surgir en este costa que fue Domingo de Pascua del Spiritu Santo decaidos del puerto quatro u cinco leguas sin que ninguno de mis Pilotos supiesen en donde estava, por lo qual me convino salir en los vergantines i buscarlo i en esto i entrar la boca del puerto nos detuvimos tres dias i tambien por no estar instructos en la canal que es un ancon que entra doze leguas i mas en la mar; tuvimos tanta dilacion que tuve necesidad de embiar a Vasco Porcallo de Figueroa mi lugar teniente General en los vergantines a tomar un pueblo [f. 1v] [unreadable] cabo del ancon, i yo mande echar to[da la] gente i cava-llos en una playa donde con harto trabajo nos fuimos a juntar con Vasco Por-callo domingo de la Santissima Trinidad; los Yndios de la costa por algunos temores que nos coxeron nos desmanpararon toda la tierra que en treinta leguas no ha parado hombre; llegado aqui, yo tuve noticia de un cristiano que estava en poder de un cacique i embie alla a Baltasar de Gallegos con 40 de a cavallo i otros tantos peones a procurar de haverlo, al qual hallo una jornada de aqui con ocho o diez Yndios que truxo a mi poder; no nos holgamos poco con el porque sabia tan bien la lengua, que tenia perdida la nuestra aunque

luego bolvio a ella, dicese Joan Ortiz natural de Sevilla e hijo de algo; pasado
esto yo fui en persona a este Cacique i lo truxe de paz i luego despache a
Baltasar de Gallegos con ochenta lansas i cien peones a entrar la tierra en la
qual ha hallado tantos maizales frisoles i calabazas i otras frutas i mantenimientos que para mui gran exercito hai, sin que padescan nesesidad; llegado
a un Cacique que se dice Urripacoxit señor destotro de paz i otros muchos le
enbie algunos Yndios para contratar de paz en la qual me scrive que andavan
i que porque andando en ella le falto de ciertas promesas le tomo i detuvo
unos 17 Yndios en que havia algunos principales porque por esta via le parecio tenerlo mas cierto; entre estos que detuvo ay algunos viejos de [f. 2r]
[unreadable] quanta en tal gente puede haver [que tie]nen noticia de la tierra
adelante; i di[cen] que a tres jornadas de alli yendo por algunos pueblos i
bohios bien poblado todo i de muchos mayzales, ay un pueblo grande que
se dice Acuera donde a mucho placer podriamos invernar; i que luego mas
adelante pasadas dos jornadas ay otro pueblo que se dice Ocale i dicen ques
tan grande i dellos tan encarecido que yo no osare decirlo aqui en el dicen
haver lo que en todos los dichos en gran abundancia, ay gallinas guanaxos
en corrales muchas, ay venados mansos que se guardan en manadas como
esto sea yo no lo entiendo ecebto sino son las bacas que traemos noticia,
dicen haver muchos mercaderes entre ellos i mucho trato i abundancia de
oro i plata i muchas perlas plega a Dios que sea ansi porque yo destos Yndios
no creo sino lo que veo, i aun bien visto puesto que saben i tienen por dicho,
que si me mienten les ha de costar la vida, questa lengua nos da la vida para
entendernos con ellos, i sin el yo no se que pudiera ser de nosotros, gloria
sea a Dios que todo lo ha encaminado por su bondad de manera que parece
quel tiene especial cuidado questo sea para su servicio como yo se lo tengo
suplicado i ofrecido. Por mar en unas barcas son ochenta peones i mi General
por tierra con 40 de cavallo a daruna junta que Joan de Añasco descubrio de
unos mill Yndios u mas, i el General vino anoche que le huyeron i aunque los
siguio no pudo haverlos por muchos [f. 2v] [unreadable] el camino, en estando todos juntos co[mo d]igo nos iremos a juntar con Baltasar de Gallegos
para de alli yr como digo juntos a invernar al Ocale, que segun dicen si es verdad no tenemos mas que desear, plega a Dios que suceda dello cosa que sea
para servicio de Dios Nuestro Señor y con que yo pueda servir a v[uestra]s
m[e]r[ce]d[e]s i a cada uno en especial como yo deseo i lo devo y porque con
todas las ocupaciones de aca yo no tengo olvidado el amor que devo a lo de
alla i la obligacion que tengo i porque no puedo visitarlo con mi presencia,
creo yo que donde v[uest]ras m[e]r[ce]d[e]s estan poco havra en que ser
menester mi persona, merced mui grande recebire que con todos los otros
cargos que tengo tenga este sobre ello con mas obligacion aun de sentirlo,
que v[uest]ras m[e]r[ce]d[e]s como quien son miren por la pasificacion i bien
del pueblo i buena administracion del, tieniendo siempre por encomendado
al Licenciado i las cosas de la justicia de tal manera que Dios i el Rey sean

muy servidos i yo reciba merced i todos gran contentamiento, i satisfecho en nosotros mismos de haver hecho el dever en todo como siempre v[uest]ras m[e]r[ce]d[e]s lo suelen hacer, pues por mi respeto no menos que suelen lo miraran de lo qual a la verdad que soy i me tendria por mui encargado, i en eso del bestion que yo dexe comensado si por ventura el descuido de no ser el presente menester huviere sido cabsa de no estar acabado merced me haran v[uest]ras m[e]r[ce]d[e]s // [f. 3r] fin en el para cada dia se ofrecen otros tiempos i que no se ofrescan es buena provicion i gran provecho i bien desa cibdad y cosa en que yo tan gran m[e]r[ce]d recibire cuyas muy nobles personas de v[uest]ras m[e]r[ce]d[e]s N[ues]tro Señor guarde i acreciente como yo deseo i v[uest]ras m[e]r[ce]d[e]s meresen. En este pueblo i puerto del Espiritu Santo de la provincia florida de Julio 9 de 1539 años.

Servidor de v[uest]ras m[e]r[ce]d[e]s
El Adelantado D. Hernando de Soto

English

[f. 1r] Transcript of a letter that the Adelantado Soto wrote to the justices and regiment of the city of Santiago of the island of Cuba.[17]

Very Noble Señor,

In being in a new land, although not very far from that one, nevertheless with some sea in between, it seems to me that it has been a thousand years that I have not had news of Your Graces, because in truth it has also been a long time that I have not seen a letter, although by three routes I left letters for you in Havana. Nevertheless, for now I have the opportunity to report to you, which is something that I must always do. I left here what seems [suitable] to me and that I believe will be agreeable to you all, as persons that I know and have always known to have good will. I left from Havana with all my armada on Sunday, May 18. Although I wrote that it would be on the 25th, I left early in order not to miss the good weather that we had, which converted into calms when we entered the gulf, however not so continuous that in eight days we were not able to arrive to anchor on this coast, which was Sunday, the Feast of the Holy Spirit,[18] four or five leagues leeward of the port, without any of my pilots knowing where they were. On account of this it was suitable for me to go forth in the brigantines and look for it. We delayed three days in this, and in entering the mouth of the port, and also by not being informed about the canal, which is a bay that enters twelve leagues and more from the sea. We had such delays that I had the need to send Vasco Porcallo de Figueroa, my lieutenant general, in the brigantines to take a town [f. 1v] at the end of the bay, and I ordered all the people and horses landed on a beach where with great effort we went to meet with Vasco Porcallo on the Sunday of the Holy Trinity.[19] The Indians of the coast, because of some fears that they developed of us, abandoned the entire land, so that in thirty leagues not a man has ended up.[20] Having arrived here, I had news of a Christian who was in the power of a cacique, and I sent Baltasar de Gallegos with 40 on horseback, and just as many foot soldiers, to endeavor to get him. He found him one day's journey from here with eight or ten Indians that he brought into my power. We take no small pleasure in him, because he knew their language so well that he had lost ours, although later he returned to it. He is called Juan Ortiz, a native of Seville, and a gentleman. After this happened, I went in person to this cacique and brought him in peace, and next I dispatched Baltasar de Gallegos with eighty lancers and one hundred foot soldiers to enter the land, in which he has found so many cornfields, beans, and squash and other fruits and sustenance that there is enough for a very large army, without suffering any need. Having arrived at a cacique called Urripacoxit, lord of this other one at peace and many others, I sent him some Indians in order to negotiate peace, which he [Gallegos] writes that he was working on, and because while he was working on it, he [Urripacoxit] failed in certain promises, he took and detained some 17 Indians, among which there were some nobles, because by this route it seemed to him he would have him more certain. Among these that he detained there are some old men [f. 2r] [of authority[21]], as much as can be had among such people, who have some news of the land farther on. And they say that three days' journey from there, going through some towns and huts, all well populated and with many cornfields, there is a large town called Acuera, where we could winter with much pleasure. And then two days' journey farther on there is another town called Ocale, and they say that it is so large, and so extolled by them that I will not dare to say it here. In it they say there is everything that is in the aforementioned towns in great abundance. There are many turkeys in corrals, [and] there are tame deer that are kept in herds. If this is true, I do not understand it, except if they are the cows that we have heard of.[22] They are said to have many merchants among them, and much trade and abundance of gold and silver and many pearls. I pray to God that it is so, because I do not believe anything that I do not see, and even well seen, since they know and have had it told to them that if they lie to me it will cost them their lives. This interpreter gives life to us in order to communicate with them, and without him, I do not know what would become of us. Glory be to God that everything has proceeded by his goodness, in such a manner that it seems that he has special care that this may be for his service, as I have implored and offered. By sea in some boats [I sent] eighty foot soldiers, and my general by land with 40 on horseback, to attack a meeting of some one thousand or more Indians that Juan de Añasco discovered, and the general came last night [saying] that they fled from him, and although he followed them he could not take them because of many [f. 2v] [obstructions on[23]] the road. Upon everyone being together like I say, we will go to join up with Baltasar de Gallegos in order to go together from there to winter at Ocale, where according to what they say, if it is true, we will have nothing more to desire. I implore God that what happens in this is a matter that is in the service of God, Our Lord, and with which I can serve your graces, and to each one in particular, as I desire and ought to, and because with all the occupations here, I have not forgotten the love that I owe to everything there, and the obligation that I have. And because I cannot visit it with my presence, I believe that wherever your graces are, my person will be little needed. I will receive very great favor, since with all the other charges that I have, I hold this above everything with even more obligation, feeling that your graces, as who you are, are looking after the pacification and good of the public, and their good administration. I am always holding this as entrusted to the *licenciado*,[24] and the affairs of justice, in such a manner that God and the King are very served, and I receive favor, and everyone great contentment, and we are satisfied in ourselves for having done our duty in everything, as always your graces normally do, since for my respect, no less than normally, you will look after it, of which in truth I am and hold myself as very responsible [for it]. And in that [matter] of the bastion that I left started, if by chance the over-sight of not being presently necessary has been the cause of it not being finished, your graces will favor me [f. 3r] [missing word or words[25]] finishing it up, because each day new times offer themselves, and if they are not offered, it is a good precaution and great benefit for the good of that city, and a matter in which I will receive great favor. Our Lord guard and advance the very noble persons of your graces as I desire, and as your graces deserve. In this town and port of Espiritu Santo of the province of Florida, July 9, 1539.

Servant of your graces,
Adelantado Don Hernando de Soto[26]

3

The Luís Cancer Expedition, 1549

Following the failed military expeditions of Pánfilo de Narváez and Hernando de Soto between 1528 and 1543, Spain ultimately acquiesced to a novel approach to the conquest of Florida: unescorted Dominican missionaries. Fray Luís Cancer de Barbastro was chosen to lead this expedition, which finally sailed from Veracruz, Mexico, in 1549 after years of planning. In retrospect, the expedition was a complete failure, resulting in the deaths of its leader and several others before abandoning the Florida coast. Nevertheless, the original handwritten diary of the expedition presented here represents one of the most unique and compelling relics of the first-contact era in Spanish Florida and provides extraordinary insight into an idealistic if misguided attempt to reach out in peace to Florida's indigenous inhabitants. One can only guess whether the expedition would have met with a less brutal fate had it not followed several decades of Spanish slaving and military presence along the Florida coastline in this vicinity.

The first document is a selection from the 1596 Dávila Padilla history of the Dominicans in New Spain, which relates the origins and background of the Cancer expedition. The next document is the complete text of the original Luís Cancer diary as completed and amended by Gregorio de Beteta. As supplements to these primary narrative accounts, selections from several letters written by Cancer prior to his departure for Florida are also included at the end. The detailed financial accounts for the Cancer expedition (Lázaro 1549; Hernández de Burgos 1549) are not included but do provide additional detail regarding the cost of outfitting the friars, ship, and crew.

Narratives

Dávila Padilla's Account of the Origins of the Luís Cancer Expedition

The following selection from a history of the Dominican province of Santiago in Mexico was published in 1596 but was initially accumulated as a series of texts written by various authors. Fray Agustín Dávila Padilla (1955) was the final editor and compiler. The details in Dávila Padilla's narrative provide a meaningful background for the earlier documents relating to the Cancer expedition itself and give some sense of Cancer's motivation for the mission to Florida, as well as the broader historical context of the expedition in the mid-sixteenth century. Dávila Padilla's subsequent recounting of the events of the Cancer expedition differs in many details from those recorded in the original expedition diary and must therefore have been based at least in part on flawed or exaggerated recollections after the expedition itself. For this reason, only the introductory material is included here as a supplement to the Cancer diary itself.

The transcription here is from the 1955 facsimile of the 1596 original and follows the norms detailed in the preface, generally preserving anachronistic orthography present in the original text except in cases where it might make it difficult for modern Spanish readers to sound out the words correctly or follow the intended sentence structure.

Spanish

Capitulo LV. De como el padre fray Luys Cancer vino á Mexico, y para hazer jornada á la Florida, fue por licencia á España, y la traxo, y fue.

Asentada nuestra Fe por mano del be[n]dito padre fray Luys Ca[n]cer en aquella Provincia de la Verapaz, desseoso de salir en otras con el mesmo efecto, se vino al conve[n]to de Mexico, donde estuvo algunos años dando maravillosa exe[n]plo, administrando á los Indios, y esperando siempre nueva occasion en q[ue] ocuparse. Siempre tenia muy assentada en su coraçon la tierra de la Florida, aunque sabian quan hostigados estavan aquellos Indios, y quan aborrecible les era el nombre de Christiano, peor que á los de la Verapaz, por aver sido mas cruel su guerra. Con el desengaño que avia conquistado la Provincia que ya dexava con religiosos, entendio plantar el Evangelio en la de la Florida; y dexando concertado co[n] fray Gregorio de Beteta que avian de acometer los dos aquella empresa, determinó el bendito padre de yr á España, y traer licencia para aquel viaje, como luego lo puso en execucion. Salio de Mexico para la corte del Emperador Carlos. V. adonde estava el buen Obispo de Chiapa Don fray Bartolome de las Casas, cuyos inte[n]tos eran los proprios que llevava el buen religioso, desseando q[ue] la predicacion Evangelica entrasse con paz, y la gozasse[n] las almas por la Fe y caridad, espera[n]do la perfecta en la gloria. Navegando el siervo de Dios para España, cayo en manos de los Turcos q[ue] le captivaron, y le pusieron luego co[n] amo. Corria[n] ento[n]ces los Turcos la costa de España, porq[ue] andavan en este tie[n]po las guerras de nuestro Emperador con el Rey Francisco de Fra[n]cia, y avian venido Turcos assalariados del Rey Fra[n]ces co[n]tra el Emperador, y los q[ue] andavan por la mar hazian el daño q[ue] podian á los Españoles q[ue] avian á las manos. No dexó de entristecerse de aquel successo el fervoroso predicador de Christo sintie[n]do q[ue] le cortasse el hilo de sus inte[n]tos: pero como rendido en todo á la voluntad de Dios, estava co[n]tento con su suerte pues q[ue] Dios se la embiava. Al dese[n]-barcar aquella nao co[n] la priessa para bolver en busca de otras, llegó á ver la gente q[ue] en ella venia un cavallero Frances muy principal, y viendo al be[n]dito padre tan religioso y compuesto, se llegó á el con sentimie[n]to de su prision, y le dixo—Que siente aora vuestra reverencia? Siento (respondio el bendito padre) q[ue] se haze en mi la volu[n]tad de Dios, y huelgome mucho desto: porque aunque yo yva á tratar negocios de no menos importancia q[ue] la salud de muchas almas, para emplear mi vida segú[n] mi profession, pero pues quiere Dios que la vida sea en captiverio, mi vida es suya, y yo lo soy, hagase su volu[n]tad. Quedó tan edificado el cavallero con aquellas palabras, q[ue] luego sin dilacion le rescató, dando al capitan lo q[ue] quiso pedir, y avió al bendito religioso para q[ue] prosiguiesse su viaje, y tomasse puerto en España, de donde estaban muy cerca. Agradecio mucho el regalo, dando gracias á nuestro Señor, á quien reconocia por autor principal de todas aquellas mercedes. Fuese derecho á la Corte del Emperador, adonde halló al buen Obispo, co[n] cuyo favor esperava tenerle para su despacho desseado. Holgose mucho el Obispo de ver aquel Apostol de la Verapaz, y estimava el santo zelo que le traia de Provincia en Provincia, y de tierra en mar, y de mar en captiverio, y de captiverio le avia llevado á la Corte, procurando conversion de infieles y salud de almas. Fueronse los dos á tratar el caso co[n] el Christianissimo Emperador Do[n] Carlos, y como el hilo q[ue] descubria el padre fray Luys Cancer era el que tenia recogido en ovillo el buen Obispo, començo á tratar la materia con la fuerça de su espiritu y con la verdad del caso, que es mayor que qualquiera espiritu de ho[n]bres, y la verdad es de Dios declarada en su Evangelio. Quadraronle al piadosissimo Principe las bien fundadas razones que oia, y dixo al padre fray Luys Cancer, que traçasse todo lo que quisiese, y como lo quisiese, porq[ue] para todo ello hallaria su voluntad y favor. Besole las manos con much agradecimiento el buen frayle, diziendo que no avia menester mas de que el Virrey de Mexico le aviase en un navichuelo con otros tres frayles, para que fuessen á la tierra de la Florida.

Mandó el Emperador que assi fuesse, y despachó luego una cedula hablando con el Virrey y Governador de Nueva España, y mandandole expressamente con grande rigor que sin dilacion hiziesse lo que el padre fray Luys Cancer pedia, dandole matalotaje, gente de mar, y todo lo que el dixesse ser neces-sario para su avio. Cobrada esta cedula trató el buen Obispo con el padre fray Luys Cancer, que no tomasse puerto en parte alguna de las que los Espa-ñoles avian atemorizado los años passados, porque toda aquella tierra estava corriendo sangre de Indios, y pidiendo vengança contra los Españoles de la condicion de los passados, les quitassen luego la vida en desembarcando: sino que pues era la costa larga, y la tierra muy espaciosa, se fuesse á otro puerto, para conseguir el que desseava dar á las almas con la paz Evangelica, como le avia dado en la tierra de la Verapaz. Con esta instruccion se despidio del buen Obispo y en la primera occasion vino á la Nueva España, parecien-dole que se tardava ya en ver á Mexico, y aviarse para su desseada jornada. Llegó á Mexico, y fue muy bien recebido de todos, en particular del padre fray Gregorio de Beteta, que le esperava con zelo no menos desseoso de la salud de las almas, y dada la provision Real al Virrey Don Antonio de Mendoça, con toda brevedad mandó que se aprestasse un navio acomodado para aquel viaje, y todo lo que el padre fray Luys Cancer pidiesse, como se hizo. Salieron de Mexico para esta empressa otros tres religiosos, y assi por todos yva[n] cinco: Fray Luys Cancer, fray Gregorio de Beteta, fray Juan Garcia, fray Diego de Tolosa, y un hermano donado que se llamava Fuentes. Fueronse al puerto de San Juan de Ulua, donde tenia la prodencia del Virrey prevenido todo lo que el padre fray Luys avia querido pedir, y encome[n]dandose á Dios se hizieron á la vela en demanda de la Florida, que no lo fue para ellos, pues se quedó en semilla el grano de sus buenos desseos sin que floreciesse, ni aun se sembrasse en aquella tierra, con llamarse Florida.

English

Chapter LV. How Father Fray Luís Cancer came to Mexico, and how, in order to make a journey to Florida, he went for permission to Spain, obtained it, and went.

Our Faith having been established in the province of Verapaz by the hands of the blessed Father Fray Luís Cancer,[1] being desirous of going forth in other [provinces] for the same effect, he came to the convent of Mexico, where he remained several years giving a marvelous example, administering to the Indians, and always waiting for a new opportu-nity in which to occupy himself. He always held the land of Florida very close to his heart, although it was known how harassed those Indians were, and how abhorrent the name of Christian was to them, worse than to those of Verapaz, on account of the war against them having been more cruel. With the knowledge that he had conquered the province that he already left with missionaries, he intended to plant the Gospel in that of Florida. And leaving it arranged with Fray Gregorio de Beteta that the two would embark on that undertaking, the blessed father determined to go to Spain and bring permission for that voyage, which he immediately placed in execution. He left from Mexico for the court of Emperor Charles V, where the good Bishop of Chiapas Don Fray Bartolomé de las Casas was, whose intentions were the same that the good missionary had, desiring that the preaching of the Gospel should enter with peace, and that souls should enjoy it in faith and charity, awaiting perfection in glory. While the servant of God was navigating toward Spain, he fell in the hands of the Turks, who captured him, and who immediately placed him with a master. The Turks were cruising the coast of Spain, because in that time the wars between our Emperor and King Francis of France were under way, and Turks hired by the French king had come against the Emperor, and those who traveled by sea did whatever damage they could to the Spaniards they had at hand. That occurrence did not fail to sadden the fervent preacher of Christ, regretting that the thread of his intentions was severed, but since he surrendered everything to the will of God, he was content with his fortune, since God sent it to him. Upon that *nao*,[2] unloading hurriedly in order to return in search of others, a very important French knight managed to see the people who came in it, and seeing the blessed father so religious and composed, he came to him in pity of his imprisonment, and asked him, "How is your reverence feeling?" "I feel" (responded the blessed father) "that the will of God is being done in me, and I am very happy for this, because I was going to deal with business of no less importance than the health of many souls, in order to employ my life according to my profession, but since God wishes that my life should be in captivity, my life is his, and I am his, and will do his will." The knight was so edified by those words that immediately and without delay he rescued him, giving the captain what he wished to ask for, and supplied the blessed missionary so that he might proceed in his voyage and make port in Spain, which was very close. [Fray Cancer] very much appreciated the gift, giving thanks to Our Lord, whom he recognized as the principal author of all those mercies. He went directly to the court of the Emperor, where he found the good Bishop, with whose favor he hoped to obtain his desired mission. The Bishop was very pleased to see that Apostle from Verapaz, and esteemed the holy zeal that he brought from province to province, and from land to sea, and from sea to captivity, and his captivity had carried him to the court, procuring the conversion of pagans and the health of souls. The two of them went to discuss the case with the Most

Christian Emperor Charles, and since the thread that Father Fray Luís Cancer discovered was that which the good Bishop had gathered into a ball, he began to discuss the matter with the force of his spirit and the truth of the case, which is greater than any human spirit, and the truth is of God, declared in his Gospel. The well-founded reasons that he heard squared well to the most pious Prince, and he told Father Fray Luís Cancer to trace out everything he might want, and however he might want it, because in everything he would find his will and favor. The good friar kissed his hands with great appreciation, saying that nothing was needed other than that the Viceroy of Mexico should supply him with a small ship with another three friars so that they might go to the land of Florida. The Emperor commanded that this should be done, and immediately dispatched a decree communicating with the Viceroy and Governor of New Spain, and commanding him expressly with great rigor that without delay he should do what Father Fray Luís Cancer asked, giving him supplies, sailors, and everything that he said was necessary for his provision. Having collected this decree, the good Bishop discussed with Father Fray Luís Cancer that he should not take port in any place where the Spaniards had terrorized in past years, because all that land was running with the blood of Indians, and seeking vengeance against the Spaniards from the condition of those in the past, they would immediately take their lives upon disembarking. Since the coast was long, and the land very spacious, they should go to another port in order to achieve that which he desired to give to the souls with the peace of the Gospel, as he had given them in the land of Verapaz. With this instruction he excused himself from the good Bishop, and on the first occasion he came to New Spain, seeming to him that he was running late in seeing Mexico and supplying himself for his desired journey. He arrived in Mexico, and was very well received by everyone, especially by Father Fray Gregorio de Beteta, who awaited him with a zeal no less desirous for the health of souls. And having given the royal provision to the Viceroy Don Antonio de Mendoza, with all brevity he commanded that a ship suitable for that voyage should be prepared, and everything that Father Fray Luís Cancer might ask for, as was done. There left from Mexico for this enterprise another three missionaries, and thus in all there were five who went: Fray Luís Cancer, Fray Gregorio de Beteta, Fray Juan Garcia, Fray Diego de Tolosa, and a lay brother named Fuentes. They went to the port of San Juan de Ulua, where the care of the Viceroy had prepared everything that Father Fray Luís had wished to ask for, and commending themselves to God, they made sail in search of Florida, which was not so for them, since the seed of their good desires failed to flower, even though it was sown in the land called Florida.[3]

Diary of the Luís Cancer Expedition, 1549

The following account is a remarkable day-by-day and moment-by-moment account of the tragic 1549 expedition of Dominican friar Luís Cancer and his companions to the gulf coast of Florida (Cancer and Beteta 1549). What makes this narrative so moving is that it was written during the expedition and that the second author (Fray Beteta) took over the narrative after the brutal murder of Fray Cancer. Included in the original dispatch to the Spanish Crown was the original diary of Cancer. The first eight folios were penned on both sides in his own handwriting (with subsequent marginal notes and corrections by Beteta), and the last three were penned by Beteta, whose handwriting was notably different. A second, more polished final version of the edited text was written entirely in the hand of Beteta and submitted with the original diary, with only a few differences and errors in transcription.

The transcription and translation here use the original texts of Frays Cancer and Beteta as the primary narrative. The beginning of the section written by Beteta is indicated by a bracketed heading. Marginal notes and corrections inserted by Beteta in Cancer's original text (and any differences between the final version and the original draft version) are set off in brackets and italicized. Extensive endnotes are provided regarding divergences between the two texts. The pagination is indicated both for the original Cancer diary and the subsequent Beteta transcription, though it should be noted that the papers of the original Cancer version were repaginated out of order in modern times at the Archivo General de Indias, resulting in the following order for the eleven folios of the manuscript on which there is writing: folio 1 (the cover page), folios 4–11, followed by folio 3, folio 2, and folio 14.

Spanish

[Relacion de la Florida para el ill[ustrisi]mo s[eñ]or el visorrey de la Nueva España la qual truxo fray Gregorio de Beteta]

[Cancer f. 1r;[4] Beteta f. 1r] Con mas espacio y tiempo de q[ue] al presente tengo comence a notar y escrivir lo que cada dia pasava en esta jornada de la Florida porq[ue] el olvido preter yntençionem[5] no me hiziese escrivir mas o menos d[e] lo q[ue] convenia, porq[ue] como este negocio es ya sido tenido por cosa muy notable de buena si acertavamos o de muy mala si herravamos sienpre crey y tuve por mi q[ue] avian de pasar cosas muy notables de gozo y de tristeza y ansi en la verdad an pasado y no menos lo traya pensado sino q[ue] avia de suçeder aun mas d[e] lo q[ue] hasta el p[re]sente emos visto y remitome a la obra q[ue] es quedarme solo en tan gran desierto aunq[ue] muy acompañado de muy firme y cierta esperança [y probabilidad][6] q[ue] n[uest]ro s[eñ]or qui est potens de lapidibus istis suscitare filios habrahe[7] los alumbrara y a mi guardara para q[ue] esta obra se haga muy en servic[i]o de n[uest]ro s[eñ]or donde los q[ue] no tiene ojos veran y los q[ue] no tiene oydos oyran como n[uest]ro señor qu[an]do quiere hazer una muy dibina y admirable obra, la pone en terminos y medios tan al pareçer d[e] los onbres perdidos q[ue] no ay esperança de bien alguno y al mejor t[iem]po levanta y alça dios su obra eligiendo p[ar]a ella no los mas rycos ni sabios ni poderosos a sus ojos sino contemtebilia mudi ut confundat que que forcia porque desto resulte q[ue] los ho[n]ores Y alabanças q[ue] se avian de dar al gran poder ryq[ue]za o sabiduria de dios n[uest]ro s[eñ]or al qual suplico me de su gr[aci]a y divino y singular auxilio y a los q[ue] esta breve relacio[n] leyeren ruego q[ue] supliquen a la mag[esta]d divina q[ue] en todo y por todo me alumbre y guarde q[ue] no le ofenda y a estas gentes convierta p[ar]a q[ue] le conoscan sirvan y amen.

[Cancer f. 1v] [*Fray Gregorio en la Havana se quiso yr al rrio q[ue] llaman de San Elena fuera de la canal de Bahama en una caravela q[ue] yva a Castilla por no yr adonde oviesen llegado españoles dexolo porq[ue] la caravela no lo quiso llevar.*]

Dexado aparte el quando y como salimos y lo q[ue] a pasado desde la Vera Cruz y desde la Havana hasta llegar a vista desta tierra que fue la vigilia de la Gloriosa Acension de N[uest]ro S[eñ]or dire brevemente lo q[ue] el tiempo me dara lugar porq[ue] estoy en la chalupa donde me llevan a tierra y do[nde] tengo de q[ue]dar y aunq[ue] conosco q[ue] fuera mejor yr pensando y llorando mis pecados como desterrado q[ue] solo Dios sabe q[ue] sera de mi huelgo enpero de tomar este trabajo por dar cuenta a quien conviene de una obra tan grande como es esta.

Llegados q[ue] fuimos a vista desta t[ie]rra q[ue] como e dicho fue a la vigilia de la Gloriosa Ascensio[n] de N[uest]ro S[eñ]or surgimos en menos de X brazas en XXVII grados poco mas u menos luego el dia siguiente q[ue] fue la fiesta salio la chalupa a t[ie]rra y con [Beteta f. 1v] cinco o seys marineros y aunq[ue] el piloto les mando q[ue] no saltasen ni llegasen a t[ie]rra m[as] de reconocerla y a si avia puerto p[ar]a surgir el navio, ellos lo hizieron al rebes q[ue] como biero[n] tan hermosas arboledas acordaro[n] de saltar en t[ie]rra y al t[iem]po q[ue] lo querian hazer uno dellos vio tres yndios y comiença a bozear diziendo yndios yndios los demas sin acordarse de vellos do[nde] estavan o como venian echaron mano los unos a la triza y los otros a los remos uno de los q[ua]les pensando q[ue] ya estavan con ellos dixo juro a tal q[ue] nos estan desfondando el barco. En fin ellos se fuero[n] y antes q[ue] llegasen al navio dales una tan grande refriega q[ue] los hizo descaer harto

del navio y por estar en peligro mando el piloto alcar las anclas y hazernos a
la vela para yr lo a guarecer q[ue] cierto holgara[n] algunos dellos antes verse
entre los yndios q[ue] en aq[ue]lla refriega.

[Cancer f. 2r] [*Aqui quiso el p[adre] fray grego[ri]o sallir a tierra co[n]
propo[si]to de q[ue]darse en ella au[n]q[ue] no parecia yndios temyendo lo
q[ue] despues succedio no le dexaro[n] sallir.*][8]

E como calmase el viento e t[iem]po mando el piloto q[ue] no desfiriesen las
velas y ellos se allegaro[n] poco a poco al navio y entrados començaron a
dezir cada uno de la feria como le fue en ella rogue al piloto q[ue] los repre-
hendiese porq[ue] otro dia se enme[n]dasen y visto q[ue] en aq[ue]lla costa
no avia señal de puerto q[ue] buscavamos q[ue] en la verdad estava bien
cerca de alli alexamonos pensando q[ue] estaba mas arriba hazia la bahia
de Miruelo o de Apalache y llegamos a los XXVIII grados y m[edi]o[9] y salio
luego la chalupa a t[ie]rra [*porq[ue] el navio no podia llegar a la costa co[n]
6 leguas*] el p[ad]re fray Jua[n] e yo fuimos en ella y a las tres leguas andadas vimos t[ie]rra y estavamos della otras tres leguas pasavamos por quatro
tres y dos braças hasta llegar a una pequeña bahia do[nde] saltamos todos
y no do[nde] yo quise q[ue] por no aver seys yndios en [e]l monte do[nde]
saltamos no venimos todos flechados, y fue hasta bobedad dexar de yr a la
çavana rasa do[nde] podiamos ser señores de los enemigos e yrnos a meter
entre mo[n]tes dormimos aq[ue]lla noche en una ysleta algo apartada de la
t[ie]rra y alli ovo otro descuydo q[ue] fue q[ue]dar la chalupa encallada en
seco q[ue] fue nec[esari]o aguardar a la creçiente de la mañana tambien alli
nos podian hazer harto mal solas dos canoas de yndios, aq[ue]lla mañana
fuemos otras tres leguas mas adelante en busca de puerto e como no vimos
cosa buena bolvimonos al navio q[ue] estava de nosotros IX leguas aunq[ue]
las tres ellos se avian acercado en n[uest]ra busca q[ue] fue tanto q[ue] a no
los hallar tan cerca nos echava bien lexos dellos una muy gra[n]de refriega y
por se aver llegado nosotros entrados y ello q[ue] llegava. Entonces y muchas
vezes avise y rogue al piloto q[ue] no nos descuydasemos tanto porq[ue]
qu[an]do ni como [Cancer f. 2v] piensan los onbres se hallan engañados
yo no osaba hablar porq[ue] no falto q[ui]en me dixo q[ue] temorizava los
marineros con mis temores [*Dezia lo fray Grego[ri]o porq[ue] los marineros
estava[n] ta[n] temerosos q[ue] cada dia se amotinavan en el navio sobre la
yda y no avia quie[n] osase yr en la chalupa a tierra ni osava[n] llegar co[n]
un tiro de arcabuz*] [Beteta f. 2r] partidos de alli bolvimos a desandar lo andado de suerte q[ue] surgimos çerca do[nde] p[rimer]o aviamos reconoçido
la t[ie]rra el piloto con los marineros y chalupa van a t[ie]rra a descubrir
puerto[10] o rastro de yndios yo fui con el y el padre fray Di[eg]o de Tolosa e
yvamos por una bahia adentro sin pensamie[n]to de ver yndios y qu[an]do no

nos catamos dize uno bohios bohios y vistos echamos el reson y eran unos
tres o quatro ranchos de pescadores: el padre fray Di[eg]o y Fuentes q[ue]
era un bueno y devoto onbre q[ue] trayamos rogaro[n]me q[ue] los dexase
saltar en t[ie]rra y como no avia ni pareçia gente y el piloto estava delevada
pareçiome q[ue] era mejor salir a ver sy avia gente q[ue] bolvernos al navio
sin nuevas porq[ue] ya algunos religiosos andava[n] por saltar en t[ie]rra y
meterse por los mo[n]tes adelante [antes por no yr a la baya del s[piritu]
s[ant]o] como veian q[ue] no hallava el piloto la bahia del Spiritu S[an]to
y viendo esto pareçiome q[ue] los devia dexar e yo no los podia estorvar
porq[ue] otro mandava mas q[ue] yo.

El religioso y el buen onbre se q[ue]rian meter la t[ie]rra dentro dos leguas y
por q[ue] no lo hiziesen dixeles [pareceme q[ue]][11] el uno a de saltar en
t[ie]rra y si no q[ui]siere yo saltare rogaron me mucho q[ue] los dexase
saltar juntos no [me][12] pareçio q[ue] convenia [por lo d[ic]ho][13] en fin salto el
religioso y dixele q[ue] si no viese yndios q[ue] se subiese en un arbol y q[ue]
desde alli sin entrar la t[ie]rra adentro veria lo q[ue] avia, el subio y estando
mirando a una p[ar]te y a otra sale un yndio y luego otro de entre los arboles y vanse p[ar]a el religioso salen mas hasta XV, o XX yndios [Cancer f. 3r]
todos nos holgamos por ver lo q[ue] buscavamos y deseavamos aunq[ue] en
parte me peso mucho porq[ue] q[ui]siera como siempre lo traya ordenado y
bien pensado de estar en la chalupa tres y quatro oras aguardando si veia-
mos gente vi q[ue] no se podia hazer porq[ue] ya andavan cansados piloto
y marineros vistos los yndios eche luego la lengua q[ue] era una yndia q[ue]
trayamos de la Havana y era de alli y con ella salio el buen onbre Fue[n]tes: el
piloto no me dexava salir e yo tenido por cierto q[ue] con la lengua y con dalles algo no harian mal al religioso alçadas las faldas sin dezir nada al piloto
echome a la mar el agua a la çinta y sabe n[uest]ro señor con quanta prisa
yva porq[ue] no despachasen al religioso antes de ser oydo a lo q[ue] yvamos
llegado a la playa hincome de rodillas y pedida la gr[aci]a y divino auxilio
subo al llano a do[nde] los halle juntos: y antes de llegar a ellos hago otra vez
lo mysmo q[ue] en la playa y levantado comienço a sacar de la manga ciertas
cosas de Flandes q[ue] aunq[ue] p[ar]a los xpianos sean pocas y de poco
preçio y valor p[ar]a ellos fue mucho y muy preçiado todo. Luego se llegan a
mi y dado p[ar]te de lo q[ue] traya voyme al religioso q[ue] venia p[ar]a mi y
abraçolo con harto plazer hincamonos entrambos de rodillas y el español y
la yndia y sacado el libro dezimos las ledanias encomendandonos a n[uest]
ro señor y a sus santos los yndios se hincaron de rodillas otros en costillas de
q[ue] harto me holgue y como se levantavan[14] dexe a medio dezir las ledanias
y sientome con ellos en una barbacoa y brevemente supe do[nde] estava el
puerto y bahia q[ue] buscavamos q[ue] estava de alli por t[ie]rra jornada y
m[edi]a diximosles n[uest]ro yntento y deseos.

[Cancer f. 3v; Beteta f. 2v] La yndia en ver tanta paz estava muy alegre y dixome padre yo no te dixe q[ue] como yo los hablase no te matarian estos son de mi t[ie]rra y este es de mi lengua sabe n[uest]ro señor quanto nos holgamos de verlos en tanta paz como nos mostravan q[ue] de tantos abraçados estava bien almagrado y aq[ue]llo y mas sufriera en los abitos: porq[ue] dexasen la carne segura. Yo por ver si estava libre y me dexarian yr a la chalupa use desta cautela q[ue] les dixe q[ue] tenia mas q[ue] les dar y q[ue] yva por ello y en la verdad ya yo lo tenia en la manga y no lo q[ui]se dar todo porq[ue] tenia yntento de hazer esto fui y bolvi, y halle tantos q[ue] me venian abraçar q[ue] no me podia apartar dellos: su amor y amicicia cierto de creer es q[ue] era mas por lo q[ue] pensavan[15] aver q[ue] por nosotros empezo como esto es camino destotro segun todos espirime[n]tamos y dezimos q[ue] obras son amores y dadivas q[ue]bra[n]tan penas holgue q[ue] nos hiziesen buen recibimi[en]to por aq[ue]l [temporal]:[16] lo demas verdadero y espiritual ello se vendria poco a poco: como el temor servil q[ue] se tiene por bueno porq[ue] despues del suçede y entra el filial y verdadero. Mucho me admire q[ue] como todos pedian cuentas cuchillos machetes q[ue] no los llevava no osavan arebatar nada de lo q[ue] delante de mi tenia, antes dandolo yo al hijo del casiq[ue] q[ue] lo repartiese me dixo q[ue] lo repartiese yo y los contentase esto me dixo con la lengua.

El piloto me dava mucha priesa q[ue] me fuese a enbarcar por do[nde] no estuve lo q[ue] convenia el religioso dixo q[ue] se q[ue]ria q[ue]dar con Fue[n]tes y la lengua e yrse por t[ie]rra yo no se lo podia enpedir porq[ue] como e dicho otro ma[n]dava mas q[ue] yo el se q[ue]do en mucha paz q[ue] fue tanta q[ue] un marinero salto a t[ie]rra dos vezes y bolvio y un yndio subio en la chalupa y dixo q[ue] lo llevasen al navio con yntento q[ue] le diesen algo [Cancer f. 4r] y dado buelvese a salir a t[ie]rra: otras muchas señales de paz vimos alli de q[ue] q[ue]damos muy alegres yo dixe al religioso q[ue] me aguardase alli mientras yva al navio y volvia p[ar]a traerlas de comer y q[ue] llevar al caçiq[ue] ydo a enbarcar entrase un yndio conmigo en [e]l batel y vamos a la nao todos con mucha alegria y con la misma fuemos recibidos de los q[ue] estavan dentro[17] luego doy de comer al yndio y de bestir y venimonos do[nde] dexavamos al religioso a tres tiros de piedra digo[18] al araez de la chalupa mala señal es en no salir el conpañero a t[ie]rra. Llegados a los dos tiros digo[19] peor es esta llegados al uno como no salia: digo[20] tened la chalupa y pongase todo como conviene p[ar]a huyr, o amp ararse de las flechas. A todo esto estavan en la playa quatro o seys yndios a vezes q[ue] nos aguardavan con el pescado en las manos: llegados dan nos bozes muchas vezes q[ue] saliesemos por ello y q[ue] el caçiq[ue] estava en los bohios con los xpianos: estuvimos en esto harto t[iem]po aguardando ellos a q[ue] nosotros saliesemos a t[ie]rra y nosotros a q[ue] ellos viniese a la chalupa. Un marinero sin dezir nada echase al agua por el pescado y pensando q[ue] estava todo muy

seguro como a la mañana lo estuvo sube a los bohios y un yndio: buena y
limpiamente llegase a el y poco a poco llevase del braço de aq[ui] p[ar]a alli.
El pobre luego devio de sentir la yerba porq[ue] me llamava [Beteta f. 3r] a
gran priesa q[ue] saliese con la +[21] yo le dixe q[ue] me fuese a llamar al religioso p[er]o el fue no se adonde y buelve con el yndio al lado y dixo q[ue] alli
çerca estava con el caçiq[ue] q[ue] saliese con la + y el pobre q[ui]siera me
coger pensando q[ue] por mi seriamos el e yo libres [Cancer f. 4v] yo como
triste onbre temi y tambien lo dixe p[ar]a guardarme p[ar]a qu[an]do mayor
nec[esida]d se ofreciese q[ue] es en la q[ue] al presente estoy[22] en fin yo le
dixe venid vos aca y luego yre yo alla respondio no me dexan salir estos, a
q[ue] vimos claramente q[ue] el religioso y el conpañero estavan de la misma
manera. Estuvimos hasta el sol puesto por aguardar si avia modo p[ar]a los
aver hasta q[ue] ellos se fuero[n] pr[eso]s y ansi nos fuimos nosotros con
harta tristeza y de otra manera q[ue] fuimos por la mañana otro dia salgo con
el padre fray Gregorio y visto q[ue] no parecio yndio sale en t[ie]rra y como
no viese gente buelvese a la chalupa y todos al navio: el q[ua]l se hizo luego
a la vela con esperança de ver al religioso y lengua en [e]l puerto [o *saber de*
todos ellos.][23]

Estuvimos mas de ocho dias en llegar a la entrada y otros tantos en entrar
dentro de la bahia q[ue] tenia seys o 7 leguas de conplido[24] entramos con
nec[esida]d de agua q[ue] tuvimos trabajo en la hallar: el dia de Corpus Cristi
salimos el padre fray Jua[n] e yo a t[ie]rra y como vimos lugar seguro p[ar]a
dezir misa diximosla entranbos y dicha llevamos el agua q[ue] buscavamos
otro dia estavamos con gran sospecha si era el puerto o no porq[ue] no podia
entrar el navio y estava en dos braças y aun no avia llegado a los bohios con
tres leguas fuimos a buscarlos: o a ver si parecia gente yo y el padre fray
Greg[ori]o y vimos un cerillo y ençima un buen bohio y a la puerta un solo
yndio q[ue] por muchos señales q[ue] hezimos q[ue] viniese por una camisa
no se mudo de do[nde] estava dexamos se la colgada en un palo en la mar
y vamos a otros bohios q[ue] estavan a mano yzquierda[25] [Cancer f. 5r] en la
costa una legua del cerrillo y visto q[ue] no avia ni pareçia gente echamos el
reson y comimos y aun dormimos todos buen rato y en todo este t[iem]po no
pareçia gente e ya q[ue] nos haziamos a la vela sale un yndio y con una varita
y ençima un manojo de plumas blancas y tras el otro yndio a grandes bozes
y corriendo diziendo amigos: amigos: bueno: bueno: estas y otras palabras de españoles nos dezian q[ue] de los xpianos q[ue] por aq[ui] pasaron
las devier[on] de [a]pre[n]der llegados a la playa llaman nos con la mano
diziendo ven aca ven aca: espada no: espada no: como si dixeran q[ue] era
gente paçifica q[ue] no tenian espadas y yo les dixe en su propia lengua he
oça uluata q[ue] q[ui]ere dezir nosotros somos onbres buenos: ellos todos
en grito y boz alta respondiero[n] lo mismo mucho hezimos porq[ue] se
llegasen[26] algunos a la chalupa enseñandoles camisas y como no se llegasen

determinamos de partir el camino saliendo el agua hasta la cinta el padre
fray Greg[ori]o con una camisa e yo con otra muy poco a poco y con harto
temor se allegavan a nosotros en fin llegados [Beteta f. 3v] el q[ue] traya
la señal de paz da la al padre y reçibe la camisa y el otro la q[ue] yo le di y
despues de aver con señales hablado un poco q[ue] nos truxesen el frayle y
cristianos y la lengua como nos lo prometiero[n] vanse a sus ranchos y nosotros al navio con harta alegria.

Aq[ui] se me olvido de dezir q[ue] despues de los dos saliero[n] de entre los
pinos XXX onbres bien dispuestos sin flechas mostrando señales de paz y
diziendo espada no daca machete ven aca daca camisa.

[Cancer f. 5v] [*Antes desto bolvimos a tierra como esta adela[n]te.*][27]

Llegados al navio pensando q[ue] llevamos grandes nuevas hallamos otras
muy mayores de plazer y de tristeza en q[ue] nos dizen aq[ui] vino y esta
un español de los soldados q[ue] truxo Soto q[ue] se a huydo de su amo en
una canoa mucho me holgue de tan buenas nuevas y harto en pro fueron de
n[uest]ro negocio si no añediera[n] otras mas terybles y tristes nuevas: en
q[ue] dixo q[ue] los yndios q[ue] avian reçibido al frayle y al conpañero los
mataron luego como los dexe: y q[ue] tenian bivo al marinero, y preguntado
como lo supo dixo yo lo [o]yo muchas vezes de otros yndios q[ue] los vieron
matar y aun yo vi el pellejo de la corona del religioso q[ue] me lo mostro un
yndio q[ue] lo traya enseñando y dixo q[ue] hazian y dezian muchas cosas
qu[an]do los matava[n]. Todo esto con ser harto terible cosa y muy peñosa
p[ar]a todos aun era pasadero y cosa que semejantes negoçios de fe traen
consigo y no menos lo pensava quantas vezes considero la grandeza deste
negoçio sino q[ue] con sangre como lo hiziero[n] los apostoles aviamos de
plantar y fundar aqui la fe y ley del q[ue] aun por nos la dar y predicar pa-
deçio y murio y por tanto pues esto es ansy y se prosupone a la predicaçion
de tan grande[28] ley no es de desmayar como ella vaya adelante, mas suçeder
tal cosa como la d[ic]ha y con esto ver como lo vi y oy aqui: que tan ynpor-
tante negoçio se deshiziese y bolviese atras q[ue] çierto no fuera adelante
bolviendo el navio a Mexico con tales nuevas fue p[ar]a mi una de las terybles cosas q[ue] en [e]l mundo podia oyr ni ver: y aun esto no era el sumo
mal [Cancer f. 6r] porq[ue] si agora no era n[uest]ro señor serbido q[ue] se
hiziese t[iem]po q[ue]dava p[ar]a ello: sino q[ue] de bolver atras con tales
nuevas apareçer y dicho casi de todos concluyrian (y mal concluydo) q[ue]
eran todos estos ynfieles dignos de muerte y mereçedores q[ue] los viniesen
a hazer guerra y tomar sus t[ie]rras aunq[ue] bien siento y tengo por çierto
q[ue] n[uest]ro Rey y sus consejeros como sabios y temerosos de ofender a
n[uest]ro s[eñ]or por solo lo hecho nunca tal cosa mandara[n].

Del s[eñ]or visorey de la Nueva España se q[ue] siente lo q[ue] yo siento
en este caso porq[ue] el conforme a la ley de xpo porq[ue] diziendo [me][29]
una vez que si açertava con este negoçio hazia una de las grandes cosas
q[ue] en las Yndias se an hecho y si no açertava hazia la peor obra q[ue] se
a hecho en Yndias, y preguntandole el porq[ue] era peor respondio porq[ue]
los asolarian a todos como no nos reçibiesen y nos matasen yo le respondi
y di las razones por donde si nos matasen luego al prinçipio a todos hazian
de su derecho y por solo ello no les podian hazer guerra su s[eñori]a como
xpiano Catolico respondio q[ue] era verdad pero q[ue] no lo dezia sino si nos
matasen despues de nos aver tenido: reçibido: y oydo mucho t[iem]po en sus
t[ie]rras porq[ue] ya entonçes pareçe q[ue] estan fuera de pasio[n] y saben
lo q[ue] hazen y lo q[ue] los religiosos pretenden esto respondio y aun en
tal caso ase pr[imer]o de mirar y mucho si los religiosos diero[n] ocasio[n]
basta[n]te a e[llo][30] [Cancer f. 6v] pero como el diablo es sutil nunca le faltan
grandes braços de onbres al pareçer santos y sabios del mundo con los
q[ua]les a las vezes acaba y haze mas con uno [Beteta f. 4r] destos p[ar]a
acometer q[ue] el rey con muchos buenos y santos p[ar]a se defender y
temiendo yo esto q[ue] no venga tan grande mal a esta t[ie]rra por mi q[ue]-
riendo les yo hazer bien pareçiome q[ue] tenia obligaçion y si no la tengo a lo
menos no me falta razon y causa legitima p[ar]a poner mi vida al ryezgo por
salvar tanta multitud de gentes esperando en n[uest]ro señor y en su gran
poder q[ue] me dara particular auxilio y a estos hombres y conoçimie[n]to
p[ar]a q[ue] yo a ellos les prediq[ue] y ellos a mi oyan y reçiben de paz, y
fuera desta grande esperança q[ue] tengo ay y tengo p[ar]a mi gran p[ro]va-
bilidad q[ue] es casi evidençia q[ue] no solo no me mataran mas me reçibiran
de paz: y oyran de muy buena gana las cosas de n[uest]ra santa fe catolica,
y si esto no tuviese por çierto no bastara todo el mu[n]do p[ar]a me detener
aq[ui]: estando en duda como lo estan mis conpañeros: q[ue] los mataran,
o los haran esclavos por lo q[ua]l ellos se buelven a mexico *[porq[ue] no
tiene[n] navio p[ar]a yr adela[n]te]*[31] e yo me q[ue]do solo en esta t[ie]rra y
el t[iem]po y obras mostrara[n] q[ue] en las obras arduysimas de n[uest]ro
señor ay mas q[ue] ver y sentir en ellos de lo q[ue] algunos piensan.[32]

[Cancer f. 7r] Aryba e dexado de contar por olvido [lo q[ue] paso] otra vez
q[ue] saltamos en t[ie]rra antes q[ue] supiesemos del xpiano q[ue] vino al
navio:

Y fue q[ue] como el dia antes [domingo 23 de junio][33] nos avian prometido
de traer la lengua y el religioso fuemos a t[ie]rra muy alegres y los traydo-
res avian se pasado a la p[ar]te contraria do[nde] p[rime]ro los hallamos
q[ue] fue hazia la vanda del leste[34] y aun p[rime]ro q[ue] saliese gente nos
hiziero[n] estar esperando gran rato pensa[n]do q[ue] nosotros saltariamos

y a cabo de rato dan nos bozes: y por llevar nos alla metense en el agua ocho
o diez yndios haziendo q[ue] yvan p[ar]a nosotros: no quisimos yr derechos a
los pinos do[nde] estavan porq[ue] nos pareçio q[ue] era çelada mas fuimos
mas adelante a lo raso y a lo q[ue] pareçio en [e]l salir de alli de mala gana
çierto tenian çelada o a lo menos sus arcos y flechas a los pies q[ue] no se
podian ver.

Llegados [ju[n]to][35] a la playa sin hazelles señal q[ue] se llegasen a nosotros
entra uno en la mar muy denodadamente q[ue] pareçia que le yva la vida en
ello y llegado dame el pescado q[ue] traya yo fue luego a dalle una camisa y
como no la pude sacar tan presto uno de mis conpañeros enojado yvale a dar
una tunica o saya suya demostro q[ue] era bueno llevar y tener q[ue] dalles
de lo q[ua]l e sido de muchos morm[ura]do por traelles estas cosas [Cancer
f. 7v] y reçibida la camisa llega otro con mas pescado no lo q[ui]se reçibir y
dile no se q[ue] cosas q[ue] tenia a mano y reçibidas pideme una + de dos
palmos o mas de palo q[ue] tenia en la mano yo pensando q[ue] la q[ue]ria
p[ar]a echalla en [e]l agua o coas semejante: no se la di pidela muchas vezes
yo dixe a mis conpañeros darsela e respondiero[n] q[ue] se la diese y dada
besala muy de veras y vase a t[ie]rra con muy gran priesa y dala a besar a la
yndia n[uest]ra lengua q[ue] aun no la conoçimos porq[ue] estava desnuda y
luego va de yndio en yndio dandosela a besar y despues q[ue] se fuero[n] va
delante de todos y con ella el mas contento del mu[n]do mucho note y me
holgue desto: p[ar]a el efecto en que al p[re]sente estoy.

La yndia davanos bozes q[ue] nos llegasemos[36] a t[ie]rra y dezia veni aca
q[ue] estos no traen ballestas uno de la chalupa dixo Madalena la lengua
[Beteta f. 4v] es[37] nadie lo pudo creer: y por mucho q[ue] la diximos q[ue] se
entrase en la mar p[ar]a q[ue] la pudiesemos oyr y conoçer no q[ui]so por los
yndios no le davan lugar en fin p[ar]a saber si era ella o no: echeme a la mar
el agua a la cinta y llegueme a medio camino y ella se llego a la playa y ansi
le pude ver hablar y conoçi q[ue] era la lengua de q[ue] mucho me holgue
dixelo a los de la chalupa y luego el padre fray Jua[n] [Cancer f. 8r] se echo
al[38] agua y llegose cabe mi y juntos supimos de la yndia muchas cosas en
espeçial nos dixo q[ue] el religioso y los dos xpianos estavan juntos en casa
de su caçiq[ue] y si ella mintio fue çierto q[ue] los caçiques la amenazaro[n]
q[ue] la mataria si lo dezia dyxo mas q[ue] toda la t[ie]rra se avia[39] aloro-
tado pensando q[ue] era armada y q[ue] ella les dixo como no veniamos
mas de quatro frayles a les predicar grandes cosas y q[ue] por eso se avian
juntado alli aquellos L[40] o sesenta onbres en esto el padre fray Gregorio
como deseava ver oportunidad p[ar]a se salir a t[ie]rra [por saber de los
co[n]pañeros][41] salta del[42] barco y pasa cabe mi q[ue] estava el agua casi a la
çinta hablado yo y el padre fray Jua[n] con la lengua y dizi[43] me q[ue]dase con
dios q[ue] yo me voy y mañana enbieme tal y tales cosas el padre fray Jua[n]

Garçia vase con el a t[ie]rra y con yntento de q[ue]darse yo me bolvi a la
chalupa sin llegar a t[ie]rra porq[ue] siempre temi las cautelas destos. Dende
a poco ruego al padre fray Jua[n] q[ue] se buelva a la chalupa p[ar]a tentar
si le dexavan y çierto segun el me dixo no le dexavan en fin el se vino a la
chalupa fray Greg[ori]o se q[ue]do: e yo fue a le hablar y conçer[*tar*]⁴⁴ como
otro dia nos viesemo[s] y el diese orden como los xpianos fuesen alli traydos
concluydo esto hago sacar⁴⁵ çierto presente p[ar]a el caçiq[ue] de hartas y
muchas cosas: y otras para los demas alli se diero[n] todas y p[ar]a todos
uno: el padre fray Jua[n] q[ue] estava a la sazo[n] en la chalupa [Cancer f. 8v]
vile çercado de yndios y estava espantado como ellos entravan tanto en
la mar: y los marineros los avian dexado llegar a la chalupa:⁴⁶ supe despues
q[ue] despojava a los marineros al uno q[ui]tava la camisa al otro el jubon
al otro el bonete p[ar]a dar aq[ue]llos yndios y despues me vi en harto trabajo en contener a los marineros y dalles en pago de lo q[ue] avian dado de
lo q[ue] trayamos aq[ui] tanbien sentiero[n] los padres quan bueno a sido
tener q[ue] dalles yo lo procure y lo truxe y como nu[n]ca me a pesado dello
menos agora y lo q[ue] agora veo con los ojos pr[imer]o lo senti con el entendimiento y lo ley en los doctores en especial Santo Thomas el Vitoria el
Gaetano y los decretos apruevan y lo tiene por muy bueno traer a los ynfieles
con buenos exemplos y dadivas de monusculos⁴⁷ [Beteta f. 5r] q[ue] q[ui]ere
dezir presentillos como son estos.

Dexado esto aparte los yndios dexanme bolver al barco y al padre fray
Greg[ori]o q[ue] se q[ue]ria q[ue]dar en t[ie]rra con ellos no lo dexaro[n] y
casi por la mano con una poca de media fuerça⁴⁸ le dixero[n] q[ue] se fuese a
la chalupa y ansi nos fuimos todos ellos a sus casas con yntento de traer los
cristianos: y nosotros al navio con yntento de los ver otro dia y dalles hachas
q[ue] nos pedian y desta vez llegados al navio supimos las nuevas dichas de
su triste muerte por cuya causa los padres y el piloto se quisiero[n] luego
bolver a Mexico: yo dixe q[ue] me q[ue]ria q[ue]dar por las razones dichas.⁴⁹

[Cancer f. 9r] [Beteta Text]

Antes q[ue] a este pu[n]to llegassemos vie[n]do el mal aparejo q[ue] en
aq[ue]l puerto avia p[ar]a lo q[ue] p[re]tendiamos sospecha[n]do q[ue] los
co[n]pañeros era[n] muertos como lo era[n] aviamos entre nosotros tratado
de yr a otra parte y visto q[ue] el navio no era p[ar]a aq[ue]lla costa porq[ue]
no podia llegar a tierra co[n] 5 o 6 leguas q[ue] no teniamos agua ni de
do[n]de poder tomar la q[ue] fuesse basta[n]te p[ar]a come[n]çar nuevo
viage toda la carne y pescado se avia echado podrido a la mar los marineros
cada dia se nos amotinava[n] q[ue] no avia quie[n] e[n] la chalupa quisiesse
yr a tierra y los mas dellos estava[n] co[n] cale[n]turas q[ue] apenas avia
quie[n] diesse a la bo[n]ba q[ue] en quatro ampolletas hazia el navio una de

agua aviamos co[n]cluydo de bolver o a la Havana o a la Nueva España y
tomar un barco y yr a otra p[ar]te de lo qual el p[adre] fray Luys no holgava
mucho y por esto se quiso poner al ult[im]o peligro q[ue] como el domingo
bispera de S[an] Jua[n] bolvimos a la nao muy desco[n]te[n]tos por no aver
visto ning[un]o de n[uest]ros co[n]pañeros au[n]q[ue] aviamos visto la yndia
especialm[ent]e fray Grego[ri]o tenia sospecha por averle los yndios asi
echado por fuerça llegados a la nao hallamos en ella un español llamado
Jua[n] Muñoz q[ue] desde el armada de Soto se avia alli q[ue]dado y ento[n]-
ces avia venido a la nao e[n] una canoa q[ue] casi ya no sabia hablar y luego
como llego a la nao como pudo dixo q[ue] avia[n] muerto los dos xpianos y
uno tenia[n] bivo y q[ue] el avia tenido el pellejo de la cabeça del religioso
en las manos lo mismo dixo qu[ando] llegamos siendo ya cierta la muerte de
los co[n]pañeros el p[adre] fray Jua[n] Gar[ci]a y fray Grego[ri]o de Beteta
dixero[n] a fray Luys pues aq[ue]llo asi avia sucedido fuesse[n] otro [Cancer f.
9v] dia como avia[n] puesto co[n] los yndios p[ar]a mas certificarnos y q[ue]
no pareciendo alg[un]o de n[uest]ros co[n]pañeros diessemos orde[n] en la
buelta o en yr a otra p[ar]te el dixo q[ue] el estava cierto q[ue] aq[ue]lla obra
no se avia de hazer sin sangre y pues alli avia muerto sus co[n]pañeros alli
q[ue]ria q[ue]dar porq[ue] alli pe[n]sava hazer[50] mas fruto y esperava ama[n]-
sarlos co[n] [Beteta f. 5v] darles lo q[ue] alli llevava determinado en esto no
quiso yr el dia de S[an] Jua[n] por escrivir ciertas cartas y aparejar las cosas
q[ue] avia de llevar no dexamos de dissuadirle la entrada todo aq[ue]l dia por
todos los medios q[ue] podimos p[er]o en el ap[ro]vecho poco n[uest]ra p[er]-
suasio[n] y ruego porq[ue] siemp[re] la tuvo por sospechosa y mas en esto.

Martes 25 de Junio de mañana entramos en la chalupa p[ar]a yr a tierra y
andados dos leguas nos da ta[n] gra[n] aguacero y vie[n]to por la proa q[ue]
pensamos p[er]ecer y muchas cosas de las q[ue] llevava p[ar]a tierra se da-
ñaron porq[ue] todas se hiziero[n] agua no podimos llegar a tierra y bolvimos
a la nao co[n] harto trabajo Jua[n] muñoz q[ue] avia sallido de la tierra q[ue]
yva co[n] nosotros le venia dizie[n]do q[ue] aq[ue]llo era q[ue] dios no q[ue]-
ria q[ue] alli saliesse porq[ue] luego lo avia[n] de matar porq[ue] ya ellos
sabria[n] q[ue] el se avia huydo y q[ue] la muerte de los otros era descubierta q[ue] no le aguardaria[n] nada y otras cosas semeja[n]tes q[ue] todos
le dezia[n] llegados a la nao aq[ue]lla noche torno a aparejar otras cosas
q[ue] llevar y miercoles 26 de Junio tornamos co[n] la chalupa a tierra y no
tuvimos menos trabajo de aguaceros aq[ue]l dia q[ue] el passado y nu[n]ca
pe[n]samos poder llegar a tierra p[er]o como siemp[re] se estava en su p[ro]-
po[si]to firme [Cancer f. 10r] de salir en aq[ue]lla tierra por no bolver otro dia
aguardamos q[ue] abona[n]çasse un poco y rema[n]do co[n] harto trabajo
de los marineros llegamos a tierra estava[n] alg[un]os yndios sobre arboles
a trechos q[ue] no lo tuvimos por buena señal luego como nos viero[n] se

baxaro[n] y fuero[n] corrie[n]do a un mo[n]tezillo do[n]de estava la ge[n]te
llegados cerca les dimos bozes y ellos respo[n]diero[n] p[er]o no uno dellos
q[ue] saliese del mo[n]te a lo raso p[re]gu[n]tados por la lengua dixero[n]
q[ue] estava en una casa lexos de alli alg[un]os passava[n] de una p[ar]te
a otra co[n] sus arcos y flechas y machanas[51] y dardos q[ue] claram[ent]e
se parecia[n] el p[adre] fray Luys se estava apareja[n]do p[ar]a sallir y fray
Grego[ri]o p[er]suadie[n]dole y roga[n]dole q[ue] no saliesse ellos p[re]gu[n]-
taro[n] de alla esta alla el yagué[52] q[ue] es el esclavo. Leva[n]tose en pie el
Jua[n] Muñoz y dixo q[ue] lo q[ue]reis yo soy pe[n]sais de matarnos como
matastes a los otros no matareis q[ue] ya se sabe co[n] esto parecio q[ue] se
turbaro[n] y el p[adre] fray Luys le dixo callad her[man]o no me los esca[n]-
dalizeis el p[adre] fray Grego[ri]o le dixo no puede[n] en el mu[n]do aver
ge[n]te mas esca[n]dalizada q[ue] esta por eso por amor de dios se dete[n]ga
un poco no salga no quiso sino arrojase al agua y vase a la tierra q[ue] esta-
riamos un tiro de ballesta del mo[n]tezillo llegado a tierra pidio una cruz
peq[ue]ña q[ue] se la avia olvidado au[n]q[ue] no avia peligro en llevarsela
yo le dixe padre por cha[rida]d venga v[uest]ra r[everencia] por ella porq[ue]
aqui no ay quie[n] la pueda llevar porq[ue] cierto esa ge[n]te esta de muy mal
arte el se fue por la playa y nosotros co[n] la chalupa [Cancer f. 10v] hazia
[Beteta f. 6r] el mo[n]tezillo do[n]de los yndios estava[n] q[ue] como viero[n]
q[ue] yvamos a ellos se come[n]çaro[n] a retraer el p[adre] fray luys nos dixo
q[ue] nos detuviessemos no le alborotassemos la ge[n]te el se llego cerca y
devio de come[n]çar a ver el peligro y hincose de rodillas y estuvo un poco
y fue se p[ar]a el mo[n]tezillo llegado cerca salio un yndio a el y abraçolo y
tomolo por un braço y llevalo algo de p[ri]sa y salle otro y otros lleva[n]do
lo a empellones a la entrada del mo[n]tezillo uno dellos diole de mano al
so[n]brero y derroçoselo de la cabeça y acudio otro co[n] una macana en la
cabeça y derroçolo nosotros estavamos bien cerca q[ue] viamos y oyamos
bie[n] claro lo q[ue] dezia e[n]to[n]ces dio un grito ay vala no le dexaro[n]
acabar q[ue] cargo ta[n]ta ge[n]te q[ue] lo acabaro[n] alli y da[n] una gra[n]
grita y sallen a flecharnos yo hize q[ue] nos hiziessemos un poco a la mar y
paramos a tiro de arco y sacaro[n] luego por alli los abitos y dada una rociada
de flechas se fuero[n] nosotros nos bolvimos a la nao no sin temor q[ue] avia
de sallir alg[un]as canoas.

Llegados a la nao luego acordamos de sallir de alli p[er]o no teniamos agua
aq[ue]l dia anduvimos a buscarla por la playa y tomamos una poca yo re-
q[ue]ri al pyloto nos llevasse a otra p[ar]te de la Florida como era obligado y el
respo[n]dio q[ue] estaria p[res]to p[er]o q[ue] no tenia agua ni la nao estava
p[ar]a come[n]çar nuevo viage q[ue] fuessemos a la Havana q[ue] era cerca y
tomado agua y p[ro]visio[n] lo haria y asi nos p[ar]timos de aq[ue]l puerto del
s[piritu] s[ant]o viernes[53] 28 de Junio p[ar]a yr a la Havana año 1549.

[Cancer f. 11r] Sallidos del p[uert]o del S[piritu] S[ant]o anduvimos co[n] suestes forçosos hasta el martes 2 de Jullio q[ue] la luna hizo quarto y parecio q[ue] se firmava en aq[ue]l vie[n]to el pyloto nos dixo q[ue] le parecia q[ue] viniessemos a la Nueva España porq[ue] hazia tiempos q[ue] no podriamos tomar la havana y teniamos falta de agua y p[ar]a la Nueva España era mas ciertos y favorables los tiempos yo estuve muy fuera de ello hasta q[ue] co[n] el p[adre] fray Jua[n] Gar[ci]a y co[n] los marineros se co[n]certaro[n] de yr a la Nueva España y por no ser solo en este parecer y porq[ue] llegado a la Havana es tarde p[ar]a come[n]çar viage nuevo y porq[ue] en la Nueva España se dara mejor corte a lo q[ue] se deviere hazer co[n]senti co[n] ellos y luego arribamos p[ar]a la Nueva España martes 2 de Jullio avie[n]doles el pyloto hecho mill jura[mien]tos y p[ro]testaciones q[ue] a[n]tes de ocho dias seria en la costa de Nueva España domingo 14 de Jullio nos hallamos en Yucata[n] costa de leste oest[e][54] en 20 g[ra]dos ta[n]to mas difficultoso de conocer do[n]de estavamos qua[n]to lexos[55] de do[n]de pe[n]savamos q[ue] era en los llanos de almeria al norte de la Vera Cruz llegamos a Sa[n]t Jua[n] de Lua[56] viernes 19 de Jullio 1549 años.

English

[Relation of Florida for the most illustrious señor the Viceroy of New Spain, which was brought by Fray Gregorio de Beteta]

[Cancer f. 1r; Beteta f. 1r] With more space and time than I have at the present, I began to note and write what happened each day on this journey to Florida, so that forgetfulness, against my intention, does not make me write more or less than is suitable. Inasmuch as this matter is now taken as a very notable thing of good if we succeed, or of great evil if we err, I always believed and held for my [part] that very notable things of pleasure and sadness had to happen, and thus in truth they have happened, and I had thought no less, but rather that even more would have to happen than we have seen. I remit myself to the work that is to remain alone in such a great desert, although very accompanied by a very firm and certain hope [and probability] that Our Lord, "who is able of these stones to raise up children to Abraham,"[57] will illuminate them and guard me so that this work is done in service of Our Lord, where those who have no eyes will see, and those who have no ears will hear. Our Lord, when he wishes to perform a very divine and admirable work, puts it in terms and means such that in the opinion of lost men there is no hope of any good, and at the best time God raises and elevates his work, choosing for it not the most rich or wise or powerful in his eyes, but rather "the contemptible things of the world, in order to confound the strong,"[58] because from this it results that the honors and praises must be given to the great power, richness, and wisdom of God Our Lord, to whom I implore that he gives me his grace and divine and singular aid. To those that read this brief relation, I pray that they implore the divine majesty that in everything and for everything, he enlightens and guards me so that I do not offend him, and so that I convert these people so that they know and serve and love him.

[Cancer f. 1v] [*Fray Gregorio in Havana wanted to go to the river called Santa Elena, outside the Bahama Channel, in a caravel that was going to Castille, in order not to go where Spaniards had arrived. This was abandoned because the caravel did not wish to carry them.*][59]

Leaving aside when and how we departed, and what has happened since Vera Cruz and since Havana until arriving in view of this land, which was on the vigil of the glorious Ascension of Our Lord,[60] I will tell briefly what time permits me, because I am in the shallop where they are carrying me to land, and where I have to remain.[61] Although I know that it would be better to think about and lament my sins as an outcast, only God knowing what will be of me, I am nonetheless delighted to take on this labor in order to give account to whom it is suitable regarding a work as great as this is.

Having arrived in view of this land, which as I have said was on the vigil of the glorious Ascension of Our Lord, we anchored in less than 10 fathoms at 27 degrees [latitude], more or less. Then the following day, which was the feast day, the shallop departed for land with [Beteta f. 1v] five or six sailors. Although the pilot commanded that they should not get off or even reach land any more than reconnoitering it and finding out if there was a port in which to anchor the ship, they did the opposite, and since they saw such beautiful groves of trees, they decided to get off on land. At the time that they wanted to do so, one of them saw three Indians, and he begins to shout, saying, "Indians, Indians," the rest of them without remembering where they were or how they were coming. Some of them laid hands on the rope, and others on the oars, and one of them, thinking that they were already upon them, said, "I swear to such-and-such that they are knocking the bottom out of the boat." In the end, they went away, and before they could arrive at the ship, they caused such a great scuffle that they made the ship drift significantly off course, and by being in danger the pilot ordered the anchors raised and to set sail to go take refuge. It is certain that some of them would enjoy seeing themselves among the Indians more than in that scuffle.

[Cancer f. 2r] [*Here Father Fray Gregorio wished to get off on land with the intention of remaining there. Although no Indians appeared, fearing what afterward happened, they did not let him leave.*]

And when the wind and weather calmed, the pilot ordered that they should not unfurl the sails, and little by little they reached the ship, and having entered, each one began to explain their part in the spectacle. I begged the pilot to reprimand them so that they would reform themselves the next day. Having seen that on that coast there was no sign of the port that we were looking for, which in truth was very near there, we distanced ourselves, thinking that it was farther up toward the bays of Miruelo or Apalache. We arrived at 28 and a half degrees [latitude] and then the shallop went forth to land [*because the ship could not reach nearer than 6 leagues from land*]. Father Fray Juan and I went in it, and after having traveled three leagues, we saw land, and we were another three leagues from it. We passed through four, three, and two fathoms until arriving at a small bay where we all got out, and not where I wanted to. If there had been six Indians in the woods where we landed, we would have all returned with arrow wounds, and it was almost idiocy not to go to the open field where we could be masters of our enemies, and to go put ourselves among woods. We slept that night on a little island somewhat separated from the land, and there was another oversight, which was that the shallop was stranded on dry land, and it was necessary to wait for the high tide of the morning. Also, just two canoes of Indians could have done us great damage there. That morning we went another three leagues farther on in search of the port, and as we saw nothing good, we returned to the ship, which was nine leagues from us, although it had approached three of them in search of us, which was so many that upon not finding us so close, they made a very great complaint from afar after we had already entered and while they were arriving.[62] Then and many times I advised and begged the pilot that we should not be so careless, because no matter when or how [Cancer f. 2v] men think, they find themselves deceived. I did not dare to speak, because I was not lacking in those who told me that I frightened the sailors with my fears. [*Fray Gregorio said so because the sailors were so afraid that each day they rebelled in the ship about the departure, and there was no one who dared to go in the shallop to land, nor did they dare approach within the distance of an arquebus shot.*][63] [Beteta f. 2r] Having departed from there, we backtracked along our route, in such a manner that we anchored near where we had first reconnoitered the land. The pilot with the sailors and shallop went to land to discover a port or any sign of Indians. I and Father Fray Diego de Tolosa went with him, and we went through an inland bay without thought of seeing Indians, and when we were not looking out for it, one of them said, "huts! huts!" Having seen them, we threw in the anchor,[64] and it was about three or four fishermen's shacks.[65] Father Fray Diego and Fuentes, who was a good and devoted man that we brought,[66] begged me to let them get out on land, and since there were no people, nor did they appear, and the pilot was ready to set sail, it seemed to me that it was better to get off to see if there were people than to return to the ship without news, because already some of the missionaries were preparing to debark on land and plunge forward into the woods [these in order not to go to the Bay of the Holy Spirit],[67] since they saw that the pilot could not find the Bay of the Holy Spirit. Seeing this, it seemed to me that I should let them go, and I could not impede them, because another commanded more than I.[68]

The missionary and the good man wished to go two leagues into the interior, and because I did not let them, [it seems to me that] I told one of them to get off on land, and if he did not wish to I would get off. They begged me much to let them get off together, but it did not seem suitable to me [on account of what I have said]. In the end, the missionary got off, and I told him that if he did not see Indians, he should climb a tree, and from there he would see what there was without entering into the interior. He climbed up and was looking from one side to the other, and an Indian came out and then another from among the trees, and they went toward the missionary. Up to another fifteen or twenty Indians also came out. [Cancer f. 3r] We were all pleased to see what we were searching for and desired, although in part it distressed me greatly because like always, I wanted things to be ordered and well thought out. From being in the shallop three and four hours waiting to see people, I saw that it could not be done, because the pilot and sailors were already tired. Then I sent out the interpreter, who was an Indian woman we brought from Havana, who was from there, and with her went the good man Fuentes. The pilot did not let me go. But since I considered it certain that with the interpreter, and with giving them something, they would do no harm to the missionary, having raised my robes, without saying anything to the pilot I jumped in the water, the water at my waist. Our Lord knows the urgency with which I went so that they would not send away the missionary before having heard why we were there. Having arrived at the beach, I kneeled down and asked for grace and divine aid. I ascended to the level ground where I found them together. And before reaching them, I did the same thing as on the beach, and having gotten up, I began to pull out of my sleeve certain things from Flanders, which although for Christians they are nothing and of little price and value, for them it was a lot, and all very esteemed. Then they reached me, and having given away part of what I brought, I went to the missionary who came toward me and embraced me with great pleasure. We both kneeled down, along with the Spaniard and the Indian woman, and having drawn out the book, we said the litanies, commending ourselves to Our Lord and his saints. The Indians all kneeled down, others prostrate, from which I was supremely pleased. When they got up, I stopped saying the litanies in the middle and seated myself with them on a bench, and in short order I found out where the port and bay we were searching for was, which was a day and a half's journey from there, and we also told them of our intentions and desires.

[Cancer f. 3v; Beteta f. 2v] The Indian woman, upon seeing such peace, was very happy, and told me, "Father, I did not tell you that since I spoke to them, they would not kill you. These are of my land, and this is my language." Our Lord knows how very pleased we were to see them in such peace, which they demonstrated to us. I was very flushed from so many embraces, but that and more I would suffer in my habit so that they would leave my skin safe.[69] In order to see if I was free, and if they would let me go to the shallop, I made use of this artifice: I told them that I had more to give them, and that I was going to get it, but in truth I already had it in my sleeve, and did not wish to give it all away because I had the intention of doing this. I left and came back, and found so many that came to embrace me that I could not separate myself from them. Their love and friendship are certain to believe, and were more than was initially thought. For us to begin like this is the road to something else.[70] As we have all experienced and said, works are love, and gifts lessen hardships. I was pleased that they received us well through that temporal means. The rest of the true and spiritual would come little by little, just as servile fear [of God] is considered good because afterward there occurs and enters that which is filial and true. I greatly admired how although they were all asking for beads, knives, and machetes that we did not carry, they did not dare to snatch away anything of what I had in front of me, but instead when I gave it to the son of the chief to distribute, he told me through the interpreter that I should distribute it, and that this would make them happy.

The pilot hurried me to go and embark, on account of which I was not where I should have been. The missionary said that he wished to remain with Fuentes and the interpreter and go by land. I could not impede him, because as I have said, another commanded more than I. He remained in much peace, which was such that a sailor got out on land two times and returned, and an Indian got up in the shallop and told them to take him to the ship with the intention that they should give him something, [Cancer f. 4r] and having given it he returned to land. We saw many other signs of peace, from which we remained very happy. I told the missionary to wait for me there while I went to the ship and brought something back to eat, and something to take to the chief. Having embarked, an Indian got in with me in the boat, and we went to the ship, all with great happiness, and we were received with the same by those who were within.[71] Then I gave the Indian something to eat and wear, and we came back where we had left the missionary. At three stones' throws distance, I said to the master of the shallop, "It's a bad sign that our companion doesn't come out on land." Having arrived at two stones' throws, I said, "This is worse." Arriving at one stone's throw, since he didn't come out, I said, "Hold the shallop, and get it ready to flee or protect yourself from arrows." During all this, there were four or six Indians at times who waited for us with fish in their hands. Having arrived, they shouted many times to us to come out for it, and that the chief was in the huts with the Christians. We were in this state a long time, with them waiting for us to get out on land, and us waiting for them to come to the shallop. Without saying anything, a sailor jumped in the water for the fish, and thinking that everything was very safe like it was in the morning, he climbed up to the huts, and an Indian easily and skillfully reached him and little by little took him by the arm from here toward there. The poor man must have felt the poison then, because he called me [Beteta f. 3r] with great urgency to get out with the cross. I told him that he should call to the missionary for me, but he went I don't know where, and returned with the Indian at his side and said that [the missionary] was near there with the chief, and that I should get out with the cross. The poor man wanted to grab hold of me, thinking that through me, he and I would both go free. [Cancer f. 4v] I was afraid, as a wretched man, and I also said it in order to preserve myself for when an even greater necessity should arise, which is the state in which I am now. In the end, I told him, "You come here, and then I will go there." He responded, "These [Indians] won't let me go," at which we saw clearly that the missionary and his companion were in the same manner. We remained until the sunset to wait and see if there was any way to get them, until they were carried away as prisoners, and thus we went away with great sadness, and in a different mood than we had gone with in the morning. The next day I came out with Father Fray Gregorio, and having seen that no Indian appeared, he got out on land, and since he did not see any people, he returned to the shallop, and everyone to the ship. Then the [ship] set sail with hopes of seeing the missionary and interpreter in the port [or of finding out about all of them].

We spent more than eight days in arriving at the entrance, and just as many in entering within the bay, which was six or seven leagues in length. We entered with need of water, and had difficulty in finding it. On the day of Corpus Christi,[72] Father Fray Juan and I got out on land, and since we saw a safe place to say Mass, we said it between the two of us, and after having said it, we got the water we were looking for. The next day we were very suspicious whether or not it was the port, because the ship could not enter, and it was in two fathoms and still had not arrived at the huts after three leagues. I and Father Fray Gregorio went to look for them, or to see if people appeared. We saw a little mound,[73] and on top of it a good hut, and at the door one solitary Indian, who despite many signals that we made for him to come for a shirt, did not move from where he was. We left it for him hanging on a stick in the ocean, and went to other huts that were on the left hand side [Cancer f. 5r][74] on the coast one league from the little mound. Having seen that there were no people, nor did they appear, we dropped the anchor and ate and even all slept a good period of time, and in all this time no people appeared. And when we were already setting sail, an Indian came out with a small pole with a handful of white feathers on top, and behind him another Indian, shouting and running, saying, "Friends, friends, good, good." These and other words of Spaniards they said to us, which they must have learned from the Christians who have passed by here. Having arrived at the beach, they called us with their hands, saying, "Come here, come here, no sword, no sword," as if they were saying that they were a peaceful people who had no swords. I said to them in their own language, "He oça uluata," which means, "We are good men." They responded the same, shouting and in loud voices. We made it so that some of them would reach the shallop, showing them shirts, and since they did not come, we determined to go ourselves, going out into the water up to the waist, Father Fray Gregorio with one shirt and I with another, very little by little. With great fear they approached us. In the end, [Beteta f. 3v] the one who brought the sign of peace arrived and gave it to the Father, and received the shirt and the other one that I gave him, and after speaking a little with signs that they should bring us the friar and Christians and the interpreter like they promised, they went to their shacks and we to the ship with great joy.

Here I forgot to say that after those two, thirty well-disposed men came forth from among the pines without arrows, showing signs of peace and saying, "No sword, *daca* machete, come here, *daca* shirt."[75]

[Cancer f. 5v] [*Before this we returned to land, as is [noted] further on.*]

Having arrived at the ship, thinking that we carried great news, we found others even greater of pleasure and sadness, in which they told us that a Spaniard, one of the soldiers that Soto brought, had fled from his master in a canoe, and came here and was here. I took great pleasure in such good news, and greatly in support of our endeavor, if they were not to have added other more terrible and sad news, that the Indians who had received the friar and his companion killed them as soon as I left them, and that they had the sailor alive. Asking how he knew this, he said, "I heard it many times from other Indians who saw them kill them, and I even saw the scalp of the missionary, which was showed to me by an Indian who was showing it around." And he said that they did and said many things when they killed them. All this, while being a tremendously terrible thing, and very painful for all, was still tolerable, and something that similar affairs of faith bring with them. And I thought no less each time I considered the greatness of this endeavor, but that it would be with blood, as was done by the apostles, that we would plant and establish here the faith and law of he who suffered and died himself in order to give it and preach it to us. And for this it is so, and it is presumed that the preaching of such a great law should not be cause for losing heart while it goes forward, even if something like the aforementioned should occur, and with this to see it as I saw it, and here today. If such an important endeavor should fall apart and turn back, it is certain that it would not go forward if the ship returned to Mexico with such news. This was for me one of the most terrible things that I could hear or see in the world. And even this was not the worst evil, [Cancer f. 6r] that if Our Lord was not served now, time would still be made for it, but rather that to turn back with such news, in the opinion and statement of almost everyone, they would conclude (and badly concluded) that all these pagans were worthy of death, and deserved to have war made upon them, and their lands taken. Nevertheless, I do feel and hold for certain that our king and his counselors, as wise and afraid of offending Our Lord, would never order such a thing on the basis of what has been done up to now.

I know that the señor Viceroy of New Spain feels as I feel in this case, because he conforms himself to the law of Christ, because he told me one time that if I succeeded with this affair, I was doing one of the greatest things that had been done in the Indies, and if I did not succeed, I was doing the worst deed that had been done in the Indies. Asking him why it would be the worst, he responded that it was because if they did not receive us and killed us, they would destroy them all. I responded to him and gave him the reasons why, if they should kill us all immediately at the beginning, they did so by their rights, and just for this His Grace could not make war on them as a Catholic Christian. He responded that it was true, but that he would not say so if they killed us after having received us and heard us for a long time in their lands, because then it would seem that they were beyond passion, and knew what they were doing, and what the missionaries were attempting. I responded that even in such a case, one would have to examine well if the missionaries gave sufficient occasion for it, [Cancer f. 6v] but since the devil is subtle, he never lacks the long arms of men who appear holy and wise in the world, with whom at times he finishes off and does more with one [Beteta f. 4r] of these, than the king with many good and holy [men] to defend himself.

Fearing this, so that such a great evil should not come to this land on account of my wishing to do good to them, it seemed to me that I had an obligation. Even if I do not have it, I do not lack legitimate reason and cause to place my life at risk in order to save such a multitude of people, trusting in Our Lord and in his great power that he will give particular aid to me and to these men, and understanding so that I might preach to them, and so that they might hear me and receive me in peace. And beyond this great hope that I have, there is, and I retain for myself, a great probability, which is almost evidence, that not only will they not kill me, but they will receive me in peace, and very willingly hear the matters of our holy Catholic faith. And if I did not hold this for certain, the whole world could not keep me here. My companions being in doubt as they are, that they will kill them or make them slaves, they are returning to Mexico [*because they have no ship with which to go forward*], and I will remain alone in this land, and time and deeds will show that in the arduous works of Our Lord, there is more to see and feel in them than some think.

[Cancer f. 7r] Above I have failed to recount through forgetfulness what happened the other time we got out on land, before we found out about the Christian who came to the ship.

And it was that since the day before, Sunday the 23rd of June, when they had promised to bring the interpreter and the missionary, we went to land very happy. The traitors had crossed to the opposite side where we first found them, which was toward the east, and even before people came out, they made us remain waiting a long time, thinking that we would get out on land. At the end of a short time they shouted to us, and eight or ten Indians got in the water to take us there, making signs that they were coming for us. We did not want to go straight to the pines where they were, because it seemed to us that it was an ambush, but instead we went farther on into the open, and based on what it appeared upon their coming out from there with bad will, it is certain they had an ambush, or at least their bows and arrows at their feet, which could not be seen.

Having arrived next to the beach, without making a signal for them to approach us, one of them entered in the ocean very boldly, so that it seemed that his life depended on it, and he arrived to give me the fish that he was carrying. I then went to give him a shirt, and since I couldn't pull it out quickly enough, one of my companions, angrily, went to give him a tunic or blouse of his. This demonstrated that it was good to carry and have something to give them, about which I have been very poorly viewed by many for bringing them these things. [Cancer f. 7v] Having received the shirt, another arrived with more fish. I didn't want to receive it, and I gave him I don't know what things that I had at hand. Having received them, he asked me for a cross of wood two palms or more in length which I had in my hand,[76] and thinking that he wanted it in order to throw it in the water or something similar, I didn't give it to him. He asked for it many times, and I asked my companions whether I should give it to him, and they responded that I should give it to him. Having given it to him, he kissed it very sincerely, and went to land in a great hurry and gave it to the Indian woman, our interpreter, to kiss. We did not even recognize her, because she was naked. And then it went from Indian to Indian, giving it to each other to kiss, and after [the others] went back, he came in front of all of them with her, the most happy man in the world. I noted this and was very pleased, for the consequence in which I am presently.

The Indian woman shouted for us to approach land, and said, "Come here, these are not carrying crossbows," and one from the chalupa said, "It's Magdalena the interpreter." [Beteta f. 4v] Nobody could believe it, and no matter how much we told her to come into the water so that we could hear and recognize her, she refused, because the Indians would not give her the opportunity. In the end, in order to find out if it was her or not, I jumped in the water up to my waist and arrived halfway, and she arrived at the beach, and thus I was able to see and speak with her, and I recognized that it was the interpreter, which pleased me greatly. I told those in the shallop, and then Father Fray Juan [Cancer f. 8r] jumped in the water and arrived next to me, and together we found out from the Indian woman many things. In particular, she told us that the missionary and the two Christians were together in the house of her chief, and if she lied, it was certain that the chiefs threatened that they would kill her if she told us. She also said that the entire land had risen up, thinking that it was an armada, and that she told them that no more than four friars were coming to preach great things, and that because of this there had gathered there those fifty or sixty men. Upon this, since Father Fray Gregorio desired to find an opportunity to go forth on land [*to find out about the companions*], he jumped from the boat and passed next to me, with the water almost up to the waist. I and Father Fray Juan having spoken with the interpreter, he told me, "Be with God; I am going, and tomorrow send me this and that thing." Father Fray Juan Garçia went with him to land, and with the intention of remaining, I returned to the shallop without reaching land, because I always feared the cunning of these [Indians]. In a short time I begged Father Fray Juan to return to the shallop in order to test if they would let him, and this was true, because according to him they would not let him. In the end, he came to the shallop. Fray Gregorio remained, and I went to talk with him and arrange how the next day we would see each other, and he should order that the Christians should be brought there. Having concluded this, I had a certain present brought out with many things, and others for the rest. All of them were given out, one for each one. I saw Father Fray Juan, who at the time was in the shallop, [Cancer f. 8v] surrounded by Indians, and he was frightened at how they entered so far in the water, and the sailors had let them reach the shallop. I found out afterward that they plundered the sailors, one of them taking off his shirt, the other his doublet, the other his hat, in order to give them to those Indians. Afterward I saw myself in great hardship containing the sailors and giving them payment for what they had given away out of what we brought. Here also the Fathers noticed how good it had been to have things to give them that I had procured and brought, and how I have never regretted it, even less now. What I now see with my eyes I first felt with my understanding, and I read it in the doctors [of the church],[77] in particular Saint Thomas, *Vitoria*, *Gaetano*, and the decrees approve and regard it as very good to attract the pagans with good examples and gifts of minuscule things, [Beteta f. 5r] which is to say little presents like these are.

Leaving this aside, the Indians let me return to the boat, and although Father Fray Gregorio wanted to remain on land with them, they would not let him, and almost by the hand, with a little force,[78] they told him that he should go to the shallop. And thus we all went away, they to their houses with the intention of bringing the Christians, and we to the ship with the intention of seeing them the next day and giving them axes, which they asked us for. This was the time, when we reached the ship, that we found out the aforementioned news of their sad death, on account of which the Fathers and the pilot then wanted to return to Mexico. I said that I wanted to remain for the aforementioned reasons.

[Cancer f. 9r] [Beteta Text]

Before we arrived at this point, seeing the poor preparation that there was in that port for what we were attempting, suspecting that our companions were dead, as they were, among ourselves we had discussed going to another place. The ship was not suitable for that coast, because it could not reach any closer than 5 or 6 leagues from land. We did not have water, or anywhere from which to take on enough in order to begin a new voyage, [and] all the meat and fish had been thrown rotten into the sea. Each day the sailors rebelled against us, with no one who wished to go to land in the shallop, and most of them had fevers, such that there was hardly anybody to work the pump, since in four hourglasses the ship took on one of water. Because of all this, we had concluded we should return to Havana or to New Spain and take a ship and go to another place. Father Fray Luís[79] was not pleased at this, and for this he wished to confront the last danger. On Sunday, the vigil of Saint John,[80] we returned to the ship very discontent, on account of not having seen any of our companions, although we had seen the Indian woman. Fray Gregorio was especially suspicious because the Indians had thrown him out by force. Having arrived at the ship, we found in it a Spaniard named Juan Muñoz, who had remained there since the armada of Soto, and had then come to the ship in a canoe. He almost did not know how to speak now, and as soon as he had arrived at the ship as best he could, he said that they had killed two of the Christians, and they had one alive, and that he had held the scalp of the missionary in his hands. He said the same thing when we arrived. The death of our companions now being certain, Father Fray Juan García and Fray Gregorio de Beteta told Fray Luís that since that had happened, they should go the next day [Cancer f. 9v] as they had arranged with the Indians, in order to assure ourselves, and that if none of our companions appeared, we should give the order to return, or to go to another place. He said that he was certain that that endeavor would not be achieved without blood, and since his companions had died there, there is where he wished to remain, because he intended to produce more fruit, and he hoped to subdue them by [Beteta f. 5v] giving them what he had carried there. Determined in this, he did not wish to go on the day of Saint John, so he could write certain letters and prepare the things that he had to carry. We did not stop dissuading him against the expedition all that day, by all the means that we could, but our persuasion and petitions were of little use, because he always held them as suspicious, and even more in this.

Tuesday, the 25th of June, in the morning we entered in the shallop to go to land, and having traveled two leagues, we were struck by such a great downpour and wind by the prow that we thought we were going to die, and many of the things that he was carrying for land were damaged, because everything was soaked. We could not reach land, and we returned to the ship with great effort. Juan Muñoz, who had come out of this land, and who went with us, told him that [the reason for] that [storm] was that God did not wish him to get out there, because they would then kill him, because they would now know that he had fled, and that the death of the others was discovered, and that they were not waiting for him at all, and other similar things that everyone told him. Having reached the ship that night, he [Cancer] again prepared other things to carry, and Wednesday, the 26th of June, we returned with the shallop to land, and we had no less hardship with downpours that day than the previous one, and we never thought we could reach land, but as always, he was firm in his intention [Cancer f. 10r] to stay in that land in order not to return. The next day, we waited for it to calm a little, and rowing with great effort by the sailors, we reached land. There were some Indians in trees at stretches, which we did not hold as a good sign. As soon as they saw us they climbed down and went running to a little grove of trees where the people were.[81] Having arrived near, we shouted to them, and they responded, but not one of them would come out of the woods into the open. Questioned about the interpreter, they said that she was in a house far from there. Some moved from one place to another with their bows and arrows and clubs and spears, which appeared clearly. Father Fray Luís was preparing himself to leave, and Fray Gregorio persuading him and begging him not to leave. They asked from there, "Is the yagué there?," which is the slave. Juan Muñoz got up and said, "You want him? I am he. Do you intend to kill us like you killed the others? You will not kill us, because now we know." With this it appeared that they got disturbed, and Father Fray Luís said, "Quiet, brother! Don't anger them!" Father Fray Gregorio told him that there could not be people in the world more stirred up than these, that on account of this, for the love of God he should delay a little and not leave. He refused, and threw himself in the water and went toward land. We were about a crossbow-shot away from the woods. Having reached land, he asked for a little cross that he had forgotten. Although there was no danger in taking it to him, I told him, "Father, for charity, Your Reverence should come back for it, because here there is no one who can carry it to you, because those people are

certainly very tricky." He went toward the beach, and we with the shallop [Cancer f. 10v] toward [Beteta f. 6r] the woods where the Indians
were. When they saw that we were going toward them, they began to
withdraw. Father Fray Luís told us to restrain ourselves, that we should
not agitate the people. He arrived close, and must have begun to see the
danger, and kneeled and remained a moment, and then went toward
the woods. Arriving near, an Indian came forth to him, and embraced
him and took him by the arm, and led him away somewhat quickly.
Another came out, and others, shoving him toward the entrance of the
woods. One struck his hat with his hand and knocked it off his head,
and another one struck him with a club in the head and knocked him
down. We were very close, and saw and heard very clearly what he
said then. He shouted, "Ay, enough!" They didn't let him finish, since
so many people charged in that they finished him off there. They made
a great yell and came forth to shoot arrows at us. I ordered that we
should withdraw a little toward the sea, and we stopped at the distance
of an arrow shot. Then they pulled out the habits [of the missionaries],
and having given us a shower of arrows, they went away. We returned
to the ship, not without fear that some canoes might come forth.

Reaching the ship, we then agreed to leave from there, but we did not
have water. That day we traveled in search of it along the beach, and we
took on a little. I asked the pilot to take us to another part of Florida, as
he was obligated, and he responded that he would be ready, but that he
had no water, nor was the ship ready to begin another voyage, and that
we should go to Havana, which was near, and having taken on water
and provisions, he would do it. Thus we departed from that port of the
Holy Spirit on Friday, the 28th of June 1549 in order to go to Havana.

[Cancer f. 11r] Having left from the port of the Holy Spirit, we traveled with strong southeasterly [winds] until Tuesday, the 2nd of July,
with a quarter moon, and it seemed that that wind was firming up.
The pilot told us that it seemed that we should come to New Spain,
because the weather would not allow us to go to Havana, and we were
lacking water, and the weather was more certain and favorable toward
New Spain. I was very opposed to this until Fray Juan García and the
sailors agreed to go to New Spain, and in order not to see myself alone
in this opinion, I consented with them, because upon reaching Havana
it would be late to begin a new voyage, and because in New Spain it
would be easier to make preparations.[82] And then we headed for New
Spain on Tuesday, the 2nd of July. The pilot having made a thousand
oaths and professions that we would be on the coast of New Spain
within eight days, on Sunday, the 14th of July, we found ourselves in

Yucatan on the east-west coast at 20 degrees [latitude]. It was very difficult to recognize where we were and how far we were from where we thought, which was in the plains of Almería to the north of Vera Cruz. We arrived at San Juan de Ulua on Friday, the 19th of July 1549.

Supplementary Document: Extract of Letter from Fray Luís Cancer to Bishop Bartolomé de las Casas

The extracted text is part of an undated letter written by Cancer before his departure from Spain (likely from Seville on February 6, 1548) to his supporter and promoter Bartolomé de las Casas and provides important details regarding the strategic planning for the expedition, including the selection of vessels and a pilot, as well as the eventual selection of the Florida Indian woman named Magdalena as an interpreter for the expedition. What is perhaps most compelling about the letter is the fact one can see the eventual seeds of destruction for the expedition in some of the advice and warnings given to Cancer during the planning stage.

The transcription here follows the norms detailed in the preface, generally preserving anachronistic orthography present in the original text except in cases where it might make it difficult for modern Spanish readers to sound out the words correctly or follow the intended sentence structure.

Spanish

Estos señores viendo que no se hallaba caravela p[r]esta al p[r]esente en este ryo acordaro[n] de enbiar a llamar a Jo[a]n Lopez que es el piloto q[ue] nos a de llevar q[ue] estaba en Guelva con su muger e hijos para con el consultar lo q[ue] convenia hazer en esto de la caravela o navio pues el la avia de llebar y regir, y llegado aqui les dixo muy a la clara q[ue] por amor de dios no se lo mandasen q[ue] era viejo e tenia hijos y muger y q[ue] no se queria poner a ryesgo de p[er]der la vida y de morir en manos de aquellos yndios. Otro dia despues desto vine a la contratacion de lo hallar q[ue] ya parecia q[ue] se le queria salir el alma y dixome lo mismo y mas adelante q[ue] [e]l Rey no fue bien ynformado en mandar hazer esta jornada con frayles q[ue] como no baya españoles nos mataran luego. . . .

. . . lo p[rime]ro q[ue] [Juan Lopez] dize es q[ue] conviene q[ue] se lleve bergantin para q[ue] si conviniere yr de la Florida a la Havana o a otras p[ar]tes q[ue] sea cosa q[ue] lo pueda hazer y no chalupa y q[ue] en la Havana se avia de formar y adereçar, y yo le dixe q[ue] no teniamos nec[esida]d de yr alli por agora porq[ue] su alteza nos mandaba visitar cada año. En fin de muchas palabras dixo verdad es que qu[an]do fue con fulano sin bergantin entraro[n]

a tomar puertos y con solos los bateles de los navios q[ue] echaro[n] a la mar
fuero[n] a reconocer el puerto por do[nde] parec[ie]re q[ue] dio a entender
q[ue] tambien se podia hazer con bergantin pero el no lo dixo luego oy me fue
a ynformar de Hernando Blas q[ue] favorece y ayuda mucho en este negocio
y le dixe lo d[ic]ho y finalmente dize lo d[ic]ho q[ue] le parece q[ue] bastara
una buena chalupete de doze o quatorze codos q[ue] la puedan llevar de
aq[ui] encima del navio lo q[ue] yo digo salvo mehor[?] judicio es q[ue] pues
estos pilotos estan diferentes en esto y en otras cosas q[ue] conviene q[ue]
de alla se enbie muy largo y bastante poder para q[ue] aqui estos señores o
en Mexico o en la Havana se pueda hazer el bergantin o chalupa o llevar de
aca la ligazon o la chalupa entera y q[ue] alla do[nde] q[uie]ra q[ue] fuere-
mos se pueda aderecar a costa de su mag[esta]d. . . .

. . . yten dize q[ue] en mexico no ay lenguas a lo q[ue] el cree de la costa de
la florida do[nde] nosotros emos de yr sino de la t[ie]rra adentro y q[ue] en la
Havana ay quatro yndios q[ue] saco el por mandado de Soto q[ue] saben la
lengua de aq[ue]lla costa y q[ue] por solos estos convenia llegarnos a la Havana. Santana dize q[ue] no ay mas de una yndia y yo dixe q[ue] no la llevaria
por todo el mundo respondieron todos q[ue] si no avia yndio q[ue] convenia
mucho llevarse, y p[ar]a esto conviene q[ue] si nos pareciere a nosotros los
religiosos y al piloto o pilotos q[ue] nos an de llevar q[ue] conviene tornar
en la Havana q[ue] se haga y q[ue] todo lo q[ue] alli conviniere gastarse en
vergantin o en cavallos q[ue] dize q[ue] mejor sera llevallos de alli q[ue] de
mexico q[ue] se murieran por la mar.[83] . . .

. . . mas dizen q[ue] en Santo Domy[ng]o esta un piloto q[ue] se llama
Fr[ancis]co del Barrio q[ue] trae un pleyto alli: dizen q[ue] sabe la costa
mexor q[ue] este piloto porq[ue] este luego se vino y sabe mejor la costa y
conviene llevalla o a alguno de los q[ue] estan en la Havana o Cuba de q[ue]
v[uest]ra R[ever]encia me escrivio. . . .

. . . yten dizen q[ue] esta otro muy buen honbre en mexico o en Santo Do-
[min]go q[ue] se llama Renteria q[ue] mas q[ue] particular sabe la costa las
entradas y salidas q[ue]todos aunq[ue] no sabra llevar el navio desde la Veracruz y q[ue] conviene mucho q[ue] pase en conpania del piloto Fr[ancis]co
del Barrio porq[ue] una cosa de tanta ynportancia dizen q[ue] no se avia de
confiar de un piloto q[ue] puede herrar y enganarse y siendo dos toma el uno
consejo del otro.

English

These señores, seeing that a caravel could not be found ready in this
river, agreed to call upon Juan López, who is the pilot that is to carry

us, who was in Huelva with his wife, in order to consult about what was appropriate to do regarding the matter of the caravel or ship, since he would have to lead and guide it. Having arrived here, he told them very clearly that for the love of God they should not command him [to go], that he was old and had children and a wife, and that he did not wish to place himself at the risk of losing his life in the hands of those Indians. The next day after this, I came to the [House of] Trade to find him,[84] and it now seemed that he was extremely worried,[85] and he told me the same, and later on that the King was not well-informed in ordering us to make this journey with friars, and that if soldiers did not go, they would kill us immediately. . . .

. . . The first thing that Juan López says is that it would be most appropriate to take a brigantine, so that if it is suitable to go from Florida to Havana, or other places, that this would be something that could be done, and not [in a] shallop, and that [the expedition] should assemble and equip in Havana. I told him that we had no need to go there for now, because His Highness ordered us to be visited each year. At the end of many words, he said that the truth is that when he went with so-and-so without a brigantine, they entered to take ports, and with only the boats of the ships that they launched into the sea, they were able to reconnoiter any port that might appear, from which one could take that it would also be possible to do this with a brigantine, but he did not say it. Then today I went to inform myself from Hernando Blas, who assists and helps much in this business, and I told him what had been said, and finally he says the aforementioned, that it seems to him that a good shallop of twelve or fourteen cubits would suffice,[86] which could be carried from here on top of the ship. What I say, without better judgment, is that since these pilots differ in this, and in other things, it is suitable that there should be sent from there a long and sufficient power [of attorney] so that these señores here or in Mexico or in Havana can make the brigantine or shallop, or carry from here the futtock-timbers or the entire shallop, and that it can be finished wherever we might be at the cost of His Majesty. . . .

. . . In addition, he says that in Mexico there are no interpreters, according to what he believes, for the coast of Florida, where we are to go, but rather for the interior,[87] and that in Havana there are four Indians who were taken by order of Soto, who know the language of that coast, and if only for this it is suitable for us to reach Havana. Santana says that there is no more than one Indian woman, and I said that I would not carry her for all the world, [but] everyone responded that if there were no Indian man, it would be very suitable to carry her. And on account of this, it is suitable that if it seems appropriate to us, the missionaries, and to the pilot or pilots that are to bring us, we should stop by Havana, and that everything that is suitable should be done there, spending on a brigantine or on horses, which they say would best be carried from there than from Mexico, since they will die on the ocean. . . .

. . . In addition, they say that in Santo Domingo there is a pilot named Francisco del Barrio who is bringing a lawsuit here. They say that he knows the coast better than this pilot, because he came recently, and knows the coast better, and it would be suitable to take him, or one of those who are in Havana or Cuba, about which Your Reverence wrote me. . . .

. . . They also say that there is another very good man in Mexico or in Santo Domingo who is named Rentería who knows in great detail the coast [and] its entrances and departures, better than anyone, although he will not know how to take the ship from Veracruz. And it would be very suitable for him to go together with the pilot Francisco del Barrio, because in an affair of such importance, they say that one should not trust in one pilot, who can err and be deceived, and being two, they can take counsel from each other.

4

The Captivity of Hernando
de Escalante Fontaneda, 1549–1566

The captivity of Hernando de Escalante Fontaneda resulted in one of the most detailed and famous ethnographic accounts regarding the Indians of South Florida (True 1944b). Subsequent research has identified several additional text fragments that were not included in the final Memorial (Worth 1995) but that nonetheless form part of Fontaneda's written legacy. These documents, combined with additional testimony transcribed more recently, have never before appeared together. Collectively, these texts constitute the majority of ethnographic information available regarding the sixteenth-century Calusa and their neighbors.

The texts presented here include the original Memorial and an addendum (the Memoranda), a lengthy list of Florida chiefs (the Memorial), several short descriptions of cultural practices of the South Florida Indians (Escalante Fontaneda, n.d.a, n.d.b, n.d.c), and an extract from a letter of Pedro Menéndez de Avilés (1566a) mentioning Fontaneda himself.

Narratives

Fontaneda's Memorial

The following Memorial was penned by Hernando de Escalante Fontaneda about 1575, evidently not long before the author's death, and seems to have been intended as a somewhat formal report to the Spanish Crown regarding Florida based on his long captivity (Escalante Fontaneda, n.d.c). Since it was signed, the authorship has long been recognized (e.g., True 1944b), though it is now clear that other contemporaneous text fragments in the Archivo General de Indias were also penned by Fontaneda around the same time and may well have formed part of a broader set of drafts intended for eventual construction into a single, longer manuscript (Worth 1995). Although the manuscript may be read as a completed narrative, it should also be viewed in light of the three subsequent sets of documents, which may have been discarded texts that might originally have been intended for inclusion with the final version presented here.

The transcription here follows the norms detailed in the preface, generally preserving anachronistic orthography present in the original text except in cases where it might make it difficult for modern Spanish readers to sound out the words correctly or follow the intended sentence structure. Perhaps curiously, and in contrast to most handwritten documents of this era, Fontaneda's writings contain relatively consistent within-text punctuation in the form of slashes throughout the text, in most cases corresponding quite well to locations where commas or periods could be placed. For my transcriptions in this chapter, I have replaced the many slashes with what seems to be the appropriate punctuation, though as indicated in the preface, I have also added periods at the end of long text sections where none were present before.

Spanish

[f. 1r]

Muy P[odero]so Señor

[*Colon las islas de Yucaio y de Ahiti*][1]
    Memoria de las cosas y costa y indios de la Florida que ninguno de quantos la an costeado no lo an sabido decalrar las yslas de Yucayo y de Ahite caen a un lado de la canal de Bahama y no ai yndios y esta entre la Habana y la Florida aunque ai otras yslas mas serca de tiera firme que corren de poniente a oriente que se disen los martires dicense los martires porque an padesido muchos ohbres y tanbien porque ai unas peñas salidas debajo de la mar que dende lejos paresen hombres que estan padesiendo, y en estas yslas aiy indios grandes de cuerpo y las mujeres muy dispuestas de buen rrostro, y en estas yslas ai dos pueblos de yndios la qual el un pueblo se llama el uno Guarugunbe quiere desir en rromanse pueblo de llanto, y el otro pueblesuelo Cuchiyaga quiere [de]zir lugar amartirisado estos yndios no tienen oro ni menos plata y menos bestido que andan en cueros si no solamente unos brageros tejidos de palma que los hombres cubren sus berguensas, y las mujeres unas yerbas que nazen de unos arboles estas yerbas paresen lana aunque son diferente, su comida ordinario es pescado y tertugas y caracoles que todo es pescado y atunes y ballenas que segun bi estando entre ellos y algunos de estos yndios comen lobos merinos no todos porque ai diferencia entre

mayores y menores ser de mayores y prinsipales. Ay otro pescado que aca
llamamos langostas y otro como a manera de chapin que no menos, y tanbien digo que en estas yslas ai benados muchos y unos animales que paresen
rraposos y no lo son sino de otra cosa diferente son muy gordos y buenos de
comer, y en otras yslas ai osos i muy grandes, y digo que como estas yslas
corren de ponyente a oriente y la tierra firme de la florida corre asia oriente a
estas yslas lo debe decau- [f. 1v] sar aber los osos porque aserca con ellas y
deben de pasar de ysla a ysla pero lo que algunos cautibos que alli y en otras
partes estabamos era mucha maravilla aber benados en las yslas de Cuchiyaga al pueblo que tengo d[ic]ho, y mas largamente contare de cada cosa
d[ic]ho mas porque tengo otros cuidados que me ban mas lo de oi en estas
yslas ay tanbien una madera que aca llamamos el palo para muchas cosas
como los fiçicos lo saben y tanbien ai mucha fruta de dibersas maneras que
no lo contare porque no acabaria. Haziea poniente destas yslas ay una canal
grande que ningun piloto se atrebe pasar con nabio grueso porque como digo
de la otra parte ay unas yslas hazia poniente sin arboles estas yslas son de
harena, nacidas que en algun tienpo, debia ser tiera de cayos que la comio la
mar con andalubios y ansi que daron sin arboles y llanas en harena ay siete
leguas de rrendondes llaman las yslas de las tertugas porque las ay i muchas
que salen de noche y desguebar en la harena son las tertugas del tamaño
de una adarga tienen tanta carne como una baca tiene de todas carnes y es
pescado.

[Capitulo de lo demas]
   Dende la Habana a la Florida corriendo de sur a norte y en d[e]r[ech]o
destas yslas a islas Tortugas y los Martires quarenta leguas de trabes beynte
leguas a los Martires, y de alli a la Florida otras beynte a la probinçia de Carlos probinçia de yndios. Quiere desir en su lenguaje pueblo feros, o lo dizen
por ser brabos, o diestros que ansi lo son señorean mucha parte de la tierra
hasta un pueblo que llaman Guacata a la laguna de Mayaimi. Llamase laguna
de Mayaimi porque [e]s muy grande y en redondes ai muchos pueblezuelos
como adelantye dire y tornando de la Habana para las leguas que ai dende
la Habana [f. 2r] a la otra parte del cabo de las yslas de los Martires que
casi ajunta con la Florida ay sesenta leguas de trabesia a las yslas postreras
porque las yslas tienen serca de setenta leguas y ansi corren de poniente a
oriente yesta canal tiene muchas maneras de trabesias y muchas diferencias
de bajuras y canalejas aunque la canal prinçipal es bien hancha y por parte
del medio hazia las yslas de la Bermuda donde tengo una poca de memoria
a d[ic]hos de yndios no lo quiero alargar boi a lo que tratava del cabo de las
yslas de los Martires hacia el norte fenesen estas yslas junto a un lugar de
yndios que an nonbre Tequesta questa a un lado de un rrio que dentra hasia
la tierra dentro esta rrio corre hasta quinse leguas y sale a otra laguna du[l]se
que disen algunos yndios que la an andado mas que yo ques braso de la

laguna de Mayaimi, y sobre esta laguna que corre por en medio de la tierra
dentro tiene muchos pueblos aunque son de treynta i quarenta [i veinte
otros tantos] lugares tienen pan de rraises ques la comida ordinario la mas
parte del tienpo aunque por caso de la laguna que crese mucho que no
alcansan estas rraises por estorbo de la mucha agua y ansi dejan de comer
algun tienpo este pan pescado mucho y muy bueno, otras rayses a manera
de turmas de las de aca du[l]ses y otras diferentes, de muchas maneras mas
quando ai casa ansi de benados como de abes entonses comen carne o abe.
Tanbien digo que ai en aquellos rios de agua du[l]ce enfinitisimas anguillas
y muy rricas y truchas grandisimas casi tamaño de un honbre las anguillas
gordas como el muslo y menores comen tanbien lagartos y culeb[r]as
y unos como ratones que andan en la laguna y galapagos y otras [f. 2v]
muchas sarvandixas que si las ubueramos de contar no acabariamos. Estos
yndios biben en tierra muy fragosa y pantanosa no tienen cosa de minas ni
cosa deste mundo andan desnudos y las mugeres con un mantellin de unas
palmas rajadas y tejidas son vasallos de Carlos y pagane tributo de todas
estas cosas que e d[ic]ho arriba de comida y raises y pellejos de los benados
y otras cosas.

*[Siete v[ecin]os de Santo Domingo me parese que fueron a buscar a las yslas
Lucayas y entre ellos me parese que fue el L[icencia]do Lucas Basques, oidor
mas como no llegaron mas de la costa aunq[ue] dise trujo yndios]*[2]

El oidor Lucas Vasques v[e]s[in]o en Santo Dimi[n]go y ot[r]os seys v[e]s[in]os
suyos me parese que partieron con nabios de que algunos yndios de las
yslas de Jeaga cabo de las yslas Lucayos a ber aquella tierra y rio de Santa
Elena cien leguas mas al norte adonde esta un pueblo que por dezir Orizta
dixeron Chicora los que fueron y el otro pueblo por llamalle Guale le llamaron
Gualdape y no bieron mas pueblos porque no pesquisaron mas o no entraron
ni costearon de beras por miedo de no tocar y perderse, y ansi no alcansaron
mas aunques berdad que no ai oro ni plata sino muy lexos de alli y ai sesenta leguas donde disen que ai minas de oro y cobre hasya la tierra corrida
adentro al norte al pie de un rio y lagunas estan pueblos de indios Otapali y
Olagatano y otros muchos ni son Chichimecas ny Jordaneros llamase el rey
mayor y gran señor en n[uest]ra lengua y en la de los yndios, Estoescertepe
en lenguaje de los yndios de Carlos. Este casique es el mayor de los reyes
fama de Montesuma, pero adonde fue Lucas Basques y otros Españoles
son jente misera, aunque ai algunas perlesillas en algunas conchas, comen
pescado ostiones asados y crudos y benados y corsos y otros animales y al
tienpo que los matan ellos las mujeres acarrean leña y agua para coser o asar
en parrillas y si algun oro allaron seria lejos benido de estas tieras y rei que
ariba digo el rio Jordan que dizen es buçion de los yndios de Cuba que era lei
uno porques berdad.

[f. 3r] Juan Ponse de Leon³ fue a buscar el rio Jordan a la Florida creyendo a
los yndios de Acha y a otros de Santo Domingo, o porque tener que entender,
o por baler mas y acabar de morir ques lo mas sierto, o sino para tornarse
moso labandose en tal rio [scratched-out line]⁴ ques lo que hase al caso, que
todo eso eran buçiones de los yndios de Cuba y de toda aquella comarca,
que por cumplir su ley desian quel rio Jordan estaba en la Florida. A lo menos estando yo catibo en muchos rios me bañe pero por mi desgracia nunca
aserte con el en la probincia de Carlos antiguamente aportaron muchos
yndios de Cuba en busca deste rio y el padre del rei Carlos que se llamaba
Senquene los tomo y hiso un pueblo dellos que hasta oi dia esta la jeneracion
y por las mismas causas quellos partieron de sus tieras que benian a buscar
el rio Jordan tomaron lengua todos los reyes y casiques de la Florida como
personas aunque salbajez a ber que rio podia ser aquel que ttan buena obra
hasia de tornar los biejos y biejas mosos y tan de pechos la tomaron que ni
quedo aroyo ni rio en toda la Florida hasta las lagunas y pantanos que no se
bañaron que hasta oi dia porfian de hallalle y nunca acaban y los de Cuba
botaban a morir por esa mar a cumplir su lei q[ue] ansi debio de ser que los
mesmos que pasaron a Carlos y se hiso un pueblo porque fueron tantos que
oi dia se hallan los hijos y biejos engañados y anse muerto muchos y es cosa
de risa lo que Juan Ponse de Leon fue a buscar al rio Jordan [en la Florida].⁵

[f. 3v] [*Rio de Cañas*]
   Digamos de la parte de Abalachi ques zerca de hacia Panuco adonde se
suena la muchedunbre de las perlas y sierto ai las entre Abalachi y Olagale
ay un rio q[ue] llaman los yndios Guasacaesgui que quiere desir rio de cañas
en nuestra platica en este rio y boca de mar y costa de la mar ay las perlas
ado[nde] se co[j]en unas hostias y conchas y se lleban a todas las probincias
y lugares de la Florida y principalmente a Tocobaga questa mas serca porque
en este pueblo esta el rei casique mayor de aquella comarca hacia mano
dere[c]ha a la benida para la habana llamase Tocobagachile tiene muchos
basallos y es rei por si vive a cabo postrero del rio hacia la tiera dentro que
ai de rio mas de quarenta leguas ado[nde] Her[nan]do de Soto penso poblar
y por su muerte no se poblo y se desbarato la jente de guerra y se fueron por
tierra y de camino ahorcaron los españoles al casique de Abalachi porque
no les quiso dar mays para mantenimy[en]to del camyno o porque dizen los
yndios de aquel pueblo de Abalachi quel casique suyo tenia al cuello unas
perlas gruesas y en medio dellas una muy grande que seria tan gruesa casi
como un guevo de paloma torcasa que las ai y añidan en unos arboles por
tienpos y esto es lo que dizen los yndios. No ai minas de oro ni plata y si las
ai no lo conosen el comer destos yndios es mais y pescado y muy mucho
matan benados y corsos y otros animales quellos comen pero lo ordinario es
pescado hacen pan de unas raises que nasen en unos pantanos como ariba
tengo d[ic]ho y mucha fruta [f. 4r] de diversas maneras ponellas aqui era no

acabar estos yndios no bisten ropa ni menos las mugeres andan desnudos los
hombres sino unos pellejos de benado curtidos hacen bragueros con que se
cubren solamente sus berguensas, y las mugeres unas pajuelas que nasen de
los arboles a manera de estopa, o lana y no es blanca sino pardo i con aquellas yerbas se cubren dellas a la redonda, de la sinta.

[*El numero de los pueblos*]
   Dejemos a Tocobaga y Abalachi y a Olagale y a Mocoso que son reinos
por si, y contare los lugares y pueblos del casique Carlos ya difunto que le
mato el Capitan Reynoso por culpado. Primeramente un lugar que se dize
Tanpa, pueblo grande, y otro pueblo que se llama Tomo, y otro Juchi, y otro
Soco, y otro que anombre, Ño, quiere dezir pueblo querido, y otro Sinapa, y
otro Sinaesta, y otro Metamapo, y otro Sa cas[?]pada, y otro Calaobe, y otro
Estame, y otro Yagua, y otro Guaya, y otro Yguebu, y otro Muspa, y otro Casitoa, y otro Tatesta, y otro Coyobea, y otro Jutun, y otro Tequemapo, y otro
que a nombre Comachicaquise, yobe, y otros dos pueblos desta comarca
que no me acuerdo [*Custevia Tavuazio*] porque a seys años que byne mas
ay otros por la tierra dentro en la laguna de Mayaimi y es pueblo primero, y
otro Cutespa, y otro Tavagemue y otro Tonsobe, y otro Enenpa, y otros beynte
pueblos que no me acerdo sus nombres y mas ay otros dos pueblos en las
yslas Yucayos que son sujetos a Carlos yndio [f. 4v] como d[ic]ho tengo mas
ariba que se llama Guarungube, y el otro Cuchiaga. Carlos y su padre eran
señores destos sinquenta pueblos hasta que le mataron como d[ic]ho tengo
y agora reina un don P[edr]o hijo de Sabastian llaman se ansi porque P[edr]o
Melendes los trujo a la Habana para regalallos y los mando nonbrar ansi,
pero tornaronse ansi peor que antes por el regalo que les hizo y mas peor
fuera si fueran bautisados pero porque ya no quise no los bautisaron porque
en su platica los entendi que no fuera lijitimo el bautismo en ellos que fueran
herejes como sean alsado otra bes y peores que antes saben la mayor parte
de n[uest]ras man[e]ras son flecheros y onbres de fuersa no ai hombre que
tanto sepa de aquella comarca como yo q[ue] lo se que la presente escrivo
porquestuve cautibo entre ellos dende niño de treze años hasta que fui de
treynta años. Se quatro lenguas, sino es la de Ais y Jeaga que es tiera que
nunca la andube.

[*Del rei de Abalachi*]
   Quiero dezsir ques gran pueblo y ricos de perlas y poco oro, porquesta lejos las minas de Onagatano, ques en las sieras nebadas de Onagatano postrer
basallo de Abalachi y Olagatano, y de Olagale y de Mogoso y la Cañogacola
que dizen los yndios que son muchos y grandes honbres de guerra aunque
andan desnudos y bestidos algunos dellos con pellejos y son pintores que
quanto ben pintan llamanse Cañogacola, que quiere desir jente bellaca sin
respeto y balientes de flecha pero las buenas armas de los españoles todavia

los benseria con muy buenas ballestas y escopetas [f. 5r] y rodelas y espadas
hanchas y agudas y buenos caballos y escupiles y una y dos personas que
los entiendan y que sean las lenguas personas buenas y fieles no como el
Biscaino que quiso bender a Pero Melendes a los yndios sino fuera por mi y
un mulato que descobrimos la traicion fueran todos muertos y io con ellos y
no muriera Pero Melendes en Santander sino en la Florida en la probincia de
Carlos, porque no ai rio ni baia que se me pueda esconder y si me trataran
como yo meresia oy dia fueran los yndios basallos de n[uest]ro poderoso rey
Don Felipe que dios guarde muchos años. Ya tengo d[ic]ho queste casiq[ue]
es señor de aquel rio de las cañas donde ai las perlas y mynas de asul y el oro
lejos postrer basalla, y pueblo de Olagale.

[Punta de Cañaberal donde reside el casique de Ais]

Un Don P[edr]o Biscaino que su mag[esta]d hiso m[erce]d de tener cuidado de los sisnes fue catibo en esta probincia si el fuera mas hombre pues
su mag[esta]d le hiso tanta m[erce]d los yndios de Ais y Guacata y Jeaga y
sus basallos fueran ya dominados y aun muchos dellos cristianos pero fue
hombre para poco y de poco entendimiento y ansi no ai que hablar don
P[edro] Biscaino sabe muy bien esta lengua de Ais y los demas nonbrados,
y aun hasta Mayaca y Mayajuaca desotra parte del norte pero yo creo que
como por mandado de Pero Melendes que lo mando ahorcar por una false-
dad que le lebantaron a Domingo Rruys conpañero de Don P[edro] Biscaino
le espantaron y se bino a España con las nuebas de la Florida y no curo de
bolber mas y si bolbio seria por traer un hijo que tenia entre los yndios segun
lo trujo y nunca bolbio mas y por ber el mal tratamy[en]to que a las [f. 5v]
lenguas se asia quiso no bolber como otros emos hecho y sin paga hasta oi
dia y benimos rotos y ansi nos dio poca gana de bolber a la Florida a serbir
sin medra ninguna. Este rei de Ais y Jeaga son yndios pobres de la tierra que
no ai minas de oro ni menos plata, y para desir por entero, son ricos de la
mar que muchos nabios se an perdido muy cargados de plata y oro como se
perdio Farfan y el mulato con su hurca y el nabio del Biscaino adonde benia
Anton Granado que fue pasajero y cautibado y el nabyo de Juan Cristobal
maese y capitan y mataron los yndios a Don Martin de Gusman y al capitan
Her[nan]do de Andino procurador de la probincia de Popayan y Juan Ortis
de Sarate fator de Santa Marta. Perdiose este nabio en el año de sinquenta y
uno y benian en esta nao dos hijos de Alonso de Mesa y un tio con ellos ricos
todos quel que menos traia fui yo pero con todo esto trai a beynte y si[n]co
mill pesos en oro fino porque quedaba en Cartajena mi padre y madre que
fueron comenderos, y sirbieron a su mag[esta]d en aquellas partes del Peru
y despues en la siudad de Cartajena y poblazon en ella donde yo i otro her-
[ma]no nacimos y de alli nos enbiaba a España a estudiar y nos perdimos en
la Florida como d[ic]ho tengo y otros nabios y la armada de la Nueba España
adonde dizen que benia el hijo de Pero Melendes por jeneral porque los

yndios tomaron un Español que salio a tiera y los yndios le cojeron muerto de
hambre e yo le bi bivo y hable con el y un Juan Rrodriges natural de Nicaragua [f. 6r] nos dijo que benian de la Nueba España y iban para Castilla y que
era el jeneral un hijo de Pero Melendes Esturiano y el que benia por marinero
de otra nao y que no supieron unos de otros hasta que los yndios se arma-
ban para ir a la costa de Ais y los bido yr y bolber con mucha rriquesa de
barras de plata y de oro y costales de reales y mucha ropa y como era recien
cautibado o hallado no entendia la lengua de los yndios. Yo y Juan Rodrigues
fuimos farautes deste hombre y de otros como ya sabiamos la lengua de los
yndios consuelo era aunque triste para los que despues se perdian en hallar
delante conpañeros cristianos con que pasar los trabajos y entenderse con
aquellos brutos muchos españoles escaparon la byda en hallar adelante
conpañeros cristianos porque los yndios que los tomaban les mandaban
bailar y cantar y no lo entendian y como los yndios son tan bellacos y mas los
de la Florida pensaban que no lo querian hazer por rebeldia, los mataban y
desian despues a su casique q[ue] por bellacos y rebeldes los mataban que
no querian hazer lo que les mandaba. Preguntando el casique porque los
mataban respondian esto que tengo d[ic]ho y un dia yo y un negro y otros dos
españoles rezien cautibos tratando el casiq[ue] con sus basallos y señores
grandes de su corte lo que tengo d[ic]ho arriba, pregunto me el casique que
era el mas ladino de todos, diziendo Escalante desinos la berdad pues ya
sabeys que hos quiero mucho quando mandamos a estos v[uest]ros conpañeros bailar y cantar y otras cosas porque son tan bellacos rebeldes que
no lo quieren hazer o hacen lo que no estiman la muerte, o por no torzer su
braso a jente contraria de su ley, desimelo y sino lo sabeys preguntase lo a
esos rezien catibos que por su culpa son catibos agora q[ue] por dioses los
teniamos abajados del zielo, y respondiendo a mi amo y señor dixe le luego
la berdad [f. 6v] señor a lo que entiendo no son rebeldes ni lo hazen de mal
proposito es porque no los entienden y ellos rabian por entendellos dixome
que no era berdad que muchas beses se lo desian y algunas beses lo hazian
y otras beses no querian por mas que les dixesen. Dixe yo con todo eso señor
no lo hazen adrede ni por rebeldia por no entender lo hazen por eso hablales
que lo bea yo y este negro horro v[uest]ro y el casique riendose dixoles
se le tega rezien benidos. Ellos preguntaron que q[ue] les desia el casique
el negro questaba junto a ellos riose y dixo al casique señor berdad hos dize
Escalante que no lo entienden y lo an preguntado a Escalante q[ue] ques lo
q[ue] desis y no se lo quiere desir hasta que se lo mandeys y entonses creyo
el casique la berdad y dixo a Escalante declaraselo Escalante que agora hos
creo de beras. Yo se lo declare que quiera desir se le tega corre mira si biene
jente al miradero miradero quere dezir tejove. Abrebian mas en la palabra
que nosotros los de la Florida. Y bisto el casique la berdad dixo a sus bazallos
que quando hallasen cristianos ansi perdidos y los cojesen que no les mandasen nada hasta abisar para que fuese uno de los que entendiese la lengua

y ansi fue este el primero ariba declarado q[ue] abia nombre, Pijiguini, y en lengua n[uest]ra quere desir Martines, marinero ariba declarado que benia en la Flota, de Mejico y se perdio. Y dexando esto aparte, quiero hablar de las riqu[ue]sas que los yndios de Ays hallaron que seria hasta myllon y mas en barras y en oro y otras [f. 7r] cosas de joias hechas de manos de yndios Mejicanos que traian los pasajeros la qual lo rrepartio el casique de Ais y Jeaga y Guacata y Mayajuaca y Mayaca y el tomo lo que le parezio, o lo mejor, con estos nabios y otros d[ic]hos y carabelas perdidas y indios de Cuba y de Honduras perdidos en busca del Rio Jordan que benian ricos y los cojian Carlos, y el de Ais y Jeaga, y las yslas de Guarugunbe, son ricos como d[ic]ho tengo de la mar y no de la tiera. Desde Tocobaga hasta Santa Elena que abra de costa seysientas leguas. No ai oro ni menos plata de natural de la tiera, sino es lo que d[ic]ho tengo por la mar no quiero desir si ai tierra para abitar, pues los yndios biben en ella abundosa para ganados y para senbrar a su cercaña no lo sabre de zierto algunas senbraron y nacieron pero como no estaba yo de sosiego quando se senbraron no bi en lo que paro—todas estas probincias que e declarado dende Tocobagachile hasta Santa Elena son grandes pescadores y nunca les falta pescado fresco son grandes flecheros y traidores y tengo por muy zierto que jamas seran de pas ni menos cristianos. Yo lo firmare de mi nombre por muy cosa sierta porque lo se si no toman mi consejo sera trabajo y peor que antes que los cojan a buena manera conbidandoles la pas y metellos debajo de las cubiertas a maridos y mugeres y rerepartillos por vasallos a las yslas y aun en tierra firme por dineros como algunos señores en España conpran al rei basallos y desta manera abria maña y amenguandolos, y esto digo—que seria cosa asertada y podrian hazer los Españoles unas granjerias para criar ganado y guarda de tantos nabios como se pierden.

[f. 7v] [*Capitulo*]

De la probincia de Sotoriba puerto de Santa Agustin y rio de San Mateo a do[nde] los luteranos de Francia tenian hecho fuerte e rrincon para rrobar a todos quantos benian de tierra firme, ora sean de Mejico, o del Peru o de otras partes como lo hacian y recojianse al rio de San Mateo como d[ic]ho tengo donde rreside este casique traidor de Sotoriba y Alimacani y otros lugares sus basallos, y en medio del rio de San Mateo sesenta leguas a la tiera dentro ay otro casiq[ue] reino por si y señor de su tierra que se llama, Utina y Seravai, y Moloa y otros muchos sus basallos hasta llegar a Mayajuaca tiera de Ais hacia el cañaberal que disen los pilotos n[ues]tros que nabegan. Estos dos casiques tomo pases Pero Melendes no tienen oro ni plata ni perlas son miserables y grandes bellacos y traidores flecheros andan desnudos como los demas q[ue] arriba tengo d[ic]ho. Por este rio de San Mateo pueden yr a Tocobaga de la otra banda de la Florida hazia poniente y no digo que siempre por el rio sino desta manera entrar por la barra de San Mateo y llegar a

Sarabai questa sincuenta o sesenta leguas a la tierra dentro del rio arriba o a la probincia de Utina y de alli desenbarcar y ir por la banda de poniente tomando por arriba den pueblo en pueblo y dar consigo a la Cañogacola basallos de Tocobaga y de alli al lugar mismo de Tocobaga que dentra otro rio muy grande adonde Soto estubo y murio y con esto fenesco. [f. 8r] Y no dize mas porque si fuera pretender la conquista desta tiera no diera mas relazion que tento dado aunque a su mag[esta]d le conbiene para la seguridad de sus armadas que ban al Peru y a la Nueba España y a otras partes de Yndias que pasan por fuersa por aquella costa y canal de Bahama y se pierden muchos nabios y perese mucha xente porque los yndios son contrarios y muy flecheros y ansi como digo conbiene aber alguna fuertejuela por do[nde] pudiesen segurar aquella canal con alguna renta que se pudiese sacar de Mejico y del Peru y de las yslas de Cuba y de todas partes de Yndias para el remedio y manteny[mien]to de los soldados de guarda en la tal fuertesuela y esto es lo que conbenia y otra cosa mas de yr a buscar las perlas pues otra riquesa no ai en aquella tiera y para ello concluyo y si fuere nesesario,

Lo firmo H[ernan]do descalante Fontaneda

English

[f. 1r]

Most Powerful Lord,

[Columbus, the Islands of Yucaio, and Ahiti]
   Memorial of the affairs and coast and Indians of Florida, which none among many have explored, nor have they known how to describe the Islands of Yucayo and Ahite.[6] They lie to one side of the Bahama Channel, and there are no Indians, and they are between Havana and Florida, although there are other islands closer to the mainland that run from west to east called the Martyrs. They are called the Martyrs because many men have perished [there], and also because there are bare rocks projecting from beneath the sea that appear from afar to be men who are dying. And in these islands there are Indians with very large bodies, and the women are very handsome with good faces. And in these islands there are two towns of Indians, of which one is called Guarugunbe, which in Spanish means "Crying Town," and the other little town Cuchiyaga, which means "Martyred Village." These Indians have neither gold nor even less silver, and less clothing, because they walk naked, with only some loincloths woven from palm with which the men cover their privates, and the women some grasses that grow in some trees. These grasses appear to be wool, although they are different.[7] Their normal food is fish and turtles and snails, and everything is

fish and tuna and whales, according to what I saw while living among them. Some of these Indians eat seals, but not all, because there is a difference between old and young, and these are for elders and nobles. There is another fish that here we call lobsters, and another in the manner of a trunkfish, which is no less [large]. And I also relate that in these islands there are many deer, and some animals that look like foxes and aren't, but rather something else different. They are very fat and good to eat. And on other islands there are bears, and very large. And I say that since these islands run from west to east, and the mainland of Florida runs to the east toward these islands, that ought to be the cause [f. 1v] for there being bears, because it is near them, and they probably pass from island to island. But what some of us captives who were there and in other places say is that it was quite a marvel that there were deer on the islands of Cuchiyaga up to the town that I have mentioned. I will relate each thing I have said at greater length, because I have other concerns that are more pressing than that of today. On these islands there is also a wood that here we call "palo," [which is useful] for many things, as the physicians know, and there is much fruit of many types, which I will not recount because I would never finish. To the west of these islands there is a large channel that no pilot dares to pass through with a large ship, because as I said earlier, there are some islands toward the west without trees. These islands are made of sand, but at some time they must have been a land of keys, which the sea ate away with floods, and thus they were left without trees and flat with sand. They are seven leagues in circumference, and the islands are called the Tortugas because there are many [turtles] that come out at night and lay their eggs in the sand. The turtles are of the size of a shield, and have as much meat as a cow. They have all types of meats, and it is a fish.

[*Chapter of the rest*]

From Havana to Florida, running from south to north, and straight from these islands to the Tortugas Islands and the Martyrs, [there are] forty leagues in traverse: twenty leagues to the Martyrs, and from there to Florida another twenty, to the province of Carlos, a province of Indians. In their language the name means "fierce town,"[8] or so they say so by being brave and cunning, as indeed they are. They dominate a great part of the land, up to a town called Guacata to the lake of Mayaimi.[9] It is called the lake of Mayaimi because it is very large, and around it there are many small towns, as I will recount later on. Turning to Havana, regarding the leagues that there are from Havana [f. 2r] to the other side at the end of the islands of the Martyrs, which almost join with Florida, there are sixty leagues in traverse, and thus they run from west to east. This canal has many types of crossings, and many differences in deep spots and little channels, although the main channel is very wide in the middle stretch toward the islands of Bermuda, where I have little memory, based on the statements of Indians. I do not wish to prolong this, so I will return to what I was dealing with about the end of the islands of the Martyrs toward the north. These islands come to an end next to a village of Indians called Tequesta, which is at one side of a river that enters toward the interior. This river runs up to fifteen leagues, and comes out at another freshwater lake, which some Indians who have traveled there more than I say is an arm of the lake of Mayaimi. And upon this lake, which runs through the middle of the interior, there are many towns, although they are of thirty and forty (and just as many with twenty) places.[10] They have bread from roots, which is the ordinary food during the greater part of the time, although in the case of the lake, which rises greatly, they cannot reach these roots due to the obstacle of high water, and thus they leave off eating this bread for some time. [They also have] much and very good fish, and other roots in the manner of truffles like the sweet ones here, and other different ones in many varieties. Furthermore, when there is game, both deer and birds, then they eat meat or fowl. I also say that in those freshwater rivers there are infinite eels, and very delicious, and very large trout, almost as large as a man, and the eels as thick as the thigh and smaller. They also eat lizards and snakes, and some [animals] like rats that walk in the lake, and turtles and many [f. 2v] other vermin that, if we were to count them, we would never end. These Indians live in a very difficult and swampy land. They have nothing from mines, or anything else [of value] in this world. They walk naked, and the women with a cloak of split and woven palm leaves.[11] They are vassals of Carlos and pay him tribute of all these things that I have stated above, including food and roots and skins of the deer and other things.

[It seems to me that seven residents of Santo Domingo went in search of the Lucayas Islands, and among them it seems to me was the Licenciado Lúcas Básques, a magistrate, and that they did not reach more of the coast, although it is said they brought Indians][12]

It seems to me that the Oidor Lúcas Vásquez, resident in Santo Domingo, and another six of its residents left with ships [with][13] some Indians from the islands of Jeaga, at the end of the Lucayos Islands, to see that land and river of Santa Elena, one hundred leagues farther to the north. There is a town there that, since it was called Orizta, those that went [with Ayllón] called it Chicora, and the other town, by being called Guale, they called it Gualdape.[14] And they did not see more towns because they did not investigate further, or enter or skirt the coastline in earnest for fear of losing sight of land and getting lost. And thus they did not achieve more, although it is true that there is no gold or silver except very far from there. It is sixty leagues to where it is said that there are mines of gold and copper, toward the interior running to the north, at the foot of a river and lake, [where] there are towns of Indians: Otapali and Olagatano and many others. They are neither Chichimecas nor Jordaneros.[15] [The chief] is called principal chief and great lord in our language, and in that of the Indians, Estoescertepe, in the language of the Indians of Carlos. This chief is the most principal of the kings, as famous as Montezuma, but where Lúcas Vázquez and other Spaniards went they are very poor people, although there are some little pearls in some shells. They eat fish, roasted and raw oysters, and large and small deer,[16] and other animals, and while [the men] kill them, the women carry firewood and water to boil[17] them or roast them on grills. And if they had found any gold, it would have come from far away, from these lands and king that I note above. The River Jordan that is talked about is a deceit of the Indians of Cuba, which was a belief,[18] and not because it is true.

[f. 3r] Juan Ponce de León went to Florida to look for the River Jordan, believing the Indians of Acha and others from Santo Domingo, or in search of understanding, or to become famous and end up dying, which is the most certain, or instead in order to become young, bathing in some river, which is what makes the case that all that was a deceit of the Indians of Cuba and all that district. In order to fulfill their belief, they said that the River Jordan was in Florida. At least while I was captive, I bathed in many rivers, but to my misfortune I never happened upon it in the province of Carlos. Long ago, there arrived many Indians from Cuba in search of this river, and the father of the king Carlos, who was called Senquene, took them and made a town of them, and their offspring remain to this day. And for the same reasons that they left from their lands to come and search for the River Jordan, all the kings and chiefs of Florida took notice, as persons, although savages, to see which river could be that which had such a good effect, making old men and women become young. And they took it so much to heart that not a stream or river remained in all of Florida, including the lakes and swamps, that was not bathed in, and they persist in their search up to the present day, and never cease. Those from Cuba hurled themselves to die in that sea in order to fulfill their belief, which must be the same ones who crossed to Carlos and made a town, because there were so many that even today the children and elders find themselves deceived, and many have died. It is a matter of laughter that Juan Ponce de León went to look for the River Jordan [in Florida].

[f. 3v] [*River of Canes*]

[Now] we speak of the region of Abalachi, which is nearby toward Panuco, where the multitudes dream of pearls, and it is true that there are [pearls] between Abalachi and Olagale. There is a river that the Indians call Guasacaesgui, which means River of Canes in our language. In this river and its mouth and the seacoast are the pearls, where they gather oysters and shells. They carry them to all the provinces and villages of Florida, and principally to Tocobaga, which is closest, because in this town is the king, principal chief of that district on the right hand when returning toward Havana.[19] He is called Tocobagachile, and he has many vassals, and is an autonomous king.[20] He lives at the farthest end of the river toward the interior, and by river there are more than forty leagues to where Hernando de Soto intended to settle, and on account of his death it was not settled and the soldiers were thwarted and went away by land.[21] Along the road, the Spaniards hanged the chief of Abalachi because he did not wish to give them corn for sustenance on the road, or because the Indians of that town of Abalachi say that their chief had some thick pearls around his neck, and in the middle of them one very large, which would be almost as thick as an egg of a woodpigeon,[22] which there are there. They nest in some trees for certain periods, and this is what the Indians say. There are no mines of either gold or silver, and if there are, they do not know about them. The food of these Indians is corn and fish, and very much of it. They kill large and small deer and other animals that they eat, but the ordinary [food] is fish. They make bread from some roots that grow in some swamps, as I have said above, and much fruit [f. 4r] of diverse types, which to put here would be unending. These Indians do not dress in clothes, not even the women. The men walk naked, except for some tanned deerskins with which they make loincloths with which they cover only their privates. And the women [wear] some fine straw that grows in the trees in the manner of flax or wool,[23] and it is not white, but rather brown, and with those grasses they cover themselves roundabout the waist.

[*The number of the towns*]

We leave Tocobaga and Abalachi and Olagale and Mocoso, which are autonomous kingdoms, and I will count the villages and towns of the chief Carlos, now deceased, who was killed by Captain Reynoso as a criminal. First, a village that is called Tanpa, a large town, and another town that is called Tomo, and another Juchi, and another

Soco, and another called Ño, which means beloved town, and another Sinapa, and another Sinaesta, and another Metamapo, and another Sacaspada, and another Calaobe, and another Estame, and another Yagua, and another Guaya, and another Yguebu, and another Muspa, and another Casitoa, and another Tatesta, and another Coyobea, and another Jutun, and another Tequemapo, and another called Comachicaquiseyobe, and another two towns of this district that I don't remember [Custevia, Tavuazio],[24] because it has been six years since I came.[25] Beyond this, there are others in the interior on the lake of Mayaimi, and it [Mayaimi] is the first town, and another Cutespa, and another Tavagemue, and another Tonsobe, and another Enenpa, and another twenty towns whose names I can't remember. There are also another two towns in the Yucayos Islands,[26] which are subject to Carlos, the Indian, [f. 4v] as I have stated above, which are called Guarungube, and the other Cuchiaga. Carlos and his father were lords of these fifty towns until they killed him as I have stated, and now there reigns one Don Pedro, son of Sebastián. They are called thus because Pedro Menéndez brought them to Havana to give them gifts, and he ordered them named thus. But they became worse than before on account of the gift that he gave them, and it would have been worse if they were baptized, but because I did not wish it, they did not baptize them, because in their language I understood that the baptism would not be legitimate for those who were heretics, since they have risen up on another occasion, and worse than before they knew the greater part of our customs. They are archers and men of force. There is no man who knows more about that district than I, because I know what I am presently writing because I was imprisoned among them from the time that I was a boy of thirteen years until I was thirty years old. I know four languages, though not that of Ais and Jeaga, which is a land that I never traveled in.

[Of the king of Abalachi]

I want to say that it is a great town, and rich in pearls and little gold, because it is far from the mines of Onagatano, which is in the snowy mountains of Onagatano, the last vassal of Abalachi and Olagatano. And of Olagale and of Mogoso and Cañogacola, the Indians say that they are many and great warriors, although they walk naked, and some of them dressed with skins. And they are painters, who paint everything they see. They call themselves Cañogacola, which means wicked people without regard, and valiant archers. But the good weapons of the Spaniards would still vanquish them with very good crossbows, and guns, [f. 5r] and shields, and broad and sharp swords, and good horses, and padded armor, and one or two persons who understand them and who would be the interpreters, persons good and faithful, not like the Biscaino who wanted to sell Pedro Menéndez to the Indians. If it were not for me and a mulatto, who discovered the treason, everyone would have been dead, and I with them, and Pedro Menéndez would not have died in Santander, but rather in Florida in the province of Carlos, because there is neither river nor bay that could hide me. And if they had treated me as I deserved, today the Indians would be vassals of our powerful king Don Felipe, whom God preserve many years. I have already said that this chief [Cañogacola] is lord of that River of Canes, where there are the pearls, and mines of cobalt, and the gold far away, with the last vassal and town of Olagale.

[*Point of Cañaveral, where resides the chief of Ais*]
   One Don Pedro Biscaino, whom His Majesty gave the favor of caring for the swans, was imprisoned in this province. If he was more of a man, since His Majesty gave him such favors, the Indians of Ais and Guacata and Jeaga and their vassals would already be dominated, and even many of them Christians, but he was a man [suited] for little, and of little understanding, and thus Don Pedro Biscaino should not speak. He knows very well this language of Ais and the rest named, and even up to Mayaca and Mayajuaca on that other side to the north,[27] but I believe that since by order of Pedro Menéndez he was ordered to be hanged on account of a falsehood that was stirred up against Domingo Ruíz, a companion of Don Pedro Biscaino, they scared him off, and he came to Spain with news of Florida. He did not try to return again, and if he returned it was to bring back a son that he had among the Indians, as he brought him, and he never returned again. And by seeing the bad treatment that was made to the [f. 5v] interpreters, he refused to return like others of us have done, and without payment up to the present day, and we came back bankrupt, and thus we had little interest in returning to Florida to serve without any prosperity.[28] This king of Ais and Jeaga are Indians who are poor from the land, since there are neither mines of gold, nor even less silver, and to tell the whole truth, they are rich from the sea, since many ships have been lost there very laden with silver and gold. Farfán and the mulatto were lost with their urca,[29] and also the ship of [Don Pedro] Biscaino where Antón Granado was a passenger and was imprisoned, and the ship of Juan Christóbal, master and captain. The Indians [also] killed Don Martín de Guzmán and Captain Hernando de Andino, procurer of the province of Popayan, and Juan Ortiz de Zarate, factor of Santa Marta. This ship was lost in the year of [fifteen] fifty-one, and in this ship came two sons of Alonso de Mesa, and an uncle with them, all of them rich. He who brought the least was me, but with all of this I brought twenty-five thousand pesos in fine gold, because in Cartagena

remained my father and mother, who were encomenderos and served
His Majesty in those regions of Peru, and later in the city of Cartagena
and in its settlement, where I and another brother were born. And from
there they were sending us to Spain to study, and we were lost in
Florida as I have stated. [There were also] other ships, and the armada
from New Spain where they say the son of Pedro Menéndez came as a
general, because the Indians took a Spaniard who came forth on land,
and the Indians captured him dying from hunger, and I saw him alive
and spoke with him. And one Juan Rodríguez, a native of Nicaragua,
[f. 6r] told us that they were coming from New Spain and were going
toward Castille, and that the general was a son of Pedro Menéndez the
Asturian, and he [Rodríguez] came as a sailor on another ship, and
they did not know one another until the Indians prepared to go to the
coast of Ais, and he saw them go and return with great riches of bars
of silver and gold and sacks of silver coins and much clothing.[30] And
since he was recently imprisoned or found, he did not understand the
language of the Indians. I and Juan Rodríguez were heralds of this
man, and of others, since we already knew the language of the Indians.
It was a consolation, although sad, for those who were lost later, in
finding before them Christian companions with whom to pass the
hardships and get along with those brutes. Many Spaniards escaped
with their lives upon finding before them Christian companions,
because the Indians who took them ordered them to dance and sing,
and they did not understand. And since the Indians are so wicked, and
even more those of Florida, they thought that they did not wish to do
so in rebellion, and they killed them, and afterward told their chief that
they had killed them as wicked and rebellious men, since they did not
wish to do what they were ordered. When the chief asked why they
killed them, they responded this way, as I have said. And one day, while
the chief was discussing what I have said above with his vassals and
great lords of his court in the presence of me and a black man and
another two recently captured Spaniards, the chief, who was the most
shrewd of them all, asked me, saying, "Escalante, tell us the truth, since
you already know that I am very fond of you all; when we command
these your companions to dance and sing and other things, why are
they so wicked and rebellious that they refuse to do so, or act as if they
do not fear death, or in order not to twist the arm of people against
their law? Tell me, and if you do not know why, ask these recent
captives, who are imprisoned now because of their own fault, who we
once regarded as gods who descended from heaven." And responding
to my master and lord, I immediately told him the truth, [f. 6v] "Lord,
according to what I understand, they are not rebels, nor do they do so
with evil intention; it is because they do not understand them, and they

long to understand them." He told me that it was not true, that many times they told them and sometimes they did it, and other times they refused no matter how many times they told them. I said, "With all this, Lord, they do not do so on purpose, or in rebellion; they do so on account of not understanding. For that, speak to them so that I and this black man can see it apart from you. Laughing, the chief said to them, "Se le tega, recent arrivals." They asked what the chief was saying to them. The black man who was next to them laughed, and told the chief, "Lord, it is true what Escalante is telling you, that they do not understand you, and they have asked Escalante what is it that you are saying, and he refuses to tell them until you command him to." And then the chief believed the truth, and told Escalante, "Declare it to him, Escalante, now I truly believe you." I told him what "se le tega" means: "run to the lookout, see if people are coming." Lookout means "tejove." Those of Florida abbreviate their words more than we do. Having seen the truth, the chief told his vassals that whenever they should find Christians lost like that and capture them, that they should not command them to do anything until sending news, so that one of those who understands the language can go. And thus was this first aforementioned who had the name Pijiguini, which means Martínez in our language, the sailor mentioned above who came in the fleet from Mexico and was lost. Leaving this aside, I wish to speak about the riches that the Indians of Ays found, which would be up to a million or more in bars and in gold and other [f. 7r] things of jewelry made by the hands of Mexican Indians, which the passengers brought. All of this was distributed by the chief of Ais and Jeaga and Guacata and Maya-juaca and Mayaca, and he took what seemed suitable to him,[31] or the best, from these ships and others mentioned, and caravels lost, and Indians from Cuba and Honduras lost in search of the River Jordan. They came rich, and they were captured by Carlos and the [chief] of Ais and Jeaga and the islands of Guarugunbe. As I have stated, they are rich from the sea, and not from the land. From Tocobaga up to Santa Elena, which will be about six hundred leagues of coastline, there is no gold or even less silver naturally from the land, but rather it is what I have said, from the sea. I do not wish to say if there is land to inhabit, since the Indians live in it. It is plentiful for livestock and for agriculture in their vicinity. I don't know for certain; some sowed seeds and they sprouted, but since I wasn't at rest when they were planting, I didn't see how they ended up. In all these provinces that I have declared about, from Tocobagachile up to Santa Elena, they are great fisherfolk, and they never lack fresh fish. They are great archers, and traitors, and I hold it for very certain that they will never be at peace, and even less Christians. I would sign it with my name as a very certain thing, because I know that if they don't take my advice it will be difficult work, and worse than before. They should capture them in a good way, inviting them in peace, and place them in captivity, husbands and wives, and distribute them as vassals to the islands, and even on the mainland, in exchange for money, like some lords in Spain buy vassals from the king.[32] In this manner they could be diminished through cunning. And I declare this—it would be a sensible thing, and the Spaniards could establish some farms to raise livestock and protect however many ships are lost.

[f. 7v] [Chapter] of the province of Sotoriba, port of St. Augustine, and river of San Mateo, where the Lutherans from France had made a fort and hideout in order to rob everyone who came from Tierra Firme, or from Mexico or from Peru, or other places. They did so and took refuge themselves at the river of San Mateo, as I have said, where there resides this traitor cacique of Sotoriba and Alimacani and other villages, his vassals. In the middle of the river of San Mateo, sixty leagues toward the interior, there is another cacique who reigns for himself, and is lord of his land, called Utina, and Seravai, and Moloa, and many other of his vassals, until reaching Mayajuaca, [in the] land of Ais, toward [Cape] Cañaveral, a name given by our pilots who navigate there. Pedro Menéndez made peace with these two caciques. They have neither gold nor silver or pearls, and are poor. [They are] great miscreants and traitors, and archers, and they walk naked like the rest that I have spoken about above. Through this river of San Mateo it is possible to go to Tocobaga on the other side of Florida toward the west, and I do not say that it is always by river, but rather in this manner: one enters through the bar of San Mateo and arrives at Sarabai, which is fifty or sixty leagues upriver to the interior, or to the province of Utina, and from there one disembarks to go toward the west, going overland from town to town and reaching Cañogacola, vassals of Tocobaga, and from there to the very village of Tocobaga, which is within another very large river where Soto was and died, and with this I finish. [f. 8r] And I say no more because if one were to endeavor the conquest of this land, I would not give any more account than that which I have given, although for His Majesty it is suitable for the security of his fleets that go to Peru and to New Spain, and other parts of the Indies who are obligated to pass by that coast, and the Bahama Channel. Many ships are lost [there], and many people perish because the Indians are very contrary, and very warlike, and thus as I say it would be suitable for there to be some small fort with which to secure that canal, with some revenue that could be drawn from Mexico and Peru and the islands of Cuba, and from all parts of the Indies, for the remedy and subsistence of the soldiers in garrison at such a fort. This is what is suitable, and one other thing, to go and look for the pearls, since there are no other riches in that land, and for this I conclude. And if it were necessary,

I sign it, Hernando de Escalante Fontaneda

Fontaneda's Memoranda

The following one-folio document is filed in a different *legajo* (document bundle) than the longer Memorial but has long been acknowledged as a manuscript penned by Hernando de Escalante Fontaneda (Escalante Fontaneda, n.d.b; True 1944b). Its handwriting style is consistent with that of Fontaneda, and it contains a paraph at the end (possibly an *F* with a raised *a*), which appears similar to features of Fontaneda's full signature in the Memorial (Worth 1995: 340). Though the Memoranda is written in a more careless, cramped style, it nonetheless contains information not included in other Fontaneda texts. It also has marginal notes by Juan López de Velasco, as do the rest of Fontaneda's secondary manuscript fragments.

The transcription here follows the norms detailed in the preface, generally preserving anachronistic orthography present in the original text except in cases where it might make it difficult for modern Spanish readers to sound out the words correctly or follow the intended sentence structure.

Spanish

[f. 1r] Colon descubrio las yslas Yucayo i de Achiti y parte de la Florida con otros v[esin]os de Santo Domyngo[33]

Las islas Lucayos son de tres suertes y es desta manera lo primero las yslas de Bahama lo segundo las yslas de los Organos lo tercero las yslas de los Martires que confirma con unos caios de las Tertugas hacia poniente y estos caios son de harena y como son de harena no se ben de lejos y por esta causa se pierden muchos nabios en toda aquella costa de la canal de Bahama y islas Tertugas y de los Martires.

[Otra rrelasion]
La Habana esta hasia el sur, la Florida esta hasia el norte y entre la una tierra de la Habana ysla de Cuba, para tierra firme de la Florida estan estas yslas de Bahama y Organos y islas de los Martires y Tertugas hace una canal de hancho por do[nde] mas estrecho beynte leguas de la Habana a los Martires y de los Martires a la Florida catorce leguas entre yslas hacia España para desir mejor hacia oriente, y por lo mas hancho deste pasaje hacia poniente ay

quarenta leguas ay muchos bajos y canales hondas pero no ay pasaje para nabios ni bergantines aunque son menores, sino ay pasaje para canoas y no mas,
y esto es hacia oriente a nordeste, pero por poniente para benir de la Habana
y yr a la Florida ai pasaje pero no para benir a España, sino es por la canal
principal de Bahama[34] entre los Martires y la Habana yslas Yucayos y punta del
Cañaberal; y otra cosa no se halla para mas atajar. Portrejo se podria hazer
por en medio de la Florida, por el rio Hacho de Tocobaga al rio de San Mateo
de poniente a oriente y no con nabios sino por tiera y por mar sirbiendose los
unos nabios a los otros de una banda a la otra, para benir a España.

Otra memoria declarare generalmente de las cosas de la Florida y de un rio
que dizen el Rio Jordan, questa a la banda del norte, y tanbien dizemos de
la parte de poniente donde murio Her[nan]do de Sot y el capitan Salinas y
tanbien Fran[cis]co de Rreynoso y otros frailes que padecieron y de los q[ue]
fueron cautibos que despues bi alguno dellos bivos y en cautiberio, y tanbien
yremos declarando los trajes y comidas y bestidos de los yndios de Abalachi y de Mogoso y otros lugares mas abajo que son Tocovaga, Osiguebede, y
Carlos y Ay[s?] [T?]onsobe y otros muchos q[ue] declarare aunq[ue] no todos
y cada cosa por su capitulo y primero declaro el capi[tu]lo arriba de las yslas
Lucayos y islas de los Martires los pueblos de yndios.

[f. 1v] De Abalachi q[ue] andan desnudos los yndios y las yndias con pan
parrillas de heno nazida de los arboles ques como lana q[ue] adelante declarare y comen benados y zorros y bacas lanudas y ot[r]os muchos animales
y estos yndios cobra[n] ziertos tributos de oro bajo questa machado en oro
fino y much[as] camusas pintadas y en un rio q[ue] este pueblo tiene tiene[n]
las perlas q[ue] adelante tiene declaradas adelante y son flecheros pero
llevandolos paña y con una lengua abisada y diestra[?] se ganaria fazilmente
y mejores yndios de la Florida q[ue] los de Tocobaga i Carlos y Ais y Tegesta
y otros q[ue] tengo declarados adelante en el proseso hasta el Rio Jordan[35]
q[ue] dizen como adelante particularmente declaro cada cosa.

Los yndios de Abalachi son sujetos a los yndios Olagale y Mogoso y otros de
hazia la tierra de la zierra Aite q[ue] son los mas ricos yndios y estos lugares
son de mas balor estube yo dos años entre ellos por oro bajo mesclado en
oro fino pero en toda la costa q[ue] adelante declaro en el memorial no ai
oro bajo ni menos fino porq[ue] lo q[ue] ellos tienen es de los nabios q[ue]
se pierden de la Nueba España y del Peru q[ue] les da tormenta en la canal de Bahama y da con ellos en Cañaberal o en los Martires q[ue] se llama
Cuchijaga cabo de los Martires hazia las yslas de las Tertugas frontero a los
Martires y la Habana hazia el sur, y la propiedad de todos y sustanzia de todo
adelante lo declaro aunq[ue] no todos los lugares por tener diversos nonbres
q[ue] no me acuerdo como, y en esto zeso.

Capitulo de Colon y Narvaes y H[ernan]do de Soto, y el Ll[icencia]do Ponce de Leon y otros

English

[f. 1r] Columbus discovered the Yucayo Islands and [the island of] Achiti and part of Florida with other residents of Santo Domingo.[36]

The Lucayos Islands are of three sorts,[37] and it is in this fashion: the first, the islands of Bahama; the second, the islands of the Organos; the third, the islands of the Martyrs, which border on the west with some keys called Las Tortugas. These keys are of sand, and since they are of sand, they cannot be seen from afar, and for this reason many ships are lost in all that coast of the Bahama Channel, and the Tortugas Islands and [the islands] of the Martyrs.

[*Another account*]

Havana is toward the south, Florida is to the north, and between the one land of Havana on the island of Cuba, toward the mainland of Florida, are the islands of Bahama and the Organos and the islands of the Martyrs and Tortugas. They make a wide channel, which at its narrowest is twenty leagues from Havana to the Martyrs, and from the Martyrs to Florida fourteen leagues among islands in the direction of Spain, or better said, toward the east. And the widest point of this passage is forty leagues toward the west. There are many shoals and deep channels, but there is no passage for ships or brigantines, even though they might be small, but rather only for canoes, and nothing else. This is toward the east-northeast, but to the west, in order to come to Havana and go to Florida, there is passage.[38] But this is not the route to Spain, which is instead through the principal channel of Bahama, between the Martyrs and Havana, the Yucayos Islands, and the point of Canaveral, and nothing else is found as a greater shortcut. One could make a portage across the middle of Florida through the River Hacho of Tocobaga to the River of San Mateo, from west to east, and not with ships but rather by land, and by sea, making use of some ships on either side in order to come to Spain.

In another memorial I will declare generally about the affairs of Florida, and about a river that is called the River Jordan, which is toward the north, and we will also speak about the region to the west where Hernando de Soto died, and Captain Salinas, and also Francisco de Reynoso and other friars who died,[39] and about those who were imprisoned, some of whom afterward I saw alive and in captivity. And we will also describe the clothing and foods and clothes of the Indians of Abalachi and of Mogoso and other places lower down, which are Tocovaga, Osiguebede, and Carlos and Ay[s?], [T?]onsobe,[40] and many others that I will relate, although not all of them, and each matter in its chapter. And first I declare the above chapter about the Lucayos Islands and the islands of the Martyrs [and] their Indian towns.

[f. 1v] Regarding Abalachi, the Indian men and women walk naked with breechcloths of moss that grows from trees,[41] which is like wool, which I will declare below, and they eat deer and foxes and wooly cows[42] and many other animals. These Indians gather certain tributes of low-grade gold,[43] which is hammered into fine gold, and many painted deerskins, and in a river that this town has they have the pearls that will be declared below. And they are archers, but by sending them cloth, and with a prudent and artful interpreter, they could be won over easily. [They are] the best Indians of Florida, [better] than those of Tocobaga and Carlos and Ais and Tegesta and others that I have declared below in the process, up to [the river] that they call the River Jordan, as I will declare in detail below.

The Indians of Abalachi are subject to the Indians [of] Olagale and Mogoso and others toward the land of the hills of Aite,[44] who are the richest Indians, and these places are of greater value. I was two years among them [looking] for low-grade gold mixed with fine gold, but in all the coast that I will declare below in the memorial, there is no low-grade gold, or even less fine [gold], because what they have is from the ships that are lost from New Spain and Peru that are struck by storms in the Bahama Channel. These strike them at [Cape] Canaveral or in the Martyrs, which are called Cuchijaga [at the] end of the Martyrs toward the islands of the Tortugas, opposite the Martyrs and Havana toward the south. And I will declare the properties of everything, and the substance of all, although not all the places, on account of having diverse names that I do not remember. And with this I finish off.

Chapter about Columbus and Narváez and Hernando de Soto and the Licenciado Ponce de León and others.[45]

Fontaneda's Memorial of the Chiefs of Florida

The following one-folio document is filed in the Archivo General de Indias alongside the Memoranda text fragment just quoted (Escalante Fontaneda, n.d.b). It appears to have been a list compiled either as an addendum to the final narrative actually sent to the Spanish Crown (the Memoir) or simply as a working document used in completing other texts. Like other Fontaneda text fragments, it contains at least one hand-written insertion in the hand of Juan López de Velasco.

The transcription here follows the norms detailed in the preface, generally preserving anachronistic orthography present in the original text except in cases where it might make it difficult for modern Spanish readers to sound out the words correctly or follow the intended sentence structure.

Spanish

[f. 2r] Memoria de todos los casiques de la Florida

[*En la tierra de Abalachi*]

El primer casique questa mas cerca de Mejico es Olaga[le] y despues, Abalachi, despues Onagatano, despues Mogoso, despues Tocobaga, despues Cañogacola, despues, Pebe, y despues, Esquega, y despues, Osigbede, y despues, Piyaya, y despues, Tanpacaste.

[*En la tierra de Carlos*]

Despues, Tanpa, y Yagua, y Estantapaca, y Queyhcha, y Juestocobaga, y Sinapa, y Tomo, y Cayuca, y Ñeguitun, y Avir, y Cutespa, y Çononoguay, y Esquete, y Tonçobe, y Chipi, y Taguagemue, y Namuguya, y Caragara, y Henhenquepa, y Opacataga, y Janar, y Escuru, y Metamapo, y Estame, y Çacaspada, y Satucuaba, y Juchi, y Soco, y Vuebe, y Teyo, y Muspa y Casitua, y Cotebo, y Coyovia, y Tequemapo y Jutun, y Custevuiya, y estos son los que sujetan a Carlos.

[*En la tierra de los Martiles*]

Y en los Martiles ay tanbien poblado de yndios y el primer casique es Guarungube, despues Cuchyaga, despues Tatesta.

Despues mas adelante esta Tegesta, y Tabuaçio, y Janar, y Cabista, y Custegiyo y Jeaga y asi muchos yndios q[ue] no les se el nonbre.

[*En la tierra de Ays*][46]

Ays primeramente, y Buacata, y Tunsa, y May[a]juaca y Maycoya, y Mayaca, y Çilili, y Potano, y Moloa, y Utina.

[f. 2v] Y en San Agustin esta Sotoriba, y Moloa el bravo, y Alimacany, y Palica y otros muchos yndios pueblos que no les se el nonbre.

Y Tacatucuru, y Guale, y Paica.

Y el casique que tiene las perlas son dos casiques y el uno se llama Aquera, y el otro Ostaga.

English

[f. 2r] Memorial of all the chiefs in Florida

[In the land of Abalachi]

The first chief nearest to Mexico is Olaga[le], and afterward Abalachi, afterward Onagatano, afterward Mogoso, afterward Tocobaga, afterward Cañogacola, afterward Pebe, and afterward Esquega, and afterward Osigbede, and afterward Piyaya, and afterward Tanpacaste.

[In the land of Carlos]

Afterward Tanpa, and Yagua, and Estantapaca, and Queyhcha, and Juestocobaga, and Sinapa, and Tomo, and Cayuca, and Ñeguitun, and Avir, and Cutespa, and Çononoguay, and Esquete, and Tonçobe, and Chipi, and Taguagemue, and Namuguya, and Caragara, and Henhenquepa, and Opacataga, and Janar, and Escuru, and Metamapo, and Estame, and Çacaspada, and Satucuaba, and Juchi, and Soco, and Vuebe, and Teyo, and Muspa, and Casitua, and Cotebo, and Coyovia, and Tequemapo, and Jutun, and Custevuiya, and these are those who are subject to Carlos.

[In the land of the Martyrs]

And in the Martyrs there is also a population of Indians, and the first chief is Guarungube, afterward Cuchyaga, afterward Tatesta. Afterward, farther on, is Tegesta, and Tabuaçio, and Janar, and Cabista, and Custegiyo, and Jeaga, and thusly many Indians that I do not know their names.

[In the land of Ays]

Ays first, and Buacata, and Tunsa, and May[a]juaca, and Maycoya, and Mayaca, and Çilili, and Potano, and Moloa, and Utina.

[f. 2v] And in St. Augustine is Sotoriba, and Moloa the fierce, and Alimacany, and Palica, and many other Indian towns that I do not know their names.

And Tacatucuru, and Guale, and Paica.

And the chief who has the pearls are two chiefs, and one is called Aquera, and the other Ostaga.

Two Unsigned Memorials regarding Florida Indian Customs

The following two brief accounts are unsigned and filed as "anonymous" reports regarding the ethnography of Florida Indians, in the vast miscellaneous section of the Archivo General de Indias titled "Indiferente General" (Escalante Fontaneda, n.d.a). On the basis of the handwritten paraph at the end of the text (possibly an *E. F.*), along with the handwriting, in concert with what is known about Hernando de Escalante Fontaneda's life experiences and other writings, I concluded in 1995 (340) that these texts were fragments written by Fontaneda for possible inclusion in a longer manuscript. They may have been excluded because of their grotesque content, which nonetheless provides important details regarding the mortuary practices and beliefs of the South Florida Indians. The three folios on which these memorials are penned are also liberally sprinkled, as other Fontaneda texts are, with handwritten notes identified as those of the royal cosmographer Juan López de Velasco.

The transcription here follows the norms detailed in the preface, generally preserving anachronistic orthography present in the original text except in cases where it might make it difficult for modern Spanish readers to sound out the words correctly or follow the intended sentence structure.

Spanish

Memoria

De lo que en la Florida pasa de los yndios de la misma tiera los de Carlos primerame[n]te tienen por costunbre cada ves que muere un hijo del casique çazrifican cada vesino sus hijos o hijas q[ue] van en conpañia de la muerte del hijo del casique. La Segunda çacrefisio es que quando el casique mismo muere o la casica matan los mismos criados del o della y este es el segundo çacrefisio.

El tersero çacrifisio es que matan cada año un cativo cristiano para dar de comer a su ydolo que adoran en el que disen que su ydolo come ojos de onbre umano y con la cabesa baylan cada año que tiene por costunbre.

Y el quarto çacrifisio es que despues del verano bienen unos hichiseros en figura del demoño con unos cuernos en la cavesa y vienen aullando como lobos y ot[r]os muchos ydolos diferentes que dan boses como anymales del monte y estan estos ydolos quatro meses que nunca çosiegan noche ni de dia que tan coriendo con mucha furia que cosa p[ar]a contar la gran bestelidad quellos hazen.[47]

Memoria de los yndios y cerimonias de los yndios de Tocobaga

Quando muere un cacique de los principales hazenlo pedazos y quesenlo en unas ollas grandes y quesenlo dos dias hasta que la carne despide de los guesos y tomanlos guesos y encaxan un gueso con otro hasta que arman el onbre como estaba y ponenlo en una casa que ellos tienen por templo mientras que lo acaban de conponer ayunan quatro dias a cabo de los quatro dias ajuntance todo el pueblo de los yndios y salen con el a la procesyon y encienrralo hazyendole mucha reberencia y estonces dizen ellos que todos los que ban a la procesyon ganan yndulxencias.

Los yndios de Tegesta que es otra provincia dende los martires hasta el Cañaberal

Quando muere un cacique u prinzipal descoyuntalo y sacanle los guesos mayores del cuerrpo y los guesos menudos lo entierran con el cuerpo y en casa del casyque ponen una caxa grande y en esta caxa hencierranlos guesos grandes y alli viene todo el pueblo adorar estos guesos tienen por sus dioces.

Y en el ynvierno salen todas las canoas a la mar entre todos estos yndios sale un yndio envixado que lleba tres estacas en la cinta[48] y echale el laço al pescuezo y mientras la vallena se ba sumiendo metele una estaca por una ventana de las narices y ansi como se cabulle no la pierde porq[ue] va sobre ella y en matandola q[ue] la mata sacanla asta q[ue] encall[e] en la arena y lo prim[er]o q[ue] le acen abrenle la cabeça y sacanle dos guesos q[ue] tiene en el casc[o] y estos dos guesos hechanlos en esta caxa q[ue] ellos meten los difuntos y en esto adoran.

[paraph]

English

Memorial

Of what happens among the Indians of the land itself, those of Carlos. First, they have as custom that each time a child of the chief dies,[49] each resident sacrifices [one of[50]] their sons or daughters, who go in company of the death of the child of the chief. The second sacrifice is that when the male chief himself dies, or the female chief,[51] they kill his or her own servants, and this is the second sacrifice.

The third sacrifice is that they kill every year one captive Christian in order to feed the idol that they worship, which they say eats the eyes of humans, and they dance with the head each year, which they have as a custom.[52]

And the fourth sacrifice is that after the summer, there come some shamans in the figure of the devil, with some horns on their heads, and they come howling like wolves, and many other different idols that shout like animals of the woods, and these idols are there four months, during which they never rest, night or day, running with great fury. What a thing to recount the great bestiality that they perform![53]

Memorial of the Indians and ceremonies of the Indians of Tocobaga

When one of the principal caciques dies, they cut him into pieces and cook him in some large jars, and cook him two days until all the meat separates from the bones. And they take the bones and attach one bone with another until they reassemble the man as he was, and they place him in a house that they have as a temple while they finish assembling him. They fast for four days, [and] at the end of the four days the entire town gathers, and they come forth with him in procession and bury him, showing great reverence, and then they say that all those who go in the procession gain indulgences.

The Indians of Tegesta, which is another province from the Martyrs up to Cañaveral

When a cacique or noble dies, they cut him up and remove the large bones of the body, and they bury the small bones with the body, and in the house of the cacique they place a large chest, and in this chest they enclose the large bones. And all the town comes there to worship these bones, which they have as their gods.

And in the winter, all the canoes go to the sea, and among all these Indians there comes forth one Indian who is sent with three stakes at his waist, and he throws a lasso around the neck of a whale, and while it is coming up, he places a stake in one of the air holes, and thus since it is tied up he does not lose it because he goes on top of it. And upon killing it as they do, they run it aground on the sand, and the first thing that they do is to open up the head and remove two bones that it has in the skull, and they place these bones in this box where they place their dead, and they worship this.

[paraph][54]

Supplementary Document: Extract from letter of Pedro Menéndez de Avilés to the Crown, October 20, 1566

The following extract from a much longer letter by the adelantado of Florida (Menéndez de Avilés 1566a) includes one of the few direct independent references to Hernando de Escalante Fontaneda as part of a longer section describing Menéndez's activities in South Florida, and in particular his interactions with the Calusa Indians. The contents of this extract also provide a framework for understanding the Solís de Merás account in the following chapter, inasmuch as there are direct references in this letter to some of the events described in that more lengthy narrative.

The transcription here follows the norms detailed in the preface, generally preserving anachronistic orthography present in the original text except in cases where it might make it difficult for modern Spanish readers to sound out the words correctly or follow the intended sentence structure.

Spanish

[f. 74v] Quando se motino la jente de San Mateo en una galeota que alli tenia que tome a los Franceses se fueron en [e]lla ciento y tantos soldados a la Havana y junto de los martires en la tierra firme desta Florida entro la fragata en un puerto a tomar agua y binieron muchos yndios abordo de p[ron]to y saltaron a tierra beynte soldados sin armas ningunas porque los yndios no se escandalicasen y huyesen entro tiempo a la fragata que le fue forcado hazer bela y los beinte soldados quedaron alli tubo se entendido que los yndios los mataran luego porque es jente la de alli muy guerrera y an muerto muchos cristianos. Yendo un bergantin mio a la Havana entro en aquel puerto y allo doze destos soldados y tomolos y llevolos a la Havana dicen que los yndios les hicieron mucha amistad y buen tratam[ient]o y que los otros soldados son todos bivos que no murio ninguno porque aunque ay de alli a Carlos aquel cacique mi amigo cien leguas son estos yndios sus amigos y sabian de la cruz que yo le di y el la adora y todos estos yndios trayan una colorada al pescuezo pequeña y que tenian otra grande en que adoravan y que yban quitando sus ydolatrias yo despache ____[55] dias un bergantin alli con una carta para los ocho soldados que alli quedaron que se esten quedos y hagan el oficio de religiosos emproqurar dotrinar los yndios con cuydado y deprender bien la lengua y descubran bien la tierra y caminos y procuren mucho tener la amistad con los yndios y que dentro de dos años yo los sacare de alli y suplicare a V[uestr]a M[a]g[estad] los perdone la traicion que cometieron en amotinarse en San Mateo y dexar el fuerte desmanparada y enbiole un presente al cacique y m[an]do que este bergantin baya de alli a Carlos con una carta

mia para el y enbio alli doze soldados los seys labradores y los otros seys
nobles la mejor jente que yo e hallado y por principal dellos a un Fran[cis]co
de Reynoso que a sido hombre de armas de V[uestr]a M[agestad] a beynte
años para que proquren conservar la hamistad deste cacique y enseñarles la
dotrina hasta que bengan religiosos y enpiecen a qultibar la tierra y enbio al
mesmo heredero de Carlos que traya conmigo que es muy buen yndio porque
se le murio un indio que traya por criado y temo no se me muera el dize que
proqurara mucho que los caciques de aquella tierra sean todos mis amigos
y enbio con el para que lo haga mejor dos cristianos que me dio Carlos que
parece que habra beynte años que los tiene cautibos que por agradecerme
lo que por ellos hize en sacarlos de alli [f. 75r] ban con grande boluntad
para ayudar en esto el uno dellos es de muy buena parte hijos de principales
padres hijo de un Garcia descalante conquistador que fue en Cartajena y la
madre se decia Doña Ana de Aldana y heste se llama Hernando descalante
heran dos hermanos y siendo muchachos de diez años ynbiabalos a Salamanca y perdiose la nao y escapo toda la jente y abia el padre deste Carlos
en estos años muerto quarenta y dos dellos y a su hermano mayor deste Escalante entre ellos avia un año halle vibos cinco y cinco mugeres todas mes-
ticas del Peru y una negra entrellas Carlos me los dio todos los dos hombres
no quisieron benir qudaronse alla ni las dos mugeres las que truxe dexe en la
Havana y de los tres hombres buelvo a ynbiar los dos y el uno llevo conmigo
a esos reynos y m[an]do al que lleva cargo deste bergantin que en hechando
estos soldados en Carlos se baya a la Havana a cargar de ganados y mayz y
otras cosas para senbrar y se lo buelba a llevar y me trayga respuesta de la
carta que escrivo a Carlos y con esta respuesta me baya a buscar a Puerto
Rico o a la Española a la parte donde entendiere que esta la harmada para
que quando baya a esos reynos lleve a V[uestr]a M[a]g[estad] la lumbre del
estado en que quedan las paces con estos yndios que yo la deseo y proquro
lo ultimo de potencia y ago en ello lo posible.

English

[f. 74v] When the people from San Mateo mutinied in a galliot that I
had there, which I took from the French, a hundred or more soldiers
went in it to Havana. Next to the Martyrs on the mainland of this Florida, the frigate entered in a port to take on water, and many Indians
came aboard quickly, and twenty soldiers disembarked on land without
any weapons, so that the Indians would not be frightened and flee.
Because of the weather the frigate was forced to set sail, and the twenty
soldiers remained there. It was understood that the Indians would
kill them immediately, because the people there are very warlike, and
have killed many Christians. When one of my brigantines was going to
Havana, it entered in that port and found twelve of these soldiers, and

took them and carried them to Havana. They say that the Indians made great friendship with them, and good treatment, and that the other soldiers are all alive. None of them died because although there are one hundred leagues from there to Carlos, that chief [who is] my friend, these Indians are his friends, and they knew about the cross that I gave him, which he worships, and all these Indians wear a small red [cross] at the neck, and they had another large one that they worshipped, and they were beginning to eliminate their idolatry. I dispatched a brigantine there in ____ days with a letter for the eight soldiers who remained there telling them to remain there, and to perform the role of missionaries in attempting to indoctrinate the Indians with care, and learn well the language, and reconnoiter well the land and roads, and endeavor greatly to have friendship with the Indians. And I told them that within two years I will retrieve them from there and will ask Your Majesty to pardon them the treason that they committed in mutinying in San Mateo and leaving the fort abandoned. And I sent a present to the chief, and I commanded that this brigantine should go from there to Carlos with a letter of mine for him. And I am sending there twelve soldiers, six of them farmers and six of them nobles, the best people that I have found, and as their leader one Francisco de Reynoso, who has been a man at arms of Your Majesty for twenty years, so that they might attempt to conserve the friendship of this chief, and instruct them in the doctrine until missionaries come, and so that they should begin to cultivate the land. I am sending the very heir of Carlos, whom I brought with me, who is a very good Indian, because an Indian that he brought as a servant died, and I fear that he may die. He says that he will endeavor greatly that the chiefs of that land should all be my friends. So that he might do this better, I am sending with him two Christians that Carlos gave me, who it seems he had imprisoned for twenty years, and in order to thank me for what I did for them in getting them out of there, [f. 75r] they are going with great resolution to help in this. One of them is of very good background, a child of noble parents, son of one García de Escalante,[56] who was a conquistador in Cartagena, and the mother was called Doña Ana de Aldana, and this one is named Hernando de Escalante. There were two brothers, and when they were boys of ten years [in age], they were sent to Salamanca, and the ship was lost, and all the people escaped. The father of this Carlos killed forty-two of them in these years, and the older brother of this Escalante among them one year before. I found alive five [men] and five women, all mixed Spanish-Indian women from Peru, and a black woman among them. Carlos gave me all of them, but two of the men did not wish to come, but remained there along with two of the women. I left those that I brought in Havana, and of the three men, I am sending the two of them back, and the other one I am taking with me to these kingdoms. I am commanding he who is in charge of this brigantine that upon delivering these soldiers to Carlos, he should go to Havana to load up with livestock and corn and other things to sow, and carry them back. He is also to bring me a reply to the letter that I am writing to Carlos, and with this reply I will go to Puerto Rico or Hispaniola or wherever it is understood that the fleet is, so that when I go to those kingdoms I will bring Your Majesty an illumination of the state in which the peace made with these Indians remains, which I desire, and endeavor for it to have the greatest strength, and I am doing everything possible in this.

5
The Pedro Menéndez de Avilés
Expeditions, 1566–1569

Less than a year after Pedro Menéndez de Avilés established St. Augustine in 1565, he embarked on a journey to make contact with the powerful Indian chiefs of South Florida. This initial expedition marked the beginning of more than three years of tenuous interaction between the Spaniards and the Indians of Florida's lower gulf coast. Establishing a primary military base at Fort San Antón de Carlos at the Calusa capital that same fall, and secondary bases at forts in Tocobaga and Tequesta in the spring of 1567, Menéndez also stationed Jesuit missionaries in these outposts, along with the recently freed Hernando de Escalante Fontaneda as interpreter. Over the course of this brief and sometimes hostile era of Spanish-Indian contact, both sides learned a great deal about one another, ultimately reinforcing the Calusa policy of isolationism for more than a century afterward.

The best narrative account of these early interactions is the lengthy Memorial of Gonzalo Solís de Merás, whose relevant portions are presented here. In addition, supplementary documents include the original gubernatorial order establishing Fort San Antón and letters by General Pedro Menéndez Márquez and Jesuit Francisco Villareal, both of which provide important detail regarding the fate of the Spanish forts along the South Florida coast.

Narrative: Solís de Merás's Account of the Menéndez Expeditions

The following narrative was selected from a much lengthier memorial by Gonzalo Solís de Merás, brother-in-law of Pedro Menéndez de Avilés and fellow participant in the colonization of Florida. Portions of the original manuscript were published in 1722, and the complete text appeared in print in 1893 (González de Barcia Carballido y Zuñiga 1723; Ruidíaz y Caravia 1893). The first English translation was published in 1923 (Connor 1923). For the purposes of this book, the following narrative covers the initial journey of Menéndez in early 1566 (chapter 14; Ruidíaz y Caravia 1893: 149–68), a subsequent visit later that year (chapter 20; 226, 227–34), and the establishment of the fort at San Antón in the fall and yet another visit by Menéndez in the spring of 1567 (chapter 25; 277–93, 296–97). While the details of this narrative are extremely significant from a historical and ethnographic point of view, it is important to recognize that this text covers only the first year of contact with the South Florida Indians; the Spaniards remained another year among the Tocobaga and Tequesta and then an additional year among the Calusa. Details of those final years are included in the supplementary documents that follow.

The transcription here follows the norms detailed in the preface, generally preserving anachronistic orthography present in the original text except in cases where it might make it difficult for modern Spanish readers to sound out the words correctly or follow the intended sentence structure.

Spanish

Capitulo XIV

E á prencipio de Enero del año venidero de 66, llegó Estébano de las Alas que era General de la armada de Vizcaya é había estado en la Yaguana, é con su llegada, que traxo 2 navíos é 200 hombres, fué grande la alegría y contento que el Adelantado con su llegada recibió, y luego mandó que en todo aquel mes se aparexasen aquellos 2 navios é los 2 que el Adelantado traxo de la Florida, é un bergantín nuevo que yendo Diego de Maya con bastimento á la Florida traxo de allá, y otro patax francés que allí compró en la Habana, y una chalupa nueva, é todos estos 7 navíos hizo calefetar y ensebar é poner á punto, é á 10 de Febrero, con 500 hombres de mar é guerra dentro dellos, se partió á la Florida, é fué á descubrir si había paraje fondable é buena navegación entre las Tortugas é los Mártires, que para las flotas de Nueva España é tierra firme, é otros cualesquier navíos que por allí navegasen, era muy necesario saberlo, y hallándola muy buena, pasó adelante á la costa de la Florida, en demanda de unos hombres é mujeres que decían había veinte años que estaban cautivos, en poder de un cacique que llaman Cárlos, é cada año mataba desta gente, haciendo sacrificio della al demonio, é que todos andaban desnudos, hechos salvaxes, como los mesmos indios, é compadeciéndose el Adelantado de estos esclavos, quiso hacer esta xornada, y de allí irse á las

provincias de S[an]ta Elena, que es 50 leguas al Norte del fuerte de Sant Mateo, que se ganó á los luteranos, porque los indios decían á los soldados que
en aquel fuerte, en el puerto de Guala, había franceses nuevamente venidos.

E habiendo hecho decir muchas misas á Santo Antón, que fuese abogado
con Nuestro Señor le encontrase con el puerto donde estaban aquellos cristianos é con los mesmos cristianos; é dentro de 8 días que partió de la Habana, encontró con ellos: fué desta manera: que salió de su nao capitana, en
que iba, dexando á Estébano de las Alas, que hizo General de aquellos navíos
é su lugarteniente, é metióse el Adelantado en un bergantín con 30 hombres,
soldados, é marineros, que no demandaba más de media braza de agua, é
mandó al Capitán Diego de Maya, que iba por Almirante de los navíos, que
con otro bergantín en que iba con 30 personas, que demandaba muy poca
agua, se fuese con él, y entrambos los dos bergantines juntos fuesen navegando al luengo de la tierra, y los más navíos por lo largo, porque era la costa
bajía, y al 3.o día se apartó de sus 5 navíos con los dos bergantines, con una
cerrazón que hubo, y al 4.o día, yendo navegando al luengo de tierra, salió
una canoa al bergantín donde iba el Capitán Diego de Maya, media legua
adelante, é venía en ella una personal vogando, é cuando llegó cerca del
bergantín, habló diciendo:

—Españoles, hermanos, cristianos, seáis bien venidos, que 8 días há que
os aguardamos, que Dios é Santa María nos ha dicho que venís, é los hombres é mujeres cristianos que aquí están vivos me han mandado venir aguar-
daros aquí con esta canoa, para daros una carta que os traigo.

El Capitán Diego de Maya é la gente que con él iba en el bergantín, recibieron gran gozo é contento de ver que habían descubierto lo que el Adelantado
buscaba, é tanto deseaba, é recibió dentro del bergantín á este hombre, que
venía desnudo é pintado, hecho indio, con sus vergüenzas cubiertas.

El Capitán le abrazó é pidió la carta.

El hombre sacó de entre el cuero de venado con que traía tapadas sus
vergüenzas, una cruz, é dióla al Capitán, diciéndole que aquella era la carta
que los españoles é cristianos que allí estaban cautivos le inviaban, y que le
pedían que por la muerte que Nuestro Señor había recebido en aquella cruz
por salvarnos, no pasase sin entrar en el puerto é procurar de sacarlos de su
cacique é llevarlos á tierra de cristianos.

En esto llegó el Adelantado con su bergantín, é pasó este hombre para él,
donde entendió más particularmente deste cristiano todo lo que pasaba, é
de la calidad de la tierra é condición de los indios; é todos puestos de rodillas adoraron la cruz, dando gracias é Nuestro Señor.

Metióse el Adelantado dentro del puerto é surgió al luengo de la tierra,
que saltaban del bergantín en tierra sin mojarse los zapatos: estaría el pueblo
media legua de allí, donde estaban algunas mujeres españolas é otros cristianos, é otros dos estaban en la tierra adentro, é otra mujer, porque de más de
200 españoles de naos de las Indias, perdidas en tierra deste cacique

20 años había, é la gente della se los llevaban todos, los habían muerto su padre y él, haciendo sus fiestas y bailes al demonio.

El Adelantado no se atrevió descubrir á este cristiano el cómo pensaba sacar los cristianos é cristianas que allí estaban, porque le pareció sabía poco, é cualquier cosa que le dixese, se lo podría decir al cacique: sólo le dixo que dixese al cacique que le traía muchas cosas para él é sus muxeres, que le viniese á ver: el cacique, sabido la poca gente que el Adelantado traía, vino otro día por la mañana, con hasta 300 indios flecheros, é junto de los bergantines, al luengo de la tierra, estando la proa del uno puesto en la popa del otro é puestos los bersos de la banda de la tierra, dentro de los mesmos bergantines, con muchos perdigones dentro para lo que se pudiese ofrecer, é hizo poner un estrado en que se sentase el cacique, é ansi se asentó, é los más sus indios principales al derredor dél. El Adelantado salió de los bergantines con 30 arcabuceros con sus mechas encendidas, é sentóse á cabe dél, haciéndole el cacique é sus principales mucha obediencia al Adelantado.

Vistióle una camisa é unos zaragüelles de tafetán é una ropeta é un sombrero, é dióle otras cosas de rescates para sus mujeres: parecía muy bien, porque era muy gentil hombre, de hasta 25 años; é también dió á sus indios principales, é dióles de comer bizcochos é miel, que lo comieron muy bien.

El cacique dió al Adelantado una barra de plata que pesaba como 200 ducados, é le dixo que le diese más cosas é más de comer.

El Adelantado le dixo que no tenía comida para tanta gente, que se metiese él en los bergantines con sus prencipales, é les daría de comer é muchas cosas para ellos é sus mujeres: con la cobdicia, el cacique lo hizo ansí, é metió consigo hasta 20 indios.

El Adelantado, con gran secretud é deligencia, mandó que cada soldado estuviese cabe su indio, é 66 cabe ellos, é si se quisiesen echar á la mar, no se lo consintiesen, é mandó largar los cabos con que los bergantines estaban amarrados á tierra, é túvose á lo largo: los indios se alteraron un poco: fuéles dicho con la lengua (intérprete) que no tuviesen miedo, porque se ponían allí, á causa que no entrasen más indios en los bergantines, porque como eran pequeños, los trastornarían.

El cacique é los indios lo creyeron, é les dieron de comer é muchas cosas, y el cacique se quiso ir.

El Adelantado le dixo que el Rey de España, su Señor, le inviaba por los hombres é mujeres que él tenía, cristianos, é que si no se los llevaba, le mandaría matar; que le rogaba se los diese, porque le daría muchas cosas por ellos y sería grande su amigo y hermano.

El cacique dixo que era contento y que él iría por ellos.

El Adelantado le dixo que si él iba, que su gente le mataría porque le dexaba ir; que le rogaba inviase algunos indios por ellos.

El cacique, con miedo, ansí lo hizo, y dentro de una hora truxeron 5 mujeres é 3 cristianos, á los cuales mandó el Adelantado dar luego unas

camisas, é de cariseas é Lóndres, que traía, mandó á 4 ó 5 sastres que allí
venían, les hiciesen de vestir, y lo mesmo los cristianos: lloraban de contento,
que era cosa de ver. El Adelantado las consolaba é regalaba mucho, é decían
que tenían mucha pena por los hijos que dexaban allí.

El Adelantado dió muchas cosas al cacique é á su gente, é le invió muy
contento, diciéndole el cacique que dentro de 3 meses le tendría allí otros 2
cristianos é una cristiana, que estaban en la tierra adentro, é que le rogaba
fuese por la mañana, antes que se partiese á su pueblo, para que sus mujeres
lo viesen. El Adelantado dixo que ansí lo haría. A la mañana invió el cacique
muchas canoas por él: estando el Adelantado sospechoso de su ida, llegó en
una canoa el cristiano que había salido en la canoa á la mar con la cruz, que
se había ido con el cacique, á visitar á sus mujeres, de parte del Adelantado,
é llevarles un presente, é dixo este cristiano al Adelantado que no fuese al
pueblo, porque tenían concertado de le matar, y los indios con las canoas,
que sabían la traición, sospecharon que aquel cristiano lo descubría, é fué-
ronse huyendo: el Adelantado, porque el cacique é indios entendiesen que él
no sabia la traición, levó las áncoras de los bergantines é con la boga se fué
á surgir junto del pueblo, é allí, tocando 2 clarines, campeando las banderas,
hizo señal que viniesen las canoas por él, porque los bergantines no podían
pasar más adelante, y como ninguna canoa quiso venir, el Adelantado salió
del puerto para buscar sus 5 navíos, y como no parecían, los cristianos le
dixeron que 50 leguas de allí más adelante, había un muy buen puerto, é que
había otros 3 cristianos cabtivos, en poder de los indios. Al Adelantado le
pareció que sus navíos habían corrido allá, y tuvo deseo de rescatar aquellos
3 cristianos, é fué allá, é no halló los navíos, ni los cristianos, y á la vuelta que
volvió, halló los 5 navíos surtos sobre este puerto de Cárlos y que Estébano
de las Alas había ido al pueblo con cient soldados, que como los indios vieron tantos navíos é gente, que fueron á reconocer con las canoas, temieron
é hicieron buen recibimiento á Estébano de las Alas: rescataron los soldados
allí más de 2.000 ducados de oro é plata con los indios, á trueco de bujerías.

El Adelantado acordó de inviar el cristiano á Cárlos, para que le diese á
entender que el Adelantado no sabía nada de la traición que le armaba para
matarle. El Cárlos lo creyó, é con cobdicia que tuvo de que le diese otras cosas, é de tomar por amigo al Adelantado, le vino á ver, con solos 5 ó 6 indios
no más, é le dixo que le quería tomar por su hermano mayor, para hacer todo
lo que le mandase, é que le quería dar por mujer una hermana que tenía,
mayor que él, á quien quería mucho, para que la llevase á tierra de cristianos y se la volviese á inviar, que cuando volviese, él iría también y se haría
cristiano, con todos sus indios, que le parecía que era mejor que no ser indio,
que le rogaba fuese por ella, ó fuese á ver á sus mujeres é pueblo.

El Adelantado dixo que otro día iría, é le regaló mucho é invió. Quisieran
los capitanes é soldados que el Adelantado no soltara este cacique, porque
decían que tenía mucho dinero, é que todo se lo daría por soltarlo. El Adelan-

tado, pareciéndole por la confianza que el cacique del hacía, que era bella-
quería, é que nunca serían cristianos, no lo quiso hacer.

Todos los capitanes, soldados, é marineros que allí estábamos, quedamos
admirados de la respuesta que el Adelantado diera, porque sabíamos lo mucho que había gastado en esta empresa, é la poca ayuda que S. M. le había
dado, é que quedaba en España endeudado, é lo mismo dexaba á sus deudos
é amigos, é lo estaba en la Habana, é había enviado á tomar dineros presta-
dos á la Nueva España, y lo tuvimos por hombre mal aconsejado, que por lo
poco sacara de aquel cacique cient mill ducados, que aunque no los tuviera,
sus indios é caciques amigos, en cuyo poder estaba algún oro é plata de
naos perdidas, que no lo conoscían, ni sabían qué cosa era, pudiera con ellos
desempeñarse, y á los que lo estaban por amor dél, é hallarse más esforza-
dos para una tan santa é buena conquista como esta, para procurar, como
procuraba, según la grande inclinación que todos veíamos tenía, de plantar
en ella el Santo Evangelio; porque los indios no sabían qué cosa era oro ni
plata, y por un naipe, que era as de oros, hubo indio que dió un pedazo de
oro que valía 70 ducados, é por unas tixeras, media barra de plata, que valía
cient ducados. Rescataron de aquella vez, todos los soldados que primero
habían llegado con Estébano de las Alas, y los que llegaron con el Adelantado
en los dos bergantines, hasta 3.500 ducados en todo, de que andaban ya
regocijados é contentos y empezaban á jugar, teniendo el dinero en poco: no
les quitó ni negó cosa el Adelantado de lo que cada uno rescató, ni él rescató
ninguna cosa, porque no entendiesen los indios que él iba á buscar aquello.
E luego otro día siguiente que el cacique Cárlos se salió de los bergantines,
fué á comer con él el Adelantado, llevando 200 arcabuceros consigo é una
bandera, 2 pífanos é atambores, 3 trompetas, una arpa é vihuela de arco é un
salterio, é un enano pequeño, gran cantador é danzador, que traía consigo.
Había como 2 tiros de arcabuz, donde desembarcó, á la casa del cacique,
que coxieran dentro della dos mill hombres, aunque no estuvieran muy
apretados: fué su gente en ordenanza hasta esta casa, que no consintió el
Adelantado entrasen dentro, sino que fuera della estuviesen á punto con sus
mechas encendidas.

Sólo se metió dentro al aposento del cacique, con hasta 20 gentiles hombres, donde había unas ventanas grandes, por donde veía su gente: estaba el
cacique en un buen aposento, sentado sólo con grande autoridad, y una india
también sentada, apartada un poco dél, en un alto medio estado del suelo,
y hasta 500 indios prencipales é otras 500 indias: los indios cerca dél, y las
indias cerca de la india, en lo baxo.

Como el Adelantado subió á aquel aposento, el cacique le dexó el lugar
que tenía, y se apartaba mucho dél.

El Adelantado le puso cabe sí, é luego se levantó el cacique, é según
costumbre dellos, fuese para el Adelantado á tomarle las manos, haciendo
cierta cerimonia, que es cuando acá besan la mano al Rey, que no se puede

hacer más cortesía entre ellos, é la que los indios vasallos suelen hacer á
sus caciques: luego vino la india, é hizo lo mesmo, é luego todos aquellos,
é indias prencipales que allí estaban, é pusiéronse más de 500 indias, de 10
años hasta 15, sentadas de la banda de fuera de la ventana, á cantar, é otros
indios á saltar é voltear: cantaron los indios é indias prencipales que cabe el
cacique estaban, que decían, según después se supo, que este era el mayor
regocijo, respeto obediencia que aquel cacique, ni otro ninguno de aquella
tierra, pudo hacer al Adelantado, porque danzaron los hermanos del cacique
é sus tíos é tías, que había indias, entre estas prencipales, de 90 é 100 años,
que danzaron: todos mostraron estar muy contentos é tener mucha alegría.

Después que hubieron acabado sus prencipales de danzar é cantar, aunque las indias que estaban fuera nunca lo dejaron de hacer, hasta que el
Adelantado se fué, é cantaban por mucha orden: estaban asentadas de 100
en 100, é las 50 cantaban un poco é callaban, é volvían á cantar las otras 50;
el cacique dixo al Adelantado, después que sus prencipales danzaron, que si
quería que trajesen la comida para él é sus cristianos.

El Adelantado le dixo que no tan presto; é llevaba escritos muchos vocablos en lenguaje de indios, los cuales eran de mucho comedimiento é amor
para hablar á la mujer prencipal de Carlos é á su hermana, é pensando que
aquella que estaba allí era la mujer prencipal del cacique, le dixo las palabras
que pensaba decirle, en su propia lengua: quedaron admirados el cacique
é los indios: pensaron que hablaba el papel é lo que en él estaba escrito, y
entendió el cacique que pensaba el Adelantado que aquella era su mujer
prencipal, é díxole con la lengua que allí tenían para entenderse, que era de
los cristianos cautivos, que aquella no era su mujer, que era su hermana, la
que le había dado por mujer al Adelantado.

Entonces se levantó el Adelantado é la tomó por la mano, é la sentó cabe
sí, en el medio dél é del cacique, é por lo que llevaba escrito le dixo en su
lengua, leyendo por el papel, muchas cosas, de que ellos é todos los indios é
indias que allí estaban, se alegraron. Era esta india de hasta 35 años, no nada
hermosa, aunque muy grave, tanto que andando el tiempo, admiró esto á
todos nosotros, porque parecía que desde su nacimiento la habían criado á
saber tener gravedad.

Pidió el Adelantado al cacique truxese allí á su mujer prencipal, el cual lo
hizo: era de 20 años, muy buen dispuesta y hermosa, de muy buenos feycio-
nes: tenía muy buenas manos é ojos, é miraba con mucha gravedad á una
parte é á otra, con toda honestidad: tenía muy buena mesura, que aunque
entre las muchas indias que allí se vió hermosas, ninguna lo era tanto como
ésta: traía las cejas muy bien hechas, é á la garganta un muy hermoso collar
de perlas é piedras é una gargantilla de cuentas de oro: estaba desnuda
como la otra hermana del cacique, con sólo sus vergüenzas cubiertas.

El Adelantado la tomó por la mano, é la puso entre la india y el cacique,
é habló con ella, en su lengua, muchas palabras, que las llevaba escritas en

el papel, de que ella se regocijó mucho; en especial, que como habían dicho al Adelantado que era muy hermosa, llevaba escrito en su lengua palabras para decírselo, de que ella mostró no le pesar, é púsosele en el rostro muy buena color, mirando á su marido con honestidad: el cacique mostró pesarle por haber traído á su mujer, é mandaba que se fuese, pensando que se la querían tomar: el Adelantado le dixo con la lengua que no la inviase é que comiese allí con él, porque tenía muchas cosas que le dar; é luego hizo traer el presente que llevaba, é hizo vestir á la hermana del cacique una camisa é otra á la mujer del cacique, é sendas ropas verdes, con que la mujer del cacique estaba harto hermosa: dióles cuentas, tixeras é cuchillos, cascabeles y espexos, con que se holgaron mucho, en especial con los espexos, cuando se miraban, y desto reían mucho los indios y las indias que allí estaban, é dió al cacique otro vestido, sin otro que antes le había dado, é otras menuden- cias de rescates, é dos hachas é dos machetes, é también dió á los indios é indias prencipales que allí estaban, algunos rescates, sin que por esto diesen al Adelantado ningún género de interés, ni él lo pidiese: mandó traer la co- mida, la cual fué muchos géneros de pescado muy bueno, asado é cocido, é ostriones crudos, cocidos é asados, sin otra cosa. El Adelantado había hecho desembarcar un quintal de bizcochos muy buenos é una botixa de vino é otra de miel de azúcar, é repartió por todos aquellos prencipales, é con la lengua les mandó truxesen escudillas para echarles de aquel miel: dióles algunas confituras é carne de membrillo, y en un plato de por sí comió el Adelan- tado, y la hermana del cacique en otro, y el cacique é su mujer en otro, pero en mesa, manteles y pañizuelos que el Adelantado había hecho llevar: bien entendieron ser nuestra comida muy mejor que la suya.

Cuando la comida se traía, tocaron las trompetas que estaban de la parte de fuera, y en cuanto comió el Adelantado, tocaron los instrumentos muy bien é bailaba el enano: empezaron á cantar 4 ó 6 gentiles hombres que allí estaban, que tenían muy buenas voces, con muy buena orden, que por ser el Adelantado muy amigo de música, siempre procura de traer consigo lo mejor que puede; alegrándose los indios extrañamente de oir aquello. Dixo el caci- que á las mozas que no cantasen, porque sabían poco, y los cristianos sabían mucho: cesó la música: rogó el cacique que hasta que él se fuese, siempre tocasen los instrumentos é cantasen: el Adelantado lo mandó ansí. Acabaron é alzóse la mesa: entonces dixo que se quería ir.

El cacique le dixo que fuese á reposar á un aposento que estaba allí, con su hermana, pues se la había dado por mujer, é si no lo hacía, que sus indios se escandalizarían, diciendo que se reía dellos é della é la tenía en poco; é había en el pueblo más de 4,000 indios é indias.

El Adelantado mostró una poca de turbación é dixole por la lengua que los cristianos no podían dormir con mujeres que no fuesen cristianas.

El cacique le respondió que ya su hermana y él y su gente lo eran, pues le había tomado por su hermano mayor.

El Adelantado le respondió que antes que fuesen cristianos, habían de saber é creer muchas cosas, é díxoles quién era Dios é su saber, poder é bondad, é que á este sólo han de adorar todas criaturas que nascen en la tierra, é hacer lo que él manda, é que los cristianos que lo hacemos, cuando morimos acá en la tierra, nos vamos para el cielo, y que allí estamos siempre sin morir y vemos á nuestra mujer, hijos, hermanos é amigos, é siempre estamos alegres, cantando é riendo, y que ellos, porque no conocen esto, no sirven ni adoran á Dios, antes sirven á un cacique muy bellaco é mentiroso, que se llama el diablo, é cuando mueren, se van para él, é perpétuamente están llorando, porque unas veces tienen mucho frío é otras veces mucho calor, y ninguna cosa les dá contento.[1] Dixo otras razones muy eficaces, y Cárlos respondió que por que había conocido en el modo de los españoles, en su música y en sus manjares, ser mejor su ley, la quería abrazar, y le había dado á su hermana, y se la volvía á dar para que se la llevase; por lo cual el Adelantado hubo de llevarla al puerto con algunos indios é indias que la acompañasen, y después de consultar el caso con sus capitanes, indicóles que[2] parecíale podría venir en rompimiento con los indios, y esto no convenía, por el desinio del Adelantado, que todo lo mostraba, dende que había partido de España, su interés particular era que los indios se volviesen cristianos; y los capitanes le respondieron que convenía hacerle mucha fiesta á ella y á los indios é indias que con ella estaban, y que hubiese aquella noche muchos regocijos é música, é la bautizasen é pusiesen nombre, é que el Adelantado durmiese con ella, porque sería este gran prencipio para que se confiasen dél é de los demás cristianos, é que todos aquellos indios é los caciques, sus vecinos, serían cristianos, é que por ninguna manera convenía hacer otra cosa.

El Adelantado mostró mucho . . .[3] procurar otro remedio, é como no se pudo tomar, ni se halló, acordó que se hiciese ansí.

Luego las cristianas que allí estaban, la hicieron lavar, tocar é vestir, que pareció harto mexor que primero, cuando estaba desnuda; é los capitanes, con industria, la alababan de muy hermosa é mesurada: pusiéronle nombre Doña Antonia, é aquel puerto Sant Antón, por la devoción que el Adelantado había tomado al señor Sant Antón, para que le encontrase aquellos cristianos é cristianas que iba á buscar: duró la cena é música é regocijo en tierra, en unas tiendas que el Adelantado tenía armadas, junto de sus navíos, hasta las dos después de media noche, que el Adelantado la tenía cabe sí, é con la lengua le decía muchas cosas que la alegraban, é respondía tan discretamente y en tan pocas palabras, que á todos nos admiraba: danzaron sus indias é las mujeres cristianas é otros soldados, é acabado esto, la llevaron á acostar á una cama que el Adelantado mandó hacer, y él se fué para ella, y á la mañana, ella se levantó alegre, é las mujeres cristianas que le hablaron, dixeron que estaba muy contenta; é luego invió con una canoa que allí estaba, á 2 indios é 2 indias, á su hermano, el cual vino á verla, y el Adelantado le recibió muy bien, é dixo que deseaba que tuviese una cruz grande, puesta cabe su casa, é que todos los días, á las mañanas, los hombres é mujeres é los niños, la fuesen á besar y adorar, é la tuviesen por su ídolo mayor, é le dixo las causas para ello, é que quitaste los demás ídolos que tenía.

El cacique dixo que sí haría, mas que sus ídolos no los podía quitar tan presto, hasta que su hermana volviese, é los indios que con ella iban, é les dixesen lo que habían de hacer.

Este cacique se llamaba Cárlos, porque se llamaba ansí su padre, é su padre se puso aquel nombre, porque los cristianos cautivos que tenía le dixeron que el Emperador Cárlos era el mayor Rey de los cristianos.

Hízose la cruz é hízola el Adelantado hincar allí, é con grande música é devoción se hincó de rodillas é la besó é lo mesmo todos los españoles que allí estábamos: luego hizo lo mesmo la india Doña Antonia é las más mujeres é indios que consigo tenía: luego la besó é adoró Cárlos é sus indios: tenía este Cárlos un Capitán, muy buen indio, que era casado con hermana del Cárlos y desta Doña Antonia, y el cacique con hermana del Capitán, y los indios, al parecer, según los cristianos decían, más temían á este Capitán que al cacique, é dixo á su cacique que él había de ser Capitán de aquella cruz, para que todos hiciesen lo que el Adelantado mandaba, irla á besar é adorar á la mañana; y ansí, se la entregó el Adelantado, é con gran reverencia, la llevó á cuestas á las canoas; é fué el Adelantado luego á embarcar, llevando consigo á doña Antonia é á los 3 indios é 4 indias é 7 cristianos é cristianas que estaban cautivos, porque otras 2 mujeres se habían ya ido á los indios é con el deseo que tenían de los hijos que dejaban; é dió orden á Estébano de las Alas se fuese á la Habana con esta india é su gente, é la entregasen al tesorero Juan de Ynistrosa, que era lugarteniente del Adelantado en aquella isla para las cosas de la Florida, é le escribió diese orden como fuese dotrinada la india é los que con ella iban, é les hiciesen todo buen tratamiento, é cuando fuese tiempo, los hiciesen cristianos, que él volvería á la Habana, dentro de 3 ó 4 meses para la llevar á su tierra; é que diese el más bastimento que pudiese, aves y ganados, á Estébano de las Alas, é le despachase luego, para que con los 5 navíos que llevaba se fuese al fuerte de Sant Agustín, á donde el Adelantado le aguardaría, para ir sobre los franceses, que decían estaban en Guale y en Santa Elena; porque él se iba con 2 bergantines, descubriendo toda aquella costa de los Mártires, á ver si hallaba algún puerto bueno en la canal de Bahama, é procurando de ir á hacer amistades con los caciques é pueblos que topase; é ansí se partieron con próspero viento, el Estébano de las Alas, con 5 navíos, á la Habana, y el Adelantado, con 2 bergantines, al luengo de los Mártires, á San Agustín.

Capitulo XX

El Adelantado . . . le dixo [al Licenciado Valderrama] . . . que él quería partirse otro día por la mañana á tierra del cacique Cárlos, y llevarle á su hermana, que estaba allí en la Habana, á causa de que se le habían muerto los indios é indias prencipales que consigo había traído, que no le habían quedado más que dos, é si aquellos y ella se morían, pensaría que los había hecho matar el Adelantado, y aquel cacique era señor de mucha tierra y de los Mártires y canal de Bahama, donde las naos de las Indias tienen el mayor peligro en aquella navegación; que convenía mucho tenerle por amigo, procurando se volviesen él é sus indios cristianos; é que dentro de 10 ó 12 días volvería. . . .

[Juan de Ynistrosa] díjole también [al Adelantado] que era muy discreta la india Doña Antonia, hermana de Cárlos, é de tanta gravedad que espantaba á los del pueblo, é que en pocos días ella y una criada suya, á quien quería mucho, habían deprendido con gran facilidad todas las cosas de oraciones é dotrina cristiana para ser bautizada, é ansí lo era ya, é que estaba muy triste por ausencia de S[u] S[eñorí]a é por la muerte de sus indios é indias, é que despues que le habían dicho que S[u] S[eñorí]a era venido, era grande su gozo y alegría, é que lloraba de placer; que era menester regalarla é hacer mucha cuenta della, que pues la quería llevar, convenía fuese diciendo mucho bien, porque él é los de la Habana habían tenido gran cuenta con ella de regalarla é que tuviese contento.

El Adelantado le dixo que el día antes, cuando desembarcaran, la inviara á vesitar, é que para hoy la iría á ver, é que ansí lo haría en acabando de comer, é ansí lo hizo, inviándole primero de lo que comía y ciertas camisas y ropa, que encomendó al tesorero que le comprase, para que la india estuviese contenta é viese que él traía alguna cosa; é llevó consigo, cuando la fué á ver, muchas personas bien tratadas que la acompañaron, é la música, que nunca el Adelantado andaba sin ella: halló la india triste, y aunque el Adelantado le hacía muchos regalos, no se quería alegrar: rogóle muchas veces con la lengua que le dixese por qué estaba triste: díxole que ella quería que Dios la matase, por que cuando desembarcaron, no inviara por ella é la llevara á su casa, para comer con el Adelantado é dormir con él.

Entendido el Adelantado ser mujer tan prencipal, de tan buen entendimiento, é que no le faltaba razón, le dijo que los cristianos que traían aquella cruz,—que es el Adelantado Caballero de la Orden de Santiago,—cuando desembarcaban de hacer jornada contra sus enemigos, no podían dormir con su mujer hasta pasar 8 días, é que él quisiera que éstos fueran pasados, porque la quería mucho.

La india se rió medio llorando, é dixo que si ella supiese que él decía verdad, que estaría alegre.

El Adelantado le rogó que lo estuviese, por que él la decía; é dixo, empezando á contar por los dedos, que ya eran pasados 2 días, é señaló los 6; que pasados aquéllos, ella se iría para su casa: el Adelantado le dijo que ansí lo hiciese, é se levantó el Adelantado, é lo abrazó con gran regocijo, é le pidió las manos, é mandó que tañesen los instrumentos, porque aquellos no los había visto en aquella tierra é que le parecían muy bien: estuvo el Adelantado allí más de una hora, regocijándola.

Tenía á su cargo esta india un regidor de aquella villa, que se llama Alonso de Rojas, que tiene una mujer prencipal, la cual fué madrina desta india cuando se bautizó, é la quería mucho é dotrinaba, que contó al Adelantado muchas cosas del buen entendimiento della, con que el Adelantado se holgó mucho. É dixo á la india que si tenía deseo de irse á su tierra: ella dixo que sí, é muy grande: el Adelantado le dixo si quería que se fuesen otro día: ella dijo que sí, é que le rogaba mucho que se fuesen: el Adelantado le dijo que ansí lo harían, é se despidió della é se fué á su posada, que era cerca de allí.

Aquella noche aconteció que, siendo pasada la media noche, estando el Adelantado durmiendo en su aposento, con una vela encendida, la india dijo á una mujer, su amiga, á quien quería mucho, de las que el Adelantado había traído de la Florida, que tenía por esclava Cárlos, su hermano, que se fuese con ella á casa del Adelantado, porque le había mandado ir allá; la mujer lo creyó, é se fué con ella, é con la india su criada, y llamó á la puerta de la posada del Adelantado: abrieron á saber quién era: conosciéronla: dijo que el Adelantado le había mandado que fuese allá con la india, y el mozo que abrió la puerta, creyendo decían verdad, las dejó entrar é metió en el aposento del Adelantado, donde estaba una vela encendida, é la india la tomó en la mano, é miró si estaba en la cama alguna mujer con el Adelantado, é despúes miró al derredor de la cama, é por bajo.

El Adelantado, aunque muy cansado é quebrantado, despertó, y como la vió con la candela en la mano, turbóse, é dixo contra la mujer que venía con ella:

—¿Qué es esto, hermana?

D[oñ]a Antonia se sentó encima de la cama con la candela, para ver lo que el Adelantado decía: la mujer respondió al Adelantado que Doña Antonia la había dicho que mandaba S[u] S[eñorí]a que se la trajesen á aquella hora, é que ella, creyéndolo, lo había hecho ansí.

El Adelantado, con alegre rostro é regocijado, riéndose mucho desto, le dijo que le dijese que holgara mucho que fueran pasados los 8 días, para que se acostara allí con él.

Doña Antonia dijo por la lengua que le rogaba la acostase consigo en un canto de la cama, é que no se llegaría á él, para que su hermano Cárlos supiese que habían dormido juntos, porque de otra manera pensaría que se reía della, é no querría ser amigo de verdad de los cristianos, ni ser cristiano como ella, de que le pesaría mucho.

El Adelantado le pareció que no le faltaba razón; mas que Dios le mataría; que si ella quería que él se muriese, que se desnudase é acostase con él: ella empezó entonces á echar los brazos al Adelantado, é dixole que porque no se muriese, no se quería con él acostar.

Llamó el Adelantado á un criado suyo, que sacase de un cofre algunas co-sas, que fueron 3 camisas é sendos espejos é gargantillas de cuenta é vidrio, que eran rescates que el Adelantado había hecho recojer aquel día, para llevar á su hermano Cárlos; é dixo á la mujer cristiana que con ella fué, que si el Adelantado no despertara, ella quería matar la candela é acostarse con él; é con esto se fueron contentas.

Luego á la mañana el Adelantado se fué á embarcar, é llevó la india con-sigo, é á su criada, é á 2 mujeres cristianas de las que habían sido allá cau-tivas: fué en un patax é una chalupeta, con hasta 30 soldados é marineros: hizo vela con próspero viento: llegó al pueblo de Cárlos á tercero día: surgió á la entrada del puerto, porque, como llevaba poca gente, no se atrevió llegarse al pueblo: entonces dijo la india al Adelantado que se desembarcase con ella é fuese al pueblo.

El Adelantado le dijo que en ninguna manera lo podía hacer, porque le convenía partirse luego á buscar cristianos, para que viviesen allí y enseña-sen á ser cristianos á su hermano é á los indios de aquella tierra, si lo quisie-sen ser, é que él le prometía entonces hacerle una casa en aquella tierra, en que viviese, en el pueblo de los cristianos; é que los parientes de los indios é indias que se murieran en la Habana, pensarían que el Adelantado los había muerto, é le querrían hacer algún mal á él é á sus soldados, de que se podría romper la guerra con su hermano, y desto le pesaría mucho, porque lo quería bien, por amor della, é lo tenía por hermano; é que luego se quería volver: la india le respondió que le pesaba mucho, porque el Adelantado no desem-barcaba, é que estuviera algunos días en tierra, hasta ser pasados los 8 días, para que durmiese con él; mas que también tenía miedo que los indios fue-sen bellacos é le hiciesen algún mal; que le rogaba viniese lo más presto que pudiese, é trujese cristianos, para que viviesen allí, é volviesen á su hermano é á los demás indios cristianos.

Luego vinieron muchas canoas, y la Doña Antonia invió á decir á su her-mano cómo estaba allí, que viniese por ella: era cosa de ver la alegría que los indios tenían con ella, é otros lloraban de pesar, de los indios é indias que se murieron, que habían ido con ella. Dentro de 2 horas, con hasta 12 canoas, é las dos dellas amarradas una con otra é cubiertas y entoldadas con sus arcos y esteras, muy bien, é primeramente metióse él y el Capitán, su cuñado, é otros 6 principales, en el patax con el Adelantado: fué cosa de ver cómo recibieron la Doña Antonia y su hermano, é las cerimonias que se hicieron: mandó el Adelantado traer de comer é tañer los instrumentos, é dar á los indios de las canoas algún maíz é cazave, é algunos cuchillos é tixeras, espexos é casabeles, y acabando de comer, dió un presente á Cárlos para él é su mujer, é dió otro al Capitón para él é su mujer, que era hermana de Doña Antonia, y dió á los indios prencipales que allí estaban, é á la Doña Antonia le dió algunas cosas que llevaba para ella: dixo el Adelantado á Cárlos si quería ser cristiano é trasquilarse, y si quería ir á tierra de cristianos, como se lo había prometido, é que le trujese los cristianos que dijo le daría cuando allí volviese.

El Cárlos le respondió que le dejasen hablar con su Capitán aparte, é que luego le daría la respuesta; é ansí se apartaron más de un cuarto de hora, é dixeron al Adelantado que por aquellos 9 meses, no podía en ninguna manera ir á tierra de cristianos, ni volverse cristiano por entonces, porque sus indios no se levantasen contra él é le matasen; que pasado aquel tiempo, volviese el Adelantado; é justicó con razones bastantes.[4]

Encargóle á Doña Antonia el Adelantado y se volvió á la Habana. . . .

Chapter XXV

Antes que el Adelantado partiese de la Florida á hacer los socorros, acordó de inviar á Fran[cis]co de Reinoso, hombre de armas de S[u] M[agestad], muy buen soldado, con 30 soldados, al cacique Cárlos, y enviarle á su primo, que era heredero suyo, que pusieron nombre Don Pedro cuando se bautizó, y á otro indio su criado, porque le pareció ser este indio heredero de Cárlos, de muy buen entendimiento é grande su amigo, é no quería el Adelantado que se le muriese, é mostraba tener muestra de buen cristiano y pretendía casarle con Doña Antonia, la india, pues habían de ser herederos del estado de Cárlos y procurarían que los indios fuesen cristianos; y nombró por capitán de aquellos 30 soldados al Fran[cis]co de Reinoso, é dióle instrucción hiciese una casa fuerte en el pueblo de Cárlos, é procurasen todos, con gran devoción, á las mañanas é á las tardes, adorar la cruz, diciendo la dotrina cristiana, para que los indios hiciesen lo mesmo, é trabaxasen de los dotrinar lo mexor que pudiesen, y que con la amistad de los indios procurasen de saber si un río que estaba 2 leguas de allí iba á dar á la laguna de Maymi, y cuántas leguas había, porque ya el Adelantado sabía las que había desta laguna á Macoya, é que había pasaje; porque iría dentro de 3 ó 4 meses á Cárlos, con bajeles suficientes, para ver si podría pasar por aquel río á S[a]n Mateo é San Agustín, que era lo que el Adelantado mucho deseaba, por el gran servicio que entendía hacía á S[u] M[agestad] y á los tratantes en las Indias y al bien general de los que andaban en la población é conquista de la Florida; é dióle un presente para Cárlos y otro para su mujer y otro para Doña Antonia la india.

Y llegado el Fran[cis]co de Reinoso, en el bergantín, á Cárlos, con sus 30 soldados é con D[on] Pedro el indio, heredero de Cárlos, é con el otro indio, echaron en tierra los dos indios, para que hablasen á Cárlos é á Doña Antonia, de que fué grande el contentamiento que todos los indios recibieron con ellos, é luego vino Cárlos al patax, ofreciendo su amistad al capitán Fran[cis]co de Reinoso é soldados, que pues el Adelantado era su hermano mayor é le inviaba á mandar que los recibiese é hiciese buen tratemiento, que él lo había de hacer, y que él ni ningún indio de los suyos le habían de hacer mal: ansí se desembarcaron con gran regocijo é contento, é los llevó á su pueblo, y le dió el Fran[cis]co de Reinoso el presente que llevaba y dió una carta, la cual él aclaró con la lengua lo que en ella decía, que era encargándole mucho fuesen bien tratados los cristianos dél y de sus indios, y ansí lo prometió Cárlos al capitán Reinoso, é le hizo hacer una casa, en que se recogieron; los cuales, arbolando cerca della una cruz, la iban á adorar á la mañana é tardes, diciendo su dotrina cristiana, y á ella acudían los indios é indias con gran devoción.

Partióse el bergantín para la Habana, con 5 ó 6 marineros, como lo había ordenado el Adelantado: llevó consigo á la india Doña Antonia, con 5 ó 6 indios prencipales, porque ansí lo había ordenado el Adelantado, por la seguridad del capitán Fran[cis]co de Reinoso é 30 soldados que con él quedaban, porque era muy poca la confianza que el Adelantado hacía del Cárlos, porque cuando le trató, le vió tener muchas muestras de traidor.

Llegada la india en el bergantín á la Habana, dentro de 6 días que partió de Cárlos, fué luego á la marina Alonso de Rojas, Regidor de aquella villa, y llevó á Doña Antonia é á sus indios á su casa, como de antes los tenía, é su mujer, que era madrina de Doña Antonia, la recibió muy bien, haciéndole mucho regalo é buen tratamiento; é luego el bergantín é otro patax cargaron de ganados vivos é algún bastimento, é fueron con ellos á Cárlos.

Escribió el capitán Fran[cis]co de Reinoso el trabajo é peligro con que vivían, é que por 2 ó 3 veces, á traición, los había querido matar Cárlos, é que inviaba á pedir á su hermana Doña Antonia é los demás indios, que tenía muy gran deseo de verlos, que luego se volverían, á fin que teniéndoles consigo, poder matar al Fran[cis]co de Reinoso é los soldados que con él estaban, porque estaba muy encarnizado este cacique y su padre, de matar cristianos, que en 20 años que había que aquellos hombres é mujeres que el Adelantado allí halló cautivos, decían que habían muerto padre é hijo más de 200 cristianos, sacrificándolos al demonio, é haciendo sus fiestas é bailes con ellos, é que eran todas gentes de naos perdidas en la carrera de las Indias, porque aunque se perdiesen 100 leguas de allí, se los llevaban á él, como era cacique de mucha costa de mar en los Mártires é canal de Bahama, que es donde las naos que van de Indias á España corren el mayor peligro; é por esto hacía grandes diligencias el Adelantado de poblar aquella costa y querer atraer los caciques de indios á su amistad. Y ansí en los 6 bergantines que sacó de la Habana con 150 hombres, el día que el Maestre de Campo partió para San Agustín con la nao cargada de bastimento é municiones que habían sobrado de la armada, que fué á . . .[5] y le había dado orden subiese por la ribera de San Mateo arriba, hasta Macoya, que él iba á saber si por la parte de Cárlos podía ir á Macoya, para de alli ir á San Agustín é San Mateo; é llevaba consigo á Doña Antonia, indios é indias que consigo tenía; é fué con próspero viento en 2 días naturales.

Llevaba consigo al Padre Rogel, de la Compañía de Jesús, muy docto é gran religioso, y al Padre Fran[cis]co (de Villareal), de la mesma Compañía: llevaba indios prencipales de Tequesta, que era donde dejó el navío que venía de

San Mateo, con la gente amotinada, los 20 soldados, que acertando á pasar
un bergantín que el Adelantado inviaba de la Florida á la Habana á buscar
bastimento, y llegando sobre aquel puerto, dióle el viento contrario, y entróse
en él y halló los cristianos que allí habían quedado destos amotinados, todos
muy buenos, que les dixeron el buen tratamiento que el cacique é sus indios
les habían hecho, por tener por mujer el Adelantado á Doña Antonia, é que 5
ó 6 dellos andaban en la tierra adentro, é la gente del bergantín tomó hasta 15
soldados destos, y el cacique invió un hermano suyo con 3 indios é 3 indias en
este bergantín, á decir al Adelantado que él é sus indios querían ser cristianos, que le fuese á ver, porque le quería tomar por su hermano mayor, para
hacer lo que les mandase; y este cacique é Cárlos tenían gran guerra, é sabido
por qué era, que el cacique Tequesta solia ser subjeto á Cárlos, é como Cárlos
los supo que tenía aquellos cristianos, invió por ellos, é no se los quiso dar, é
después invió para que los matasen á traición: súpolo el Tequesta, defendiólos
y mató dos indios suyos que andaban tratando de matar los cristianos.

Y el Adelantado llevaba consigo esta tercera vez estos mensaxeros de
Tequesta, con la Doña Antonia, todos juntos, para tratar paces y amistades
entre el Cárlos é Tequesta; é como entró el Adelantado en el puerto de Cárlos, a días desque partió de la Habana, como está dicho, fué descubierto por
el Capitán Fran[cis]co de Reinoso é sus soldados, é por el cacique Cárlos é su
gente; luego acudieron con las canoas á los bergantines: saltó el Adelantado
en tierra: fué muy bien recebido de los cristianos é indios: hizo hacer junto
de la casa de los cristianos, una casa á la Doña Antonia, é una capilla, donde
el Padre rogel decía misa: pedricó[sic] otro día siguiente á los soldados, que
tenían harta necesidad de ser dotrinados, é por los buenos exemplos que les
dió, pidieron al Adelantado que los dexase con ellos, porque de otra manera,
presto serían salvajes, como los mesmos indios; y esto era que las indias los
querian mucho, de tal manera, que si el Adelantado entonces allí no llegara,
el Cárlos é sus indios, aunque perdieran á Doña Antonia, su hermana, é á
los seis indios é indias que consigo tenía, estaban determinados de matar al
Fran[cis]co de Reinoso é á todos los cristianos que con él estaban, aunque
con el aviso que las indias daban á los cristianos, que Cárlos é sus indios los
querían matar, vivian con gran recatamiento.

Informó el Fran[cis]co de Reinoso capitularmente al Adelantado de las
costumbres é condiciones de Cárlos é de sus indios, é de las muchas veces
que los habían querido matar, é que era grande la devoción que iban tomando á la cruz, aunque el Cárlos estaba muy aperreado é se reía de nuestras cerimonias. El Adelantado regocijó mucho al Cárlos é á toda su gente:
llevóle á comer consigo dos veces, é á su mujer, indios é indias prencipales.

Supo el Adelantado que el pasaje que é buscaba no le había por allí, é que
50 leguas adelante, en un pueblo que llamaban Tocobaga, hallaría pasajes.

El cacique de aquella tierra era grande enemigo de Cárlos é le hacía mucha guerra.

Había pedido el Cárlos al Adelantado é al Fran[cis]co de Reinoso fuesen con él é su gente á hacer la guerra á Tocobaga.

El Fran[cis]co de Reinoso dijo al Cárlos que sin orden del Adelantado no lo había de hacer, por que si lo hacía, le mandaría cortar la cabeza.

Y el Adelantado respondió al Cárlos que el Rey de España, su Señor, no le inviaba á aquella tierra á hacer la guerra con los caciques indios, é que si estaban reñidos, procurar de hacerlos amigos, é decirles si querían ser cristianos, é los que lo quisieren ser, enseñarles la dotrina de la manera que lo han de ser, para que cuando se muriesen en la tierra, fuesen con Dios, Señor de todo el mundo, al cielo; que ansí él quería ser amigo de Tocobaga; que él iría á tratar las paces con él.

Pesóle mucho á Cárlos de que el Adelantado no fuese á hacer la guerra á Tocobaga, é díjole que él quería ir con él en sus bergantines á Tocobaga, con hasta 20 indios prencipales de los suyos, é que allá trataría el Adelantado de las paces.

El Adelantado holgó dello, é trató luego con el Cárlos las paces é amistades entre él y el cacique Tequesta, con su hermano, que allí tenía, é otros 2 indios é 3 indias: efectúaronse muy bien: dejó el Adelantado confirmada mucha amistad entre los indios é soldados: dejó allí hasta que volviese de Tocobaga los indios de Tequesta con los cristianos, é á los dos padres de la Compañia.

El Padre Rogel dábase prisa á deprender con vocabulario la lengua de Cárlos é Tocobaga, para empezar á predicar á los indios.

El Padre Fran[cis]co deprendía la lengua de Tequesta, porque pretendió el Adelantado, vuelto de Tocobaga, dejar allí al Padre Rogel, é llevar á Tequesta el Padre Fran[cis]co.

Dentro de 3 días que estuvo en Cárlos, se partió con todos los 6 bergantines, la vuelta de Tocobaga: llevó consigo al Cárlos é á otros 20 principales suyos: llegó el 2.o día á la noche por el puerto, é vivía el cacique 20 leguas por la tierra adentro, é se iba hasta el borde de su casa por un brazo de agua salada: un indio de los que iban con Cárlos, aunque era de noche é no hacía luna, por el Norte, guió de tal manera, que llevando viento próspero, una hora antes del día, llegó el Adelantado junto de la casa de Tocobaga, sin ser descubierto, y mandó con gran secreto surgir los bergantines.

El Cárlos rogó al Adelantado que saltasen en tierra, é quemasen el pueblo, é matasen los indios.

El Adelantado no lo quiso hacer, diciéndole que el Rey de España, su señor le mandaría cortar la cabeza, porque Tocobaga, ni sus indios, nunca le habían hecho mal, é que si se lo hubieran hecho, que él hiciera lo que Cárlos decía: quedó desto muy triste Cárlos, é dijo al Adelantado que le echasen en tierra á él, é á su gente, que él iría á dar fuego á la casa del cacique é se volvería á nado á los bergantines.

El Adelantado le dijo que no lo hiciese, ni se lo había de consentir, pues iba con él para tratar las paces é amistades: enojóse mucho dello el Cárlos, é lloraba de pesar.

El Adelantado le consoló lo mexor que pudo é le dijo que él procuraría hiciese paces muy honrosas con Tocobaga, é que le diese 10 ó 12 indios é indias que le tenía cautivos. Con esto se alegró mucho Cárlos, porque había entre ellos una hermana suya é de Doña Antonia, é dixo al Adelantado que con aquello estaba contento. Mandó el Adelantado que á junto de la casa del cacique se llegase una chalupeta con 8 bogadores é un cristiano de aquellos que habían estado cautivos en Cárlos, que sabían la lengua de Tocobaga, y mandó que junto de la casa del cacique, le dijese con altas voces, en su lengua, que no hubiese miedo, que los navíos que allí estaban, toda la gente que traían eran cristianos de verdad, sus amigos; é habiéndolo hecho ansí, los indios despertaron, é vieron los navíos junto de las casas, y echaron á huir, con sus mujeres é hijos.

El cacique se estuvo quedo con 5 ó 6 indios é una mujer, y en siendo de día, invió un cristiano que tenía al Adelantado á decirle que le agradecía mucho en que no le hubiese muerto á él ni su gente, ni quemado su pueblo, é que aquel cristiano tenía é no más, que lo inviaba, que su gente había huído, é que él se había quedado con su casa de su oración é sus dioses, que primero quería morir que desampararlos; que si quería que fuese á sus navíos, iría, y si el Adelantado quería ir é tierra, á darle la vida ó la muerte, que lo podía hacer, porque él lo estaba aguardando.

El Adelantado se holgó mucho con el recaudo é con el cristiano que le llevaba, el cual era portugués, de Tavila, que es en el Algarbe: dixo que había 6 años que estaba allí cautivo, que iban en una barca con maíz é gallinas, mantas é miel, dende Campeche á Nueva España, é que la tormenta los había echado allí al través, é que los indios los mataron é todos dentro de una hora; que este se escondiera al monte, que no le pudieron hallar, y anduviera por él un mes escondido, comiendo palmitos, bellotas é algún marisco, é que acaso unos indios pescadores le vieron é le prendieron é llevaron á este cacique; que les servía de traer agua é leña é hacerles de comer, é que del día que se perdieron hasta entonces, cada día suplicaba á Nuestro Señor lo sacase de cautivo, y ocho días había que estaba aguardando á cristianos, que soñaba cada noche destos 8 días que cristianos iban allí á vivir, de que estaba muy contento: contó al Adelantado las cosas de aquella tierra, aunque sabía muy poco, que nunca había salido 20 leguas fuera de aquel pueblo; é no quiso el Adelantado decir á este cristiano que Cárlos venía allí, ni que viniese Tocobaga al navío, por amor de Cárlos: invióle á decir que él iría en tierra á hablarle é que no tuviese miedo, y encargó al cristiano que le esforzase, que ningún mal le haría, é que inviase á decir á sus indios é indias que se volviesen al pueblo; é ansí se fué el cristiano con esta respuesta, y á las 8

de la mañana fué el Adelantado á tierra: habló al cacique, el cual recibió el
Adelantado muy bien, é lo sentó cabe sí, en un lugar más alto é preminente:
tenía consigo 6 indios y una india: dixo al Adelantado con la lengua que no
pensaba que los cristianos eran tan buenos; que bien conoscía que le pudieran matar á él é á su gente y quemar sus ídolos é pueblo; que había muchos
días que sabía que cristianos andaban en aquella tierra y habían inviado á
decir á caciques, sus amigos, que les diesen maíz, si no, que los matarían,
é porque no se lo daban, mataban muchos, y que él les tenía mucho miedo,
y que después vinieron otros cristianos é matáran á estos, y que decían que
á estos postreros que los caciques é los indios los querían mucho; que de
cuáles eran ellos.

El Adelantado le respondió que él y su gente eran de los cristianos postreros que vinieran á matar aquellos cristianos primeros que venían á hacer los
caciques é indios esclavos, é que eran cristianos de mentira, é que por esto
los matara; que él y su gente eran cristianos de verdad, é que no los venían
á matar, ni hacer esclavos, ni á tomarles su maíz; que sólo iban á decirles si
querían ser cristianos y enseñarles cómo lo habían de ser y tenerles por amigos y hermanos, y que no iba á hacer la guerra, ni matar á ningún cacique ni
indio, ecepto á los que le quiesieran hacer mal é matar algún cristiano; é que
si él é su gente querían ser cristianos, que holgaría dello.

El cacique se holgó mucho de lo que el Adelantado le dixo, é levantóse: él
é sus 6 indios, hicieron al Adelantado grande humildad y obediencia, é le be-
saron las manos, é luego se volvieron á sentar. Entonces dixo el Adelantado
al cacique que él era amigo de Cárlos é tenía cristianos en su tierra, é que no
por eso había de ser enemigo del Tocobaga; que tenía consigo á Cárlos en los
bergantines, que le llevaba para tratar paz é amistad con él é le volviese las
12 personas que tenía cautivas, y que si él y sus indios quisiesen ser cristianos, que holgaría mucho dello é que le dejaría allí cristianos, como en Cárlos,
para que los defendiesen de sus enemigos y los enseñasen á ser cristianos.

Contestó que él tenía su gente é los prencipales é caciques, sus subjetos é
amigos, lejos de allí, y que sin que viniesen é les hablase, no podría respon-
derle; que aguardase el Adelantado 3 ó 4 días, é los inviaría á llamar.

El Adelantado dixo que era contento, y ansí invió el cacique á llamar sus indios prencipales é caciques, é rogó al Adelantado mandase á sus soldados no
llegasen á la casa de sus dioses, á quien este cacique tenía gran veneración.

Fuese aquella noche el Adelantado con su gente á dormir á los bergantines; y otro día por la mañana, el cacique Tocobaga le fué á ver: habláronse
él y Cárlos y tuvieron algunos dares é tomares: quisiera el Cárlos desembarcar con Tocobaga é con sus indios, é por tener el Adelantado á Cárlos por
muy traidor, no se atrevió, pensando le diría mal dél é de sus cristianos, é se
conformarían los 2 caciques para que el Cárlos matase á los cristianos que
allí tenía, y el Tocobaga los que allí dexase. Por otra parte, no se atrevía el
Adelantado enojar al Cárlos, é por esto le dejó saltar en tierra, con 2 lenguas

que siempre anduviesen cabo él, porque no hablase al cacique é á los indios mal de los cristianos.

Acudieron en aquellos 3 días más de 1.500 indios, toda gente de muy buena disposición, con sus arcos é flechas.

El Adelantado, como vido tanta gente, dijo al cacique que sus soldados estaban alegres, porque pensaban que sus indios querían ser bellacos, é pelear con ellos; que dejase los principales consigo, para tratar de las paces, é inviase los otros. El cacique lo hizo ansí.

Al cuarto día, estando juntos 29 caciques é como otros 100 indios principales que consigo dejaron, invió el cacique llamar al Adelantado, que fuese á tratar las paces; é ansí fué, llevando consigo al Cárlos, y estando juntos, el Adelantado, sentado en un lugar más preminente, el cacique Tocobaga le dijo que él había dicho á aquellos caciques é indios que allí estaban, todo lo que el Adelantado había dicho, é que si él decía aquellas cosas de verdad, que todos holgaban de tomarle por hermano mayor é volverse cristianos, é hacer las paces con Cárlos, é darle su gente; con que si Cárlos volviese hacer la guerra con él, que el Adelantado le ayudase, é que si él la rompiese con Cárlos, ayudase el Adelantado á Cárlos; por que él quería hacer las paces con los cristianos de verdad, é no de mentira, é que le dexase otro capitán con 30 cristianos, para que enseñasen á él é á sus caciques á ser cristianos: todo se hizo desta manera, quedando las paces hechas con Cárlos, é vuéltole su gente; que el Adelantado dexó allí 30 soldados, é con cargo dellos é por Capitán á García Martínez de Cos, el cual quedó harto contra su voluntad, y el Adelantado lo dexó por que estaba contra él desabrido, por cierta desobediencia que había tenido; mas por que era de buen entendimiento é buen cristiano, le dejó, y por que Tocobaga dijo al Adelantado que no podía ir á Macoya con tan poca gente, por que eran muchos é bellacos.

Luego se partió de allí con sus bergantines, dentro de 4 días que llegó, é dentro de 8 volvió á Cárlos á su pueblo, y en el camino fué grandísima la soberbia y enojo que conosció tenía Cárlos, por la amistad tan buena que el Adelantado dexaba hecha en Tocobaga, y procuraba mucho el Adelantado alegrarle: no podía. Pasando un marinero por delante de Cárlos, acertó á caerle un cabo de cuerda delgada sobre la cabeza de Cárlos, y pensando que el marinero lo hiciera adrede, dale un gran bofetón en la cara y cerró con él á brazos para le querer echar á la mar: acude el Adelantado, é quítalo: era el marinero de los más principales que allí iban: sintióse mucho desto, é mucho más lo sintió el Adelantado, é como le llevaba en su bergantin, é lo había sacado de su tierra, parecióle que era obligado á volverle á ella, que de otra manera, túvose entendido que lo mandaría ahorcar por el bofetón y tambien por que había entendido de las lenguas que amenazaba al Adelantado é á sus cristianos, que daría orden que ninguno se le escapase.

Dejóle el Adelantado en su pueblo: hizo fortificarse los cristianos mexor de lo que estaban: dejóles á complemento de 50 soldados sobre los que allí

estaban, é ciertos bersos, é al Padre Rogel, de la Compañia de Jesús, para
que dotrinase los indios: partióse con el Padre Fran[cis]co, su compañero, é
con los indios de Tequesta, para los llevar á su cacique y decirles las paces que entre él é Cárlos quedaban hechas: dejó el Adelantado allí á Doña
Antonia, con los cristianos: no traía della bueno concepto, y estaba mucho
de la parte de su hermano Cárlos, é muy triste por las paces que había hecho
en Tocobaga: dixo palabras muy sentidas al Adelantado, porque no habían
quemado é muerto á Tocobaga é sus indios é quemádoles el pueblo é casa de
sus ídolos, é que tenía dos corazones, uno para sí, otro para Tocobaga, é que
para ella, ni su hermano, no tenía ninguno.

El Adelantado la satisfizo lo mexor que pudo, y la dexó, y se fué á embarcar para ir á Tequesta, y estando en los navíos para hacer vela é irse á
Tequesta, á llevar los indios que allí tenía, á confirmar las paces é de allí á
los fuertes de San Agustín é San Mateo, vió entrar por el puerto un navío, de
que se espantó, no sabiendo qué podía ser, y llegando á surgir, conosció ser
un patax suyo, que había dejado en el puerto de San Agustín, cuando salió de
armada contra los cosarios, el cual habían despachado los capitanes de los
fuertes de San Agustín, San Mateo é Sant Felipe, á la Habana, dando aviso al
Adelantado socorriese de bastimento, y llegado este bergantín á la Habana,
el tesorero Juan de Ynistrosa, teniente del Adelantado en aquella villa é isla,
para las cosas de la Florida, le inviaba con aviso al Adelantado, y también
llevaba cartas de todos los regidores de la Habana. . . . El Adelantado, como
vió estos despachos, invió los indios á Tequesta, y él se vino á la Habana, y
llegó dentro de 3 días . . . y dejando en el mejor recaudo que pudo lo de allí,
con algún bastimento que se cogió é otros navíos que invió á Campeche á
cargar de maíz, se fué á la Florida, al Tequesta, donde fué muy bien recebido de aquel cacique é indios: hizo con ellos grandes paces: tomáronle por
hermano mayor: dejó allí 30 soldados, é por capitán dellos . . . , y dejóles una
sierra é carpinteros que hiciesen una casa fuerte: arboló una cruz con gran
devoción: los indios la adoraron: dejó allí al Padre Fran[cis]co, de la Compañia de Jesús: estuvo 4 días en aquel pueblo: fué grande su contento de ver
que á las mañanas é á las tardes, todos los indios é indias, grandes é pequeños, acudían á adorar la cruz é besarla con gran devoción: dió el cacique al
Adelantado un hermano suyo é dos indios prencipales, que el uno era capitán
de un pueblo de Cárlos, para que los trujese á España, é partióse con ellos el
Adelantado, con buen tiempo, é al tercero día llegó á San Mateo. . . .

English

Chapter XIV

At the beginning of January of the next year of [15]66, there arrived
Estébano de las Alas, who was general of the armada of Viscaya, who

had been in Yaguana. He brought 2 ships and 200 men, and with his arrival, the Adelantado felt great joy and contentment. He immediately ordered that during that entire month those two ships should be outfitted, along with the 2 that the Adelantado brought from Florida, and a new brigantine that Diego de Maya brought from Florida after having delivered supplies,[6] and another French patache that he bought there in Havana,[7] and a new launch. All these 7 ships were caulked and oiled and put in good condition, and on the 10th of February, with 500 sailors and soldiers in them, they departed for Florida, and went to discover if there was a deep enough passage to navigate between the Tortugas and the Martyrs, which was very necessary to know for the fleets from New Spain and Tierra Firme, and whichever other ships that might navigate there. Finding a suitable place, they passed onward to the coast of Florida in search of some men and women that were said to have been captive for twenty years in the power of a chief called Carlos. Each year he killed some of these people, making a sacrifice of them to the devil, and they were all naked, turned into savages like the Indians themselves. Sympathizing with these slaves, the Adelantado wished to make this journey, and from there to go to the provinces of Santa Elena, which is 50 leagues to the north of the fort of San Mateo, which was won from the Lutherans,[8] because the Indians told the soldiers that in that fort, in the port of Guala,[9] there were newly arrived Frenchmen.

And having had many Masses said to Saint Anthony,[10] so that he should intercede with Our Lord so that they might find the port where those Christians were, and the Christians themselves, they found them within 8 days after having departed from Havana. And it was in this manner: the Adelantado left the flagship in which he was traveling, leaving Estébano de las Alas in his place as General of those ships, and put himself in a brigantine with 30 men, soldiers and sailors, which drafted no more than half a fathom of water. And he commanded Captain Diego de Maya, who went as Admiral of the ships, to go with him in the brigantine in which he [Maya] was traveling with 30 people, which also drafted little water. Between the two brigantines together they went navigating along the length of the land, the rest of the ships far off, because the coast was shallow. On the 3rd day he was separated from his 5 ships with the two brigantines on account of fog, and on the 4th day, navigating alongside the land, a canoe came forth to the brigantine in which Captain Diego de Maya was traveling, half a league farther on, and there was a person in it rowing, and when he arrived near the brigantine he spoke, saying,

"Spaniards, brothers, Christians! You are quite welcome. We have been waiting for you 8 days; God and Saint Mary told us you were coming. The Christian men and women who are alive here have sent me to wait for you here with this canoe, in order to give you a letter that I bring you."

Captain Diego de Maya and the people who were traveling with him in the brigantine received great joy and contentment in seeing that they had discovered what the Adelantado was searching for and so desired. They received this man, who came naked and painted, as an Indian, with his privates covered, inside the brigantine.

The Captain embraced him and asked for the letter.

The man drew forth a cross from within the deerskin that he covered his privates with, and gave it to the captain, telling him that that was the letter that the Spaniards and Christians who were captive sent him, and that they asked him for the sake of the death that Our Lord had received on that cross in order to save us, not to pass without entering in the port and attempting to save them from their chief and carry them to the land of Christians.

At this point the Adelantado arrived with his brigantine, and this man crossed over to him, where he found out more specifically from this Christian everything that had happened, and about the quality of the land and the condition of the Indians. And all on their knees, they worshipped the cross, giving thanks to Our Lord.

The Adelantado went inside the port and anchored alongside land so that they could get out of the brigantine on land without getting their shoes wet. The town was half a league from there, where there were some Spanish women and other Christians. And another two were in the interior, and another woman, because out of more than 200 Spaniards on ships from the Indies lost on the lands of this cacique in the past 20 years, they had carried off all their people, and his father and he had killed them, conducting their festivals and dances to the devil.

The Adelantado did not dare reveal to this Christian how he intended to get the Christian men and women that were there out, because it seemed to him that he knew little, and whatever thing he might tell him, he could tell to the chief. He only told him to tell the chief that he was bringing many things for him and his wives, and that he should come and see them. The chief, finding out how few people the Adelantado brought, came the next day in the morning with up to 300 Indian archers. The brigantines were placed alongside the land, with the prow of one placed at the stern of the other, and the culverins within the brigantine placed on the landward side,[11] with many loads of shot inside for whatever might happen.[12] Next to the brigantines [the Adelantado] had a platform placed for the chief to sit on, and thus he sat down, and most of his noble Indians round about him.[13] The Adelantado came forth from the brigantines with 30 arquebusiers with their fuses lit, and sat down next to him, with the chief and his nobles displaying much obedience toward the Adelantado.

He had him dressed in a shirt and taffeta pants and a short jacket and a hat,[14] and he gave him other trade goods for his wives.[15] He looked very good, because he was a very genteel man, of up to 25 years old. He also gave gifts to his noble Indians, and gave them biscuits and honey to eat, and they ate it very well.

The chief gave the Adelantado a bar of silver that weighed about 200 ducats, and asked him to give him more things, and more to eat.

The Adelantado told him that he did not have food for so many people, and that he should get in the brigantines with his nobles, and he would feed them and give them many things for them and their wives. With his greed, the chief did so, and came aboard with up to 20 Indians.

The Adelantado, with great secrecy and diligence, ordered each of his 66 soldiers to remain next to his Indian, and that if he should wish to jump into the sea, they should not consent to it. He commanded the cables with which the brigantines were tied to land to be loosed, and to hold them at a distance. The Indians became a little disturbed, but they were told through the interpreter[16] that they should have no fear, and that the reason they had put themselves there was so that no more Indians would enter in the brigantines, because since they were so small, they would overturn.

The chief and the Indians believed it, and they [the Spaniards] fed them and gave them many things, and the chief wished to go.

The Adelantado told him that the King of Spain, his Lord, sent him for the Christian men and women that he had, and if he did not bring them to him, he would order him killed. He implored him to give them to him, because he would give him many things for them, and he would be his great friend and brother.

The chief said that he was content, and that he would go for them.

The Adelantado said that if he went, his people would kill him because he let him go, so he requested him to send some Indians for them.

The chief, with fear, did so, and within an hour they brought 5 women and 3 Christian [men], to whom the Adelantado immediately ordered be given some shirts, and of serge from London, that he brought. He ordered 4 or 5 tailors that came there to make clothes for them and for the Christian [men] the same. They wept from happiness, which was something to see. The Adelantado consoled them and gave them many gifts, and they said that they were very sad because of the children that they left there.

The Adelantado gave many things to the chief and to his people, and he sent them away very content, the chief telling him that within three months he would have there another 2 Christian men and one Christian woman who were in the interior, and that he implored him to go in the morning, so that his wives might see him before he departed his town. The Adelantado said that he would do so. In the morning, the chief sent many canoes for him. The Adelantado being suspicious of his departure, there arrived in a canoe the Christian who had come forth to the sea with the cross, and who had gone with the chief to visit his wives on behalf of the Adelantado and take them a present. This Christian told the Adelantado that he should not go to the town, because they had arranged to kill him. The Indians with the canoes who knew about the treason suspected that that Christian had revealed it, and fled. So that the chief and Indians would think that he did not know about the treason, the Adelantado raised the anchors of the brigantines and rowed over to anchor next to the town. There, with two bugles, raising the flags, he made a signal that the canoes should come for him, because the brigantines could not go any farther. Since no canoe wished to come, the Adelantado left from the port in order to search for his 5 ships, and as they did not appear, the Christians told him that 50 leagues farther on from there was a very good port, and that there were another 3 Christians captive in the power of the Indians. It seemed to the Adelantado that his ships must have gone there, and he desired to rescue those 3 Christians, so he went there and did not find either the ships or the Christians. Upon his return, he found the 5 ships anchored upon this port of Carlos, and that Estébano de las Alas had gone to the town with one hundred soldiers, and when the Indians saw so many ships and people, which they went to reconnoiter with the canoes, they were afraid, and gave a good reception to Estébano de las Alas. The soldiers bartered more than 2,000 ducats of gold and silver with the Indians there, in exchange for trinkets.

The Adelantado decided to send the Christian to Carlos, so that he would make him believe that the Adelantado knew nothing of the treason that they were preparing in order to kill him. And Carlos believed it, and with the greed that he had for him to give him other things, and to take the Adelantado as a friend, he came to see him with no more than only 5 or 6 Indians, and he told him that he wanted to take him as his elder brother, in order to do everything that he should command, and that he wanted to give him as a wife a sister that he had, older than him, whom he loved very much, so that he might take her to the land of Christians and send her back. And when she returned, he would go also and become a Christian with all his Indians, which seemed better to him than being an Indian. He implored him to come for her, or go to see his wives and town.

The Adelantado said that the next day he would go, and he gave him many gifts and sent him away. The captains and soldiers wanted the Adelantado not to let this chief go, because they said that he had much money, and that he would give it all away to free himself. It seemed to the Adelantado that that would be a dirty trick, given the trust that the chief had in him, and that they would never become Christians, so he did not wish to do so.

All of us captains, soldiers, and sailors who were there admired the reply that the Adelantado gave, because we knew how much he had spent in this enterprise, and the little aid that His Majesty had given him, and that he was in debt in Spain, and had left his relatives and friends the same, and he was also [in debt] in Havana, and had sent to New Spain for a loan of money. We considered him a poorly advised man, since he could have at least gotten a hundred thousand ducats from that chief, and even if he didn't have that many, the Indians and chiefs who were his friends would, in whose power was some of the gold and silver from lost ships. They did not understand [gold and silver], nor did they know what things they were, and he could have gotten himself out of debt, and those who were [in debt] out of love for him. And [they would] find themselves more energized for such a holy and good conquest as this, in order to try, as he was trying, according to the great inclination that we all saw he had, to plant the Holy Gospel in it. Because the Indians did not know what gold or silver was, and for a playing card, which was the ace of coins,[17] there was an Indian who gave a piece of gold that was worth 70 ducats, and for some scissors, half a bar of silver that was worth one hundred ducats. All the soldiers who had first arrived with Estébano de las Alas, and those who arrived with the Adelantado in the two brigantines, bartered up to 3,500 ducats in all during that time, from which they were now all joyful and content, and began to gamble, holding the money in little [value]. The Adelantado did not take away or deny anything of what each one bartered, nor did he barter a single thing, so that the Indians would not think that he went in order to search for that. And then the next day after the chief Carlos returned from the brigantines, the Adelantado went to eat with him carrying with him 200 arquebusiers and a flag, 2 fifes and drummers, 3 trumpets, a harp and guitar,[18] and a psalter, and a small dwarf, a great singer and dancer, whom he brought with him. It was about 2 arquebus shots from where they disembarked to the house of the chief, which could fit two thousand men inside it, even if they weren't crowded together. His people went in an orderly fashion to this house, and the Adelantado did not consent for them to enter inside, but rather that they should remain outside, ready with their fuses lit.

Only [the Adelantado] with up to 20 gentlemen went inside the room of the chief,[19] where there were some large windows through which to see his people. The chief was in a good-sized room,[20] seated alone with great authority, and an Indian woman also seated, a little separated from him, at a height of half a rod from the floor.[21] [There were also] up to 500 noble Indians and another 500 Indians, the Indian men near him, and the Indian women near the Indian woman, below her.[22]

When the Adelantado ascended to that room, the chief gave him the place that he had, and withdrew far from him.

The Adelantado put himself next to him, and then the chief got up, and according to their custom, he went toward the Adelantado to take his hands, performing a certain ceremony, which is [the same as] when here they kiss the hand of the King, and greater courtesy cannot be expressed among them, and it is that which the Indian vassals normally do to their chiefs. Next came the Indian woman, and she did the same, and then all of the noble Indian men and women that were there. Then more than 500 Indian girls from 10 to 15 years old, seated on the outside of the window, began to sing, and other Indians to jump and whirl,[23] and the noble Indian men and women who were next to the chief sang. They said, as was later found out, that this was the greatest celebration, respect, and obedience that that chief, or any other in that land, could offer the Adelantado, because the brothers and sisters of the chief danced, and his uncles and aunts, and there were Indian women among these nobles of 90 and 100 years who danced. Everyone showed that they were very happy and joyful.

His nobles finished dancing and singing, though the Indian girls who were outside never stopped doing so until the Adelantado went away. They sang with great orderliness; they were seated 100 by 100, and 50 of them sang a little and were quiet, and then the other 50 began singing again. After his nobles danced, the chief asked the Adelantado if he wanted them to bring the food for him and his Christians.

The Adelantado said not so quickly, since he was carrying many words written in the language of the Indians, which were of great courtesy and love, in order to speak to the principal wife of the chief. He said the words that he intended to tell her in her own language, and the chief and the Indians were astonished. They thought that the paper and what was written on it were talking. And the chief understood that the Adelantado thought that that [woman] was his principal wife, and he told him through the interpreter that they had there in order to understand each other, who was one of the captive Christians, that that was not his wife, that it was his sister, whom he had given to the Adelantado as a wife.

Then the Adelantado got up and took her by the hand, and seated her beside him, between him and the chief, and by what he carried in writing, he told her many things in her language, reading the paper, of which they and all the Indian men and women who were there rejoiced. This Indian woman was up to 35 years old, not at all pretty, although very dignified,[24] so much so that as time passed, all of us admired this, because it seemed that since her birth they had raised her to know how to have dignity.

The Adelantado asked the chief to bring his principal wife there, which he did. She was up to 20 years old, very pretty and beautiful, of very good features. She had very nice hands and eyes, and looked with much dignity from one side to the other, with all honesty. She was very composed,[25] so that although there were many beautiful Indian women to be seen there, none were as [beautiful] as this one. Her eyebrows were very well formed, and at her throat a very beautiful necklace of pearls and stones, and a necklace of beads of gold. She was naked like the chief's sister, with only her privates covered.

The Adelantado took her by the hand, and placed her between the Indian woman and the chief, and spoke many words with her in her language, which he had written on the paper, of which she took great joy. In particular, since they had told the Adelantado that she was very beautiful, he carried written in her language words to tell her so, of which she showed no regret, and her face took on a pleasing color, looking at her husband with honesty. The chief showed that he regretted having brought out his wife, and he ordered her to go away, thinking that they wanted to take her. The Adelantado told him with the interpreter that he should not send her away, and that she should eat there with him, because he had many things to give her, and then he had the present that he was bringing brought out, and he had the chief's sister dressed in a shirt, and another for the chief's wife, and both were green clothing, with which the wife of the chief was beyond beautiful. He gave them beads, scissors, and knives, bells and mirrors, with which they were very pleased, and particularly with the mirrors when they looked at themselves, at which the Indian men and women who were there laughed greatly. He gave the chief another set of clothes, in addition to the other one that he had given him, and other odds and ends of trade goods, and two axes and two machetes. And he also gave the noble Indian men and women who were there some trade goods, without them giving any item of interest to the Adelantado in return, nor did he request anything. The food was ordered to be brought, which consisted of many types of very good fish, roasted and stewed, and raw, stewed, and roasted oysters, without anything else. The Adelantado had had a hundred pounds of very good biscuits offloaded, and a jar of wine and another of molasses,[26] and he distributed it among all those nobles, and with the interpreter he ordered them to bring bowls in which to pour the molasses. He gave them some preserves and quince jelly, and the Adelantado ate from his own plate, and the sister of the chief from another, and the chief and his wife from another, but with a table, tablecloths, and napkins that the Adelantado had had carried. Well they understood that our food was much better than theirs.

When the food was brought, they sounded the trumpets that were on the outside, and when the Adelantado had eaten, the instruments were played very well, and the dwarf danced. There began to sing 4 or 6 gentlemen who were there, who had very good voices, with very great order, since the Adelantado, by being a great friend of music, always endeavored to bring the best that he could with him. The Indians were strangely happy to hear that. The chief said that the young girls should not sing, because they knew little, and the Christians knew much. The music ceased, and the chief implored that until [the Adelantado] went away, they should always play the instruments and sing, and the Adelantado commanded thus. They finished up, and he got up from the table and then said that he wished to go.

The chief told him that he should go to sleep in a room that was there, with his sister, since he had given her to him as a wife, and that if he did not do so, that his Indians would be upset, saying that they were laughing at them and at her, and that he regarded her poorly. And there were more than 4,000 Indian men and women in the town.

The Adelantado showed a little perturbation, and told him through the interpreter that Christians could not sleep with women who weren't Christian.

The chief responded that now his sister and he and his people were [Christian], since he had taken him as his elder brother.

The Adelantado responded that before they could be Christians, they had to know and believe many things. And he told them who God was, and about his knowledge, power, and goodness, and that all creatures that are born on the earth are to worship only him, and to do what he commands. When we Christians who do so die here on the earth, we go away toward heaven, and that there we remain always without dying, and we see our wives, children, siblings and friends, and we are always happy, singing and laughing. And because they do not know this, not serving or worshipping God, but rather serving a very warlike and deceitful chief called the devil, when they die they will go away toward him, and will be perpetually weeping, because sometimes they will be very cold, and other times very hot, and nothing will make them happy. He said other effective explanations, and Carlos responded that because he had found out about the way of the Spaniards, in their music and in their dishes, their law was better, and he wished to embrace it. And he had given him his sister, and he was giving her to him again so that he would take her away, because of which the Adelantado had to take her to the port with some Indian men and women who would accompany her. After consulting about the case with his captains, he indicated to them that it seemed to him that this could result in a break with the Indians, and this was not suitable, because of the designs of the Adelantado, which he had demonstrated since he had left from Spain, that his particular interest was that the Indians should become Christians. The captains responded that it would be appropriate to make much festivity to her and to the Indian men and women who were with her, and that there should be much rejoicing and music that night. They should baptize her and give her a name, and that the Adelantado should sleep with her, because this would be a great beginning so that they would trust him and the rest of the Christians, and all those Indians and their neighboring chiefs would be Christians, and that in no way would anything else be suitable.

The Adelantado showed much . . .[27] to look for another solution, and since nothing could be done, nor was a way found, he agreed that it should be done thus.

Then the Christians that were there had her washed, touched up, and dressed, so that she appeared immensely better than at first, when she was naked. And the captains, on purpose, praised her as very beautiful and dignified. They gave her the name Doña Antonia, and the name San Antón to the port, because of the devotion that the Adelantado had shown to the señor Saint Anthony, so that he might find those Christian men and women that he was looking for. The supper and music and rejoicing [took place] on land in some tents the Adelantado had assembled next to his ships, and lasted until two in the morning. The Adelantado had [Doña Antonia] next to him, and with the interpreter he said many things to her that made her happy, and she responded so discreetly and in so few words that we marveled. Her Indians and the Christian women and other soldiers danced, and having finished this, they took her to sleep in a bed that the Adelantado ordered made, and he went to her. In the morning, she woke up happy, and the Christian women that spoke with her said that she was very content. And then with a canoe that was there, they sent 2 Indian men and 2 Indian women to her brother, who came to see her. The Adelantado received him very well, and said that he wished him to have a large cross placed next to his house, and that every day in the morning, the men and women and children should go to kiss it and worship it, and they should have it as their principal idol, and he told them the reasons for this, and that he should remove all the rest of the idols that he had.

The chief said that yes, he would do this, but also that he could not remove his idols so quickly, until his sister returned along with the Indians that were going with her, and they would tell them what they had to do.

This chief was named Carlos, because his father was named thus, and his father gave himself that name because the captive Christians that he had told him that Emperor Charles was the principal King of the Christians.

The cross was made, and once made, the Adelantado kneeled there with great music and devotion, and kissed it. All of us Spaniards who were there did the same, and then the Indian woman Doña Antonia did the same, and the rest of the Indian women and men whom she had with her. Then Carlos and his Indians kissed and worshipped it. This Carlos had a captain, a very good Indian, who was married to a sister of Carlos and this Doña Antonia, and the chief with a sister of the captain. To all appearances, according to what the Christians said, the Indians feared this captain more than the chief. And he said to his chief that he would be the captain of that cross, so that everyone would do what the Adelantado commanded, to go and kiss and worship it in the mornings, and thus the Adelantado turned it over to him, and with great reverence he carried it on his shoulders to the canoes. And the Adelantado then went to disembark, taking with him Doña Antonia and the 3 Indian men and 4 Indian women and 7 Christian men and women who were prisoners, because another 2 women had already gone to the Indians, longing for the children that they left. And he gave an order to Estébano de las Alas to go to Havana with this Indian woman and her people, and deliver her to the treasurer Juan de Ynistrosa, who was deputy of the Adelantado on that island for the affairs of Florida. And he wrote an order how the Indian woman and those who were going with her should be indoctrinated, and that they should make all good treatment to them, and when it was time, they should make them Christians. He would return to Havana within 3 or 4 months to take her to her land. He should also give as many supplies as he could to Estébano de las Alas, birds and livestock, and dispatch him immediately with the 5 ships that he led to go to the fort of St. Augustine, where the Adelantado would wait for him in order to go against the French, whom they said were in Guale and in Santa Elena. [All this happened] because he was going with 2 brigantines, discovering all that coast of the Martyrs, to see if he could find some good port in the Bahama Channel, and endeavoring to go make friends with the chiefs and towns that he ran across. And thus they departed with a fortunate wind, Estébano de las Alas with 5 ships to Havana, and the Adelantado with 2 brigantines along the length of the Martyrs to St. Augustine.

Chapter XX

. . . The Adelantado . . . told [Licenciado Valderrama] . . . that he wanted to depart the next day in the morning for the land of chief Carlos, and take him his sister, who was there in Havana, on account of the fact that the noble Indian men and women that she had brought with her had died, and that no more than two were remaining, and if these and her were to die, [Carlos] would think that the Adelantado had had them killed. That chief was lord of much land, and of the Martyrs and the Bahama Channel, where the ships[28] from the Indies had the greatest danger in navigation, and it was very appropriate to have him as a friend, endeavoring that he and his Indians should become Christians. And within 10 or 12 days he would return. . . .

. . . [Juan de Ynistrosa] also told [the Adelantado] that the Indian woman Doña Antonia, sister of Carlos, was very discreet, and of such dignity that she amazed those of the town, and that in a few days she and a female servant of hers, whom she loved greatly, had learned with great facility all the affairs of prayers and Christian doctrine in order to be baptized, which she was now. And she was very sad by the absence of His Lordship, and on account of the death of her Indian men and women, and after they had told her that His Lordship had come, her joy and happiness were great, and she wept from pleasure. And [he said] that it was necessary to give her gifts and pay much attention to her, and since he wished to take her away, it was suitable that she should go away saying many good things, because he and those of Havana had paid great attention to her in giving her gifts, and keeping her happy.

The Adelantado said that the day before they disembarked he would send someone to visit her, and that for today he would go to see her, and that he would do so upon finishing eating. He did so, sending first something of what he was eating, and certain shirts and clothes that he entrusted the treasurer to buy her, so that the Indian woman would be content, and would see that he brought something. When he went to see her, he took with him many well-treated persons to accompany her, and the music, which the Adelantado never traveled without. He found the Indian woman sad, and although the Adelantado gave her many gifts, she refused to cheer up. He implored her many times with the interpreter that she should tell him why she was sad. She told him that she wished that God would kill her, because when they disembarked, he did not send for her, or take her to his house, in order to eat with the Adelantado and sleep with him.

The Adelantado understanding that she was such a noble woman, and of such great understanding, and that she was not lacking in reason, told her that the Christians who wore that cross—the Adelantado is a Knight of the Order of Santiago[29]—when they disembarked from making a journey against their enemies, they could not sleep with their wife until 8 days had passed, and that he wished that these were passed, because he loved her greatly.

The Indian woman laughed, half weeping, and said that if she found out that he was telling her the truth, she would be happy.

The Adelantado implored her to be [happy], because he said so, and he said, beginning to count with his fingers, that 2 days had already passed, and he indicated the 6, that when they had passed, she would go to his house. The Adelantado told her that he would do this, and the Adelantado got up and embraced her with great joy. She asked for his hands, and told him to play the instruments, because they had not seen those in that land, and they seemed very good to her. The Adelantado remained there another hour more, cheering her up.

This Indian woman had at her charge an alderman of that villa, called Alonso de Rojas, who has a noble wife, who was the godmother of this Indian woman when she was baptized. She loved her greatly and indoctrinated her, and told the Adelantado many things about her good understanding, with which the Adelantado was very pleased.

And he asked the Indian woman if she desired to go away to her land. She said yes, and very much. The Adelantado asked her if she wanted to go the next day. She said yes, and that she implored him greatly that they should go. The Adelantado said that they would do thus, and took his leave of her and went to his room,[30] which was near there.

It happened that night that, when midnight had passed, while the Adelantado sleeping in his room with a candle lit, the Indian woman told a woman, her friend, whom she loved greatly, that she should go with her to the house of the Adelantado, because he had ordered her to go there. [This woman] was one of those that the Adelantado had brought from Florida, whom Carlos, her brother, had held as a slave. The woman believed it, and went with her, and with the Indian woman, her servant, and called at the door of the room of the Adelantado. They opened to see who it was, and recognized her. She said that the Adelantado had ordered her to go there with the Indian woman, and the boy who opened the door, believing that they told the truth, let them enter. She entered in the Adelantado's room, where there was a candle lit, and the Indian woman took it in her hand, and looked to see if there was some woman in the bed with the Adelantado, and afterward she looked around the bed, and underneath.

Although he was very tired and exhausted, the Adelantado woke up, and when he saw her with the candle in her hand, he got upset, and said against the woman who came with her,

"What is this, sister?"

Doña Antonia sat on the bed with the candle to see what the Adelantado was saying. The woman responded to the Adelantado that Doña Antonia had told her that His Lordship ordered her to bring her at that hour, and that she, believing it, had done so.

The Adelantado, joyful and with a happy face, laughing greatly at this, said that he had told her that he would be very pleased if the 8 days had already passed, so that she could go to bed with him there.

Doña Antonia said through the interpreter that she implored him to let her sleep with him on a corner of the bed, and that she would not touch him, so that her brother Carlos would know that they had slept together, because in another manner he would think that he was laughing at her, and he would not want to be a true friend of the Christians, or to be a Christian like her, which she would greatly regret.

It seemed to the Adelantado that she was not wrong, but that God would kill him, and that if she wished for him to die, she should take her clothes off and get into bed with him. Then she began to throw her arms around the Adelantado, and told him that so he would not die, she did not wish to go to bed with him.

The Adelantado called a servant of his, so that he might get some things out of a chest, which were 3 shirts and as many mirrors and necklaces of beads and glass, which were trade goods that the Adelantado had had gathered that day in order to take to her brother Carlos. And he told the Christian woman who went with her that if the Adelantado had not woken up, she wished to put out the candle and go to bed with him. And with this they went away happy.

Then in the morning the Adelantado went to embark, and took the Indian woman with him, and her servant woman, and 2 of those Christian women who had been imprisoned there. He went in a patache and a small launch, with up to 30 soldiers and sailors. He set sail with a favorable wind, and arrived at the town of Carlos on the third day. He anchored at the entrance of the port, because since he carried few people, he did not dare to reach the town. Then the Indian woman told the Adelantado that he should disembark with her and go to the town.

The Adelantado told her that in no way could he do so, because it was suitable to depart immediately to look for Christians, so that they could live there and instruct her brother and the Indians of that land to be Christians, if they wished to be so. And he promised her then to make a house in that land in which to live, in the town of the Christians. And [he also said] that the relatives of the Indian men and women who died in Havana would think that the Adelantado had killed them, and they would want to do some evil to him and to his soldiers, from which a war could break out with her brother, and he would regret this greatly, because he loved him greatly, for the love of her, and he held him as a brother, and that he wished to return immediately. The Indian woman responded that she regretted greatly that the Adelantado was not disembarking, and would not remain several days on land until the 8 days had passed, so that she might sleep with him. And beyond this, she also feared that the [other] Indians would be warlike and would hurt him. She implored him to come back as quickly as he could, and to bring Christians to live there, and make Christians of her brother and the rest of the Indians.

Then many canoes came, and Doña Antonia sent to say to her brother that she was there, and that he should come for her. It was something to see the joy that the Indians had with her, and others wept in regret for the Indian men and women that died, who had gone with her. Within 2 hours, [her brother came] with up to 12 canoes, and two of them tied together and covered and outfitted very well with awnings of arches and mats. He and the captain, his brother-in-law, got on the patache with the Adelantado first, and another 6 nobles. It was something to see how Doña Antonia and her brother received each other, and the ceremonies that they performed. The Adelantado ordered food to be brought and the instruments to be played, and that the Indians in the canoes should be given some corn and manioc, and some knives and scissors, mirrors and bells. Having finished eating, he gave a present to Carlos for him and his wife, and he gave another to the captain for him and his wife, who was the sister of Doña Antonia, and to the noble Indians who were there. And he gave Doña Antonia some things that he was carrying for her. The Adelantado asked Carlos if he wished to become Christian and cut his hair, and if he wished to go to the land of the Christians, as he had promised, and that he would bring the Christians that he said he would give him when he returned there.

Carlos responded that he should let him speak with his captain privately, and that then he would give him his answer. And thus they separated themselves for more than a quarter of an hour, and told the Adelantado that for those 9 months, they could in no way go to the land of the Christians, nor become Christians at that time, so that their Indians would not rise up against him and kill him, and that after that time had passed, the Adelantado should return. And he justified himself with sufficient reasons.

He entrusted Doña Antonia to him, and returned to Havana. . . .

Chapter XXV

Before the Adelantado departed from Florida to bring aid, he decided to send Francisco de Reinoso, man at arms of His Majesty, a very good soldier, with 30 soldiers to the chief Carlos.[31] [He also wanted] to send him his cousin, who was an heir of his, to whom they gave the name Don Pedro when he was baptized, and another Indian, his servant, because this Indian heir of Carlos seemed to him to be of very good understanding, and a great friend of his, and the Adelantado did not wish for him to die. He showed signs of being a good Christian, and he intended to marry him to Doña Antonia, the Indian woman, since they would be heirs of the estate of Carlos, and would endeavor for the Indians to become Christians. And he named Francisco de Reinoso as captain of those 30 soldiers, and gave him instruction to make a strong house in the town of Carlos, and that they should all endeavor to worship the cross with great devotion, in the mornings and in the afternoons, speaking about the Christian doctrine, so that the Indians might do the same, and they should indoctrinate them as well as they could. With the friendship of the Indians, they should endeavor to find out if a river, which was 2 leagues from there,[32] went to connect with the lake of Maymi, and how many leagues there were, because the Adelantado already knew how many there were from this lake to Macoya, and that there was a passage.[33] [The Adelantado] planned to go to Carlos within 3 or 4 months with sufficient vessels to see if he could pass through that river to San Mateo and St. Augustine, which was what the Adelantado greatly desired, for the great service that he understood it would be for His Majesty and for the merchants in the Indies, and for the general good of those who worked in the settlement and conquest of Florida. And he gave him a present for Carlos and another for his wife, and another for Doña Antonia the Indian woman.

And when Francisco de Reinoso reached Carlos in the brigantine with his 30 soldiers, and with Don Pedro the Indian, heir of Carlos, and with the other Indian, they put the two Indians out on land so that they would speak to Carlos and to Doña Antonia. Great was the contentment that all the Indians received upon seeing them, and Carlos immediately came to the patache, offering his friendship to Captain Francisco de Reinoso and the soldiers, [saying] that since the Adelantado was his elder brother, and he sent to command that they should receive them and give them good treatment, he would do so. Thus they disembarked with great joy and contentment, and he took them to his town, and Francisco de Reinoso gave him the present that he was carrying and gave him the letter, the contents of which he explained with the interpreter, which was that he [the Adelantado] was entrusting him greatly that the Christians would be treated well by him and his Indians, and Carlos promised this to Captain Reinoso. And he had a house made for him, in which they gathered. Erecting a cross near it, they went to worship it in the morning and afternoons, reciting their Christian doctrine, and the Indian men and women attended with great devotion.

The brigantine departed for Havana with 5 or 6 sailors, as the Adelantado had ordered. It took with it the Indian woman Doña Antonia with 5 or 6 noble Indians, because the Adelantado had ordered this for the security of Captain Francisco de Reinoso and the 30 soldiers that remained with him, because the Adelantado had little confidence in Carlos, because when he dealt with him, he saw that he had many signs of a traitor.

After the Indian woman arrived in Havana in the brigantine within 6 days after departing from Carlos, Alonso de Rojas, alderman of that villa, then went to the marina and took Doña Antonia and her Indians to his house, as he had had them before, and his wife, who was the godmother of Doña Antonia, received her very well, giving her many gifts and good treatment. And then the brigantine and the other patache loaded up with livestock and some supplies, and went with them to Carlos.

Captain Francisco de Reinoso wrote about the hardship and danger with which they lived, and that 2 or 3 times, in treason, Carlos had wished to kill them. He sent to ask for his sister Doña Antonia and the rest of the Indians, and he had very great desire to see them, and wished them to return immediately, with the goal that once he had them with him, he could kill Francisco de Reinoso and the soldiers who were with him. This chief and his father were very bloodthirsty to kill Christians, such that in the 20 years that he had those men and women that the Adelantado found imprisoned there, they said that father and son had killed more than 200 Christians, sacrificing them to the devil, and performing their festivals and dances with them. They were all people from ships lost en route from the Indies, because although they might be lost 100 leagues from there, they were carried to him, since he was chief of much of the seacoast in the Martyrs and the Bahama Channel, which is where the ships that go from the Indies to Spain run the greatest risk.[34] For this reason the Adelantado made great efforts to settle that coast, and wished to attract the Indian chiefs to his friendship. And thus in the 6 brigantines that he took from Havana with 150 men, on the day that the Field Master departed for St. Augustine with the ship loaded with supplies and munitions that had been left over from the armada that went to . . . ,[35] and he had given him an order to ascend through the river of San Mateo upriver to Macoya,[36] and he [the Adelantado] was going to find out if he could go to Macoya through the territory of Carlos, so that from there he could go to St. Augustine and San Mateo. And he carried with him Doña Antonia, and the Indian men and women that she had with her, and arrived with favorable wind in 2 natural days.[37]

He carried with him Father Rogel, of the Company of Jesus, a very learned and great missionary, and Father Francisco (de Villareal), of the same Company. They were carrying noble Indians from Tequesta, which is where the ship that was coming from San Mateo with the mutinous people left the 20 soldiers. A brigantine that the Adelantado was sending from Florida to Havana to look for supplies succeeded in passing, and having arrived at that port, the wind turned against them, and they entered within it and found the Christians that had remained out of these mutineers, all very well. They told them of the good treatment that the chief and his Indians had given them, on account of the Adelantado having Doña Antonia as a wife, and that 5 or 6 of them were in the interior. The people of the brigantine took up to 15 of these soldiers, and the chief sent a brother of his with 3 Indian men and 3 Indian women in this brigantine, to tell the Adelantado that he and his Indians wished to be Christians, and that he should come to see him, because he wanted to take him as his elder brother, in order to do what he might command them. This chief and Carlos had a great war, and they found out why, which was that the chief Tequesta was normally a subject to Carlos, and when Carlos found out that he had those Christian [mutineers], he sent for them, and he [Tequesta] refused to give them up, and afterward he sent to have them killed for treason. Tequesta found out, and defended them and killed two of his Indians that were trying to kill the Christians.

The Adelantado took with him this third time these messengers from Tequesta, with Doña Antonia, all together, in order to negotiate peace and friendship between Carlos and Tequesta. And when the Adelantado entered in the port of Carlos, days after he departed from Havana, as is stated, he was discovered by Captain Francisco de Reinoso and his soldiers, and by the chief Carlos and his people. They immediately came up to the brigantines with the canoes, and the Adelantado got out on land.

He was very well received by the Christians and Indians. He had a house made for Doña Antonia next to the house of the Christians, and a chapel where Father Rogel said Mass. He preached the next day to the soldiers, who had tremendous need to be indoctrinated, and because of the good examples that he gave them, they asked the Adelantado to leave him with them, because without him, they would quickly become savages like the Indians themselves. And this was because the Indian women loved them greatly, in such a manner that if the

Adelantado had not arrived there, Carlos and his Indians were determined to kill Francisco de Reinoso and all the Christians who were with him, even if they might lose Doña Antonia, his brother, and the six Indian men and women that she had with her. But with the warnings that the Indian women gave to the Christians that Carlos and his Indians wished to kill them, they lived with great caution.

Francisco de Reinoso informed the Adelantado in detail about the customs and conditions of Carlos and his Indians, and about the many times that they had wanted to kill them, and how great was the devotion that they were developing for the cross, although Carlos was very irritated and laughed at our ceremonies. The Adelantado cheered up Carlos and all his people, bringing him to eat with him two times, and his wife and noble Indian men and women.

The Adelantado found out that the passage that he was looking for was not there, and that 50 leagues farther on, in a town called Tocobaga, he would find passages.

The chief of that land was a great enemy of Carlos and made much war on him.

Carlos had asked the Adelantado and Francisco de Reinoso to go with him and his people to make war on Tocobaga.

Francisco de Reinoso told Carlos that without order from the Adelantado he could not do so, because if he did so, he would command his head to be cut off.

And the Adelantado responded to Carlos that the King of Spain, his Lord, did not send him to that land to make war with the Indian chiefs, and that if they were on bad terms with each other, he should endeavor to make them friends, and to ask them if they wished to be Christians. Those that wished to be so would be instructed in the doctrine about the manner in which they should be [Christian], so that when they died on the Earth, they would go with God, Lord of all the world, to heaven. Therefore he wished to be a friend of Tocobaga, and he would go to negotiate peace with him.

Carlos regretted greatly that the Adelantado would not go to make war on Tocobaga, and he told him that he wanted to go with him in his brigantines to Tocobaga with up to 20 of his noble Indians, and that there the Adelantado would negotiate peace.

The Adelantado was pleased with this, and then with Carlos he negotiated peace and friendship between him and the chief Tequesta, with his brother, whom he had there, and another 2 Indian men and 3 Indian women. This was implemented very well, and the Adelantado left great friendship confirmed between the Indians and soldiers. He left the Indians from Tequesta with the Christians, and the two fathers of the Company [of Jesus], until he returned from Tocobaga.

Father Rogel hurried to learn with vocabulary the language of Carlos and Tocobaga, in order to begin to preach to the Indians.

Father Francisco learned the language of Tequesta, because the Adelantado intended, when he returned from Tocobaga, to leave Father Rogel there, and to take Father Francisco to Tequesta.

Within 3 days after arriving in Carlos, he departed with all 6 brigantines toward Tocobaga. He took with him Carlos and another 20 of his nobles. He arrived at the port at night on the 2nd day, and the chief lived 20 leagues into the interior, and one reached up to the edge of his house through a branch of salt water.[38] One of the Indians who was going with Carlos guided toward the north in such a manner that, although it was nighttime and there was no moon, with a favorable wind the Adelantado arrived next to the house of Tocobaga one hour before daylight, without being discovered. He ordered the brigantines to be anchored with great secrecy.

Carlos implored the Adelantado that they should get out on land and burn the town and kill the Indians.

The Adelantado did not wish to do so, telling him that the King of Spain, his lord, would order his head to be cut off, because neither Tocobaga nor his Indians had ever done any evil to him, and that if he had done so, he would do what Carlos said. Carlos was very sad at this, and asked the Adelantado to let him and his people off on land, and he would go to set fire to the house of the chief, and would return swimming to the brigantines.

The Adelantado told him he would not do so, nor would he consent to it, since he went with him in order to negotiate peace and friendship. Carlos was greatly angered by this, and wept in regret.

The Adelantado consoled him as best he could, and told him that he would endeavor to make a very honorable peace with Tocobaga, and that he should give him 10 or 12 Indian men and women that he had imprisoned. With this, Carlos cheered up, because among them there was a sister of his and of Doña Antonia, and he told the Adelantado that he was happy with that. The Adelantado ordered that a small launch with 8 oarsmen and one of those Christians who had been imprisoned in Carlos, who knew the language of Tocobaga,[39] should arrive next to the house of the chief, and there he should tell them in a loud voice, in their language, that they should have no fear, that all the people on the ships that were there were true Christians, their friends. And having done so, the Indians woke up and saw the ships next to their houses, and they began to flee with their wives and children.

The chief remained with 5 or 6 Indians and a wife,[40] and when it was daylight, he sent a Christian that he had to the Adelantado to tell him that he was very thankful that he had not killed him or his people, or burned his town, and that he had only that Christian whom he sent, and no more, and that his people had fled, and that he had remained with his house of his prayer and his gods, and he would sooner die than abandon them. And if he wished him to go to his ships, he would go, and if the Adelantado wished to go on land, and grant him life or death, that he could do so, because he was waiting for him.

The Adelantado was very pleased with the message, and with the Christian who carried it, who was a Portuguese man from Tavila, which is in the Algarve. He said that he had been imprisoned there for 6 years, and that they were traveling in a small boat with corn and hens, blankets and honey, from Campeche to New Spain, and that the storm had driven them across there, and the Indians killed them all within one hour, and this man hid in the woods so that they could not find him, and spent a month in hiding, eating palm hearts, acorns, and some shellfish. And by chance some Indian fishermen saw him and caught him and took him to this chief, and he served them in bringing water and firewood, and making food for them, and that from the day when they were lost until then, each day he begged Our Lord to free him from captivity. He had been waiting for Christians for eight days, and dreamed every night of these 8 days that Christians were going there to live, from which he was very happy. He related to the Adelantado the affairs of that land, although he knew very little, since he had never traveled more than 20 leagues outside that town. And the Adelantado did not wish to tell this Christian that Carlos had come there, or that Tocobaga should come to the ship, for the love of Carlos. He sent to say to him that he would go on land to speak to him, and that he should have no fear, and he charged the Christian with encouraging him, that he would do no evil to him, and that he should send to tell his Indian men and women that they should return to the town. And thus the Christian went with this reply, and at 8 in the morning the Adelantado went to land. He spoke to the chief, who received the Adelantado very well, and he seated him next to him, in a higher and more preeminent place. He had with him 6 Indian men and an Indian woman. He said to the Adelantado with the interpreter that he did not think that Christians were so good, that he knew well that they could kill him and his people and burn his idols and towns, and that for many days he had known that there were Christians in that land, and they had sent word to tell the chiefs, their friends, that they should give them corn, and that if they did not, they would kill them. And because they did not give it up, they killed many, and thus he was very afraid of them. Afterward, other Christians came and killed these, and it was said of these later ones that the chiefs and Indians loved them greatly. Of which [group] were they?

The Adelantado responded that he and his people were of the later Christians who came to kill those first Christians who came to make slaves of the chiefs and Indians, and who were false Christians, and for this he killed them.[41] He and his people were true Christians, and they did not come to kill them, or make them slaves, or take their corn, but instead they came to ask them if they wished to be Christians, and to instruct them how they should be [Christian], and to have them as friends and brothers. He did not come to make war, or to kill any chief or Indian, except those who wished to do evil and kill some Christian, and that if he and his people wished to be Christians, he would be very pleased.

The chief was very pleased by what the Adelantado told him, and he and his 6 Indians got up and performed great humility and obedience to the Adelantado, and kissed his hands, and then seated themselves again. Then the Adelantado told the chief that he was a friend of Carlos, and that he had Christians in his land, and that not because of this would he be an enemy of Tocobaga. He had Carlos with him in the brigantines, whom he carried in order to negotiate peace and friendship with him, and he should return the 12 persons that he had imprisoned to him, and that if he and his Indians wished to be Christians, he would be very pleased, and would leave him Christians there, as in Carlos, so that they would defend him against his enemies and instruct them to be Christians.

He replied that he had his people and the nobles and chiefs, his subjects and friends, far from there, and without them coming to speak with him, he could not respond, and that the Adelantado should wait 3 or 4 days, and he would call them.

The Adelantado said that he was content, and thus the chief sent to call upon his noble Indians and chiefs, and implored the Adelantado to command his soldiers not to approach the house of his gods, of whom this chief had great veneration.

The Adelantado went away that night with his people to sleep on the brigantines, and the next day in the morning, the chief Tocobaga came to see him. He and Carlos spoke, and bickered some. Carlos wished to disembark with Tocobaga and with his Indians, and because the Adelantado believed Carlos to be a great traitor, he did not dare, thinking that he would speak ill of him or of his Christians, and the 2 chiefs would agree that Carlos would kill the Christians he had there [in his town], and Tocobaga those that might be left there [in Tocobaga]. On the other side, the Adelantado did not dare to make Carlos mad, and for this he let him get off on land, with 2 interpreters who always stayed next to him, so that he would not speak ill of the Christians to the chief and the Indians.

In those 3 days there arrived there more than 1,500 Indians, all people of very good disposition, with their bows and arrows.

The Adelantado, since he saw so many people, told the chief that his soldiers were happy, because they thought that his Indians wished to be brave, and fight with them, and that he should leave the nobles with him in order to negotiate peace, and send away the others. The chief did so.

On the fourth day, when 29 chiefs and about another 100 noble Indians who remained with them were all together, the chief sent to call upon the Adelantado so that he would go to negotiate peace. And thus he went, taking Carlos with him. When they were together, the Adelantado seated in the most preeminent place, the chief Tocobaga told him that he had told everything the Adelantado had told him to those chiefs and Indians who were there, and that if he was saying those things in truth, that everyone would be pleased to take him as elder brother and become Christian, and make peace with Carlos, and give him his people. With this, if Carlos should once again make war on him, the Adelantado would help him, and if he should break [into war] with Carlos, the Adelantado would help Carlos, because he wished to make peace with the true Christians, and not the false ones. [For this] he should leave him another captain with 30 Christians, so that they might instruct him and his chiefs to be Christians. All was done in this manner, peace having been established with Carlos, and his people having been returned. The Adelantado left 30 soldiers there, and in charge of them, and as Captain, García Martínez de Cos, who remained completely against his will. The Adelantado left him because he was embittered against him on account of a certain disobedience that he had shown, and he also left him because he was of good judgment, and a good Christian, and because Tocobaga told the Adelantado that he could not go to Macoya with so few people, because [the Indians] were many and warlike.

Then they departed from there with their brigantines, less than 4 days after arriving, and within 8 [days] they returned Carlos to his town, and on the voyage it was recognized that Carlos had tremendously great haughtiness and anger on account of the great friendship that the Adelantado had made in Tocobaga. The Adelantado tried greatly to cheer him up, but could not. While a sailor was passing in front of Carlos, one end of a thin cord managed to fall on Carlos's head, and thinking that the sailor had done it deliberately, he gave him a great punch in the face and wrapped his arms around him, wanting to throw him in the ocean. The Adelantado reached him and pulled him off. The sailor was one of the most noble that was there, and resented this greatly. The Adelantado resented it much more, but since he was carrying him in his brigantine, and he had taken him from his land, it seemed to him that he was obligated to return him to it, but were it any other way, he made it understood that he would order him hanged for the punch, and also because he had understood from the interpreters that he was threatening the Adelantado and his Christians, and that he would order that none should escape him.

The Adelantado left him in his town. He had the Christians fortify themselves better than they were, and left them a complement of 50 soldiers in addition to those that were there, and certain artillery, and Father Rogel, of the Company of Jesus, so that he might indoctrinate the Indians. He departed with Father Francisco, his companion, and with the Indians from Tequesta, in order to take them to their chief and tell them about the peace that had been established between him and Carlos. The Adelantado left Doña Antonia there with the Christians. He did not bring away a good opinion of her, and she was very much in favor of her brother Carlos, and very sad about the peace that he had made with Tocobaga. She said very regrettable words to the Adelantado, because they had not burned and killed Tocobaga and his Indians, and burned his town and the house of their idols, and that he had two hearts, one for himself, another for Tocobaga, and that for her, or her brother, he had none.

The Adelantado satisfied her as well as he could and left her, and left to embark for Tequesta. While the ships were ready to set sail and go to Tequesta in order to carry the Indians that they had there and confirm the peace, and go from there to the forts of St. Augustine and San Mateo, he saw a ship enter the port, at which he was startled, not knowing what it could be. When it arrived to anchor, he discovered that it was a patache of his, which he had left in the port of St. Augustine when he left in his fleet against the corsairs, and which the captains of the forts of St. Augustine, San Mateo, and San Felipe had dispatched to Havana, reporting that the Adelantado should aid them with supplies. Upon its arrival in Havana, the treasurer Juan de Ynistrosa, lieutenant of the Adelantado in that villa and island for the affairs of Florida, sent it with news to the Adelantado, and it also carried letters from all the aldermen of Havana. . . . The Adelantado, when he saw these dispatches, sent the Indians to Tequesta, and he came to Havana, and arrived within 3 days . . . leaving everything there with the best precautions that he could, with some supplies that were gathered, and other ships that he sent to Campeche to load up with corn. He went to Florida, to Tequesta, where he was very well received by that chief and Indians. He made great peace with them, and they took him as elder brother. He left 30 soldiers there, and as their captain . . . ,[42] and he left them a saw and carpenters to make a strong house. He erected a cross with great devotion, and the Indians worshipped it. He left there Father

Francisco, of the Company of Jesus. He remained 4 days in that town, and great was his contentment to see that in the mornings and in the afternoons, all the Indian men and women, large and small, came to worship the cross and kiss it with great devotion. The chief gave the Adelantado a brother of his and two principal Indians, one of whom was captain of a town of Carlos, so that he might bring them to Spain. The Adelantado departed with them, with good weather, and on the third day he arrived at San Mateo. . . .

Supplementary Documents

Order by Menéndez establishing Fort San Antón de Carlos, October 15, 1566

The following order (Menéndez de Avilés 1566c) was transcribed from the original manuscript given to Captain Francisco de Reinoso and later submitted by him in 1569 in Madrid as part of his formal petition to recover his salary, after the withdrawal of the fort (Reynoso 1569). The original document, therefore, physically traveled from St. Augustine to Fort San Antón de Carlos, then three years later to Havana and Madrid, where it became part of the Spanish governmental archives. Within the text is a description of Menéndez's original plan for the Calusa fort, which formed the hub of his planned network of Spanish garrisons in South Florida.

The transcription here follows the norms detailed in the preface, generally preserving anachronistic orthography present in the original text except in cases where it might make it difficult for modern Spanish readers to sound out the words correctly or follow the intended sentence structure.

Spanish

Yo Pedro Menendez de Avilez Gobernador y Capitan General por su magestad de la tierra y costas de las probincias de la Florida y adelantado dellas por su magestad, digo que al servicio de su magestad y bien unibersal de los navios que nabegan en las Yndias y desembocan la canal de bahama conbiene allanar toda la costa de Carlos y los Martires y la cabeca dellos que es el principio de la canal de Bahama que es por donde los navios de las yndias bienen a estos reynos y procurar atraer los yndios a la obidiencia de la yglesia y de su magestad por lo qual nombro por Capitan a bos Francisco de Reinoso que hagais un fuerte en el puerto de Sant Anton para la defensa de aquel puerto que es en el mismo pueblo donde el cacique Carlos vvive el qual es mi amigo

y para lo poder hazer os mando dar un bergantin con piloto y doce marineros
y cinquenta soldados con sus armas y municiones de los que traxo Sancho
de Archiniega a estas provincias y quatro soldados de los biejos que conmigo
an estado en aquel fuerte y al padre Rrogel teatino de la compania de Jesus
y al Hermano Francisco su conpanero y a Grabiel de Solis y a Juan Menendez
ninos para que rrecen la dotrina xpiana a los Yndios y por yncurrir en bos las
calidades que se rrequieren y por lo mucho y bien que abeys servido a Su
Magestad en ellas despues que yo a ellas vine y aberos allado en la muerte
de Juan Rribao y los mas Luteranos ansi en el rrio de la Matanca como en
ganar el fuerte del Canaberal en nombre de su magestad bos nonbro por
capitan del dho fuerte y gente y governador de aquel dest[acament]o y como
a tal toda la gente de mar y guerra navios merchantes y de armada que por
alli fueren y aportaren y todas las personas de qualquiera calidad y condicion
que fueren bos obedezcan y acaten y rrespeten por tal y cunplan vuestros
mandamyentos no siendo las personas de los capitanes Estebano de las Alas
y Pedro Menenedez Marquez porque el dho Estebano de las Alas de mi lugar
tenyente de toda la tierra de la Florida y fuertes que su magestad en ellas
tuviere y el dho capitan Pedro Menendez de la conquista y descubrimiento de
la costa, puertos, y baxios y a vos vos mandara su magestad pagar el sueldo
de tal capitan segun y como ganan los demas capitanes que rresiden en estos
presidios de la Florida y a los dhos soldados y ofiziales que tubiere del ni mas
ni menos y conforme esta vieren asentados por sus nonbres en las listas que
estan en la casa de la contratacion al tiempo que se enbarcaron con el capitan Sancho de Archiniaga y para usar y exercerse dho officio todo el tiempo
que en el estuviere [?] os doy poder cunplido segun que de su magestad
lo tengo fecho en el fuerte de San Agustin destas provincias de la Florida a
quince dias del mes de Otubre de mill y quinientos y sesenta y seys anos. Ba
entre renglones, estovala, y borrado aquello no vala. Va entre renglones pa lo
qual nonbro por Capitan a vos Francisco de Reynoso vala.

Pedro Menendez

Por mandado de su senoria, Fernando de Miranda

English

I, Pedro Menéndez de Avilés, Governor and Captain General for His
Majesty of the land and coasts of the provinces of Florida, and Adelantado of them for His Majesty, say that in the service of His Majesty and
the universal good of the ships that navigate in the Indies and travel the
Bahama Channel, it is suitable to pacify all the coast of Carlos and the
Martyrs, and their head, which is the beginning of the Bahama Channel, which is where the ships from the Indies come through toward

these kingdoms, and to endeavor to attract the Indians to the obedience of the Church and of His Majesty, for which I name you, Francisco de Reinoso, as Captain, so that you shall make a fort in the port of San Antón for the defense of that port, which is in the same town where the chief Carlos lives, who is my friend. And so that you can do this, I command to be given to you a brigantine with a pilot and twelve sailors and fifty soldiers with their weapons and munitions, of those that Sancho de Archiniega brought to these provinces, and four of the old soldiers that have been with me in that fort, and Father Rogel, Jesuit of the Company of Jesus,[43] and Brother Francisco, his companion, and Grabiel de Solís and Juan Menéndez, boys, so that they might pray the Christian doctrine to the Indians. And because the required qualities concur in you, and because of your lengthy and good service to His Majesty in [these provinces] after I came to them, and having been present at the death of Juan Ribao and the rest of the Lutherans, both in the river of Matanzas and in winning the fort of Cañaveral, in the name of His Majesty I name you as captain of the aforementioned fort and people and governor of that detachment. And as such, I order all the sailors and soldiers of merchant ships and [military] fleets that might go there and reach port, and all the persons of whatever quality and condition they may be, to obey and observe and respect you as such, and to fulfill your commands, not including the persons of Captains Estébano de las Alas and Pedro Menéndez Márquez, because the aforementioned Estébano de las Alas is my deputy of all the land of Florida and the forts that His Majesty has in them, and the said Captain Pedro Menéndez [is deputy] of the conquest and discovery of the coast, ports, and bays. And His Majesty shall order you paid the salary of captain, according to and as the rest of the captains that reside in these presidios of Florida earn, and the aforementioned soldiers and officials that you have [will not earn] either more or less and in conformity with what is seen inscribed by their names in the lists that were in the House of Trade at the time that they disembarked with Captain Sancho de Archiniaga. And in order to make use of and exercise the aforementioned office all the time in which you may occupy it, I give you full power according to that which I have from His Majesty. Signed in the fort of St. Augustine in these provinces of Florida on the fifteenth of the month of October of fifteen sixty-six. Between the lines,[44] "this" is valid, and crossed out "that" is not valid. Between the lines "for which I name you, Francisco de Reynoso, as captain" is valid.

Pedro Menéndez

By order of his lordship, Fernando de Miranda

Letter of Pedro Menéndez Márquez, March 28, 1568

The following selection is from a previously unpublished letter written by Pedro Menéndez Márquez, nephew of the Adelantado Pedro Menéndez de Avilés and future governor of Florida. Menéndez Márquez supervised many maritime expeditions throughout South Florida during the period from 1566 to 1569 and was thus ultimately selected to provide detailed geographic information to royal cosmographer Juan López de Velasco (Lyon 1989: 160–61; López de Velasco 1894: 157–70). Menéndez Márquez, writing from Havana, describes the voyage during January 1568 in which he discovered the massacre of the Tocobaga garrison, as well as a subsequent expedition to Tequesta that revealed the uprising and abandonment of that garrison, resulting in the movement of all survivors at Fort San Antón de Carlos (Menéndez Márquez 1568).

The transcription here follows the norms detailed in the preface, generally preserving anachronistic orthography present in the original text except in cases where it might make it difficult for modern Spanish readers to sound out the words correctly or follow the intended sentence structure. There are several illegible or only partially legible sections of the text indicated with question marks in brackets, some including possible missing text.

Spanish

Fui a Tocobaga en principio de henero y fue dios servydo q[ue] halle dos cristianos muertos en la playa de flechaços y los mas no los bi ny yndio ny [?] no sabemos q[ue] es la causa aguarde tres dias tirando tiros y [?] yndio ny cristiano entiendo q[ue] son todos muertos. Bisto q[ue] no venyan quemeles el pueblo y todos sus ydolos y bolvime a Carlos donde reforce la gente con otra mas y dejeles comida p[ar]a quatro meses y vine a esta villa donde halle aviso de Est[eban]o de las Alas q[ue] le socoriese q[ue] no comyan sino a media libra de mahiz solo conpre aqui treci[ent]os hanegas a diez y seis r[eale]s y enbieselas en la fregata grande [?] y de camyno mandele hechar veynte y cinco hanegas en Tequesta las quales hechos despues por no tener aqui que hacer fuime a los Martiles a hacer que los yndios ynbiasen el tributo a Carlos q[ua]l me lo avia rogado y estando con ellos me dijeron q[ue] los cristianos de Tequesta abian muerto al Rey viejo yo como lo supe fui alla y llegue a tan buen t[iem]po con seis arcabuceros que halle los yndios rrebueltos con los cristianos q[ue] ya avian muerto tres cristianos y herido uno. Los yndios quando me vieron metreronse en el monte y tomaron el agua de manera q[ue] no era posible aver agua para llebar y tanbien los cristianos no tenian munycion q[ue] se les yba acabando ny yo le llebaba cojilos todos en la chalupa y quatro pipas de mahiz y trujelos a los Martiles y assi los deje por no me atreber a atrabesar asta villa en tan chico barco y llegado aqui ynbie un barco grande y mandele q[ue] los llevase a Carlos p[ar]a q[ue] ally ubiese mas gente y enbielas mahiz y escrivi al padre teatino y a Rreinoso tubiesen grande centinela y no se descuydase y supiesen porq[ue] Carlos avia mandado matar el cacique y otros dos yndios de Tatesta un pueblo de los martiles porq los yndios de alli me dijeron q[ue] los avyan muerto porq[ue] tenyan amistad con nosotros y q[ue] de todo me diese aviso el barco no a venydo y ansi no podre dar desto mi aviso a V[uestra] S[eñoria] a zelodado [?]. Yo digo cierto q[ue] ay poco q[ue] fiar dellos y ques menester el remedio de el mano de dios.

English

I went to Tocobaga at the beginning of January, and God was served that I found two Christians dead on the beach from arrow wounds, and the rest I did not see, neither Indian nor [Christian?]. We do not know what is the cause. We waited three days, firing shots, and [saw neither?] Indian nor Christian. I understand that they are all dead. Having seen that they were not coming, I burned the town and all its idols, and returned to Carlos where I reinforced the garrison with more people, and left them food for four months. And I came to this villa [of Havana], where I found news from Estébano de las Alas that I should help him and that they were only eating half a pound of corn. I only bought here three hundred fanegas of corn at sixteen *reales*, and I sent it in the large frigate [?], and along the way I commanded it to unload twenty-five fanegas in Tequesta. All of this being done, since I had nothing else to do here, I went to the Martyrs to make the Indians send tribute to Carlos, which he had implored me to do. And while I was with them, they told me that the Christians at Tequesta had killed the old king. As soon as I found out, I went there and arrived with six arquebusiers with such good timing that I found the Indians in rebellion with the Christians, having already killed three Christians and wounded one. When they saw me, the Indians went into the woods and took the water, so that it was not possible to get water to carry. Also, the Christians did not have munitions, which were dwindling, and I was not carrying any, so I gathered them all in the launch along with four pipas of corn and brought them to the Martyrs. I left them there, because I did not dare cross to this villa [Havana] in such a small boat, and having arrived here I sent them a large boat and ordered it to carry them to Carlos, so that there would be more people there, and I sent them corn. I wrote to the Jesuit father and to Reinoso that they should keep close watch and not be careless, and that they should find out why Carlos had ordered the killing of the chief and another two Indians from Tatesta, a town of the Martyrs, because the Indians from there told me that they had killed them because they had friendship with us, and that they should give me news about everything. The boat has not come, and thus I cannot give news from this to Your Lordship [?]. I would say for certain that they should not be trusted much and that the hand of God will be needed in remedy.

Letter of Francisco Villareal to Francisco Borgia, March 5, 1570

The following selection is part of a letter from Jesuit lay brother Francisco Villareal to his superior Francisco Borgia and was taken from a published transcript included in a comprehensive collection of sixteenth-century Jesuit letters regarding Florida (Zubillaga 1946: 415–16). Selections from several of Juan Rogel's contemporaneous letters regarding the South Florida missions have been translated (Hann 1991: 230–98), but Villareal's letter also has important details that bear on the Menéndez era, particularly regarding the long-anticipated return of the Adelantado to the Calusa capital in 1569.

Villareal was originally stationed in the Spanish fort at Tequesta, in present-day downtown Miami, but was forced to withdraw to the Calusa capital early in 1568 after an Indian uprising (described by Pedro Menéndez Márquez in the previous letter). Stationed at Fort San Antón de Carlos for the last year of its existence, Villareal provides the only known details regarding the final interactions between the Calusa chief Felipe and Pedro Menéndez de Avilés during the winter of 1568–69, as well as the deterioration of relations the following spring and the deaths that ultimately led to the Spanish withdrawal from South Florida in June.

The transcription here follows the norms detailed in the preface, generally preserving anachronistic orthography present in the original text except in cases where it might make it difficult for modern Spanish readers to sound out the words correctly or follow the intended sentence structure.

Spanish

1. Pax Chri[sti] etc. Estando yo en el fuerte de Carlos, de que ya V[uestra] P[aternidad] terná noticia, escreví otra dando quenta de lo que avía sucedido en las partes que estado en la Florida. Esta servirá de lo mismo para que V[uestra] P[aternidad] sea mejor informado deste negocio.

2. Yo vine juntamente con el Padre Rogel y estuve en un fuerte que llaman Tequesta con algunos soldados. Los indios parecía que heran los más pacíficos

que yo avía visto; y allí enseñava la doctrina a los niños y la deprendían bien:
los grandes no venían a ella sino algunas vezes, ni preguntavan ninguna cosa,
ni davan muestra de querer saber las cosas de Dios; antes me parece que
oí dezir que dezian que los grandes ya no harían nada, que los chicos depren-
diesen la doctrina; y poco tiempo después que llegamos allí dezían que ya
sabían la doctrina, que nos fuésemos de su tierra. Al fin estuvimos allí como
diez meses; y por una afrenta que un indio viejo de allí, que avía sido cacique,
que dezían que avía hecho a un soldado, los cristianos le mataron; y después
los indios mataron algunos cristianos; y assí se salieron de allí los cristianos
por orden del Governador que dexó el Adelantado para este fuerte y los
demás. En este tiempo también se supo cómo otro fuerte que avía dexado
el Adelantado en Tocobaga con veinte cristianos, pocos más o menos, se
avía deshecho y los indios mataron a los cristianos.

3. Como se acabó este fuerte donde yo estava, me fui a Carlos, donde estava
el Padre Rogel, el qual viendo que hazia allí poco fruto, se vino a la Habana y
me dexo allí para dezir la doctrina a los indios y cristianos. Este cacique que
avía en Carlos, que los cristianos le nombraron, porque avían muerto a su an-
tecesor, porque dizen que los quería matar, desde luego començó a dar grandes esperanças de que avía de quemar sus ídolos y ser cristiano, en viniendo
el Adelantado de España; y con esto se procedía con él con amor, dándole
algunas cosas y a sus indios. Vino el Adelantado y traxo al cacique con
algunos de los suyos a la Habana, para que viese las cosas de los cristianos;
y creo le procuraron regalar dándole algunas cosas con que se bolvió a su
tierra; y de allí a poco tiempo el Adelantado fue allá juntamente con el Padre
Viceprovincial y el Padre Sedeño y el Padre Alamo, que antes estava allá; y
estando allí el Adelantado, habló aparte con el cacique, el qual, otro día por
la mañana, juntamente con algunos de sus indios, quemó sus ídolos, y luego
se vino el Adelantado y el Padre Viceprovincial y el Padre Sedeño; y supimos
de las lenguas y del mismo cacique cómo de miedo y temor avía quemado los
ídolos. Yo no supe ni entendí que los Padres le hablasen para [que] quemase
los ídolos. Después desto, diziendo que este cacique nos armaba traición,
los cristianos le mataron a él y a otros catorze o quinze indios, principales los
más dellos, y a otros hirieron malamente, y a las reinas traxeron a la Habana,
y aquí se están enseñando la doctrina y las cosas de Dios; los indios todos
se fueron, dexando la tierra sola, y a los cristianos sacaron de allí, y venimos
todos a la Habana, donde agora estamos.

English

1. The Peace of Christ, etc. While I was in the fort of Carlos, about
which Your Paternity already has notice,[45] I wrote another [letter]

recounting what had happened in the places that I had been in Florida. This will serve in the same way, so that Your Paternity is better informed about this affair.

2. I came together with Father Rogel and was in a fort that they call Tequesta with some soldiers. It seemed that the Indians were the most peaceful that I had seen, and there I taught the doctrine to the children and they learned it well. The adults did not come more than a few times, nor did they ask anything, or give any sign of wanting to learn about the affairs of God. Rather, it seems to me that I heard it said that they said that the adults would do nothing now, that the young should learn about doctrine. And a little time after we arrived there, they said that now they knew the doctrine, so we should go away from their land. In the end we were there about ten months, and on account of an affront that they said an old Indian from there, who had been chief, made to a soldier, the Christians killed him. And afterward the Indians killed some Christians, and thus all the Christians left from there by order of the governor that the Adelantado left for this fort and the rest. In this time it was also discovered that another fort that the Adelantado had left in Tocobaga with twenty Christians, more or less, had been unmade, and the Indians killed the Christians.

3. Since this fort where I was had been finished off, I went to Carlos, where Father Rogel was. Seeing that little fruit was obtained there, he came to Havana and left me there to teach the doctrine to the Indians and Christians. This chief who was there in Carlos, whom the Christians had named because they had killed his predecessor because they said that he wished to kill them,[46] immediately began to offer great hopes that he would burn his idols and become a Christian when the Adelantado came back from Spain. With this, he was treated with love, giving him and his Indians some things. The Adelantado came and brought the chief to Havana with some of his [Indians], so that he might see the things of the Christians, and I believe they attempted to regale him, giving him some things with which he returned to his land. And a very short time later the Adelantado went there together with the Father Vice-Provincial, and Father Sedeño, and Father Alamo, who was there before. And while the Adelantado was there, he spoke individually with the chief, who, on the morning of the next day, together with some of his Indians, burned his idols. Then the Adelantado went with the Father Vice-Provincial and Father Sedeño, and we found out from the interpreters and from the chief himself that he had burned his idols out of terror and fear. I did not know or understand that the

Fathers spoke with him so that he would burn the idols. After this, saying that this chief was plotting to betray us, the Christians killed him and another fourteen or fifteen Indians, most of them nobles, and others they wounded badly. They brought the queens to Havana, and here they are learning about the doctrine and the affairs of God. The Indians all went away, leaving the land alone, and they withdrew the Christians from there, and we all came to Havana, where we are now.

Notes

Chapter 1. The Juan Ponce de León Expeditions, 1513–1521

1. The navigational term *quarta* refers to the otherwise unnamed halfway points between the sixteen named directions on the compass, including the eight principal directions (N, NE, E, SE, S, SW, W, NW) and their eight combinations (NNE, ENE, ESE, SSE, SSW, WSW, WNW, NNW). Together, the sixteen named directions and the sixteen *quartas* made up thirty-two divisions, or "winds" (*vientos*), of the 360-degree compass. In this case, one "quarter" to the north from due northwest was $\frac{1}{32}$ of the compass (equaling 11.25 degrees) from exactly 315 degrees, equaling 326.25 degrees. In English terminology, this was called "northwest and by north."

2. A nautical day, or *singladura*, was normally measured from noon to noon.

3. The Lucayos is another name for the Bahamas, and the Caicos Islands still exist today under the same name.

4. The sixteenth-century *bergantín* was a small, one-masted, lateen-rigged vessel with oars, very different from the more familiar image of the much larger two-masted brigantines of the eighteenth and nineteenth centuries.

5. A *barca* is a small rowboat, presumably used for landing in shallow waters.

6. The term *palo*, which literally means "stick," probably refers in this context to the common war club typically used by Southeastern Indians in hand-to-hand combat.

7. The term *bara* (*vara*), or stick, clearly refers to spears here.

8. The phrase *para que aprendiesse la lengua* presumably means the Indian was to learn Spanish in order to serve as an interpreter, a common practice during such coastal explorations during this era.

9. The phrase *dexo en el labrada una de canteria con un letrero* could refer to an individual piece of carved stone or might refer to a carving made from an existing rock outcrop along the riverbank.

10. This translation of *unas isletas, que se hazian fuera a la mar* is based on the interpretation that this passage refers to the barrier islands along the Southwest Florida coastline, but the wording is ambiguous enough to be translated in several ways that might refer to different geographic features.

11. The term *guanin* is previously defined by Herrera y Tordesillas as "a metal they called Guanin . . . having assayed it where it was found, which of thirty-two parts, eighteen were of gold, six of silver, and eight of copper" (1601: 100, 129). Paul Hoffman defines *guanines* as "gold objects of low carat" (1980: 422), and presuming that this was an item being traded by the Florida Indians, it might be identified as copper, though it is at least remotely possible that the Indians already had access to some shipwreck gold from Spanish sources prior to 1513.

12. This passage implies a specific expectation of the distance from the Tortugas Islands to Cuba, which was presumably based on calculations of their position using log entries but which could possibly be interpreted to mean there was some prior knowledge of the distance between Cuba and the islands to its north.

13. This recounting of the now-famous story of the "fountain of youth" likely derives from Herrera's use of the late sixteenth-century narrative of Hernando de Escalante Fontaneda, who describes precisely the same details at greater length in his handwritten manuscript dating to ca. 1575 (see the introduction and chapter 3).

14. The phrase *hasta oy dura aquella generación de los de Cuba* might also be translated to mean that there were still survivors alive from the original generation that emigrated from Cuba to Florida, but in this context and at this date (1601), it seems more likely that the term *generación* refers to offspring or descendants.

15. The initial exploration of the South Carolina coast was actually carried out by Pedro de Quejos in 1521, five years earlier than the colonial expedition of Lúcas Vázquez de Ayllón.

16. There is a blank space in the original manuscript here.

17. *Staves* refers to the official staff that was a tangible insignia for such positions.

18. Oviedo's date here is incorrect, referring instead to the date when his first contract was issued. The actual date of Ponce de León's voyage was 1513.

19. The term *adelantamiento* refers to the territory granted to the adelantado as the Spanish Crown's representative in frontier zones. Juan Ponce de León was one of the first recipients of this title in the New World (see Hill 1913: 652–56).

20. As stated in note 16, the original manuscript left this space blank, but the 1521 letters translated in this chapter suggest the date of departure was in February, unless the expedition was delayed beyond the expected departure on February 15 or 16.

21. Oviedo's original date of 1520 is in error and should be 1521.

22. Here Oviedo renders one of his typical scathing critiques of the Spanish explorers of Ponce's era.

23. The date provided by Las Casas is erroneous; it should be 1521.

24. The *Casa de Contratación*, or "House of Trade," had been recently established in 1503 as a regulatory institution for Spanish colonial commerce.

25. The *diezmo* was an obligatory 10 percent ecclesiastical tax, or tithe, charged on agricultural produce and livestock.

26. The *repartimiento* was a specific socioeconomic institution of the Spanish colonial period in which Indians within colonized territories were divided and distributed among designated Spanish colonists, who were to benefit from the fruits of their labor.

27. The *quinto*, or fifth, was the standard royal tax levied on earnings in the Spanish colonial world, and thus the benefit to the first settlers in Ponce de León's expedition was to have this 20 percent tax waived during the first five years after discovery and settlement of the new land, during which the tax rate rose incrementally from 10 percent to 20 percent.

28. The abbreviation *xpo* or *xpto* was a common Spanish shorthand for "Christ" and was derived from the Greek rendering of the name. Here the phrase *in xpo* simply means "in Christ."

29. This word was mistakenly left out of this version of the contract but appears in the other version (Spanish Crown 1514b).

30. The *Requerimiento*, or "requirement," was a formal statement to be read three times in legal form before Indians in newly discovered lands. It detailed the conditions under which they could either submit to the authority of the pope and the Spanish Crown or be subjected to military conquest under principles of just war. An early version of this text is found in the orders issued to Pedrarias Dávila on folios 20r–22v of Ramo 5 in Patronato 26 in the Archivo General de Indias, as presented in translated form by Helps (1855: 379–82) and Hanke (1938: 26–28).

31. The measurement of a *tapia* was based on a single portion of a masonry wall, generally ten feet long by five feet high, corresponding to fifty square feet of surface area. In this passage, it refers to the minimum height of stone construction to be used in houses (five feet), above which earthen construction was acceptable.

32. See note 28.

Chapter 2. The Pánfilo de Narváez and Hernando de Soto Expeditions and the Captivity of Juan Ortiz, 1528–1539

1. These royal officials accompanied Narváez on his first entry into the interior, including the author as the expedition's treasurer.

2. The Río de las Palmas was actually located far to the west, along the northern gulf coast of Mexico, north of modern Tampico (see Hoffman 1994: 51–52).

3. This location is at modern Tampico.

4. An *auto* is a broad term referring to a formal legal proceeding recorded in writing.

5. This parenthetical remark relative to the inadequacy of the Spanish term *cavallero* (*caballero*) for knight (derived from *caballo*, or "horse") furthermore provides important ethnographic commentary relative to an apparent rank distinction between nobles and high nobles (*nobles* and *nobilissimos*) among Florida Indians in this region, which the author distinguishes by using the terms *hombres nobles* and *caballeros*. It is uncertain whether he intended to characterize *caballeros* as low nobles or high nobles in this sense.

6. This episode in Garcilaso's Ortiz narrative has been asserted by some authors to be the origin of John Smith's subsequent (and now familiar) story of his rescue from Chief Powhatan by his daughter Pocahontas (see, e.g., Hubbell 1957: 283).

7. Here the author provides a remarkably detailed description of the term *barbacoa*, which colonial Spaniards adopted from the Taino Indians of the

Caribbean and which was variously applied in Florida to beds and benches, as well as raised grills, all of which had a similar form described here as "Barbacoa, que es un lecho de madera, de forma de parrillas, una vara de medir alta del suelo." The Arawak term is the origin of the modern word *barbecue*.

8. This is doubtless a reference to the Florida panther.

9. The term *dardos* probably refers to light spears thrown either by hand or with the aid of a spear thrower, or atlatl.

10. This colloquial expression (*la mano sabrosa*) is difficult to render into English but might best be expressed in noting that Ortiz's shot was so good that he could "taste" it.

11. Here Garcilaso makes explicit reference to one of his sources, Soto expedition survivor Alonso de Carmona, presumably in order to provide a citation for this particular detail, which might not have appeared among his other sources.

12. This incident serves to illustrate the confusion caused by poor translations, in this case resulting in the hearing of the Spanish surname Ortiz as a nonexistent word *orotiz*, which the best interpreters at the time rendered as an Indian expression meaning that there was much *oro* (Spanish for "gold") in the land. The actual testimony must have simply noted the presence of a captive Spaniard named Ortiz.

13. One *braça* (*braza*) was equivalent to 1.67 meters (5.5 feet), making this feathered headdress roughly 83 cm (2.7 feet) tall.

14. Here Garcilaso mentions Juan Coles, who presumably was the sole source for this element of the story.

15. Here Garcilaso refers to all of *La Florida*, meaning the entire southeastern United States traversed by Soto's army.

16. The pagination here is my own, since the microfilm copy of Smith's papers does not permit his original pagination (apparently beginning on page 231) to be read clearly. In addition, at the top of Smith's transcription is the following note regarding the text's original location in the papers of Juan Muñoz: *[Tom]o LXXXI, Simancas Cartas, leg[ajo] 31, 1539.*

17. This title was actually placed by Muñoz at the end of his transcription, where he noted *En la cubierta dice:* (On the cover it says:), suggesting that this was likely a title or filing note placed on the outside of the paper on which the original sixteenth-century transcription was made.

18. Pentecost Sunday fell on May 25, 1539.

19. Trinity Sunday fell on June 1, 1539.

20. The phrase *en treinta leguas no ha parado hombre* could also be translated as "in thirty leagues not a man has been stopped," but since Soto uses the verb *detener* later in reference to detaining Indians, this rendering seems less likely.

21. My translation is based on Smith's (1866) own translation of the unreadable word or words in this corner of the microfilmed page. The last two letters of the unreadable portion are *ta*.

22. The phrase *ecebto sino son las bacas que traemos noticia* could also be translated as "except if they are the cows that we bring news of," suggesting that Soto thought the Indians were reporting on cows that they had learned about from the Spaniards themselves. I believe it more likely that Soto already had reports of "cows" (presumably bison) from previous Spanish expeditions to the

Southeast and suspected that these Indian informants were talking about such creatures.

23. Here again I follow Smith's (1866) published translation, since the corresponding word is unreadable in the corner of the microfilm copy.

24. This refers to the *licenciado* Bartolomé Ortiz, appointed by Soto to govern Cuba in his absence. The title *licenciado* indicates he had received formal education in law.

25. In the bottom left margin of the Smith transcription is the following note in Spanish: *aqui hai blanco en el orig. donde sin duda falta de poner* (here there is a blank in the original where doubtless something has not been placed). Since the other notes by Smith in the transcription are in English, this may be a note by Muñoz in reference to the original transcription of the 1539 letter.

26. At the base of the Smith transcription are notes both by the original transcriber, Juan Muñoz, in Spanish and by Buckingham Smith in English. In addition to his surname, Muñoz included the title said to have been placed "on the cover" of the original document. Smith inserted a note saying, "Handwriting of my wife" and concluded with "A correct transcript of the copy certified by Muñoz in the Royal Academy of History. Madrid: October 10th 1852, Buckingham Smith."

Chapter 3. The Luis Cancer Expedition, 1549

1. Cancer had been a missionary in Verapaz, Guatemala, during the early 1540s.

2. A *nao* was a specific type of large merchant vessel of the colonial era.

3. Here the author makes poetic reference to the irony of a seed that fails to sprout even in a land called *Florida*, which can be taken to mean "florid" or "flowering" as a double meaning.

4. The first four folios of Cancer's diary appear to have been paginated in Arabic numerals by Cancer himself in the bottom right corner of each folio's front side.

5. Like most educated priests during the colonial era, Cancer inserts occasional Latin phrases, as is the case in several places in his Florida diary.

6. This phrase was inserted within the original text in what appears to be Fray Cancer's handwriting, though it is possible that it was inserted by Beteta along with other marginal notes.

7. As noted in Smith's (1857: 190) transcription, this Latin passage is extracted from the Vulgate New Testament, Matthew 3:9.

8. This marginal insertion was written by Beteta above the main text of Cancer's original diary and corresponded to a "//" symbol also inserted alongside the text below, between the words *enme[n]dasen* and *y visto*. Despite this apparent original positioning, Beteta's final transcription simply inserted the addition between the text for the two pages, as is reproduced here.

9. Fray Beteta here underlined Cancer's text and inserted *a 29* in the right margin, but his later transcript of the journal correctly noted *28 grados y m[edi]o*, though in a script that could easily be mistaken for *23 grados y m[edi]o*.

10. Although Cancer's original journal clearly uses the phrase *van a t[ie]rra a descubrir puerto* here, Beteta's later transcription erroneously renders it *van a tierra a descubrir tierra*.

11. This marginal insertion appears to be in Cancer's handwriting, based on its style and the size of the letters, and similarly appears in Beteta's later transcription.

12. This word was clearly inserted by Cancer.

13. This phrase was also clearly inserted by Cancer.

14. Beteta mistranscribed this as *se levantan*.

15. Beteta mistakenly wrote *mas que esperava* here in his transcription.

16. This marginal insertion was probably penned by Cancer.

17. The original Cancer manuscript has a marginal note apparently written by Beteta saying *no de todos* in the left margin, with the text phrase *estavan (estaban) dentro* underlined, suggesting that Cancer's comment that everyone in the boat was happy was not entirely correct. Despite this marginal note, Beteta's final transcription of the Cancer manuscript does not include this comment.

18. Beteta's transcription changed the tense of this verb from present to past, though the original Cancer text clearly has *digo* instead of *dixe*.

19. The tense was also changed here from present to past in Beteta's version.

20. The tense was changed here also.

21. Here Cancer simply drew a cross with four dots in the spaces around it, whereas Beteta in his transcription wrote *cruz*.

22. The handwriting in this section, and on this page in general, seems far more careless and sloppy than in previous portions of the diary, suggesting that it was written either in some haste or under conditions that were not ideal, as suggested by the very words that Cancer was writing on the page at that moment.

23. The original Cancer manuscript has the word *todos* inserted by Beteta between *esperança* and *de ver*, while there is a marginal note to the left inserted after *puerto* saying *o saber de ellos*. The final Beteta transcription is worded as noted in the text here.

24. Beteta changed *de conplido* [*cumplido*] to *de largo*.

25. Cancer's text is very difficult to read on its own here at the bottom corner of the page, but Beteta's text clearly reads *yzquierda*.

26. Here and on the next line Beteta's transcription reads *se allegasen*.

27. This sentence was inserted at the top margin of this page by Beteta in the original Cancer manuscript and set apart as an individual paragraph section within Beteta's later transcription.

28. Beteta's transcription shortens this from *grande* to *gran*.

29. This word was inserted, probably by Cancer himself, above the line of text.

30. The last part of this word is missing from the edge of the page in Cancer's original diary, but Beteta's transcription fills in the gap.

31. This marginal explanatory note was inserted by Beteta in Cancer's diary and also appeared within the final Beteta transcript.

32. Cancer had originally added *y creen* after this word but apparently crossed it out, and Beteta's text leaves it out as well.

33. This marginal note was probably added by Cancer himself, but the handwriting could possibly be Beteta's.

34. Beteta's transcription reads *del este*.

35. Cancer inserted this word above the line here.

36. Beteta transcribed this as *nos allegasemos*.

37. Beteta wrote *esto* lightly here in his transcription instead of Cancer's clear *es*.

38. Cancer had originally written *se llego a* and then crossed it out, replacing it immediately with *se echo al*.

39. Cancer mistakenly wrote *se avia* twice without correcting the error. Beteta's text transcribes only one.

40. Cancer used the Roman numeral here, while Beteta wrote *cinq[uen]ta* in his transcription.

41. Beteta wrote this passage in the left margin of the Cancer manuscript and inserted the phrase within his transcription at this point.

42. Cancer had originally written *sal de* and then crossed it out and replaced it with *salta del*.

43. Cancer's handwriting is difficult to read here, but he seems to have intended *dize me* instead of what Beteta wrote in his transcription, *dixo me*.

44. Cancer's text does not include the *-tar* that is in Beteta's transcription, and since the word fragment *conçer* is at the far right side of the paper, it seems likely that he accidentally wrote the end of the word off the paper's edge but did not correct it on the next line.

45. Cancer wrote *sasar*, but Beteta's transcription corrects the error. Cancer seems to have been making an increasing number of errors at this point in the diary.

46. Cancer originally wrote *entrar en la chal* but crossed this out and wrote *llegar a la chalupa* instead.

47. This term, derived from the Latin, is explained in the next phrase.

48. Beteta inserted a marginal note here saying *fuerça bie[n] gra[n]de*, suggesting that he disagreed with Cancer's evaluation of *media fuerça*. Nevertheless, the insertion did not appear in the final Beteta transcription.

49. These were the last words written by Fray Cancer in his diary. The next three folios of the diary are in a different handwriting, corresponding to that used later by Fray Gregorio de Beteta in his retranscription of the entire diary. In addition, there are subtle but clear differences in language, wording, and spelling, suggesting a different author was writing.

50. Beteta's transcript reads *pensava el hazer*.

51. Beteta wrote *macanas* in his retranscription of this section of the diary, which is the most common spelling of this Arawakan word for war clubs.

52. The text includes a rare accent mark here above the last vowel, which probably indicates that Beteta was trying to indicate the pronunciation of this local Indian word.

53. Beteta originally wrote *sabado* but crossed it out and wrote *viernes* next to it.

54. Beteta's transcription of this reads *de este oeste*.

55. Beteta wrote *qua[n]to lexos* twice in the original diary but only once in his later transcription.

56. Beteta wrote *San Jua[n] de lua* in the transcription.

57. This and subsequent Vulgate New Testament translations are drawn from the 1582 Douay-Rheims translation.

58. This is quoted from 1 Corinthians 1:27–28 (Smith 1857: 190).

59. This important disculpatory note was inserted by Fray Beteta on the second page of Fray Cancer's original diary and was obviously intended to indicate

that Fray Beteta had originally been opposed to the gulf coast landing site of the expedition and had unsuccessfully attempted to obtain passage on a caravel to the River of Santa Elena. It also represents the first of several insertions that Beteta blended in with the original text in his rewrite of the original Cancer manuscript.

60. Like many Spaniards of this era, and particularly priests, Cancer frequently refers to dates of specific feast days or saints on the ecclesiastical calendar. The vigil of the Ascension in 1549 would have been on Wednesday, May 29.

61. A *chalupa*, or shallop, was a small one-masted, oared vessel often used to go to shore from larger ships with deeper drafts and thus fell into the same class of watercraft as sixteenth-century brigantines and frigates.

62. My translation of this confusing passage is somewhat loose and tentative, though the meaning seems likely.

63. Clearly Fray Beteta was explaining here an obvious (though anonymous) reference to his own advice in Cancer's text.

64. The term *reson* (*rezón*) refers to a small anchor used for small vessels like the ones in which Cancer was traveling.

65. The term *ranchos de pescadores* could easily be translated as "fishing camps," but given the context of this incident and Cancer's note regarding the sailor's earlier exclamation about *bohios* or "huts," the usage here implies that Cancer was clarifying his description of the settlement and that the term *ranchos* is being used to describe a somewhat less elaborate structure than a "hut," since during the sixteenth century *rancho* normally connoted something impermanent and rural.

66. The financial accounts for the expedition reveal the name of this man to have been Estéban de Fuentes, who was noted to be a farmer contracted for a year of service (Hernández de Burgos 1549).

67. This marginal insertion by Beteta is reduced to *por no yr a la baya del s[piritu] s[ant]o* in his later transcription and seems to be a change in the overall meaning of the passage. Whereas Fray Cancer seems to be implying that some of the other missionaries wished to disembark there because the pilot could not find their destination at the Bay of the Holy Spirit, Beteta's addition suggests that the friars did not wish to go to the Bay of the Holy Spirit, foreshadowing his posthumous argument that he and the other friars were afraid of that location because of previous Spanish contacts but that Cancer chose to continue the search that ultimately led to his death.

68. On several occasions, Cancer explicitly refers to his belief that God was more in command of the expedition than he.

69. This phrase is colloquial and very difficult to interpret, but Cancer seems to be indicating that he was willing to be embarrassed by so many hugs if it would protect his life.

70. This phrase is loosely translated, but in the context of subsequent comments in this section, its meaning seems likely.

71. Beteta inserted "not by everyone" in the margin of Cancer's diary here, though he did not transcribe this for his final version.

72. This would have been on Thursday, June 20, 1549.

73. The term *cerrillo* literally means "little hill," but given the topography of the Tampa Bay area and the fact that native Indian structures are known archaeologically to have been located commonly on top of shell mounds, I have chosen the term "little mound" to correspond to *cerrillo*.

74. The page number on this fifth folio is written in Roman numerals, as are the rest of the folios of the original Cancer diary. The color and style of the writing suggest that this and subsequent page numbers were written by Beteta after Cancer's death; thus, Cancer probably stopped paginating his diary at this page, though he continued writing through the back of folio 8.

75. The term *daca* may be a direct phonetic rendering of an indigenous word, but since it obviously means "give," it may simply be a variant of the Spanish verb *dar* (such as *da la camisa* or "give the shirt"). Nevertheless, since this is unclear and the handwriting is clearly *daca*, the word remains as is for this text.

76. A *palmo* was a Spanish measure of length equaling one quarter of a *vara* (yard), or half a *codo* (cubit), and is equivalent to nearly 21 cm in length.

77. As of 1549, the Catholic Church had granted the title Doctor of the Church to only four saints: Saint Ambrose, Saint Augustine, Saint Gregory the Great, and Saint Jerome. Saint Thomas Aquinas was the next to receive the title, bestowed in 1567 by Pope Pius V.

78. Beteta's marginal comment "very great force" suggests that Cancer may have underestimated the degree of force.

79. This is the first direct reference to Fray Luís Cancer within the diary, confirming the fact that this section was written after his death.

80. This was Sunday, June 23, 1549, the day before the feast day of Saint John the Baptist.

81. The term *montezillo* (*montecillo*) here could mean "grove of trees" or "mound," but one reference below to the "entrance" of the *montezillo* suggests that the former is intended.

82. This phrase is very loosely translated, capturing what is probably the general sense of this part of the sentence.

83. Here Cancer first began to write *por el c[amino]* but crossed this out and wrote *por la mar*.

84. This building, the House of Trade, was later converted into the Archivo General de Indias, where the letter would ultimately be housed.

85. Cancer literally said here that his soul wanted to burst out of his body.

86. Twelve to 14 cubits is about 5–6 meters (16–19 feet) in length.

87. This statement undoubtedly refers to the many captive Indians in Mexico taken from across the interior southeastern United States during the Soto expedition, who had no specific knowledge of the languages of the coast. Four of these captives were later brought on the 1559 expedition of Tristán de Luna, who planned specifically to penetrate the deep interior on his way to the Atlantic coastline (Priestley 2010).

Chapter 4. The Captivity of Hernando de Escalante Fontaneda, 1549–1566

1. As noted in the preface, the extensive marginal headings and other marginal notes written in Fontaneda's own hand are inserted within the transcribed and translated text in italicized text within brackets.

2. Inserted here was the following text in script different from Fontaneda's: *puerto cuelar año de 27 Lucas Vazq[ue]z 1527*. This text, and other similar ones on this and other Fontaneda documents, are indicated on the folder within which this manuscript is held at the Archivo General de Indias to have been

authored by the cosmographer Juan López de Velasco (1894), whose research for his 1575 book doubtless included the Fontaneda memoirs (see also Worth 1995). These texts are not included in the English translations but appear in the endnotes for this book.

3. The name Juan Ponce is written in the right margin here in López de Velasco's hand.

4. It is difficult to say whether Fontaneda scratched this line out himself or whether it was done by López de Velasco. The latter inserted the words *Rio Jordan* and *sacado* in the right margin here.

5. This last phrase was inserted by Fontaneda in the right margin at the bottom of the page.

6. In this section Fontaneda distinguishes the then-uninhabited islands east of the Bahama Channel from the inhabited ones on the west side—the Martyrs, or Florida Keys.

7. This presumably refers to Spanish moss.

8. The original Spanish text could also be translated as "fierce people."

9. It is unclear whether Fontaneda was saying that the town of Guacata was actually on the lake of Mayaimi or whether he was outlining two distinct northern "boundaries," running from Guacata to the lake of Mayaimi. Given independent evidence from Fontaneda's Memorial of the Chiefs of Florida (later in the chapter), the latter seems more likely.

10. This phrase is extremely ambiguous yet pivotal in ethnographic importance. Fontaneda seems to be saying that each *pueblo* comprised between twenty, thirty, and forty *lugares*, which literally means either "places" or "villages" (as was commonly used later in Spanish Florida). This might imply that his usage of the term *pueblo* referred less to individual towns and more to localized clusters of small communities, though the number of communities mentioned seems abnormally high. Instead, it is possible that Fontaneda meant to say that each *pueblo* had between twenty and forty inhabitants or residents, which would also fit with the context of this phrase, contrasting the "many towns" with the small number of inhabitants per town.

11. Fontaneda's term *mantellín* presumably derives from the term *mantilla*, referring to a type of woman's shawl that extends from the head to below the waist; the term *mantellina* appears as a synonym for *mantilla* in the 1734 *Diccionario de la lengua castellana* (Real Academia Española 1734: 487–88).

12. The marginal insertion here is translated as "Puerto Cuellar, year of '27, Lúcas Vázquez, 1527."

13. The passage here is difficult to interpret. Although it mentions "Indians from the islands of Jeaga" (presumably referring to captives from the documented province along the southern Atlantic coast of Florida in the vicinity of modern Boca Raton), it is unclear whether Fontaneda is implying that they were simply a source for Lúcas Vázquez de Ayllón's information or were actually onboard the ships. Neither option squares well with what is documented elsewhere about the specific origins of the Ayllón expeditions of 1525–26 (Hoffman 1980, 1990, 1992).

14. This is the earliest known correlation between Guale of the 1560s and Gualdape of the 1520s, and although Fontaneda almost certainly based it on hearsay or his own unsupported personal interpretation, it supports recent scholarly assertions in that regard (Hoffman 1990, 1992).

15. Here Fontaneda distinguishes these towns reputed to possess gold from both the "Jordaneros" (presumably referring to the Indians met by Ayllón) and the "Chichimecas" of northern New Spain.

16. Fontaneda uses the terms *benados* (*venados*) and *corsos* (*corzos*), or literally "deer" and "roe deer," which probably refers to the larger deer common on the mainland to the north and the smaller "Key deer" common on the Florida Keys.

17. The term *cocer* can mean simply "to cook," but in this context Fontaneda seems to be specifying the use of water for boiling or stewing, as contrasted with grilling.

18. Fontaneda uses the term *lei* (*ley*), literally meaning "law," but in context he is doubtless asserting that it was a widespread belief or devotion.

19. Fontaneda's wording here is difficult to interpret, since Tocobaga is well known to have been located in modern Tampa Bay and would thus not have been on the right-hand side of the route of anyone sailing by ship toward Havana. Given that Fontaneda's lengthiest stay in Florida was at the Calusa capital in modern Estero Bay on the lower gulf coast, I suspect he is referring to the fact that Tocobaga would have been to the right-hand side of any ship beginning its return to Havana from Mound Key.

20. The phrase *es rei por si* literally means he "is king for himself" but is best understood as an autonomous leader without an overlord.

21. Fontaneda is clearly misinformed about Hernando de Soto, who survived another three years after his landing at Tampa Bay and eventually died hundreds of miles away along the Mississippi River. This may have been a report fabricated by the Apalachee Indians of modern Tallahassee, who skirmished with Soto's army through the winter of 1539–40 before departing northward into the interior.

22. Fontaneda's *paloma torcasa*, or "wood-pigeon," almost certainly is a reference to the extinct passenger pigeon, known to have been extremely abundant in the southeastern United States during this era.

23. The term *pajuela* can also refer to fibrous material such as twisted cotton that can be used as tinder. Here Fontaneda is almost certainly describing Spanish moss, which grows extensively across the northern Florida peninsula and extends as far south as the Calusa domain.

24. These two names were inserted by Fontaneda in the right margin of the text, immediately adjacent to his statement about the two forgotten towns. Custevia was originally written *Custebiya* and then crossed out and replaced.

25. Since Fontaneda is documented to have left fort San Antón de Carlos by June 15, 1569, and arrived in Madrid by November of the same year, this provides a clue that the undated manuscript was written in 1575.

26. This is obviously a reference to the Florida Keys, though Fontaneda uses the term *Yucayos*, referring to the Lucayos Islands, or Bahamas.

27. Fontaneda here refers to towns and provinces on the "other" (Atlantic Ocean) side of Florida and considerably farther north than the Calusa domain.

28. Fontaneda had testified in Francisco Reinoso's 1569 lawsuit soliciting his salary as captain of Fort San Antón, but according to this memoir, Fontaneda's own salary as interpreter seems not to have been paid as late as 1575.

29. An *urca* was a large, broad-hulled cargo vessel.

30. Fontaneda uses the term *reales* here, referring to the standard unit of silver coinage at that time, the *real*. Eight *reales* made up a single *peso*, accounting

for the phrase "pieces of eight," which came literally from *pesos de a ocho*, or *pesos* of eight *reales*.

31. It is unclear whether Fontaneda here is specifically referring to Carlos taking the best of the treasure from all the chiefs or simply to each chief taking the best for himself, but archaeological evidence suggests that items salvaged from Spanish shipwrecks on the Atlantic coast were indeed sent inland and westward, where many ended up in the Calusa domain on the gulf coast (e.g., Luer 1994; Wheeler 2000).

32. The founder of St. Augustine and Florida's first governor, Pedro Menéndez de Avilés, made a nearly identical proposal in 1573, a year before his own death, regarding the enslavement of South Florida's Indians (Menéndez de Avilés 1573). The Spanish Crown ultimately rejected the formal proposal, though it was accompanied by extensive testimony documenting many attacks, imprisonments, and murders of Spaniards in this region during the preceding seven years.

33. Surrounding this heading are a number of notes evidently inserted by cosmographer Juan López de Velasco, including the following names and date: *florida, chicora, 1511, Rio Jordan, Jo[a]n Ponce, Lucas Vazq[ue]z, Soto,* and *Salinas,* as well as the note *ojo,* or "look," often used by the person reading or reviewing a manuscript in order to draw attention to particular sections of the text.

34. Inserted at the margin by López de Velasco here is the note *sacado ya puesto en su lugar,* meaning "removed, now put in its place."

35. The name Rio Jordan was reiterated in the margin by López de Velasco here.

36. Christopher Columbus never saw Florida, but Fontaneda correctly mentions the explorations of Lucas Vásquez de Ayllón and his partners based in Santo Domingo.

37. Fontaneda defines the Lucayos Islands of the Bahama archipelago expansively, incorrectly including the Florida Keys (Los Mártires).

38. Here Fontaneda distinguishes a deepwater passage through the western Florida Keys that facilitated travel between Havana and Florida's lower gulf coast, from the main route between Havana and Spain, which was through the Bahama Channel (the Florida Strait).

39. While Fontaneda did indeed elaborate on some of these points in his longer Memorial, this sentence is nonetheless confusing, since Fontaneda clearly must have known that Captain Francisco de Reynoso survived the abandonment of Fort San Antón de Carlos (where both of them served) because he testified on his behalf in Madrid in 1569.

40. The letters are unclear under an ink spill here, and while there is obviously no *y* (and) between these two possible names, that both town names appear in Fontaneda's other writings suggests that this was what he intended.

41. The term *parrillas* refers to breechcloths or loincloths made from the leaves of vines and designed to cover the privates from the waist.

42. *Bacas (vacas) lanudas* must be a reference to the American bison, skins of which are documented to have been traded well into the southeastern United States during this era.

43. This statement regarding gold is obviously a reference to hammered copper known archaeologically from Apalachee, but Fontaneda's description of the process by which it was converted from low-grade to high-grade copper through hammering is ethnographically correct.

44. The term *zierra* (*sierra*) is commonly translated as "mountain range," but in Spain it is commonly applied simply to hilly regions elevated above the lower plains.

45. This seems to have been a note or "placeholder" on these draft pages for additional sections in Fontaneda's planned manuscript.

46. Here López de Velasco inserted the note *cerca de Sanct Agustin*.

47. The original handwritten manuscript on this page has marginal notes at the bottom and on the back side, as well as on the following otherwise blank fold of the same paper, written in a completely different hand (presumably that of Juan López de Velasco) with the following text: "Caciques, guarugumbe [1U] en la punta de los martires subietos suyos con cuchiaga mas adelante 40 en la mesma cabeça; tatesta mas adelante 80; desde los martires a Sant Agustin, tequesta, gega, ais, saturiba St. agustin y a Sanct mateo por la coasta; por la ti[er]ra adentro utina, potano, m[aya]ca, mayguaya, moloa; carlos 20U; tocobaa 6U; mocoço U; abalachi 20U; [unreadable at bottom of page]; En lo de lo Carlos el capitan Reynoso con 40; en St. Agustin Estevano de las Alas y Bartolome Melendez con [3]00; St. Mateo esta desapa[re]zido [cegado] pazaro[n] a Tacatacoru adonde se paso el artilleria esta Vasco Cavala con 200 hombres; en Sancta Elena Pe[d]ro Melendez Marques con 500, con 48 casados; P[edr]o Menendez; Capitan Reynoso, governador de las provincias de Carlos y fuerte de Sant Anton q[ue] se paza cincuenta leguas mas adelante de St. Mateo [?]; Capitan Aguirre; Florencio de Esquivel; Capitan Jua[n] Pardo; Hernando de Miranda; Salzedo natural de Madrid; don Anto[ni]o page q[ue] fue del arçobispo; capitan Antonio del Prado; Escalante; estan alla; Estevan de las Alas, teniente general; Capitan P[edr]o Menéndez Márques descobridor de la costa y governador y alcayde de Sancta Elena; Bartolome Menéndez alcayde y governador de Sanct Agustin; Vasco Çaval capitan y governador de Catacoru; Di[eg]o Garcia de Sierra governador de Guale; y ay alcaldes y regidores en todos cinco governaciones digo en las dos q[ue] son Sancta Elena y Sant Agustin."

48. The handwriting after this word becomes much less neat and carefully formed and appears to be more informal, though both seem to be written by the same author. This portion of the text has a final paraph that appears to be that of Hernando de Escalante Fontaneda, when compared with his signature at the end of his longer Memorial.

49. This text could literally mean "son" only, but given Fontaneda's own use of the word *casica* (*cacica*) a few lines later for female chiefs among the Calusa, it seems more likely that this refers to any child, male or female, of the chief.

50. Although Fontaneda's original text could be read to imply that each resident sacrificed all his or her children, it seems more likely that only a single child might have been expected in sacrifice.

51. This is the only known reference to the existence of female chiefs (*cacicas*) among the Calusa.

52. The reference here to dancing with human heads is consistent with several independent contemporary sources relating that the heads of sacrificed Spaniards and rebellious subordinate chiefs alike were displayed on poles and, in at least one case, collected en masse at the base of a tree (e.g., Rogel 1946c; Soto 1573; Alvaro Pérez 1573; Antonio Pérez 1573). Dávila Padilla (1955: 189) likewise recounts the practice of drinking from the skulls of victims inland from Fray Luís Cancer's landing at Tampa Bay.

53. The marginal insertion here is translated as follows: Chiefs / Guarugumbe [1,000] on the point of the Martyrs, his subject with Cuchiaga farther on 40 on the very head; Tatesta farther on 80; from the Martyrs to St. Augustine, Tequesta, Gega, Ais, Saturiba, St. Augustine, and to St. Augustine and to San Mateo along the coast; across the interior Utina, Potano, M[aya]ca, Mayguaya, Moloa, Carlos, 20,000; Tocobaa, 6,000; Mocoço, 1,000; Abalachi, 20,000; [unreadable at bottom of page]; In that of Carlos is Captain Reynoso with 40; in St. Augustine Estevano de las Alas and Bartolomé Menéndez with [3]00; San Mateo has disappeared, closed; they passed to Tacatacoru, where the artillery was placed. Vasco Cavala is there with 200 men; in Santa Elena Pedro Menéndez Márquez with 500 [men], with 48 married; Pedro Menéndez; Captain Reynoso, governor of the provinces of Carlos and fort of San Antón, which passes fifty leagues farther on from San Mateo [?]; Captain Aguirre; Florencio de Esquivel; Captain Jua[n] Pardo; Hernando de Miranda; Salzedo, native of Madrid; Don Anto[ni]o, who was page of the archbishop; Captain Antonio del Prado; Escalante; there are; Estevan de las Alas, lieutenant general; Captain Pedro Menéndez Márques, discoverer of the coast and governor and mayor of Santa Elena; Bartolomé Menéndez, mayor and governor of St. Augustine; Vasco Çaval, captain and governor of Catacoru; Diego Garcia de Sierra, governor of Guale; and there are mayors and regidors in all five governments, rather in the two, which are Santa Elena and St. Augustine.

54. The paraph, or mark, here at the base of the document is far from clear but somewhat resembles a portion of Fontaneda's signature at the end of his primary Memorial.

55. Menéndez left a blank space in the text here.

56. The name of Hernando's father is independently documented to have been Juan de Escalante de Fontaneda (Spanish Crown 1553, 1569).

Chapter 5. The Pedro Menéndez de Avilés Expeditions, 1566–1569

1. The original manuscript evidently was missing the section following this sentence up to the next endnote, but the text was replaced by the editor's use of printed versions.

2. The missing portion of the original manuscript ended here.

3. The text is missing in this portion of the volume.

4. The original manuscript is again missing for the following section.

5. There is another gap in the text here.

6. During the sixteenth century, a *bergantín*, or brigantine, was a small vessel propelled by ten or twelve sets of oars. The later use of the term "brigantine" or "brig," referring to a larger sailing vessel with both fore-and-aft rigging and square rigging, is not implied here.

7. A *patax*, or patache, was a small, flat-bottomed warship or tender commonly used to reconnoiter coastlines or carry messages.

8. The French colony at Fort Caroline on the south bank of the modern St. Johns River had previously been seized by the Spaniards and rechristened Fort San Mateo. The Spaniards often used the generic term "Lutherans" in reference to the Protestant French Huguenots during this period.

9. This undoubtedly refers to the provincial capital of Guale on St. Catherines Island, Georgia.

10. Saint Anthony was the patron saint of lost things, and his name was used to denote the Spanish Fort San Antón de Carlos at the Calusa capital and the baptismal name of the chief's elder sister Doña Antonia.

11. The term *bersos* (*versos*) refers to small artillery pieces called culverins.

12. *Perdigones* refers to the small shot used in shotguns, or in this case for artillery, serving as an effective weapon against crowds of people.

13. The term *indios prencipales* or simply *prencipales* is a clear reference to nobility, based not only on later usage of this same term for noble Spaniards in Havana within this same text but also on common usage with reference to Indians in Spanish Florida during the period.

14. *Zaragüelles* presumably refers to wide, knee-length trousers made of pleated fabric. *Ropeta* here apparently refers to a short jacket meant to be worn over the shirt.

15. *Rescates* is normally used in the Spanish colonial era to refer to items of little value that were commonly traded with or given to Indians, which are now commonly referred to as "trade goods."

16. Here Solís used the term *lengua* and in parentheses defined the term as *intéprete*, both of which are translated as "interpreter" in English.

17. The *as de oros*, or ace of [gold] "coins," referred to a card (*naipe*) in one of the four suits in a Spanish deck of cards (*baraja*), which included (and includes today) *copas* (cups, equivalent to hearts in the familiar French-style deck), *oros* (coins/diamonds), *espadas* (swords/spades), and *bastos* (clubs).

18. The *vihuela de arco* was an early form of the guitar.

19. The term *aposento*, meaning "an individual room within a house," is used here instead of *casa*, which was used previously in reference to the large structure called the *casa del cacique*. In addition, the phrase is worded such that there is a clear indication that Menéndez and his people went first *within* the house and then *to* the chief's room. These details suggest clearly that the immense structure called the chief's house had at least one smaller room within which the chief received visitors.

20. The phrase *buen aposento* could simply refer to a "good room," but given the overall context of the phrase and typical usage for the era, I have interpreted the phrase to mean "good-sized room," suggesting that the Spanish visitors did not view the chief's room as small.

21. The term *estado* refers to a unit of measurement equivalent to a *braza*, or fathom, and was equal to two Spanish *varas*, or yards. The seat referred to here was therefore about one *vara* from the ground, or roughly 84 centimeters (2.7 feet).

22. The phrase *en lo baxo* might refer to being seated on the ground itself but might simply mean that their seats were considerably lower than that of the woman seated beside the chief.

23. The term *voltear* might also refer to somersaults.

24. The term "grave" could be taken to mean "serious," but since the author appears to be providing a counterpoint to her lack of physical beauty, I use the alternative translation "dignified."

25. The term *mesura* used here is different from the previous term *gravedad*, or "grave," employed in reference to the chief's sister, but their meanings are similar. In the 1734 Spanish *Diccionario de la lengua castellana*, *mesura* is defined as "dignity, seriousness, and composure of face and body," suggesting

something slightly broader in connotation than simply "dignified" (Real Academia Española 1734: 556).

26. *Botixa* (*botija*) was a term used for what archaeologists call an "olive jar" and would have normally contained about an *arroba* of liquid volume, or just over 16 liters (about 4.25 gallons).

27. The intended word here was missing from the original Spanish manuscript.

28. The actual term used here was *naos*, referring to a specific type of large cargo vessel used during this period.

29. The Order of Santiago is a Spanish military order of knights established in the twelfth century and requires, among other things, proven ancestry that is both noble and Christian. Pedro Menéndez, like several other later Florida governors, was a member of this order and would have been able to wear the red insignia of the Cross of Saint James on his clothing.

30. The term *posada* refers here to the place where Menéndez was staying in Havana.

31. The original order, dated October 15, 1566, is presented in the supplementary documents.

32. The distance between the entrance to Estero Bay (where the Calusa capital on Mound Key was located) and the entrance to San Carlos Bay (where the Caloosahatchee River emptied into the Gulf of Mexico) was just over two Spanish nautical leagues.

33. The lake of Maymi (or Mayaimi as spelled by Fontaneda) was modern Lake Okeechobee, and Menéndez erroneously believed that there was a continuous water route between it and the village of Macoya on the upper St. Johns River, which he had previously visited.

34. The extent to which the Calusa chief actually exercised control over the lower Atlantic coastline and Keys of Florida is unclear, although Fontaneda makes this same claim. Archaeological evidence for the distribution of items and materials salvaged from Spanish shipwrecks, however, seems to match the claim here that much of it flowed westward across the southern Florida peninsula instead of remaining near the wrecks on the Atlantic side (see Luer 1994).

35. The destination is blank in the original manuscript.

36. The river of San Mateo is the St. Johns River.

37. Time onboard ship was commonly measured from noon to noon, but the author clarifies here that Menéndez arrived in two days counted from sunrise to sunset.

38. The original Spanish text suggests that the phrase *brazo de agua salada* refers to an arm or branch of the port or bay itself, at the end of which was the town of Tocobaga, some twenty leagues inland from the mouth of the bay. This description fits the Safety Harbor site on the northern end of Tampa Bay.

39. The Spanish text here uses the plural, indicating that more than one (and possibly all) of these former captives knew the language of Tocobaga, confirming the author's earlier assertion that Father Rogel was learning the language common to both Carlos and Tocobaga, while Father Villareal was learning the more distinct language of Tequesta.

40. While the generic term *mujer* might simply mean "woman," the author generally used the term *india* for that purpose, reserving the term *mujer* for wives.

41. This refers to the Spanish capture of Fort Caroline and the massacre of most of its French inhabitants in 1565.

42. The name here was absent from the original manuscript.

43. The term *teatino* was commonly used in reference to Jesuits during this era, but its origin was in Saint Cajetan of Venice, who in 1524 founded the Congregation of Clerks Regular at Rome, also known as the Theatines.

44. These notes were inserted at the end of the transcript of the original order and confirmed the presence of insertions and corrections made by the original notary in his own handwriting, thus preventing subsequent tampering with the original wording. This was standard practice for colonial notaries.

45. This formal title was used by Villareal to address his superior in the Jesuit order.

46. This unnamed chief was Felipe, who succeeded his cousin Carlos after the Spaniards killed him.

References

Adorno, Rolena. 1999. *Alvaro Núñez Cabeza de Vaca: Sus logros, su vida y la expedición de Pánfilo de Narváez*. Lincoln: University of Nebraska Press.

Alegre, Francisco Javier. 1956. *Historia de la Provincia de la Compañia de Jesus de Nueva España*. Vol. 1, bks. 1–3. New edition by Ernest J. Burrus and Felix Zubillaga. Rome: Institutum Historicum Societatis Iesu.

Allerton, David, George M. Luer, and Robert S. Carr. 1984. "Ceremonial Tablets and Related Objects from Florida." *Florida Anthropologist* 37: 5–54.

Almy, Maranda M. 2001. "The Cuban Fishing Ranchos of Southwest Florida, 1600s–1850s." Master's thesis, Department of Anthropology, University of Florida, Gainesville.

Altamira, Rafael. 1938. "El texto de las Leyes de Burgos de 1512." *Revista de Historia de América* 4: 5–79.

Alvarez de Pineda, Alonso. 1519. "Mapa de las costas de tierra firme." Mapa 5, Mapas y Planos—México, Archivo General de Indias, Seville, Spain.

Añasco, Juan de. 1544. Petition and service record, May 30, 1544. Legajo 57, Ramo 4, No. 1, Patronato Real, Archivo General de Indias, Seville, Spain.

Boyd, Mark F., and José Navarro Latorre. 1953. "Spanish Interest in British Florida, and in the Progress of the American Revolution." *Florida Historical Quarterly* 32 (2): 92–130.

Cancer, Luís. n.d. Letter to Bartolomé de las Casas, February 6. Legajo 252, Ramo 11, Patronato Real, Archivo General de Indias, Seville, Spain.

———. 1548. Letter to Diego de Çarate, November 22, 1548. Legajo 280, Audiencia de México, Archivo General de Indias, Seville, Spain.

Cancer, Luís, and Gregorio Beteta. 1549. "Diary of the Expedition to Florida." Legajo 19, Ramo 4, Patronato Real, Archivo General de Indias, Seville, Spain.

Castellanos, Juan de. 1589. *Primera parte, de las elegias de varones illustres de Indias*. Madrid: Casa de la viuda de Alonso Gomez.

Chang-Rodríguez, Raquel, ed. 2006. *Beyond Books and Borders: Garcilaso de la Vega and la Florida del Inca*. Lewisburg, PA: Bucknell University Press.

Chaunu, Huguette, and Pierre Chaunu. 1955. *Séville et l'Atlantique (1504–1650), première partie: Partie statistique, le mouvement des navires et des marchandises entre l'Espagne et l'Amérique, de 1504 à 1650*. Vol. 2, *Le trafic, de 1504 à 1560*. Paris: Librairie Armand Colin.

Chaves, Alonso de. 1977. "Libro cuarto de la cosmografía práctica y moderna llamado espejo de navegantes." In *Alonso de Chaves y el libro IV de su "Espejo de navegantes*," edited by P. Castañeda, M. Cuesta, and P. Hernández, 43–160. Madrid: Industrias Gráficas España.

Clayton, Lawrence A., Vernon James Knight Jr., and Edward C. Moore, eds. 1993. *The De Soto Chronicles: The Expedition of Hernando de Soto to North America in 1539–1543*. 2 vols. Tuscaloosa: University of Alabama Press.

Connor, Jeannette Thurber, trans. and ed. 1923. *Pedro Menéndez de Avilés, Adelantado, Governor, and Captain-General of Florida: Memorial by Gonzalo Solís de Merás*. Deland: Florida State Historical Society.

———. 1925. *Colonial Records of Spanish Florida*. Vol. 1, *Letters and Reports of Governors and Secular Persons, 1570–1577*. Deland: Florida State Historical Society.

———. 1930. *Colonial Records of Spanish Florida*. Vol. 2, *Letters and Reports of Governors, Deliberations of the Council of the Indies, Royal Decrees, and Other Documents, 1577–1580*. Deland: Florida State Historical Society.

Covington, James W. 1954. "A Petition from Some Latin-American Fishermen, 1838." *Tequesta* 14: 61–65.

———. 1959. "Trade Relations between Southwestern Florida and Cuba, 1660–1840." *Florida Historical Quarterly* 38 (2): 114–28.

Dávila Padilla, Agustín. 1955. *Historia de la fundación y discurso de la Provincia de Santiago de México de la Orden de Predicadores*. Facsimile edition of 1596 edition. Mexico City: Editorial Academia Literaria.

Davis, Dave D. 1974. "The Strategy of Early Spanish Ecosystem Management on Cuba." *Journal of Anthropological Research* 30 (4): 294–314.

Davis, T. Frederick. 1935. "Juan Ponce de León's Voyages to Florida." *Florida Historical Quarterly* 14 (1): 1–70.

Díaz del Castillo, Bernal. 1939. *Historia verdadera de la conquista de la Nueva España*. Edited by Joaquín Ramírez Cabañas. Mexico City: Editorial Pedro Robredo.

Escalante Fontaneda, Hernando de. n.d.a. "Dos breves memorias sobre los costumbres de los indios de la Florida." Legajo 1529, Indiferente General, Archivo General de Indias, Seville, Spain.

———. n.d.b. Memoranda, with appended "Memoria de los caciques de la Florida." Legajo 19, Ramo 32, Patronato Real, Archivo General de Indias, Seville, Spain.

———. n.d.c. "Memoria de las cosas y costa y indios de la Florida." Legajo 18, Ramo 1, No. 5, Patronato Real, Archivo General de Indias, Seville, Spain.

———. 1569. Testimony in petition by Francisco de Reynoso, November 19, 1569. Legajo 1001, Ramo 2, No. 1, Justicia, Archivo General de Indias, Seville, Spain.

Esquivel, Gonzalo de. 1570. Letter to Francisco Borgia, September 26, 1570. Transcription in Zubillaga, *Monumenta Antiquae Floridae*, 441–46.

Estrada Monroy, Agustín. 1979. *El mundo K'ekchi' de la Vera-paz*. Guatemala City: Editorial del Ejército.

Favata, Martin A., and José B. Fernández. 1993. *The Account: Alvar Núñez Cabeza de Vaca's Relación*. Houston: Arte Público Press.

Fernández de Olivera, Juan. 1612. Letter to the Crown, October 13, 1612. Legajo 229, ff. 540r–542v, Audiencia de Santo Domingo, Archivo General de Indias, Seville, Spain.

Fernández de Oviedo y Valdés, Gonzalo. 1851. *Historia general y natural de las Indias, islas y tierra-firme del mar océano*. Vol. 1. Edited by José Amador de los Rios. Madrid: Imprenta de la Real Academia de la Historia.

———. 1853. *Historia general y natural de las Indias, islas y tierra-firme del mar océano*. Vol. 2. Edited by José Amador de los Rios. Madrid: Imprenta de la Real Academia de la Historia.

———. 1992. *Historia general y natural de las Indias*. Edited by Juan Pérez de Tudela Bueso. 5 vols. Madrid: Ediciones Atlas.

Galloway, Patricia. 1997. "The Incestuous Soto Narratives." In *The Hernando de Soto Expedition: History, Historiography, and "Discovery" in the Southeast*, edited by Patricia Galloway, 11–44. Lincoln: University of Nebraska Press.

Gannon, Michael V. 1965. *The Cross in the Sand: The Early Catholic Church in Florida, 1513–1870*. Gainesville: University of Florida Press.

Goggin, John M., and William C. Sturtevant. 1964. "The Calusa: A Stratified Nonagricultural Society (with Notes on Sibling Marriage)." In *Explorations in Cultural Anthropology: Essays in Honor of George Peter Murdock*, edited by W. H. Goodenough, 179–219. New York: McGraw-Hill.

González de Barcia Carballido y Zuñiga, Andrés. 1723. *Ensayo cronológico para la historia general de la Florida*. Madrid: Nicolás Rodríguez Franco.

Granberry, Julian. 1957. "Anthropological Reconnaissance of Bimini, Bahamas." *American Antiquity* 22 (4): 378–81.

Hanke, Lewis. 1938. "The 'Requerimiento' and Its Interpreters." *Revista de Historia de América* 1: 25–34.

Hann, John H. 1986. *Spanish Translations*. Florida Archaeology, no. 2. Tallahassee: Florida Bureau of Archaeological Research.

———. 1988. *Apalachee: The Land between the Rivers*. Gainesville: University Presses of Florida.

———. 1991. *Missions to the Calusa*. Gainesville: University Press of Florida.

———. 1993. *Visitations and Revolts in Florida, 1656–1695*. Florida Archaeology, no. 7. Tallahassee: Florida Bureau of Archaeological Research.

———. 2003. *Indians of Central and South Florida, 1513–1763*. Gainesville: University Press of Florida.

Helps, Arthur. 1855. *The Spanish Conquest in America, and Its Relation to the History of Slavery and to the Government of Colonies*. London: John W. Parker and Son.

Hernández de Burgos, Pedro. 1549. Accounts of the Luís Cancer expedition, March 15–October 31, 1549. Legajo 876, Contaduría, Archivo General de Indias, Seville, Spain.

Herrera y Tordesillas, Antonio de. 1601. *Historia general de los hechos de los Castellanos en las islas i tierra firme del mar oceano*. Vol. 1. Madrid: Imprenta Real.

Hill, Roscoe R. 1913. "The Office of Adelantado." *Political Science Quarterly* 28 (4): 646–68.

Hoffman, Paul E. 1980. "A New Voyage of North American Discovery: Pedro de Salazar's Visit to the 'Island of Giants.'" *Florida Historical Quarterly* 58 (4): 415–26.

———. 1990. *A New Andalucia and a Way to the Orient: The American Southeast during the Sixteenth Century.* Baton Rouge: Louisiana State University Press.

———. 1992. "Lúcas Vázquez de Ayllón." In *Columbus and the Land of Ayllón: The Exploration and Settlement of the Southeast,* edited by Jeannine Cook, 27–49. Darien, GA: Lower Altamaha Historical Society.

———. 1994. "Narváez and Cabeza de Vaca in Florida." In *The Forgotten Centuries: Indians and Europeans in the American South, 1521–1704,* edited by Charles M. Hudson and Carmen Chaves Tesser, 50–73. Athens: University of Georgia Press.

Hubbell, Jay B. 1957. "The Smith-Pocahontas Story in Literature." *Virginia Magazine of History and Biography* 65 (3): 275–300.

Hudson, Charles. 1990. *The Juan Pardo Expeditions: Exploration of the Carolinas and Tennessee, 1566–1568.* Washington, DC: Smithsonian Institution Press.

———. 1997. *Knights of Spain, Warriors of the Sun: Hernando de Soto and the South's Ancient Chiefdoms.* Athens: University of Georgia Press.

Hussey, Ronald D. 1932. "Text of the Laws of Burgos (1512–1513) concerning the Treatment of the Indians." *Hispanic American Historical Review* 12 (3): 301–26.

Kelley, James E., Jr. 1991. "Juan Ponce de Leon's Discovery of Florida: Herrera's Narrative Revisited." *Revista de Historia de América* 111: 31–65.

Knight, Vernon James, and John E. Worth. 2006. "A Cuban Origin for Glades Pottery? A Provocative Hypothesis Revisited." Paper presented at the symposium Jerry's Kids: Papers in Honor of Jerald T. Milanich at the sixty-third annual meeting of the Southeastern Archaeological Conference, Little Rock, Arkansas.

Krieger, Alex D., trans. 2003. *We Came Naked and Barefoot: The Journey of Cabeza de Vaca across North America.* Austin: University of Texas Press.

Lankford, George E. 2008. *Looking for Lost Lore: Studies in Folklore, Ethnology, and Iconography.* Tuscaloosa: University of Alabama Press.

Las Casas, Bartolomé de. 1875. *Historia de las Indias.* Vol. 3. Edited by the Marqués de la Fuensanta del Valle and José Sancho Rayon. Madrid: Imprenta de Miguel Ginesta.

Lawson, Edward W. 1946. *The Discovery of Florida and Its Discoverer Juan Ponce de León.* St. Augustine, FL: Edward W. Lawson.

Lázaro, Juan. 1549. Accounts of the Luís Cancer expedition, September 22, 1548–February 10, 1549. Legajo 876, Contaduría, Archivo General de Indias, Seville, Spain.

López de Gómara, Francisco. 1554. *La historia general de las Indias, con todos los descubrimientos, y cosas notables que han acaescido en ella, dende que se ganaron hasta agora.* Antwerp, Belgium: Casa de Juan Steelsio.

López de Velasco, Juan. 1894. *Geografía y descripción universal de las Indias.* Edited by Justo Zaragoza. Madrid: Real Academia de la Historia.

Lowery, Woodbury. 1911. *The Spanish Settlements within the Present Limits of the United States, 1513–1561.* New York: G. P. Putnam's Sons.

Luer, George M. 1994. "A Third Ceremonial Tablet from the Goodnow Mound, Highlands County, Florida; with Notes on Some Peninsular Tribes and Other Tablets." *Florida Anthropologist* 47 (2): 180–88.

Lyon, Eugene. 1976. *The Enterprise of Florida: Pedro Menéndez de Avilés and the Spanish Conquest of 1565–1568.* Gainesville: University Presses of Florida.

———. 1989. "Pedro Menéndez's Plan for Settling La Florida." In *First Encounters: Spanish Explorations in the Caribbean and the United States, 1492–1570,* edited by J. T. Milanich and S. Milbrath, 150–65. Gainesville: University Presses of Florida.

Marquardt, William H. 1987. "The Calusa Social Formation in Protohistoric South Florida." In *Power Relations and State Formation,* edited by T. C. Patterson and C. W. Gailey, 98–116. Washington, DC: Archeology Section, American Anthropological Association.

———. 1988. "Politics and Production among the Calusa of South Florida." In *Hunters and Gatherers,* vol. 1, *History, Evolution, and Social Change in Hunting and Gathering Societies,* edited by Tim Ingold, David Riches, and James Woodburn, 161–88. London: Berg.

———. 2004. "Calusa." In *Handbook of North American Indians,* vol. 14, *Southeast,* edited by R. D. Fogelson, 204–12. Washington, DC: Smithsonian Institution.

Marquardt, William H., and Karen J. Walker, eds. 2013. *The Archaeology of Pineland: A Coastal Southwest Florida Village Complex, A.D. 50–1700.* Gainesville, FL: Institute of Archaeology and Paleoenvironmental Studies.

Martire d'Anghiera, Pietro. 1511. *Martyris Angli Mediolanensis Opera, Legatio Babylonica, Oceani Decas, Poemata, Epigrammate.* Seville: Jacobu Corumberger.

———. 1530. *De Orbe Novo.* Alcalá de Henares, Spain: Michaele d'Egui.

———. 1912a. *De Orbe Novo: The Eight Decades of Peter Martyr D'Anghera.* Vol. 1. Translated by Francis Augustus MacNutt. New York: G. P. Putnam's Sons.

———. 1912b. *De Orbe Novo: The Eight Decades of Peter Martyr D'Anghera.* Vol. 2. Translated by Francis Augustus MacNutt. New York: G. P. Putnam's Sons.

Menéndez de Avilés, Pedro. 1566a. Letter to the Crown, October 22, 1566. Legajo 115, ff. 167r–171v, Audiencia de Santo Domingo, Archivo General de Indias, Seville, Spain.

———. 1566b. Letter to the Crown, October 22, 1566. Legajo 115, ff. 174r–176v, Audiencia de Santo Domingo, Archivo General de Indias, Seville, Spain.

———. 1566c. Order to Captain Francisco de Reynoso, October 15, 1566. In "Petition for Payment of Salary for Service in Florida," by Francisco de Reynoso, 1569. Legajo 1001, Ramo 2, No. 1, Justicia, Archivo General de Indias, Seville, Spain.

———. 1573. Proposal regarding the Indians of the coast of Florida, January 16, 1573. Legajo 257, Patronato Real, Archivo General de Indias, Seville, Spain.

Menéndez de Avilés the Younger, Pedro. 1573. Testimony regarding the Indians of South Florida, January 16, 1573. Legajo 257, Ramo 20, G. 3, No. 1, Patronato Real, Archivo General de Indias, Seville, Spain.

Menéndez Márquez, Pedro. 1568. Letter to the Crown, March 28, 1568. Legajo 115, Audiencia de Santo Domingo, Archivo General de Indias, Seville, Spain.

———. 1573. Testimony regarding the Indians of South Florida, January 16, 1573. Legajo 257, Ramo 20, G. 3, No. 1, Patronato Real, Archivo General de Indias, Seville, Spain.

Milanich, Jerald T. 1994. *Archaeology of Precolumbian Florida*. Gainesville: University Press of Florida.

Milanich, Jerald T., and Charles Hudson. 1993. *Hernando de Soto and the Indians of Florida*. Gainesville: University Press of Florida.

Milanich, Jerald T., and Nara B. Milanich. 1996. "Revisiting the Freducci Map: A Description of Juan Ponce DeLeon's 1513 Florida Voyage?" *Florida Historical Quarterly* 74 (3): 319–28.

Narváez, Pánfilo de. 1526. Letter to the Crown, May 27, 1526. Legajo 18, Ramo 2, No. 3, Patronato Real, Archivo General de Indias, Seville, Spain.

Núñez Cabeza de Vaca, Alvar. n.d. "Relation of Cabeza de Vaca, Who Was Treasurer in the Conquest." Legajo 20, Ramo 3, No. 5, Patronato Real, Archivo General de Indias, Seville, Spain.

———. 1989. *Naufragios*. Edited by Juan Francisco Maura. Madrid: Ediciones Cátedra.

Peck, Douglas T. 1992. "Reconstruction and Analysis of the 1513 Discovery Voyage of Juan Ponce de León." *Florida Historical Quarterly* 71 (2): 133–54.

———. 1998. "Anatomy of an Historical Fantasy: The Ponce de León–Fountain of Youth Legend." *Revista de Historia de América* 123: 63–87.

Pérez, Alvaro. 1573. Testimony regarding the Indians of South Florida, February 28, 1573. Legajo 257, Ramo 20, G. 3, No. 1, Patronato Real, Archivo General de Indias, Seville, Spain.

Pérez, Antonio. 1573. Testimony regarding the Indians of South Florida, February 28, 1573. Legajo 257, Ramo 20, G. 3, No. 1, Patronato Real, Archivo General de Indias, Seville, Spain.

Pichardo Viñals, Hortensia. 1986. *La fundación de las primeras villas de la Isla de Cuba*. Havana: Editorial de Ciencias Sociales.

Pichardo Viñals, Hortensia, and Fernando Portuondo. 1947. *En torno a la conquista de Cuba*. Havana: Editorial Selecta.

Ponce de León, Juan. 1521a. Letter to the Cardinal of Tortosa, February 10, 1521. Legajo 176, Ramo 9 (2), Patronato Real, Archivo General de Indias, Seville, Spain.

———. 1521b. Letter to the Spanish Crown, February 10, 1521. Legajo 176, Ramo 9 (1), Patronato Real, Archivo General de Indias, Seville, Spain.

Priestley, Herbert Ingram. 2010. *The Luna Papers, 1559–1561: Volumes 1 and 2*. 1928. Reprint, Tuscaloosa: University of Alabama Press.

Real Academia Española. 1734. *Diccionario de la lengua castellana*. Vol. 4. Madrid: Los Herederos del Hierro.

"Relation of the Lots of Gold and Silver That Are Coming from the City of Nombre de Dios in the Nao of Which Joan Canelas Is Master, the Register of Which Was Received in This House of Trade of the Indies on August Tenth, Fifteen Forty-Nine." 1549. Legajo 1802, Indiferente General, Archivo General de Indias, Seville, Spain.

Reynoso, Francisco de. 1569. Petition for payment of salary for service in Florida, November 1569–October 1571. Legajo 1001, Ramo 2, No. 1, Justicia, Archivo General de Indias, Seville, Spain.

Rogel, Juan. 1946a. Letter to Diego Avellaneda, January 30, 1567. Appended to letter to Diego Avellaneda, November 1566. In Zubillaga, *Monumenta Antiquae Floridae*, 128–40.

———. 1946b. Letter to Francisco Borgia, July 25, 1568. In Zubillaga, *Monumenta Antiquae Floridae*, 317–29.

———. 1946c. Letter to Francisco Borgia, November 10, 1568. In Zubillaga, *Monumenta Antiquae Floridae*, 330–43.

———. 1946d. Letter to Francisco Borgia, February 5, 1569. In Zubillaga, *Monumenta Antiquae Floridae*, 377–84.

———. 1946e. Letter to Jerónimo Ruíz del Portillo, April 25, 1568. In Zubillaga, *Monumenta Antiquae Floridae*, 272–311.

———. 1946f. Letter to Pedro Menéndez de Avilés, December 9, 1570. In Zubillaga, *Monumenta Antiquae Floridae*, 471–80.

———. 1946g. Report on the Florida missions, transcribed in *Historia Novae Hispaniae ab Anno 1571 ad 1580*, by Juan Sánchez. In Zubillaga, *Monumenta Antiquae Floridae*, 604–16.

Romera Iruela, Luís, and María del Carmen Galbis Díez. 1980. *Catalogo de pasajeros a Indias durante los siglos XVI, XVII, y XVIII*. Vol. 5, bk. 2, *1575–1577*. Seville: Ministerio de Cultura.

Ruidíaz y Caravia, Eugenio. 1893. *La Florida: Su conquista y colonización por Pedro Menéndez de Avilés*. Madrid: Real Academia de la Historia.

Ruíz, Diego. 1574. Testimony regarding the Indians of South Florida, March 16, 1574. Legajo 257, Ramo 20, G. 3, No. 1, Patronato Real, Archivo General de Indias, Seville, Spain.

Sauer, Carl Ortwin. 1966. *The Early Spanish Main*. Berkeley: University of California Press.

Schober, Theresa M., and Corbett McP. Torrence. 2002. *Archaeological Investigations and Topographic Mapping of the Estero Island Site (8LL4), Lee County, Florida*. Cultural Resource Management Program Report No. 1. Fort Myers: Florida Gulf Coast University.

Sears, William H., and Shaun O. Sullivan. 1978. "Bahamas Prehistory." *American Antiquity* 43 (1): 3–25.

Sedeño, Antonio. 1946a. Letter to Francisco Borgia, November 17, 1568. In Zubillaga, *Monumenta Antiquae Floridae*, 346–58.

———. 1946b. Letter to Juan Rogel, December 19, 1568. In Zubillaga, *Monumenta Antiquae Floridae*, 372–73.

Segura, Juan Bautista de. 1946a. Letter to Francisco Borgia, November 18, 1568. In Zubillaga, *Monumenta Antiquae Floridae*, 358–70.

———. 1946b. Letter to Jerónimo Ruíz del Portillo, June 19, 1569. In Zubillaga, *Monumenta Antiquae Floridae*, 384–86.

———. 1946c. Letter to Juan de Hinistrosa, December 18, 1568. In Zubillaga, *Monumenta Antiquae Floridae*, 370–71.

Smith, Buckingham. 1854. *Letter of Hernando de Soto, and Memoir of Hernando de Escalante Fontaneda*. Washington, DC: George W. Riggs Jr.

———. 1857. *Colección de varios documentos para la historia de la Florida y tierras adyacentes*. London: La Casa de Trübner y Compañia.

————. 1866. *Narratives of the Career of Hernando de Soto in the Conquest of Florida As Told by a Knight of Elvas and in a Relation by Luys Hernandez de Biedma, Factor of the Expedition.* Vol. 1. New York: Bradford Club.

Solís de Merás, Gonzalo. 1893. "Memorial que hizo el Doctor Gonzalo Solís de Merás, de todas las jornadas y sucesos del Adelantado Pedro Menéndez de Avilés, su cuñado, y de la conquista de la Florida y justicia que hizo en Juan Ribao y otros franceses." In *La Florida: Su conquista y colonización por Pedro Menéndez de Avilés,* by Eugenio Ruidíaz y Caravia, 1–336. Madrid: Real Academia de la Historia.

Soto, Juan de. 1573. Testimony regarding the Indians of South Florida, February 28, 1573. Legajo 257, Ramo 20, G. 3, No. 1, Patronato Real, Archivo General de Indias, Seville, Spain.

Spanish Crown. 1511. Decree to Juan Ponce de León, July 21, 1511. Legajo 418, Libro 3, f. 93, Indiferente General, Archivo General de Indias, Seville, Spain.

————. 1512a. Contract with Juan Ponce de León, February 23, 1512. Legajo 415, Libro 1, ff. 13r–15v, Indiferente General, Archivo General de Indias, Seville, Spain.

————. 1512b. Decree to the Royal Officials of Hispaniola, February 23, 1512. Legajo 418, Libro 3, ff. 252r–252v, Indiferente General, Archivo General de Indias, Seville, Spain.

————. 1514a. Capitulation with Juan Ponce de León, October 27, 1514. Legajo 415, Libro 1, ff. 11v–12v, Indiferente General, Archivo General de Indias, Seville, Spain.

————. 1514b. Capitulation with Juan Ponce de León, October 27, 1514. Legajo 419, Libro 5, ff. 293r–295r, Indiferente General, Archivo General de Indias, Seville, Spain.

————. 1514c. Title of Adelantado to Juan Ponce de León, September 27, 1514. Legajo 419, Libro 5, ff. 252v–253v, Indiferente General, Archivo General de Indias, Seville, Spain.

————. 1517a. Decree to the Jeronimyte judges, July 22, 1517. Legajo 419, Libro 6, f. 641v, Indiferente General, Archivo General de Indias, Seville, Spain.

————. 1517b. Decree to the Jeronimyte judges, July 22, 1517. Legajo 419, Libro 6, f. 650r–651r, Indiferente General, Archivo General de Indias, Seville, Spain.

————. 1526. Decree to Pánfilo de Narváez, December 11, 1526. Legajo 415, Libro 1, ff. 98v–105v, Indiferente General, Archivo General de Indias, Seville, Spain.

————. 1537. Contract with Hernando de Soto, April 20, 1537. Legajo 415, Libro 1, ff. 41r–45r, Indiferente General, Archivo General de Indias, Seville, Spain.

————. 1553. Decree to the governor of Cartagena regarding the estate of Juan de Escalante de Hontaneda, February 19, 1553. Legajo 987, Libro 3, ff. 81r–81v, Audiencia de Santa Fé, Archivo General de Indias, Seville, Spain.

————. 1569. Decree to the governor of Cartagena regarding Hernando de Escalante, son of Juan de Escalante, October 27, 1569. Legajo 987, Libro 3, ff. 383v–384r, Audiencia de Santa Fé, Archivo General de Indias, Seville, Spain.

Swanton, John R. 1985. *Final Report of the United States DeSoto Expedition Commission.* 1939. Reprint, Washington, DC: Smithsonian Institution Press.

Thompson, Victor D., and John E. Worth. 2011. "Dwellers by the Sea: Native American Adaptations along the Southern Coasts of Eastern North America." *Journal of Archaeological Research* 19 (1): 51–101.

True, David O. 1944a. "The Freducci Map of 1514–1515: What It Discloses of Early Florida History." *Tequesta* 4: 50–55.

———. 1944b. *Memoir of D.º d'Escalante Fontaneda respecting Florida, Written in Spain, about the Year 1575.* Translated by Buckingham Smith. Coral Gables, FL: Glade House.

Vega, Garcilaso de la. 1605. *La Florida del Ynca.* Lisbon: Pedro Crasbeek. Available at https://archive.org/details/lafloridadelynca00vega.

Villarreal, Francisco. 1946a. Letter to Francisco Borgia, March 5, 1570. In Zubillaga, *Monumenta Antiquae Floridae*, 413–21.

———. 1946b. Letter to Juan Rogel, January 23, 1568. In Zubillaga, *Monumenta Antiquae Floridae*, 234–40.

Weddle, Robert S. 1985. *Spanish Sea: The Gulf of Mexico in North American Discovery, 1500–1685.* College Station: Texas A&M University Press.

Wheeler, Ryan. 2000. *Treasure of the Calusa: The Johnson/Willcox Collection from Mound Key, Florida.* Tallahassee, FL: Rose Printing.

Widmer, Randolph J. 1988. *The Evolution of the Calusa: A Nonagricultural Chiefdom on the Southwest Florida Coast.* Tuscaloosa: University of Alabama Press.

Worth, John E. 1993a. "'Account of the Northern Conquest and Discovery of Hernando de Soto,' by Rodrigo Rangel." In *The De Soto Chronicles: The Expedition of Hernando de Soto to North America in 1539–1543*, edited by Lawrence A. Clayton, Vernon James Knight Jr., and Edward C. Moore, 247–306. Tuscaloosa: University of Alabama Press.

———. 1993b. "'Relation of the Island of Florida,' by Luys Hernandez de Biedma." In *The De Soto Chronicles: The Expedition of Hernando de Soto to North America in 1539–1543*, edited by Lawrence A. Clayton, Vernon James Knight Jr., and Edward C. Moore, 221–46. Tuscaloosa: University of Alabama Press.

———. 1995. "Fontaneda Revisited: Five Descriptions of Sixteenth-Century Florida." *Florida Historical Quarterly* 73 (3): 339–52.

———. 1998a. *The Timucuan Chiefdoms of Spanish Florida.* Vol. 1, *Assimilation.* Gainesville: University Press of Florida.

———. 1998b. *The Timucuan Chiefdoms of Spanish Florida.* Vol. 2, *Resistance and Destruction.* Gainesville: University Press of Florida.

———. 2003. "The Evacuation of South Florida, 1704–1760." Paper presented at the sixtieth annual meeting of the Southeastern Archaeological Conference, Charlotte, North Carolina.

———. 2004. "A History of Southeastern Indians in Cuba, 1513–1823." Paper presented at the sixty-first annual meeting of the Southeastern Archaeological Conference, St. Louis, Missouri.

———. 2006. "The Social Geography of South Florida during the Spanish Colonial Era." Paper presented at the symposium From Coast to Coast: Current Research in South Florida Archaeology at the seventy-first annual meeting of the Society for American Archaeology, San Juan, Puerto Rico.

———. 2007. *The Struggle for the Georgia Coast*. 1995. Reprint, Tuscaloosa: University of Alabama Press.

———. 2008. "An Ethnohistorical Perspective on Hunter-Gatherer Complexity in South Florida." Paper presented at the symposium The Emergence of Hunter-Gatherer Complexity in South Florida at the seventy-third annual meeting of the Society for American Archaeology, Vancouver, British Columbia.

———. 2012. "Creolization in Southwest Florida: Cuban Fishermen and 'Spanish Indians,' ca. 1766–1841." *Historical Archaeology* 46 (1): 142–60.

———. 2013. "Pineland during the Spanish Period." In *The Archaeology of Pineland: A Coastal Southwest Florida Village Complex, A.D. 50–1700*, edited by William H. Marquardt and Karen J. Walker, 767–92. Gainesville, FL: Institute of Archaeology and Paleoenvironmental Studies.

Wright, Irene. 1970. *The Early History of Cuba, 1492–1586*. 1916. Reprint, New York: Octagon Books.

Zubillaga, Felix. 1946. *Monumenta Antiquae Floridae*. Rome: Monumenta Historica Societatis Iesu.

Index

Page numbers with *f* or *t* indicate figures or tables. Page numbers in bold italics indicate Spanish narrative; page numbers in bold indicate English translation of narrative.

John E. Worth is associate professor of historical archaeology in the Department of Anthropology at the University of West Florida in Pensacola, where he specializes in archaeology and ethnohistory focusing on the Spanish colonial era in the southeastern United States. A Georgia native, Dr. Worth received his doctorate in anthropology from the University of Florida in 1992 and spent fifteen years in public archaeology program administration in Georgia and Florida, including six years with the Florida Museum of Natural History at the Randell Research Center at Pineland, before becoming a member of the faculty at UWF in 2007. He is the author of two books—*The Timucuan Chiefdoms of Spanish Florida* and *Struggle for the Georgia Coast*—and numerous other professional and lay publications.

RIPLEY P. BULLEN SERIES

Florida Museum of Natural History

Tacachale: Essays on the Indians of Florida and Southeastern Georgia during the Historic Period, edited by Jerald T. Milanich and Samuel Proctor (1978)

Aboriginal Subsistence Technology on the Southeastern Coastal Plain during the Late Prehistoric Period, by Lewis H. Larson (1980)

Cemochechobee: Archaeology of a Mississippian Ceremonial Center on the Chattahoochee River, by Frank T. Schnell, Vernon J. Knight Jr., and Gail S. Schnell (1981)

Fort Center: An Archaeological Site in the Lake Okeechobee Basin, by William H. Sears, with contributions by Elsie O'R. Sears and Karl T. Steinen (1982)

Perspectives on Gulf Coast Prehistory, edited by Dave D. Davis (1984)

Archaeology of Aboriginal Culture Change in the Interior Southeast: Depopulation during the Early Historic Period, by Marvin T. Smith (1987)

Apalachee: The Land between the Rivers, by John H. Hann (1988)

Key Marco's Buried Treasure: Archaeology and Adventure in the Nineteenth Century, by Marion Spjut Gilliland (1989)

First Encounters: Spanish Explorations in the Caribbean and the United States, 1492–1570, edited by Jerald T. Milanich and Susan Milbrath (1989)

Missions to the Calusa, edited and translated by John H. Hann, with an introduction by William H. Marquardt (1991)

Excavations on the Franciscan Frontier: Archaeology at the Fig Springs Mission, by Brent Richards Weisman (1992)

The People Who Discovered Columbus: The Prehistory of the Bahamas, by William F. Keegan (1992)

Hernando de Soto and the Indians of Florida, by Jerald T. Milanich and Charles Hudson (1993)

Foraging and Farming in the Eastern Woodlands, edited by C. Margaret Scarry (1993)

Puerto Real: The Archaeology of a Sixteenth-Century Spanish Town in Hispaniola, edited by Kathleen Deagan (1995)

Political Structure and Change in the Prehistoric Southeastern United States, edited by John F. Scarry (1996)

Bioarchaeology of Native Americans in the Spanish Borderlands, edited by Brenda J. Baker and Lisa Kealhofer (1996)

A History of the Timucua Indians and Missions, by John H. Hann (1996)

Archaeology of the Mid-Holocene Southeast, edited by Kenneth E. Sassaman and David G. Anderson (1996)

The Indigenous People of the Caribbean, edited by Samuel M. Wilson (1997; first paperback edition, 1999)

Hernando de Soto among the Apalachee: The Archaeology of the First Winter Encampment, by Charles R. Ewen and John H. Hann (1998)

The Timucuan Chiefdoms of Spanish Florida, by John E. Worth: vol. 1, *Assimilation*; vol. 2, *Resistance and Destruction* (1998)

Ancient Earthen Enclosures of the Eastern Woodlands, edited by Robert C.

Mainfort Jr. and Lynne P. Sullivan (1998)

An Environmental History of Northeast Florida, by James J. Miller (1998)

Precolumbian Architecture in Eastern North America, by William N. Morgan (1999)

Archaeology of Colonial Pensacola, edited by Judith A. Bense (1999)

Grit-Tempered: Early Women Archaeologists in the Southeastern United States, edited by Nancy Marie White, Lynne P. Sullivan, and Rochelle A. Marrinan (1999)

Coosa: The Rise and Fall of a Southeastern Mississippian Chiefdom, by Marvin T. Smith (2000)

Religion, Power, and Politics in Colonial St. Augustine, by Robert L. Kapitzke (2001)

Bioarchaeology of Spanish Florida: The Impact of Colonialism, edited by Clark Spencer Larsen (2001)

Archaeological Studies of Gender in the Southeastern United States, edited by Jane M. Eastman and Christopher B. Rodning (2001)

The Archaeology of Traditions: Agency and History Before and After Columbus, edited by Timothy R. Pauketat (2001)

Foraging, Farming, and Coastal Biocultural Adaptation in Late Prehistoric North Carolina, by Dale L. Hutchinson (2002)

Windover: Multidisciplinary Investigations of an Early Archaic Florida Cemetery, edited by Glen H. Doran (2002)

Archaeology of the Everglades, by John W. Griffin (2002)

Pioneer in Space and Time: John Mann Goggin and the Development of Florida Archaeology, by Brent Richards Weisman (2002)

Indians of Central and South Florida, 1513–1763, by John H. Hann (2003)

Presidio Santa Maria de Galve: A Struggle for Survival in Colonial Spanish Pensacola, edited by Judith A. Bense (2003)

Bioarchaeology of the Florida Gulf Coast: Adaptation, Conflict, and Change, by Dale L. Hutchinson (2004)

The Myth of Syphilis: The Natural History of Treponematosis in North America, edited by Mary Lucas Powell and Della Collins Cook (2005)

The Florida Journals of Frank Hamilton Cushing, edited by Phyllis E. Kolianos and Brent R. Weisman (2005)

The Lost Florida Manuscript of Frank Hamilton Cushing, edited by Phyllis E. Kolianos and Brent R. Weisman (2005)

The Native American World Beyond Apalachee: West Florida and the Chattahoochee Valley, by John H. Hann (2006)

Tatham Mound and the Bioarchaeology of European Contact: Disease and Depopulation in Central Gulf Coast Florida, by Dale L. Hutchinson (2006)

Taino Indian Myth and Practice: The Arrival of the Stranger King, by William F. Keegan (2007)

An Archaeology of Black Markets: Local Ceramics and Economies in Eighteenth-Century Jamaica, by Mark W. Hauser (2008; first paperback edition, 2013)

Mississippian Mortuary Practices: Beyond Hierarchy and the Representationist Perspective, edited by Lynne P. Sullivan and Robert C. Mainfort Jr. (2010; first paperback edition, 2012)

Bioarchaeology of Ethnogenesis in the Colonial Southeast, by Christopher M.

Stojanowski (2010; first paperback edition, 2013)

French Colonial Archaeology in the Southeast and Caribbean, edited by Kenneth G. Kelly and Meredith D. Hardy (2011; first paperback edition, 2015)

Late Prehistoric Florida: Archaeology at the Edge of the Mississippian World, edited by Keith Ashley and Nancy Marie White (2012; first paperback edition, 2015)

Early and Middle Woodland Landscapes of the Southeast, edited by Alice P. Wright and Edward R. Henry (2013)

Trends and Traditions in Southeastern Zooarchaeology, edited by Tanya M. Peres (2014)

New Histories of Pre-Columbian Florida, edited by Neill J. Wallis and Asa R. Randall (2014)

Discovering Florida: First-Contact Narratives from Spanish Expeditions along the Lower Gulf Coast, edited and translated by John E. Worth (2014; first paperback edition, 2016)

Constructing Histories: Archaic Freshwater Shell Mounds and Social Landscapes of the St. Johns River, Florida by Asa R. Randall (2015)

Archaeology of Early Colonial Interaction at El Chorro de Maíta, Cuba, by Roberto Valcárcel Rojas (2016)

Fort San Juan and the Limits of Empire: Colonialism and Household Practice at the Berry Site, edited by Robin A. Beck, Christopher B. Rodning, and David G. Moore (2016)

Rethinking Moundville and its Hinterland, edited by Vincas P. Steponaitis and C. Margaret Scarry (2016)

Printed in the USA
CPSIA information can be obtained
at www.ICGtesting.com
JSHW020324271123
52535JS00004B/130